Special Message

As everyone knows, Hurricane Katrina devastated New Orleans, including the legendary restaurants, nightspots, hotels and attractions included in this guide. Though their doors may be closed at present, we are continuing to list them in the hope and expectation that they will soon reopen. Meanwhile, we join with the rest of the world in wishing the city a swift and full recovery.

For information on how you can help, visit www.redcross.org. Aid specifically targeted to hospitality workers is being organized by the New Orleans Hospitality Workers Disaster Relief Fund; see www.ghcf.org. For an up-to-date list of hospitality industry events taking place in cities across America to benefit the Gulf Coast region, please visit www.zagat.com.

Nina and Tim

Nina & Tim Zagat

New York, NY
September 17, 2005

ZAGATSURVEY®

2006

AMERICA'S TOP RESTAURANTS

Editor: Troy Segal

Published and distributed by
ZAGAT SURVEY, LLC
4 Columbus Circle
New York, New York 10019
Tel: 212 977 6000
E-mail: americastop@zagat.com
Web site: www.zagat.com

Acknowledgments

Our special thanks to the thousands of surveyors who have shared their views with us and made this nationwide *Survey* possible, as well as our editors and coordinators in each city: Alicia Arter, Olga Boikess, Amanda Boyd, Nikki Buchanan, Miriam Carey, Lauren Chapin, Suzi Forbes Chase, Ann Christenson, Andrea Clurfeld, Pat Denechaud, Victoria Elliott, Jeanette Foster, Lorraine Gengo, Rona Gindin, Meesha Halm, Lynn Hazelwood, Brad Johnson, Marty Katz, Michael Klein, Marilyn Kleinberg, Rochelle S. Koff, Gretchen Kurz, Sharon Litwin, Jennifer Mathieu, Christina Melander, Lori Midson, Shannon Mullen, Maryanne Muller, David Nelson, Jan Norris, Josh Ozersky, Ann Lemons Pollack, Joe Pollack, Virginia Rainey, Laura E. Reiley, Heidi Knapp Rinella, Shelley Skiles Sawyer, Helen Schwab, Deirdre Sykes Shapiro, Merrill Shindler, Jane Slaughter, Ruth Tobias, Joshua Tompkins, John Turiano, Jill Van Cleave, Alice Van Housen, Carla Waldemar and Kay Winzenried. We are also grateful to our assistant editor, Victoria Elmacioglu, and editorial assistant, Leah Hochbaum, as well as the following members of our staff: Betsy Andrews, Catherine Bigwood, Jason Briker, Caren Weiner Campbell, Reni Chin, Larry Cohn, Carol Diuguid, Griff Foxley, Schuyler Frazier, Jeff Freier, Shelley Gallagher, Curt Gathje, Randi Gollin, Natalie Lebert, Mike Liao, Dave Makulec, Emily Parsons, Robert Poole, Josh Rogers, Robert Seixas, Thomas Sheehan, Joshua Siegel, Daniel Simmons, Carla Spartos, Erinn Stivala, Donna Marino Wilkins, Yoji Yamaguchi and Sharon Yates.

Contents

About This Survey 4
What's New 5
Ratings & Symbols 6
Top Food Rankings by Area. 7
Most Popular by Area 10
RESTAURANT DIRECTORY
  Names, Addresses, Phone Numbers,
  Web Sites, Ratings and Reviews
    • Atlanta. 14
    • Atlantic City 23
    • Baltimore/Annapolis 25
    • Boston. 30
    • Charlotte. 40
    • Chicago. 45
    • Cincinnati 54
    • Cleveland 59
    • Connecticut. 64
    • Dallas 72
    • Denver/Mtn. Resorts 81
    • Detroit. 91
    • Ft. Lauderdale. 96
    • Ft. Worth 100
    • Honolulu 105
    • Houston 110
    • Kansas City. 119
    • Las Vegas 124
    • Long Island. 133
    • Los Angeles 142
    • Miami 152
    • Milwaukee 160
    • Minneapolis/St. Paul 165
    • New Jersey. 170
    • New Orleans. 179
    • New York City 188
    • Orange County, CA 198
    • Orlando. 203
    • Palm Beach. 212
    • Philadelphia 217
    • Phoenix/Scottsdale 226
    • Portland, OR 231
    • Salt Lake City/Mtn. Resorts 236
    • San Diego. 241
    • San Francisco Bay Area. 246
    • Seattle. 256
    • St. Louis 265
    • Tampa/Sarasota 270
    • Tucson. 275
    • Washington, DC 280
    • Westchester/HRV 289
  Cuisines by Area Index 300
  Alphabetical Page Index 321
  Wine Chart 332

About This Survey

Here are the results of our *2006 America's Top Restaurants Survey,* covering 1,352 restaurants across the country. This guide's list of the top restaurants in the 41 major markets contained herein demonstrates the fact that dining throughout the U.S. just keeps getting better and better.

This marks the 27th year that Zagat Survey has reported on the shared experiences of diners like you. What started in 1979 as a hobby involving 200 of our friends rating NYC restaurants has come a long way. Today we have over 250,000 active surveyors and now cover entertaining, golf, hotels, resorts, spas, movies, music, nightlife, shopping and tourist attractions. All of these guides are based on consumer surveys. They are also available on PDAs, cell phones and by subscription at zagat.com, where you can vote and shop as well.

By regularly surveying large numbers of avid customers, we hope to have achieved a uniquely current and reliable guide. More than a quarter-century of experience has verified this. In effect, this is the restaurant industry's report card, with each place's ratings and review being a freemarket study of its own consumers. Over 115,000 restaurant-goers contributed to this book. Of these surveyors, 47% are women, 53% men; the breakdown by age is 13% in their 20s; 26%, 30s; 22%, 40s; 23%, 50s; and 16%, 60s or above. Our editors, most of whom are professional food writers, have synopsized these surveyors' opinions, with their comments shown in quotes. We sincerely thank each of these people; this book is really "theirs."

While all the restaurants in this guide were chosen for their high quality, we have prepared two separate lists to facilitate your search: see Top Food Rankings by Area (pages 7–9) and Most Popular by Area (pages 10–12). To assist you in finding just what you want when you want it, we have also provided various handy indexes.

Finally, we invite you to join any of our upcoming *Surveys* – just register at zagat.com. Each participant will receive a free copy of the resulting guide (or a comparable reward). Your comments and even criticisms of this guide are also solicited. There is always room for improvement with your help. Just contact us at americastop@zagat.com.

New York, NY
November 7, 2005

Nina and Tim Zagat

What's New

Economical Eating: Americans may be feeling a bite at the gas pump nowadays, but prices are steady at the dining table: our surveyors show the average national meal cost rose only 3%, from $31.51 to $32.60, this year. Among the top restaurants listed in this guide, we estimate that the increase was 4.4%.

Designer Digs: High-profile chefs require high-style settings. Indeed, the celebrity decorator is often a selling point in his own right, with designers such as Frank Gehry, Richard Meier, Todd Oldham, David Rockwell and Adam Tihany becoming as prominent as the top toques they serve.

Adieu, Haute Cuisine: The recent closings of such formal French bastions as Boston's Maison Robert, Cincinnati's Maisonette and NYC's Le Cirque, La Côte Basque and Lutèce illustrate the dwindling of *haute cuisine* dining. Not that Americans have gone off Gallic fare: they just desire more easygoing environs, as shown by a boom in bistros and brasseries.

Dressing Down: Further evidence of the informal mode that now dominates the dining scene is the decline of the dress code. Just a few years ago, jacket and tie were *de rigueur* at fine restaurants (unless you lived in LA, perhaps); today, they're *de rigor mortis* – "jacket suggested" is the most formal requirement that all but a few *America's Tops* places make. Even that ultimate symbol of fine dining, the white tablecloth, has become something of a rarity.

Homegrown: The disappearance of *haute cuisine* also suggests a shift in the public palate, away from rich, elaborate preparations and toward natural flavors and regional produce. Given the consumer's desire (and willingness to pay) for ultrafresh foods, the mark of an acclaimed chef today seems to lie less in his recipes and more in his ties with local suppliers to obtain the "best possible ingredients."

Spreading Rays of the Rising Sun: Long popular on the West Coast, Japanese restaurants are featured in virtually every city this year, and score in the Top Food Rankings in many of them. In contrast, the growth of fine Chinese cooking, which 10 years ago dominated Asian cuisine in the U.S., has seemingly stalled.

Future Hope: Since September, our hearts and minds have been with New Orleans, which at press time is just starting to recover from Hurricane Katrina. Nevertheless, we have included the Crescent City's section here, in the hope and faith that one of America's richest restaurant capitals will rise again.

New York, NY
November 7, 2005

Nina and Tim
Nina and Tim Zagat

Ratings & Symbols

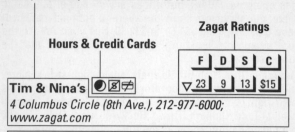

Name, Address, Phone Number & Web Site

Zagat Ratings

Hours & Credit Cards

	F	D	S	C
	▽ 23	9	13	$15

Tim & Nina's ● 🖾 ⊄

4 Columbus Circle (8th Ave.), 212-977-6000;
www.zagat.com

"You're the tapas", croon contented connoisseurs of
the Chinese-Castilian cheap cuisine at this "cramped"
concrete-clad compound at Columbus Circle; diners can
select "savory" small plates from passing dim sum carts
to assemble a "tasting menu that's attuned to their tastes";
however, detractors declare Tim and Nina "push the
concept too far" with dishes such as sweet-and-sour
sardines, Szechuan seviche and Beijing-Barcelona
bouillabaisse, with service that comes from Spain in the
'30s and China in the '40s.

Review, with surveyors' comments in quotes

Top Spots: Places with the highest overall ratings, popularity
and importance are listed in BLOCK CAPITAL LETTERS.

Hours: ● serves after 11 PM
🖾 closed on Sunday

Credit Cards: ⊄ no credit cards accepted

Ratings are on a scale of **0 to 30.** Cost **(C)** reflects our
surveyors' estimate of the price of dinner with one
drink and tip.

F Food	D Decor	S Service	C Cost
23	9	13	$15

0–9 poor to fair	**20–25** very good to excellent
10–15 fair to good	**26–30** extraordinary to perfection
16–19 good to very good	▽ low response/less reliable

For newcomers or survey write-ins listed without ratings,
the price range is indicated as follows:

I	$25 and below	**E**	$41 to $65
M	$26 to $40	**VE**	$66 or more

Top Food Rankings by Area

Atlanta
- **29** Bacchanalia
- **28** Ritz Buckhead Din. Rm.
- **27** Tamarind
   Aria
   Sia's

Atlantic City
- **27** White House
- **26** Chef Vola's
   Brighton
- **25** Capriccio
   Suilan

Baltimore/Annapolis
- **28** Charleston
- **27** Prime Rib
   O'Learys
   Joss Cafe
   Hampton's

Boston
- **29** Oishii
- **28** L'Espalier
   Aujourd'hui
- **27** No. 9 Park
   Hamersley's Bistro

Charlotte
- **29** Barrington's
- **28** Volare
- **27** McIntosh's
   Sullivan's
- **26** Nikko

Chicago
- **28** Tallgrass
   Carlos'
   Tru
   Ambria
   Mirai Sushi

Cincinnati
- **29** Jean-Robert at Pigall's
- **28** Daveed's at 934
- **27** Boca
   BonBonerie
   Palace

Cleveland
- **28** Johnny's Bar
- **27** Chez François
   Phnom Penh
   Lolita
   Blue Point Grille

Connecticut
- **28** Thomas Henkelmann
   Le Petit Cafe
- **27** Ibiza
   Jeffrey's
   Jean-Louis

Dallas
- **28** French Room
   Lola
- **27** York Street
   Teppo
   Cafe Pacific

Denver/Mtn. Resorts
- **28** Mizuna
- **27** Highlands Garden
   Del Frisco's
   L'Atelier
   Sweet Basil

Detroit
- **28** Rugby Grille
   Lark
   Emily's
- **27** Zingerman's
   Tribute

Ft. Lauderdale
- **28** Sunfish Grill
- **27** La Brochette
   Cafe Maxx
- **26** Canyon
   Cafe Martorano

Ft. Worth
- **28** Lonesome Dove
- **27** Saint-Emilion
   La Piazza
- **26** Boi NA Braza
   Kincaid's

Top Food

Honolulu
28 Alan Wong's
27 La Mer
26 Hoku's
    Roy's
    Chef Mavro

Houston
28 Mark's
    Chez Nous
27 Pappas Bros.
26 Cafe Annie
    Indika

Kansas City
27 Bluestem
26 Stroud's
    Oklahoma Joe's
    Le Fou Frog
    American Rest.

Las Vegas
28 Nobu
27 Picasso
    Malibu Chan's
    Le Cirque
    Rosemary's

Long Island
28 Kotobuki
    Polo
27 Kitchen a Bistro
    Peter Luger
    Mill River Inn

Los Angeles
28 Mélisse
    Matsuhisa
    Katsu-ya
27 Brandywine
    Nobu Malibu

Miami
28 Francesco
27 Romeo's Cafe
    Nobu Miami Beach
    Chef Allen's
    Matsuri

Milwaukee
29 Sanford
27 Dream Dance
    Ristorante Bartolotta
26 Immigrant Room
    Heaven City

Minneapolis/St. Paul
28 Bayport Cookery
    La Belle Vie
27 D'Amico Cucina
    Vincent
    Manny's

New Jersey
28 Nicholas
    Ryland Inn
27 DeLorenzo's
    Cafe Panache
    Cafe Matisse

New Orleans
27 Peristyle
    Bayona
    Jacques-Imo's
    Dick & Jenny's
    Brigtsen's

New York City
28 Le Bernardin
    Daniel
    per se
    Bouley
    Sushi Yasuda

Orange County, CA
27 Ramos House
    Studio
26 Black Sheep
    Basilic
    Zov's Bistro

Orlando
27 Le Coq au Vin
    Victoria & Albert's
    Chatham's Place
    Del Frisco's
26 Manuel's on the 28th

Palm Beach
27 11 Maple St.
    Chez Jean-Pierre
    Four Seasons
    Little Moirs
26 Kathy's Gazebo

Philadelphia
28 Fountain
    Le Bec-Fin
    Le Bar Lyonnais
    Django
    Birchrunville Store

Phoenix/Scottsdale
28 Pizzeria Bianco
    Sea Saw
27 Marquesa
    Binkley's
    Barrio Café

Portland, OR
27 Genoa
    Paley's Place
    Higgins
    Saburo's
    Heathman

Salt Lake City/Mtn. Resorts
27 Tree Room
    Red Iguana
    Mariposa
26 Michelangelo
    Seafood Buffet

San Diego
27 Pamplemousse Grille
    El Bizcocho
26 Tapenade
    Sushi Ota
    WineSellar & Brasserie

San Francisco Bay Area
29 Gary Danko
28 French Laundry
    Manresa
    Erna's Elderberry Hse.
    Sushi Ran

Seattle
29 Mistral
28 Cafe Juanita
    Nishino
    Herbfarm
    Tosoni's

St. Louis
27 Tony's
    Sidney St. Cafe
    Trattoria Marcella
26 Crossing, The
    Dominic's

Tampa/Sarasota
28 Beach Bistro
    Restaurant B.T.
27 SideBern's
26 Six Tables
    Selva Grill

Tucson
28 Dish
26 Vivace
    Grill at Hacienda del Sol
    Le Rendez-Vous
    Cafe Poca Cosa

Washington, DC
28 Makoto
    Inn at Little Washington
    Maestro
    Citronelle
    L'Auberge Chez François

Westchester/HRV
29 Freelance Café
    Xaviar's at Piermont
27 Rest. X & Bully Boy Bar
    Blue Hill at Stone Barns
    Buffet de la Gare

Most Popular by Area

Atlanta
1. Bacchanalia
2. Bone's
3. Chops/Lobster Bar
4. BluePointe
5. Nava

Atlantic City
1. P.F. Chang's
2. Chef Vola's
3. White House
4. Dock's Oyster House
5. Suilan

Baltimore/Annapolis
1. Charleston
2. Ruth's Chris
3. McCormick & Schmick's
4. Cheesecake Factory
5. Clyde's

Boston
1. Legal Sea Foods
2. Blue Ginger
3. No. 9 Park
4. L'Espalier
5. Hamersley's

Charlotte
1. Barrington's
2. Upstream
3. Mickey & Mooch
4. Bonterra
5. Palm

Chicago
1. Tru
2. Charlie Trotter's
3. Frontera Grill
4. Everest
5. Gibsons Steakhouse

Cincinnati
1. Jean-Robert at Pigall's
2. Montgomery Inn
3. Palomino
4. Jeff Ruby's
5. Precinct

Cleveland
1. Blue Point Grille
2. Lolita
3. Johnny's Bar
4. Hyde Park Prime
5. Baricelli Inn

Connecticut
1. Thomas Henkelmann
2. Union League
3. Barcelona
4. City Limits Diner
5. Jean-Louis

Dallas
1. Abacus
2. Bob's
3. Mansion on Turtle Creek
4. P.F. Chang's
5. French Room

Denver/Mtn. Resorts
1. Sweet Basil
2. Flagstaff House
3. Mizuna
4. Del Frisco's
5. 240 Union

Detroit
1. Lark
2. Tribute
3. Zingerman's
4. Emily's
5. Common Grill

Ft. Lauderdale
1. Cheesecake Factory
2. Houston's
3. Mark's Las Olas
4. Casa D'Angelo
5. Ruth's Chris

Ft. Worth
1. Del Frisco's
2. Reata
3. Joe T. Garcia's
4. Texas de Brazil
5. Bistro Louise

Honolulu
1. Alan Wong's
2. Roy's
3. Hoku's
4. La Mer
5. Duke's Canoe Club

Houston
1. Mark's
2. Brennan's
3. Cafe Annie
4. Churrascos
5. Américas

Kansas City
1. McCormick & Schmick's
2. Fiorella's Jack Stack
3. Plaza III
4. Lidia's
5. Grand St. Cafe

Las Vegas
1. Picasso
2. Aureole
3. Delmonico
4. Bellagio Buffet
5. Prime

Long Island
1. Peter Luger
2. Cheesecake Factory
3. Coolfish
4. Bryant/Cooper Steak
5. Mill River Inn

Los Angeles
1. A.O.C.
2. Campanile
3. Café Bizou
4. Cheesecake Factory
5. Spago

Miami
1. Joe's Stone Crab
2. Cheesecake Factory
3. Nobu Miami Beach
4. Houston's
5. Norman's

Milwaukee
1. Maggiano's
2. Sanford
3. P.F. Chang's
4. Lake Park Bistro
5. Eddie Martini's

Minneapolis/St. Paul
1. Oceanaire
2. Manny's
3. Vincent
4. Zelo
5. St. Paul Grill

New Jersey
1. Ryland Inn
2. Scalini Fedeli
3. Bernards Inn
4. Frog and the Peach
5. Amanda's

New Orleans
1. Commander's Palace
2. Galatoire's
3. Bayona
4. Brennan's
5. Emeril's

New York City
1. Gramercy Tavern
2. Union Square Cafe
3. Babbo
4. Daniel
5. Le Bernardin

Orange County, CA
1 Cheesecake Factory
2. Ruth's Chris
3. P.F. Chang's
4. Houston's
5. Roy's

Orlando
1. California Grill
2. Emeril's Orlando*
3. Victoria & Albert's
4. Flying Fish Café
5. Cheesecake Factory

Palm Beach
1. Cheesecake Factory
2. Houston's
3. Ke-e Grill
4. P.F. Chang's
5. Café L'Europe

Philadelphia
1. Buddakan
2. Le Bec-Fin
3. Fountain
4. Lacroix/Rittenhouse
5. Django

Phoenix/Scottsdale
1. T. Cook's
2. Roy's
3. P.F. Chang's
4. Mary Elaine's
5. Mastro's

Portland, OR
1. Jake's Famous Crawfish
2. Higgins
3. Heathman
4. Wildwood
5. McCormick & Schmick's

---

* Indicates a tie with restaurant above

By Popularity Rank

Salt Lake City/Mtn. Resorts
1. Market St. Grill
2. New Yorker Club
3. Wahso
4. Chimayo
5. Red Iguana

San Diego
1. George's at the Cove
2. Ruth's Chris
3. Sammy's Woodfired
4. Pamplemousse Grille
5. Roppongi

San Francisco Bay Area
1. Gary Danko
2. Boulevard
3. French Laundry
4. Slanted Door
5. Chez Panisse Café

Seattle
1. Wild Ginger
2. Dahlia Lounge
3. Metropolitan Grill
4. Canlis
5. Rover's

St. Louis
1. Tony's
2. Sidney St. Cafe
3. Trattoria Marcella
4. Annie Gunn's
5. Harvest

Tampa/Sarasota
1. Bern's
2. Columbia
3. Armani's
4. Bijou Café
5. SideBern's

Tucson
1. Cafe Poca Cosa
2. Grill/Hacienda del Sol
3. Terra Cotta
4. Wildflower
5. Janos

Washington, DC
1. Kinkead's
2. Jaleo
3. Citronelle
4. L'Auberge Chez François
5. TenPenh

Westchester/HRV
1. Crabtree's Kittle House
2. Xaviar's at Piermont
3. Harvest on Hudson
4. La Panetière
5. Blue Hill at Stone Barns

Restaurant Directory

Atlanta

TOP FOOD RANKING

Restaurant	Cuisine
29 Bacchanalia	New American
28 Ritz Buckhead Din. Rm.	French
27 Tamarind	Thai
Aria	New American
Sia's	Asian/Southwestern
Bone's	Steakhouse/American
MF Sushibar	Japanese
Floataway Cafe	French/Italian
Chops/Lobster Bar	Seafood/Steakhouse
26 Park 75	New American
Pano's & Paul's	Continental
Nan Thai	Thai
Seeger's	Continental
Nikolai's Roof	Continental/French
McKendrick's	Steakhouse
Joël	French
di Paolo	Northern Italian
Sotto Sotto	Northern Italian
La Grotta	Northern Italian
South City Kitchen	Southern

OTHER NOTEWORTHY PLACES

Atlanta Fish Market	Seafood
Babette's Cafe	European
BluePointe	Asian/New American
Canoe	New American
dick and harry's	Seafood/New American
Food Studio	New American
Hsu's Gourmet	Chinese
Iris	Continental
Kyma	Greek
La Tavola	Italian
Madras Saravana	Indian/Vegetarian
Nava	Southwestern
Quinones Room	New American
Rathbun's	New American
Restaurant Eugene	New American
Thumbs Up	American
Tierra	Pan-Latin
TWO. urban Licks	Southwestern/New Amer.
Wisteria	Southern
Woodfire Grill	Californian

ARIA ⌨   27 | 25 | 26 | $49
490 E. Paces Ferry Rd. (Maple Dr.), 404-233-7673; www.aria-atl.com
Surveyors sing the praises of this "suave Buckhead" boîte
with an "entirely original and elegant" aura that "continues to
shine" thanks to the "superlative" New American cuisine of chef-
owner Gerry Klaskala, who "gets it" when it comes to "making
customers feel welcome", setting an example for the "unobtrusive"
staff; it occupies a "glamorous", "renovated house" with a
"dynamite contemporary decor" that's "heavy on the comfort
factor" and, despite somewhat "poor acoustics", "perfect for
a special evening."

Atlanta Fish Market   23 | 19 | 20 | $36
265 Pharr Rd. (bet. Peachtree St. & Piedmont Rd.), 404-262-3165;
www.buckheadrestaurants.com
A "huge variety" of "eerily fresh fish" "made any way you want it"
reels in "schools" of finatics to this "warehouse-size" Buckhead
Life Group seafooder; service varies from "solid" to "abysmal" and
"long waits" are to be expected in the "loud", "fun-filled" setting
that's "too damn noisy" for many; foes feel this fin-fare "factory"
"for the masses" has "lost its freshness", while enthusiasts
exclaim "holy mackerel, this place rocks!"

Babette's Cafe   24 | 20 | 23 | $30
573 N. Highland Ave. (Freedom Pkwy.), 404-523-9121;
www.babettescafe.com
Chef-owner "Marla Adams never disappoints" at her midpriced
Poncey-Highlands European "staple" that's "highly recommended"
for "well-seasoned", "casual" fare offering a "superb blend of
fancy and simple", as well as "one of the best Sunday brunches in
town"; the "renovated Victorian cottage" is "comfy" and *très, très*
homey", and the "fantastic" "servers are as pleasant as the food."

BACCHANALIA ⌨   29 | 25 | 28 | $69
Westside Mktpl., 1198 Howell Mill Rd. (bet. 14th St. & Huff Rd.),
404-365-0410; www.starprovisions.com
A "feast for the senses", this Westside "culinary shrine" hits a
double-header as Atlanta's Most Popular destination and No. 1 for
Food, thanks to chef-owners Anne Quatrano and Clifford Harrison's
"exquisitely prepared" New American creations that are a "joy to
serious foodies" "without scaring off amateurs"; the service is
"exquisite" "but subtle", while the "lovely, contemporary" space
in a former meatpacking plant "betrays its industrial roots"; "the
only bad thing is how hard it is to get in."

BLUEPOINTE   24 | 26 | 21 | $47
3455 Peachtree Rd. (Lenox Rd.), 404-237-9070;
www.buckheadrestaurants.com
"Quintessential new Atlanta – sleek, hip and better than you
expect" is how groupies describe this "upscale" Buckhead
showcase for "vibrant, terrific" Asian-accented New American
cuisine, where "movers and shakers" mingle with "tremendous
eye candy" at the "electrifying neon bar" and the "wow factor"
extends to the "sharp room" with "high ceilings", towering
windows and a "sweeping staircase"; the jaded, however, jeer
"if only the customers and staff were as cool as the place";
N.B. the arrival of chef Doug Turbush (ex Nava) may outdate
the Food score.

BONE'S
27 | 22 | 27 | $53

3130 Piedmont Rd. (Peachtree Rd.), 404-237-2663;
www.bonesrestaurant.com
Carnivores counsel "bring a big appetite and lots of money" to
this "ridiculously decadent power steakhouse" that "beats those
chains" "hands down" with an American menu of "consistently
superb", "soft, buttery" steaks and a "comprehensive wine list"; a
"warm, knowledgeable and accommodating" staff will make you
feel like "an old friend who has been away too long" in a "dark"
and "elegant" "old-school" setting where "dealmakers and hotshot business types" abound.

Canoe
25 | 26 | 23 | $41

Vinings on the River, 4199 Paces Ferry Rd. (I-75), 770-432-2663;
www.canoeatl.com
"The charm is infectious" at this "well-loved" "special-occasion"
destination in Vinings that's "got it all" – chef Carvel Grant Gould's
"excellent" New American cuisine that makes "exceptional use of
fresh local ingredients", "idyllic" "riverside" surroundings featuring
"stellar gardens" and a "warm" atmosphere that feels "more
comfortable than home" and "attentive" service from a staff that's
"knowledgeable" "without being long-winded"; in sum, a "super-
romantic" spot to "impress a date" or "out-of-town visitors."

CHOPS/LOBSTER BAR
27 | 24 | 26 | $52

Buckhead Plaza, 70 W. Paces Ferry Rd. (Peachtree Rd.),
404-262-2675; www.buckheadrestaurants.com
"Superlatives" abound for this "exceptional" steakhouse in
Buckhead that's "ground zero for meat eaters" who "slash away" at
"beautiful", "melt-in-your-mouth" cuts in a "tony", "masculine"
setting, while downstairs in the "more intimate" Lobster Bar,
afishionados tuck into "sophisticated, fabulous", "always-fresh" fin
fare in a "fab art deco" room with a "younger" vibe; an "efficient",
"impeccable" staff "makes you feel like Trump" in both areas,
which are "buzzing" to the "power pulse" of "expense-account"
meals and "special occasions."

dick and harry's ☒
25 | 18 | 23 | $38

Holcomb Woods Vlg., 1570 Holcomb Bridge Rd. (½ mi. east of GA 400),
Roswell, 770-641-8757; www.dickandharrys.com
"Exceptional" fish dishes are the "highlight" of the "superb" New
American cuisine (the "spicy" crab cakes are "some of the best
around") at this "upscale" Roswell production where "classy
service" makes "well-dressed" diners "feel special", and "sitting
at the chef's counter" near the back of the "stainless steel"–
accented dining room (so "'90s", critics sigh) is always a "great
experience"; budget hawks grouse about the "pricey" tabs, but
many feel it's "worth the drive" to suburbia.

di Paolo
26 | 21 | 24 | $33

Rivermont Sq., 8560 Holcomb Bridge Rd. (Nesbitt Ferry Rd.),
Alpharetta, 770-587-1051; www.dipaolorestaurant.com
"As good as any inside the Perimeter", this "friendly" Alpharettan
is "worth the drive from wherever you are" for an "educated"
menu of "upscale" Northern Italian cuisine that's "unique and
filling"; there's "always a warm welcome" from "outstanding"
owner Susan Thill, and her "superb" staff delivers "personalized"
service in a "dark" and "sexy", yet "homey", dining room; N.B. the

post-*Survey* installment of chef Michael Gaylor may outdate the above Food score.

Floataway Cafe ⊠   27 | 24 | 23 | $41
Floataway Bldg., 1123 Zonolite Rd. (bet. Briarcliff & Johnson Rds.), 404-892-1414; www.starprovisions.com
"You'll need a GPS to find" "Bacchanalia's little sister", located "in the middle of an industrial park" near Emory, but it's "well worth the excursion" for chef Anne Quatrano's "stunning" French-Italian cuisine that fans swear is "every bit as good" as (and "more affordable" than) its elder sibling's; the "serious", "if not always friendly", staff "can't be beat" for "professional" service, while the "airy", "post-industrial" space is "relaxing", framing an "ultracool" scene for an "arty crowd" that's "top of the line and quite divine."

Food Studio   25 | 26 | 25 | $42
King Plow Art Ctr., 887 W. Marietta St. (bet. Ashby St. & Howell Mill Rd.), 404-815-6677; www.thefoodstudio.com
Foodies "drop bread crumbs" so they can "find their way back" to this Westside New American "favorite" that "feels a world away", and not just because of its "obscure location"; new chef Mark Alba was appointed post-*Survey,* which may outdate the Food score for creations served in "one of the most romantic places around", a "dark, luxurious" space that's "all candles and fireplace"; the "smooth" service adds to the "special-occasion" atmosphere.

Hsu's Gourmet   25 | 16 | 23 | $23
192 Peachtree Center Ave. (International Blvd.), 404-659-2788; www.hsus.com
Arguably the "best authentic Chinese in the Southeast" according to local loyalists, this Downtown Szechuan is seen as Atlanta's leading Sino spot, thanks to "generous portions" of "fabulous" dishes such as the Spicy Anna seafood noodle soup that are "worth every penny"; "multiple servers" "cater to your every need" with "attention to detail", making it "popular for lunch" with conventioneers and the business crowd.

Iris   25 | 21 | 22 | $32
1314 Glenwood Ave. (Haas Ave.), 404-221-1300; www.irisatlanta.com
This "oasis of big-city chic with a small-town attitude" is a "top-notch addition" to East Atlanta, offering a Continental-inspired organic menu that's "creative" "without being alienating", as well as "professional" service by an "earnest, attentive" staff and the "modernist" digs of a "dressed-up gas station"; an "interesting clientele" of locals mixes with those willing to venture into this "gentrifying part of town."

Joël ⊠   26 | 26 | 25 | $54
The Forum, 3290 Northside Pkwy. (W. Paces Ferry Rd.), 404-233-3500; www.joelrestaurant.com
At Joël Antunes' "haute" Buckhead eatery, "mind-blowing", "flawless" "high-concept" French cuisine (with Asian and Med inflections) by a "world-class talent" and an "extensive wine list" that "reads like *War and Peace*" are served by an "excellent" staff in a "sizzling", "stunning modern" space with "awesome" bathrooms and a "gorgeous" bar; dissenters may demur at the "odd location", "haughty" attitude and "big dollars", but most agree "many cities would be happy to have this one"; P.S. the "$39 prix fixe is an outstanding value."

Kyma ☒　　　　　　　24 | 24 | 23 | $45
3085 Piedmont Rd. (E. Paces Ferry Rd.), 404-262-0702;
www.buckheadrestaurants.com
"No wonder the Greeks get credit for civilization" marvel Med
heads who munch on "incredibly fresh" fish that's "flown in daily"
to this "haute" Hellenic in Buckhead – but "watch your wallet" as
"FedEx from the Adriatic does not come cheap"; a "helpful" staff
"ensures a superb meal" in the "refreshing" "bright-blue-and-
white" room with "columns of marble" and a "starlit ceiling."

La Grotta ☒　　　　　　26 | 22 | 26 | $46
Crowne Plaza Ravinia Hotel, 4355 Ashford Dunwoody Rd.
(Hammond Dr.), 770-395-9925
2637 Peachtree Rd. (bet. Lindbergh Dr. & Wesley Rd.), 404-231-1368
www.la-grotta.com
This "old-world" Northern Italian duo is the "top choice" of many
for "consistently excellent", "flawless" offerings on a "deep and
satisfying menu" and "impeccable" service from a "well-trained"
staff that'll "do anything to make you feel comfortable"; while
some prefer the "gorgeous room" and "outstanding views" of the
Dunwoody location, others are partial to the "relaxing, luxurious"
ambiance of the "original" "grande dame" in Buckhead; whichever
spot you choose, it's a "pleasure from start to finish."

La Tavola　　　　　　　　24 | 21 | 23 | $30
992 Virginia Ave., NE (N. Highland Ave.), 404-873-5430;
www.latavolatrattoria.com
A "bright spot in the Va-Highlands dining scene", this trattoria "has
found its groove" with "delicious, inventive" Italian cooking that's
"heaven on a plate" for ardent fans who also laud the "impeccable"
wine list and "attentive", "but not overbearing" service; the "sleek"
dining room is "refreshing and cool", but "always packed"; luckily,
those who feel "cramped" can retreat to the "comfortable" patio
for a more "relaxing" repast.

Madras Saravana Bhavan　　　25 | 11 | 15 | $15
Cub Foods Shopping Ctr., 2179 Lawrenceville Hwy. (N. Druid Hills Rd.),
Decatur, 404-636-4400; www.madrassaravanabhavan.net
This Decatur destination dazzles diners with "unbelievably good"
and "savory" vegetarian dishes that represent "some of the best"
cooking from the subcontinent "this side of Madras"; "bountiful
portions" ("don't miss the six-ft.-long dosai" for a group) are
always "satisfying" and the "lunch buffet is a bargain"; the
service is "friendly" and the "kitschy" space (a "redone Folks")
has a "funky-bamboo" and "vinyl-booth" "flair"; P.S. it's "MSB to
those in-the-know."

McKendrick's Steak House　　26 | 22 | 24 | $46
Park Place Shopping Ctr., 4505 Ashford Dunwoody Rd., NE
(bet. Hammond Dr. & Perimeter Ctr.), 770-512-8888;
www.mckendricks.com
A "suburban Bone's" "without the markup" carnivores crow
about this "top-notch" Dunwoody "old faithful" serving "tender"
"brontosaurus"-size steaks and seafood "to savor" in a "clubby",
"noisy" setting with an "attentive" staff providing "outstanding"
service; though it's "less pretentious" and somewhat "easier to get
into" than similarly "upscale" intown venues, wallet-watchers still
advise "bring lots of $$$" or a "corporate charge card."

MF Sushibar
27 | 24 | 19 | $35

265 Ponce de Leon Ave. (Penn St.), 404-815-8844; www.mfsushibar.com
"In a world of McSushi", "this is the real deal", swear "completely addicted" "slaves" of this "unsurpassed" Midtown Japanese that's "raised the bar" for sushi savants with "amazing" raw fin fare "so fresh it gives you a buzz"; the "wicked cool", "minimalist" decor matches the "cosmopolitan" crowd, and while cold fish carp about "appalling prices" and "too much attitude", a sea of supporters are "saving up their cash."

Nan Thai Fine Dining
26 | 28 | 24 | $40

1350 Spring St., NW (17th St.), 404-870-9933; www.nanfinedining.com
The "absolutely stunning", "dramatic" space of this "refined, elegant" Midtown Thai was designed by the Johnson Studio (BluePointe, Canoe, Joël, among others); complementing the "wow factor" of the room are "perfect", "superbly presented" cuisine and "kind", "warm" service; chef/co-owner "Nan has outdone herself" at this "upscale sibling" of Tamarind, where acolytes come to "worship her in all her glory", while others "would make this a regular spot, if [they] could afford it."

NAVA
25 | 25 | 22 | $39

Buckhead Plaza, 3060 Peachtree Rd., NE (W. Paces Ferry Rd.), 404-240-1984; www.buckheadrestaurants.com
"Another Buckhead Life Group" spot that "does not disappoint", this "sophisticated" Southwesterner satisfies with "creative", "vibrant" cuisine that's "fan-freaking-tastic" "from beginning to end", served in a "pleasing", "upscale Santa Fe"—esque setting, where "alfresco dining" "by the fountain" is always a "treat"; the staff is "friendly yet thoroughly professional" and gives you the "royal treatment"; in sum, "they know what they're doing here"; N.B. a post-*Survey* chef change to Tom Harvey may outdate the above Food score.

Nikolai's Roof ⊠
26 | 26 | 27 | $72

Hilton Atlanta, 255 Courtland St., NE (bet. Baker & Harris Sts.), 404-221-6362; www.nikolaisroof.com
"Splurge on caviar" and "sip on flavored vodkas" like a "noble" at this "elegant" "treat" atop Downtown's Hilton, where the "fine" French-Continental cuisine with a Russian accent is "impeccable"; with a "knowledgeable" staff that's "on top of everything" and a "wonderful" room that's graced with "beautiful table settings" and truly "breathtaking skyline views", it's a "spectacular" experience (and tab) "you'll never forget"; N.B. the Food score doesn't reflect the post-*Survey* appointment of chef Olivier De Busschere.

Pano's & Paul's ⊠
26 | 23 | 24 | $56

West Paces Ferry Shopping Ctr., 1232 W. Paces Ferry Rd. (Northside Pkwy.), 404-261-3662; www.buckheadrestaurants.com
"Simply timeless", this "star of the Buckhead Life Group" is "worth the splurge" for a "platinum-dining" experience featuring chef Gary Donlick's "phenomenal" Continental cuisine that's "nothing short of spectacular" in "superb presentations", and "flawless service"; the "rich and sumptuous" setting is like a "home away from home" for Buckhead's "old-money crowd" and a "perfect celebration" spot, so even if some find the scene "stuffy", others marvel over how it "manages to stay fresh" after 25 years.

Park 75   26 | 24 | 27 | $54
Four Seasons Atlanta, 75 14th St. (bet. Peachtree & W. Peachtree Sts.), 404-253-3840; www.fourseasons.com

Fumbling fans give all "10 thumbs up" to this "elegant" New American in Midtown that's "worth the splurge" for "unsurpassed service" from a "professional and caring staff"; chef Robert Gerstenecker was appointed post-*Survey* (possibly oudating the Food score), but you can still enjoy a power lunch in the "intimate" room; P.S. for an "over-the-top experience", "eat in the kitchen."

Quinones Room at Bacchanalia 🖂   – | – | – | VE
Courtyard of Bacchanalia, 1198 Howell Mill Rd Nw (bet. 14th & Huff Sts.), 404-365-0410; www.starprovisions.com

Foodies from far and wide are scurrying to sample the latest jewel from chef-owners Anne Quatrano and Clifford Harrison of Bacchanalia fame, housed in the same Westside complex; more refined than its industrial-chic parent, this new venture delivers a leisurely, lavish prix fixe feast of Southern-inspired New American creations, many crafted from ingredients grown on the family farm; the intimate room exudes elegance, with heavy drapes, Venetian glass chandeliers and warm mushroom and cream shades – a big lot of charm in a small (38-seat) space.

Rathbun's 🖂   – | – | – | M
Stove Works, 112 Krog St. (bet. Edgewood & Lake Aves.), 404-524-8280; www.rathbunsrestaurant.com

Gratified gourmets gather to graze at this Inman Parker, a striking industrial-chic space in a circa-1890 building that also boasts a year-round patio with fountain; in the kitchen, chef-owner Kevin Rathbun (ex Nava) turns out New American specialties with a frequent foreign flair (such as his signature dish, lobster soft taco with poblanos and cascabel cream), while on-site pastry chef Kirk Parks (also from Nava) provides the happy endings (e.g. malted milk brûlée); the select cellar holds 125 boutique wines.

Restaurant Eugene 🖂   – | – | – | E
The Aramore, 2277 Peachtree Rd. (Peachtree Memorial Dr.), 404-355-0321; www.restauranteugene.com

Nestled in the bottom of the Aramore building in South Buckhead, this sophisticated and intimate boîte beckons with warm earth tones, sultry drapes and sensual artwork that serve as a subtle backdrop for the New American cuisine of chef/co-owner Linton Hopkins; expect a seasonal, local focus (foie gras with Rainier cherries, Vidalia onion compote and beaten biscuits) and gracious service from a staff that includes partner and wife Gina Hopkins.

RITZ-CARLTON BUCKHEAD DINING ROOM 🖂   28 | 27 | 28 | $76
Ritz-Carlton Buckhead, 3434 Peachtree Rd., NE (Lenox Rd.), 404-237-2700; www.ritzcarlton.com

"Those who like pampering" call this "jacket-only" affair the "gold standard" for "world-class dining" on "endlessly creative" French cuisine "with a Japanese accent", "perfectly paired" with options from an "extensive wine list"; the service is "flawless" from a staff that "anticipates your every thought" in a "magical room" where "nothing is overlooked", and though you need a "fat wallet", it's "well worth every penny"; N.B. the Food score may not reflect a post-*Survey* chef change.

Seeger's ⌧　　　　　　　　26 | 24 | 23 | $86 |
111 W. Paces Ferry Rd. (E. Andrews Dr.), 404-846-9779;
www.seegers.com
"Gastronauts" reach "nirvana" at this Buckhead Continental
showcasing "über-chef" Guenter Seeger's "inspiring", "knockout"
cuisine that "pushes the edge" in a "romantic" setting (a full interior
renovation is planned for October 2005); "stratospheric prices" and
"frosty, alienating service" by "surly" staffers "too in love with
themselves" inspire "active hatred" in clamorous critics, but
admirers call it one of "the finest dining experiences in any city."

SIA'S ⌧　　　　　　　　　27 | 24 | 25 | $44 |
10305 Medlock Bridge Rd. (Wilson Rd.), Duluth, 770-497-9727;
www.siasrestaurant.com
"Hats off to the kitchen" exclaim enthusiasts of this "memorable"
Asian-Southwestern in Duluth that "lays to rest the notion that you
can't find gourmet food outside the Perimeter" with "excellent,
innovative creations" that shine with "skillfully blended" flavors;
owner "Sia Moshk is a charming and attentive host" and "friendly"
"servers know what they're doing" in a "beautiful" room graced
with "white tablecloths and candlelight" that "makes you forget
you're in a strip mall"; N.B. a post-*Survey* chef change may outdate
the above Food score.

Sotto Sotto ⌧　　　　　　　26 | 19 | 21 | $34 |
313 N. Highland Ave. (Elizabeth St.), 404-523-6678;
www.sottosottorestaurant.com
At this Inman Park "treasure", *amici* advise just "close your eyes
and point" at the "well-rounded menu" of "modern" Northern
Italian "heaven on a plate", including "divine homemade pastas"
and "risotto that shines", presented in "perfect portions" by an
"efficient, knowledgeable" (though sometimes "snooty") staff; a
"diverse, arty crowd" flocks to the "relaxed", "sexy" space for a
"fashionable night out", and while "bad acoustics and close tables
make for major noise", the "great food makes it tolerable."

South City Kitchen　　　　　26 | 22 | 23 | $34 |
1144 Crescent Ave., NE (14th St.), 404-873-7358; www.fifthgroup.com
"You don't even have to like Southern cooking" to appreciate the
"unconventional" "taste of the New South" at this "excellent"
Midtown "staple" where "inventive, flavor-packed offerings"
are "suitable for royalty"; the staff is "pleasant", and there's an
"energetic" "let-your-hair-down atmosphere" in the "sleek",
"renovated" "old house", but the downstairs room can get
"irritatingly loud", so many insiders "try to get a table upstairs";
N.B. a post-*Survey* chef change to Timothy Magee (ex La Tavola)
may oudate the above Food score.

TAMARIND　　　　　　　　27 | 20 | 24 | $29 |
80 14th St., NW (bet. Spring & Williams Sts.), 404-873-4888
"Year after year", this "upscale", "dependable treat" in Midtown
has "maintained its reputation" as the "best Thai in town", serving
"simply superb", "perfectly prepared and presented" "food for the
gods"; it's run by a husband-and-wife team who lend a "personal
touch" to the "exotic", "uplifting setting", aided by a "friendly",
"gracious" staff, and though it's "expensive" and the "parking's
difficult", devotees agree it's "worth it"; P.S. it has a newer sibling,
Nan, located "just a few blocks north" in Midtown.

Thumbs Up 🍴　　　　　　　25 | 16 | 20 | $11
573 Edgewood Ave. (Bradley St., SE), 404-223-0690
1617 White Way (bet. East Point & Main Sts.), East Point, 404-768-3776
This "classic diner" in Inman Park (with a newer branch in East Point) "makes it look easy" with "scrumptious", "all-American breakfasts" that "put all other brunch spots to shame"; there's a "neighborhood feel" and "people-watching" possibilities in the space graced with "nice artwork", but "get there early to avoid weekend crowds", and don't forget the cash (no credit cards).

Tierra 🖻　　　　　　　　25 | 19 | 23 | $31
1425B Piedmont Ave., NE (Westminster Dr.), 404-874-5951;
www.tierrarestaurant.com
At this "cozy" Pan-Latin "tucked away" in a strip of stores in Piedmont, "creative, sublime flavors" from an "ever-changing" yet "consistently delightful" seasonal menu "defy description" (though a "handy dandy glossary" helps); they're paired with an "interesting selection of South American wines", and if you "leave without dessert", cognoscenti caution, you will be "committing a serious crime"; the chef/co-owners are "very involved" and their "friendly" staff "goes out of its way" to make your experience "pleasant and exceptional."

TWO. urban licks ☽　　　　　– | – | – | E
820 Ralph McGill Blvd., NE (Freedom Pkwy., NE), 404-522-4622;
www.twourbanlicks.com
Bob Amick and Todd Rushing have done it again with this über-trendy urban hangout where finger-lickin' fans groove to the beat of chef Scott Serpas' (ex Sia's) New American eats with a Southwestern–New Orleans flair, and enjoy wine-by-the-barrel (the stainless-steel containers are displayed in the dining room); the Johnson Studio–designed former warehouse digs have skyline views, floor-to-ceiling gas lights and a 14-ft. tower of fire in its kitchen-in-the-round; N.B. live blues play Wednesday–Saturday.

Wisteria　　　　　　　　25 | 22 | 23 | $33
471 N. Highland Ave. (bet. Colquitt Ave. & Freedom Pkwy.),
404-525-3363; www.wisteria-atlanta.com
The "food speaks for itself" at this "incredible" Inman Park "nouveau Southern" production, but fans can't help weighing in on chef Jason Hill's "extraordinary", "fabulously prepared" cuisine featuring "in-season ingredients and local specialties"; the "low-key" service is "spot-on", and the "intimate" space, "hidden from the hubbub", shines with an "understated elegance", all of which leads groupies to gush, "twist me around this vine anytime."

Woodfire Grill　　　　　　24 | 22 | 22 | $38
1782 Cheshire Bridge Rd. (Piedmont Ave.), 404-347-9055;
www.woodfiregrill.com
"What's fresh on the farm" "ends up in the kitchen" at this "warm and popular spot" in an "out-of-the-way, edgy" Cheshire Bridge location, the showcase for chef Michael Tuohy's "rustic" Northern Californian cuisine highlighted by "immaculate ingredients and bold flavors", "fabulous cheeses" kept in a special aging cabinet and an "awesome wine list" that "doesn't cost an arm and a leg"; "smoky aromas" waft through a "relaxing", "homey" room where an "outstanding" staff is "quick to please"; N.B. there are plans to open a cafe and take-out area by late summer 2005.

Atlantic City

TOP FOOD RANKING

Restaurant	Cuisine
27 White House	Sandwich Shop
26 Chef Vola's	Italian
Brighton	Steakhouse
25 Capriccio	Italian
Suilan	Chinese/French

OTHER NOTEWORTHY PLACES

'Cesca	Italian
Dock's Oyster House	Seafood/American
Los Amigos	Mexican/SW
Old Homestead	Steakhouse
P.F. Chang's	Chinese

F	D	S	C

BRIGHTON STEAKHOUSE `26 | 24 | 24 | $55`
*Sands Hotel & Casino, 136 S. Kentucky Ave. (Pacific Ave.),
609-441-4300; www.acsands.com*
The odds are stacked in your favor at this slabhouse in the Sands
serving some of the "best steaks in AC"; fans take comfort in the
"excellent" service and "fabulous" decor, but they also pray that
someone else picks up the bill, 'cause the beef isn't the only thing
that's "premium" here.

CAPRICCIO 🗷 `25 | 25 | 25 | $64`
*Resorts Atlantic City Casino & Hotel, 1133 Boardwalk
(North Carolina Ave.), 609-340-6789*
Consider playing the slots to pay for a meal at this "pretty" Italian
in the Resorts, where fans say you've "hit the jackpot" since the
food is "superb", the staff is "excellent" and the big bonus is the
"ocean view" (though "not visible at night"); "even if you're not
comped", it's "worth every poker chip" in your pocket.

'Cesca `– | – | – | VE`
Harrah's, 1725 Brigantine Blvd. (Marina Blvd.), 609-345-2311
Sashay around the slots in Harrah's and settle into this bold offshoot
of a Manhattan favorite that's setting a new standard in AC for
contemporary Italian eats, from fig-glazed veal to rice balls plumped
with truffled mushrooms and fontina; a wine list that's a tribute to
the red, white and green rounds out a *perfetto* experience.

CHEF VOLA'S 🗗 `26 | 10 | 22 | $44`
111 S. Albion Pl. (Pacific Ave.), 609-345-2022
You may have to "know the right people" who can get you in to
this reservations-only "find" in an AC "basement", "one of the
more original places around" that delivers with "sensational"
Italian fare, "incredible hospitality" and a "quirky" "non-decor"
that's "part of the charm"; P.S. "bring cash", and don't forget a
bottle, since it's BYO.

DOCK'S OYSTER HOUSE | 24 | 19 | 22 | $47 |

2405 Atlantic Ave. (Georgia Ave.), 609-345-0092;
www.docksoysterhouse.com
Those who like to "escape the casinos" for a while and feast on
"delicious" seafood recommend this "tried-and-true" Atlantic City
"institution" (100 years and counting) known for its "fabulous
assortment of pristine oysters" and "outstanding" service; though
you may have to wait for a table, it's still "hard to beat", especially
with "free parking."

Los Amigos | 23 | 19 | 19 | $26 |

1926 Atlantic Ave. (bet. Michigan & Ohio Aves.), 609-344-2293 ☽
461 Rte. 73 N. (Franklin Ave.), West Berlin, 856-767-5216
www.losamigosrest.com
There's "always a party" at these "busy" Mexican-Southwestern
hermanos in West Berlin and AC, where the festivities feature
"exciting", "innovative" fare and "mesmerizing margaritas"; so
"keep the salsa and chips coming", say supporters, since this
duo's "as good as gold."

Old Homestead | 24 | 25 | 23 | $68 |

Borgata Hotel, Casino & Spa, 1 Borgata Way (Atlantic City Expwy.,
exit 1), 866-692-6742; www.theborgata.com
"Beef is what it's all about" at this NYC import in the heart of the
Borgata Hotel, where "if you can afford the Kobe beef", you may
have "one of the best meals of your life"; "*Flintstone*-size portions"
of steak and an "extensive and expensive" single-malt scotch
menu (not to mention a 400-bottle vino list) lure diners "from the
loud gaming floor" into a "fabulous", bi-level setting.

P.F. CHANG'S CHINA BISTRO ☽ | 22 | 22 | 20 | $28 |

The Quarter at the Tropicana, 2801 N. Pacific Ave. #101 (Iowa Ave.),
609-348-4600; www.pfchangs.com
"Chain dining at its best" brings plaudits to this "high-decibel"
Asian, AC's Most Popular eatery, whose "delicious" food and
"reasonable prices" ensure that fans leave "shaking heads"
and "wondering how they pull it off"; the few who quip about
"Americanized" "fast food in disguise" are overruled.

SUILAN | 25 | 26 | 24 | $61 |

Borgata Hotel, Casino & Spa, 1 Borgata Way (Atlantic City Expwy.,
exit 1), 609-317-7725; www.theborgata.com
Susanna Foo brings her trademark Chinese-French fusion fare to
Atlantic City in the form of this "spectacular", "very upscale" entry
in the Borgata's all-star lineup; "from potstickers to sashimi to
complex preparations of fresh fish", "you'll be in for the experience
of a lifetime" and be "doted on" by the staff amid "soothing" digs.

WHITE HOUSE ⊅ | 27 | 8 | 15 | $12 |

2301 Arctic Ave. (Mississippi Ave.), 609-345-1564
"Hail to the chief" of cheese steaks, hoagies, subs – whatever you
want to call them, since this "landmark", AC's No. 1 for Food, is
known to have patrons who've "driven the 100-mile round-trip on
many occasions" just to pick up the "best sandwiches on earth";
now listen, there's "no decor except the wall-to-wall pictures of
famous clientele", and ya bettah unnerstan' you can't reserve a
table even "if you're Jerry Vale."

Baltimore/Annapolis

TOP FOOD RANKING

Restaurant	Cuisine
28 Charleston	New American
27 Prime Rib	Steakhouse
O'Learys	Seafood
Joss Cafe	Japanese
Hampton's	New American
Les Folies	French Bistro/Seafood
Bicycle, The	Eclectic
Linwoods	New American
Helmand	Afghan
Boccaccio	Northern Italian

OTHER NOTEWORTHY PLACES

Cantler's Riverside	Crab House
Cheesecake Factory	American
Clyde's	American
Corks	New American
Costas Inn Crab House	Crab House
McCormick & Schmick's	Seafood
Pazo	Mediterranean
Ruth's Chris	Steakhouse
Samos	Greek
Timothy Dean's	French/New Amer.

F	D	S	C

Bicycle, The ☒   27 | 22 | 23 | $42
1444 Light St. (bet. Birckhead St. & Fort Ave.), Baltimore, 410-234-1900
"Brilliant" Barry Rumsey rules at this "amazing" Asian-tinged Eclectic in South Baltimore with "creative but not too out there" fare; there's an "electric vibe" to the "funky" digs, but ask the "attentive", if "oh-so-cool", staff "for a courtyard table" for "comfy" dining in summer; P.S. "don't forget the 18 bottles of wine for $18."

Boccaccio   27 | 22 | 24 | $51
925 Eastern Ave. (bet. Exeter & High Sts.), Baltimore, 410-234-1322; www.boccaccio-restaurant.com
"Simple dishes speak lovingly" at "Little Italy's most sophisticated" "institution" where "superior Northern" dishes and "old-style service" turn any meal into a "special occasion"; "formal", "elegant and unhurried", it "caters to upscale, loyal regulars" and "big-event celebrants" who sometimes "dine in the private wine room for small-group intimacy" and gush they'll "have one of everything."

Cantler's Riverside Inn   22 | 12 | 17 | $29
458 Forest Beach Rd. (Browns Woods Rd.), Annapolis, 410-757-1311; www.cantlers.com
There's "virtually no decor – unless you count the boats passing by" – but there are "crabs, crabs, crabs", "heaped high" on

"paper-covered tables" on the deck at this "creekside hideaway" outside Annapolis; it's "crowded", so to avoid "sitting in the lot" waiting for parking, "arrive early"; then "order a bucket of beers", "get the jumbos", "roll up your sleeves and get ready."

CHARLESTON 🗷   28 26 27 $64
1000 Lancaster St. (Exeter St.), Baltimore, 410-332-7373;
www.charlestonrestaurant.com
It's "culinary heaven" with "celestial cooking and prices to match" at Baltimore's No. 1 for Food and Most Popular spot where chef-owner Cindy Wolf's "magical" New American creations are conjured with a "sublime soupçon of a Southern touch"; the "divine fried oysters", "a to-die-for tasting menu" and "outstanding cheese cart" are matched by co-owner Tony Foreman's "phenomenal" wine list, while "highly professional service" and "posh" Inner Harbor East locale make it the place "to impress and be impressed"; N.B. a summer 2005 redo and repricing may outdate the scores.

CHEESECAKE FACTORY   19 17 16 $25
Harborplace Pratt St. Pavilion, 201 E. Pratt St. (South St.), Baltimore, 410-234-3990; www.thecheesecakefactory.com
At this mall-based, midpriced American, "everything is huge": "menu, portions, slabs of cheesecake and the lines", but most of that sums up their "gluttonous" appeal; "tons of choices", plenty of "leftovers" "and, of course", their "amazing" signature dessert have legions of hungry fans shrugging at the "get 'em in, get 'em out" game plan and strategizing to cope with the "interminable" wait ("put your name in and shop awhile" around Harborplace).

CLYDE'S ●   18 19 18 $28
10221 Wincopin Circle (Little Patuxent Pkwy.), Columbia, 410-730-2829;
www.clydes.com
A "local tradition", this popular American bistro "gets the basics right" with "affordable", "updated" tavern "classics", "seasonally appropriate specials", a "hopping bar" and some of the "best brunches", making it Columbia's "go-to place" for virtually any age or occasion, set amid a "warm, brass-and-wood", "Ralph Lauren–fantasy" atmosphere.

Corks   26 20 25 $45
1026 S. Charles St. (bet. E. Cross & W. Hamburg Sts.), Baltimore, 410-752-3810; www.corksrestaurant.com
"Home away from home" for "wine connoisseurs (and those pretending to be)" is this "unassuming" South Baltimore rowhouse, "transformed" into a restaurant "unlike any other in town", where smashing New American fare "rises to the challenge" of a 200-plus all-American list of "unusual" labels "from small vintners"; with a "knowledgeable staff" and "suggested pairings" for each "sublime creation", "you'll not be at a loss for a delicious" sip.

Costas Inn Crab House & Restaurant ●   23 9 18 $33
4100 N. Point Blvd. (New Battle Grove Rd.), Dundalk, 410-477-1975
"Don't be put off by the proximity of the steel mill" or the "karaoke bar next door" because "trays of steaming, peppery crabs and beer" are "spread out on paper-covered tables" for "serious" "down 'n' dirty" eating at this "traditional Maryland house" of hardshells in Dundalk; it's "not fancy", but it is "genuine", and if "service is spotty", that's because "the place is packed"; however, "they do accept reservations", so make one or "wait."

HAMPTON'S

| 27 | 28 | 27 | $68 |

Harbor Court Hotel, 550 Light St. (bet. Conway & Lee Sts.), Baltimore, 410-347-9744; www.harborcourt.com

The "thoughtful service" is the "best on earth" – or at least in Baltimore – while a "beautiful room" with water views also rates high at the Harbor Court Hotel's "exquisite", "extraordinary-in-all-respects" restaurant, "the ultimate place for the meal of a lifetime"; "beautifully presented by a master chef" and "arriving under silver domes", the seasonally changing New American fare is "sublime"; "you'll never [again] feel so pampered while dressed formally", especially "if someone else is paying."

Helmand, The

| 27 | 20 | 23 | $26 |

806 N. Charles St. (bet. Madison & Read Sts.), Baltimore, 410-752-0311; www.helmand.com

"Expand your mind" at the "effortlessly exotic" Mt. Vernon "legend" that both "herbivores and carnivores dream about"; this "polished, Afghan" offers an "explosion of flavors" in dishes like "don't-miss" *kaddo borawni* (pumpkin in garlic yogurt) at "reasonable prices"; with "dressy theater adventurers" joining "casual" students in "gustatory bliss", it's "busy", so service is "rushed."

JOSS CAFE & SUSHI BAR

| 27 | 18 | 23 | $31 |

195 Main St. (Church Circle), Annapolis, 410-263-4688; www.josscafe-sushibar.com

"Wait in line" to sit "on each others' laps, fighting for attention" at this "odd, little" "upbeat" "place in the tourist zone", where the raw fish "can turn non–sushi eaters into devotees"; "fresh and fabulous, world-class" cuts, "inventive concoctions" and a "delicious" "selection of cooked Japanese food" are "worth the drive in rush-hour traffic" to Annapolis to "run up a tab."

Les Folies Brasserie

| 27 | 22 | 25 | $43 |

2552 Riva Rd. (Aris T. Allen Blvd.), Annapolis, 410-573-0970; www.lesfoliesbrasserie.com

"Raw oysters from all the best areas" satisfy a "dress-and-spend crowd" at this "slice of Paris" in Annapolis, which serves a "daily selection of fresh shellfish" and "sumptuous" French "comfort food"; it's a "class act" "with great attention to detail", where everything from the "copper-topped bar" to the cassoulet is "authentic", except the staff – "they'll treat your Valentine better than you do."

Linwoods

| 27 | 25 | 25 | $49 |

McDonogh Crossroads, 25 Crossroads Dr. (McDonogh & Reisterstown Rds.), Owings Mills, 410-356-3030; www.linwoods.com

This "sleek", "sophisticated" New American is a "suburban-chic" "destination" for "haute Owings Mills" thanks to "high-caliber", "hands-on management" and an atmosphere "without pretense"; admirers who sit around the central exhibition kitchen "to watch them prepare" "top-drawer" fare note though it's "geared toward captains of industry", you don't have to "spend megabucks."

MCCORMICK & SCHMICK'S

| 21 | 20 | 19 | $38 |

Pier 5 Hotel, 711 Eastern Ave. (President St.), Baltimore, 410-234-1300; www.mccormickandschmicks.com

There's "nothing fishy" about this "classy" chain link in the Inner Harbor that hooks fans on "seafood at its best" cooked in seemingly "a hundred different ways"; a mutinous crew sinks "spotty" service and "lackluster presentation", but the "hands-down best" happy-hour "bargains" go over swimmingly well.

O'LEARYS SEAFOOD   27 | 22 | 25 | $46

310 Third St. (Severn Ave.), Eastport, 410-263-0884; www.olearys-seafood.com

"The staff's knowledge" is so "stellar" it's "almost not human" at this "seriously good" piscatorial Eastporter where new chef Brendan Keegan now oversees the preparation of "ultrafresh seafood choices"; the "wine list is well chosen" to go with "glorious" crispy grouper and other "excellent" fish – "just make sure your credit-card limit is high."

Pazo ●   – | – | – | E

1425 Aliceanna St. (bet. S. Caroline & S. Spring Sts.), Baltimore, 410-534-7296; www.pazorestaurant.com

In a renovated factory on the fringes of Fells Point, this plush, romantic restaurant/lounge from Charleston's Tony Foreman lures hipsters for rich Mediterranean small plates served in a soaring, multilevel setting featuring cozy, canopied booths, a mezzanine perfect for people-watching and an 18-person communal table; no matter where you're seated, settle back to the sounds of world music and a sip from the well-priced wine list; N.B. on request they'll clear tables away to create a dance floor.

PRIME RIB ●   27 | 26 | 27 | $56

Horizon House, 1101 N. Calvert St. (Chase St.), Baltimore, 410-539-1804; www.theprimerib.com

"Take your credit card and somebody sexy" to this steakhouse, a "place to go in your little black dress" and your mandatory jacket "for a night of red meat and romance"; "satisfy your ravenous appetite" with "gargantuan cuts" "served by tuxedoed waiters in the plush" if "faded glory" of "leopard print and mirrors" while you wait for the "Rat Pack to walk in any moment" to jam with the "excellent jazz" musicians; reservations are strongly recommended, though they're "not great" at honoring times on "crazy Saturdays."

RUTH'S CHRIS STEAK HOUSE   24 | 22 | 23 | $53

Pier 5 Hotel, 711 Eastern Ave. (S. President St.), Baltimore, 410-230-0033
600 Water St. (bet. Gay St. & Market Pl.), Baltimore, 410-783-0033
www.ruthschris.com

It's "all about the beef and nothing but the beef" at this "excellent" Inner Harbor duo where "sinful steaks swimming in butter" are served by a "phenomenal" staff in a setting of "dark woodwork" with an "old-school boys' club–meets–power scene" "charm"; be forewarned, you "pay big-time for the privilege" of partaking in that "divine" "mountain of meat."

Samos 🗷≠   26 | 12 | 21 | $18

600 S. Oldham St. (Fleet St.), Baltimore, 410-675-5292; www.samosrestaurant.com

"It's a minor miracle that a short-order kitchen can provide some of the area's best food", say supporters of this "real Greek for real Greeks" in (where else?) Greektown; the spartan spot is "not fancy", and "no reservations and wild popularity" mean a "long wait", but this cash-only BYO "will blow your taste

buds away" with "outstanding gyros", "delicious salad" and "excellent calamari", prepared with a "warm spirit" in "big portions at reasonable prices."

Timothy Dean's Bistro

1717 Eastern Ave. (Regester St.), Baltimore, 410-534-5650;
www.tdbistro.com

Urban sophisticates are delighted with top-flight DC chef Timothy Dean's truffle-infused, French-inspired New American cuisine – think crab cakes over leeks – served in a warm, brick-arched Fells Point setting; he monitors the room regularly, as casually dressed couples (and the occasional power broker) chat at copper-topped tables to the sounds of background jazz; N.B. the valet's a useful perk, and there's also a calmly cool Sunday brunch.

Boston

TOP FOOD RANKING

Restaurant	Cuisine
29 Oishii	Japanese
28 L'Espalier	New French
Aujourd'hui	New French
27 No. 9 Park	French/Italian
Hamersley's Bistro	French/New American
Blue Ginger	Asian Fusion
Mistral	Med./New French
Icarus	New American
Il Capriccio	Northern Italian
Oleana	Mediterranean
Clio	New French
Carmen	Italian
Rialto	Mediterranean
Coriander	French Bistro
Craigie St. Bistrot	French Bistro
26 Sage	Northern Italian
Helmand	Afghan
Salts	New American
Saporito's	Northern Italian
Radius	New French

OTHER NOTEWORTHY PLACES

B&G Oysters	Seafood
Dalí	Spanish/Tapas
East Coast Grill	Barbecue/Seafood
EVOO	Eclectic
Franklin Café	New American
Grotto	Italian
Harvest	New American
Legal Sea Foods	Seafood
Le Soir	French Bistro
Locke-Ober	Continental
Meritage	New American
Neptune Oyster	Seafood
Petit Robert Bistro	French Bistro
Pigalle	French Bistro
Restaurant L	Asian Fusion
Sibling Rivalry	New American
Tamarind Bay	Indian
Taranta	Peruvian /S. Italian
Troquet	French/New American
UpStairs on the Square	New American

AUJOURD'HUI
28 | 27 | 28 | $72

Four Seasons Hotel, 200 Boylston St. (bet. Arlington & Charles Sts.), 617-351-2172; www.fourseasons.com
As "the gold standard" for "special occasions", this New French in the Back Bay's "outstanding Four Seasons" Hotel is itself "cause for celebration": it features a staff that "takes attentive to a whole new level", making you "feel like royalty" as you dine on "superlative" cuisine "cooked to perfection" and proffered against a recently renovated backdrop of "elegance layered upon elegance" – so "book a windowside table, order a magnum of bubbly and let someone else pick up the tab."

B&G Oysters
26 | 22 | 23 | $40

550 Tremont St. (Waltham St.), 617-423-0550; www.bandgoysters.com
"Truly a pearl", this "sleek, smart" South End raw bar from No. 9 Park's Barbara Lynch showcases the "aphrodisiac" effects of "innumerable varieties" of "fantastically fresh" (if "pricey") oysters, paired with "sublime wines by the glass" and rounded out by a "limited" but "innovative" seafood menu; it's "popular", so there's "not always a table", but you can "sit at the bar and watch the choreography of the open kitchen" as you glean "vast knowledge" from your savvy server.

BLUE GINGER ⍁
27 | 22 | 24 | $49

583 Washington St. (Rte. 16), Wellesley, 781-283-5790; www.ming.com
"The culmination of Ming Tsai's quest for the perfect balance of East meets West", this Wellesley "perennial" arguably serves the "best Asian fusion in the country", as the celeb chef-owner "transcends the sometimes pretentious nature of the genre" with his "brilliant" creations; a handful – perceiving "occasional lapses" in the "crisp, professional service" and decrying the "spare" decor as "ordinary" – conclude it's "coasting on its reputation", but most, insisting "Ming's still got zing", retort with "just one word: go!"

Carmen
27 | 22 | 22 | $39

33 North Sq. (Richmond St.), 617-742-6421
"Defying cliches" and space constraints alike, this North End neighbor to Paul Revere's house "is a special place" whose "cubicle-sized kitchen turns out" "innovative", "sophisticated" – heck, "fantastic" – Italian dishes, from "delicious" cicchetti to crespelle Bolognese; though you'd best "forget privacy", remember that "rubbing shoulders with your neighbors" "is sometimes comforting", sometimes even "sexy" (just "don't tell the tourists").

Clio
27 | 25 | 25 | $68

Eliot Suite Hotel, 370A Commonwealth Ave. (Mass. Ave.), 617-536-7200; www.cliorestaurant.com
With "a genius" and "madman" like Ken Oringer in the kitchen, this Back Bay "showstopper" "continues to reign" "supreme", converting numerous critics of "la-di-da dining" via "wonderfully strange" New French "masterpieces" showcased against an "understated" backdrop; still, the remaining skeptics – who "leave having experienced food but actually eaten very little" – complain that their "wishes come second" to "ideas", a "risky" state of affairs "given the price tag"; P.S. meanwhile, adjoining sashimi bar Uni "rocks the palates" of piscivores.

Coriander Bistro ⚐   27 | 22 | 26 | $48 |
5 Post Office Sq. (bet. Billings & S. Main Sts.), Sharon, 781-784-5450;
www.corianderbistro.com
Urbanites whose culinary expectations head south when they do
are downright "shocked" to discover Sharon's French "star";
owners Kevin and Jill Crawley have "put their hearts into this bistro,
and it shows in every way", from the "all-around excellent"
"gourmet" meals sprinkled with "elegant little extras" to an
"engaging" "attention to service"; *c'est cher, naturellement,* but
"for a special occasion", it "ranks up there with the best in Boston."

Craigie Street Bistrot   27 | 20 | 25 | $46 |
5 Craigie Circle (bet. Brattle St. & Concord Ave.), Cambridge,
617-497-5511; www.craigiestreetbistrot.com
"Chef-on-the-rise" Tony Maws' "mission and talent are pure"
to the many "serious foodies" who have made this French bistro
"sleeper" "in the basement of an apartment building" outside
Harvard Square their "teeny-tiny" "home away from home";
"sparkling flavors" distinguish "one tantalizing dish after another"
on the "constantly changing menu", and the "educated, eager"
"staff thoroughly spoils" you with "spot-on advice about wine
pairings"; no wonder a majority calls its kitchen "the little
engine that could."

Dalí   25 | 25 | 23 | $32 |
415 Washington St. (Beacon St.), Somerville, 617-661-3254;
www.dalirestaurant.com
"Baroque", "electric" and "magical", this "perpetually crowded"
Spanish "restaurant that put Somerville on the map" still treats
its customers to "an event, not just a meal" – "teasing all of their
senses" with "rich, delectable tapas" and "fruity sangria" served
"in a kaleidoscope" of rooms by an "effervescent" staff "that seems
to love the place, too"; no wonder only a small minority says they're
"frankly over it."

East Coast Grill & Raw Bar   26 | 18 | 21 | $35 |
1271 Cambridge St. (Prospect St.), Cambridge, 617-491-6568;
www.eastcoastgrill.net
"There's nobody quite like [chef-owner] Chris Schlesinger", whose
"energy" imbues every "multifaceted" inch of this "jumping" joint in
Inman Square, "assuring great food is the focus" – namely "spicy,
smoky, adventurous" seafood and BBQ that skew tropical to match
the "flaming cocktails" from the in-house tiki lounge; meanwhile,
the staff remains consummate "professionals" no matter how
"freaking crowded" the place gets, even during its celebrated
Sunday "brunch with a punch" and on notorious Hell Nights (when
chile-chompers test their mettle).

EVOO ⚐   26 | 20 | 23 | $45 |
118 Beacon St. (Washington St.), Somerville, 617-661-3866;
www.evoorestaurant.com
"Duck, oxtail, rabbit – the zoo was never this much fun" joke
otherwise "serious" gourmands about this "exemplary" Eclectic
bistro in Somerville that has "firmly established itself" in their
esteem: now "rich", now "ethereal", chef Peter McCarthy's
"seasonal menu" "just gets better and more interesting", while
his wife, Colleen, oversees a "well-informed" and "extremely
nice" staff in a "casual", "comfy setting"; perhaps, then, the

'E' is not only for 'extra' (as in 'extra virgin olive oil') but also "stands for excellent."

Franklin Café ☽   25 | 18 | 20 | $32
278 Shawmut Ave. (Hanson St.), 617-350-0010; www.franklincafe.com
An "all-time favorite" among South Enders, this "dimly lit", "rollicking" joint "fires on all cylinders" with a "limited" and "understated" but "ravishing" New American menu, "much better than many that are twice as expensive"; it's always "filled to the brim", so expect "a two- or three-martini wait" and a "noise level" that can be "too much to take" – indeed, it only "gets louder as it gets later", since the "kitchen's open late", a "rare find" in Boston.

Grotto   25 | 18 | 22 | $37
37 Bowdoin St. (bet. Beacon & Cambridge Sts.), 617-227-3434; www.grottorestaurant.com
Making "the short list" of "inspired" places, this "subterranean" "bit of vintage Greenwich Village" on Beacon Hill brooks "no silliness" even as its "fantastic", "monthly changing" Italian menu "riffs on old favorites to create something entirely new" (including "interesting" as well as "delicious spaghetti and meatballs"); indeed, served by a "gracious" staff, "the food more than makes up for" a "quirky" space that's "a little uncomfortable" for legroom-lovers (yet plenty "cozy" to "romantics").

HAMERSLEY'S BISTRO   27 | 24 | 25 | $56
553 Tremont St. (Clarendon St.), 617-423-2700; www.hamersleysbistro.com
"Pioneer" "Gordon Hamersley just keeps on trucking" in "the open kitchen" of his "bright, airy" "South End classic" – arguably the "best bistro in New England" – "and all without putting on airs": the "hearty, harvest-inspired" French–New American dishes exhibit "dash" but eschew fads ("the usual kudos" go to the worthy roast chicken) and the staff displays "enduring commitment and energy"; so for each cynic who spurns the "hype", there is a satisfied – make that "spoiled" – "loyalist."

Harvest   25 | 23 | 23 | $46
44 Brattle St. (Church St.), Cambridge, 617-868-2255; www.the-harvest.com
Not only has it "aged gracefully", this Harvard Square "old-timer" is "still worthy of a magazine spread", sigh the starry-eyed while seated among "the campus glitterati, waxing eloquent" over "sensational, seasonal" New American meals; a "reliably excellent feeding place, it's not flashy but respectful" of New England culinary traditions, and of you – as exhibited by the "down-to-earth staff's" "perfect pacing"; a bit "tweedy" and "faculty loungish" in tone, it's nonetheless "worth smartening yourself up for."

Helmand   26 | 22 | 20 | $29
143 First St. (Bent St.), Cambridge, 617-492-4646
"Bored? – then eat" at this "class act" on "a godforsaken strip" of "industrial blight" in East Cambridge, where a simple meal becomes "a pure delight and an education"; the "exotic yet accessible" Afghani cuisine "far exceeds expectations" ("they do wonders with pumpkin and lamb") "in a setting with the warmth and comfort of a living room" – albeit one more evocative, some say, of Pottery Barn

than Kandahar; while the "prompt" servers are not themselves so "warm and fuzzy", "the prices are kind."

Icarus
27] 24] 25] $54]

3 Appleton St. (bet. Arlington & Berkeley Sts.), 617-426-1790;
www.icarusrestaurant.com

"There's something to be said for a chef who stays in one place", "quietly doing it right": after 20-some years, Chris Douglass' "subdued", mildly "art deco" supper club in the South End remains the "crème de la crème" of New American "gourmet" dining, "not too nouveau" but plenty "intriguing"; since it "doesn't get overwhelmed by 'in' crowds or tourists", "you're able to talk" or listen to a "delicious" "jazz combo on Friday nights", aided by "unobtrusive" servers that "bring it all together."

Il Capriccio ☒
27] 22] 25] $52]

888 Main St. (Prospect St.), Waltham, 781-894-2234

Showing "originality within the framework" of a Northern Italian menu that's alternately "earthy" and "polished", this *magnifico* Waltham winner is known "among the cognoscenti" for its "sparkling wine list", while "crisp service" from a "personable staff" makes "a special occasion special" – assuming you don't mind "sharing conversations with neighboring tables"; still, scrimpers label the tab "excessive" no matter the event.

LEGAL SEA FOODS
22] 18] 20] $35]

Copley Pl., 100 Huntington Ave. (bet. Dartmouth & Exeter Sts.),
617-266-7775
26 Park Plaza (Columbus Ave.), 617-426-4444
Long Wharf, 255 State St. (Atlantic Ave.), 617-227-3115
South Shore Plaza, 250 Granite St. (I-95, exit 6), Braintree,
781-356-3070
Burlington Mall, 1131 Middlesex Tpke. (Rte. 128), Burlington,
781-270-9700
5 Cambridge Ctr. (bet. Ames & Main Sts.), Cambridge,
617-864-3400
20 University Rd. (Eliot St.), Cambridge, 617-491-9400
The Mall at Chestnut Hill, 43 Boylston St. (Hammond Pond Pkwy.),
Chestnut Hill, 617-277-7300
50-60 Worcester Rd./Rte. 9 (Ring Rd.), Framingham,
508-766-0600
Northshore Mall, 210 Andover St./Rte. 114 (Rte. 128), Peabody,
978-532-4500
www.legalseafoods.com

Loyalty to this "ubiquitous" seafood franchise remains "high" – indeed, it's Boston's Most Popular because it's a "well-oiled machine" that "manages to maintain its identity" and preserve the status quo even as it "keeps reinventing itself" and "revitalizing its menu" (besides, "the clam chowder really is all that"); while the culinary elite may criticize its "vanilla" "cafeteria atmosphere", the vast majority insists this "quality" experience "will change the way you think about chains."

Le Soir
25] 23] 23] $54]

51-53 Lincoln St. (bet. Chester & Columbus Sts.), Newton Highlands,
617-965-3100; www.lesoirbistro.com

"When only the best will do", this "understated" yet "memorable" Newton Highlands bistro "does it – beautifully and serenely";

"one of the Frenchest spots around", it rekindles the passion for "candlelit dinners" with a "small" but "polished" menu – "suburban star" chef Mark Allen knows "what works and what doesn't" – proffered by "always solicitous" servers; pooh-poohers of the "too-too" aura, however, would prefer "a little more soul."

L'ESPALIER ☒ 28 | 27 | 27 | $84

30 Gloucester St. (bet. Commonwealth Ave. & Newbury St.), 617-262-3023; www.lespalier.com

This "favorite" offers a "once-in-a-blue-moon experience" of "unparalleled gustatory extravagance"; an "enchanting" Back Bay townhouse sets the stage for a "succulent" New England–accented "nouveau French" menu born of Frank McClelland's "painstaking" technique and brought to table by veritable "mind-readers" who know "royal treatment"; still, it's "not for everyone" say those who find the "elegant atmosphere" "intimidating" ("be sure to know proper etiquette").

Locke-Ober ☒ 23 | 24 | 23 | $60

3 Winter Pl. (bet. Tremont & Washington Sts.), 617-542-1340; www.locke-ober.com

"All spiffy" since a much-heralded "redo" by co-owner Lydia Shire, this "venerable institution" Downtown remains "a throwback to the days when fine dining meant fine dining": "the silver gleams, the service cossets" and "the preservation of haute Yankee cuisine" proves "noble", since "it is the old signature dishes that mean so much" (like the "divine lobster stew", JFK's purported fave) – though what they signify to hipsters who dismiss the Continental menu's token "innovative" gestures is "soul food for WASPs."

Meritage 26 | 26 | 25 | $63

Boston Harbor Hotel, 70 Rowes Wharf (Atlantic Ave.), 617-439-3995; www.meritagetherestaurant.com

"Forget your preconceptions about hotel restaurants" – this "sleek" "celebration" "does an extraordinary job" with a "brilliant concept": the "entrancing" "avant-garde" New American eats from "master" chef Daniel Bruce come in "half or full portions to allow lots of tastings", for which the highly "wine-savvy" (but "not condescending") staff provides "dead-on pairing" picks from an "exquisite", "comprehensive" list; granted, "the tab can be shocking", but it pales beside the "swoon"-eliciting experience – complete with "dramatic views" of the waterfront.

Mistral 27 | 26 | 25 | $59

223 Columbus Ave. (bet. Berkeley & Clarendon Sts.), 617-867-9300; www.mistralbistro.com

"Even better than when it opened", this "sexy" South End French-Med "cultural" "happening" has "matured" into a "classic" that still hits the "heights of chic" – as the "beautiful people, including the staff", around the "hot bar" attest; "masterful cooking" and "hard-to-find gems" by the bottle are the keys to its "success", though the value-conscious complain about "price-gouging" by a crew that "takes itself too seriously."

Neptune Oyster – | – | – | M

63 Salem St. (Cross St.), 617-742-3474

Say *ciao* to the red-sauce kitsch of the prior trattoria: now this tiny but "cheery" North End space houses a clean, spare raw bar with an old-fashioned feel (thanks to etched glass, subway tiles and a pressed-tin ceiling) but a modern menu – which nonetheless puts a "clever" Italian spin on the seafood entrees it features along with the traditional shucked shellfish; N.B. there's a savvy wine list too.

NO. 9 PARK ⊠   27 | 24 | 26 | $61

9 Park St. (bet. Beacon & Tremont Sts.), 617-742-9991; www.no9park.com

"When it really matters", gourmets head to Barbara Lynch's always "au courant" "heavy hitter" on Beacon Hill to be "treated like honored guests" by the "sharp staff" – and to be "left speechless" by the "dynamite" country French–Italian menu and its "casual yet precise execution", abetted by "wines chosen for taste, not label"; so though non-subscribers to the "less is more" philosophy squint at the "astronomically priced, minuscule portions" set against a "stark" backdrop, converts chant "time and time and time again, No. 9 is a 10."

OISHII   28 | 11 | 19 | $35

612 Hammond St. (Boylston St.), Chestnut Hill, 617-277-7888
Mill Vlg., 365 Boston Post Rd./Rte. 20 (Concord Rd.), Sudbury, 978-440-8300
www.oishiisushi.com

"Proud Bostonians" may debate whether these twin Japanese "gastro-temples" in Chestnut Hill and Sudbury are simply No. 1 for Food in the metro area, or whether they actually cut and roll the "best sushi in New England" (or even America itself) – but all agree the "mind-altering" "masterpieces", be they "melt-in-your-mouth maki" or "tender", "thick slices" of sashimi, trounce the "frustrating" waits for "precious" seats in the "criminally small" dining rooms amid "insane crowds"; N.B. a new South End branch is in the works.

Oleana   27 | 23 | 23 | $43

134 Hampshire St. (bet. Columbia & Prospect Sts.), Cambridge, 617-661-0505; www.oleanarestaurant.com

"Culinary goddess" Ana Sortun's self-described groupies "sing the praises" of her "original" Eastern "Med mecca" near Inman Square: the "daring" yet "carefully crafted", "titillating" yet "ethereal" menu's "execution is equal to the ideas" it conveys – a "very rare" achievement, whether relished in the "romantic" if "cramped quarters" or out on the "pretty, peaceful" "garden patio"; though the usually "knowing" but occasionally "standoffish" waitrons can be "a tad slow", "all is forgiven" by the time "you leave, stuffed and in heaven."

Petit Robert Bistro   – | – | – | M

468 Commonwealth Ave. (Charlesgate W.), 617-375-0699; www.petitrobertbistro.com

This classic French bistro occupying two floors of a Kenmore Square townhouse marks the comeback of Jacky Robert (of the erstwhile institution Maison Robert), who re-creates the workaday Parisian experience with fairly priced *plats* like rabbit moutarde and sardines en baguette; between lunch and dinner, a pastry bar presents mostly time-honored sweets like profiteroles – though nontraditionalists will find that all the menus here contain a surprise or two.

Pigalle
26 | 22 | 24 | $53

75 Charles St. S. (bet. Stuart St. & Warrenton Pl.), 617-423-4944;
www.pigalleboston.com
"Serious foodies" agree this "Theater District destination" "richly
deserves the kudos" it receives for "doing everything with quiet
style": you'll watch (and taste) French Bistro "classics evolve" into
the "imaginative" yet "mature" creations of chef Marc Orfaly, while
manager Kerri Foley and their "sweet" crew "make you feel
comfortably pampered"; while "low lighting sets the mood for
romance", their "perfect pacing" clinches it.

Radius ⊠
26 | 25 | 25 | $64

8 High St. (bet. Federal & Summer Sts.), 617-426-1234;
www.radiusrestaurant.com
A "serious address" in any gastronome's directory, this New French
"gold" mine still sets the Financial District "buzzing"; Michael
Schlow's "superlative" "art on a plate" "always comes first", but
"gorgeous" servers who act more like "personal butlers" thrill the
"fashion-forward crowd" too; true, the indifferent feel a "chill"
emanating from the kitchen (it "sometimes overemphasizes
technique") and the dining room ("too edgy to be completely
comfortable"), but most would gladly "refinance their homes"
to eat here.

Restaurant L ⊠
23 | 20 | 20 | $47

Louis Boston, 234 Berkeley St. (Newbury St.), 617-266-4680;
www.louisboston.com
"Cotton candy, Pop Rocks and Kobe beef live in harmony" at
Louis Boston's "cutting-edge" in-store bistro in the Back Bay:
though "not too many people seem to know about" "superb"
"young" chef Pino Maffeo, his "tricky" Asian fusion creations
sure taste "delicious" – except to straight-shooters who (after
"leaving hungry, without understanding what they ate") call the
"minimalist-cool" vibe "cold."

Rialto
27 | 24 | 24 | $57

Charles Hotel, 1 Bennett St. (University Rd.), Cambridge, 617-661-5050;
www.rialto-restaurant.com
"Doing for food what Harvard does for education", the Charles
Hotel's signature dining room, now a decade old, remains "a
tour de force" of Mediterranean cuisine: supporters say "Jody
Adams is such a smart and well-traveled chef", and it shows in
the "wonders [she] works" with a menu that's "inventive without
being unapproachable"; some suggest that perhaps "the space
could use an update – it still feels like a hotel restaurant" – but it's
sufficiently "elegant" and "romantic" to "cherish" "with your
significant other", especially since the staff, though "bright" and
"eager", isn't "overbearing."

Sage ⊠
26 | 19 | 22 | $43

69 Prince St. (Salem St.), 617-248-8814; www.sageboston.com
"Resisting the peer pressure" of nearby "pasta shacks", this
North End "must-visit" "continues to turn out fresh", "ethereal"
New American–accented Northern Italian faves ("no one does
rabbit like chef-owner Anthony Susi", whose "gnocchi float" like
"clouds"); granted, the mostly "accommodating" staff "couldn't
shoehorn even one more person" into the "plain-looking" "closet"
of a dining room, but "the wise know" "size isn't everything."

Salts ⑤
26 22 25 $51

798 Main St. (Windsor St.), Cambridge, 617-876-8444;
www.saltsrestaurant.com

Satisfied surveyors suggest you take this "quiet, romantic"
"detour" from the "student-oriented eateries" of Central Square
and have yourself an "unforgettable experience"; while the much-
touted "duck for two is divine", "you'll migrate here for the rest"
of new chef-owner Gabriel Bremer's "earthy", "meticulously"
"handcrafted" New American dishes as well; true, it's "very small"
while the prices are quite "large", but it still feels like a "warm"
"home away from home."

Saporito's
26 19 24 $40

11 Rockland Circle (George Washington Blvd.), Hull, 781-925-3023;
www.saporitoscafe.com

"You wouldn't even know" this "quaint" Northern Italian getaway
was under "new management" – the food is "still fantastic" and the
"unpretentious staff" still "tries to do everything for its patrons";
occupying a "secluded" "seaside bungalow" in Hull, it may be an
"unkept secret", but scoring a reservation is "worth the effort."

Sibling Rivalry
– – – E

525 Tremont St. (Berkeley St.), 617-338-5338;
www.siblingrivalryboston.com

"Family feuds can be ugly", but Kinkead brothers Robert (of
Washington, DC's famed Kinkead's) and David (of local fame) are
betting "competition brings out the best" in them – hence the high
concept of this "unique" South End newcomer, whereby each
chef presents his own "unusual" New American menu based
on shared main ingredients; naturally, the large, urbane, earth-
toned space features an exhibition kitchen so diners can catch all
the explosive action.

Tamarind Bay
∇ 26 19 22 $26

75 Winthrop St. (JFK St.), Cambridge, 617-491-4552

"Definitely different than any other Indian restaurant you've ever
visited", this "phenomenal addition" to Harvard Square adds "a
whole new dimension of flavor" to the genre via "cooked-to-order"
dishes that "delight the palate" with "the complexity of their
spicing"; a "courteous" staff oversees the "crowded" but "warm"
renovated basement space where a "fun and inexpensive prix
fixe menu" replaces the "typical buffet" come lunchtime.

Taranta
24 21 23 $37

210 Hanover St. (Cross St.), 617-720-0052; www.tarantarist.com

An "exciting" North End "experiment", this "modern"-looking
"multilevel" "star" shines with the "successful fusion of Southern
Italian" and, "of all things, Peruvian" cuisines, highlighted by an
equally uncommon wine list; though the "gregarious owner" is
usually on hand "to make sure everything works", the staff is
equally "informed" and "helpful."

Troquet ⑤
26 21 24 $54

140 Boylston St. (bet. S. Charles & Tremont Sts.), 617-695-9463;
www.troquetboston.com

"It's grown-up time" for the oenophiles who take "great joy in
this well-run", "informal" yet "serious" Theater District wine bar,
where a "small" French–New American menu, "glistening" with

"neatly prepared, simple bistro dishes", brings out the "breadth and depth" of the *carte du vins*; even if it's "no bargain", "what's not to love about a place that serves imported butter by the ice cream scoop?"

UpStairs on the Square   24 | 25 | 23 | $51

91 Winthrop St. (JFK St.), Cambridge, 617-864-1933;
www.upstairsonthesquare.com
"A worthy successor" to the much-"loved" UpStairs at the Pudding, this New American "fantasyland" in Harvard Square is "actually two restaurants"; the "pink", "mirrored" Soirée Room, resembling "a life-size jewel box" or "dollhouse", "sparkles" along with its "magic" menu, while the more casual Monday Club Bar is like "*Alice in Wonderland*'s tea party"; expect "over-the-top service upstairs" and "pleasantly brisk service downstairs", but "stop at the bank first"; P.S. though one of its "top chefs", Amanda Lydon, left post-*Survey,* Susan Regis remains to run both kitchens.

Charlotte

TOP FOOD RANKING

	Restaurant	Cuisine
29	Barrington's	New American
28	Volare	Italian
27	McIntosh's	Seafood/Steakhouse
	Sullivan's	Steakhouse
26	Nikko	Japanese
	Upstream	Seafood
	ONEO	New American
	Toscana	Northern Italian
	Noble's	Continental/Italian
	Luce	Northern Italian

OTHER NOTEWORTHY PLACES

Restaurant	Cuisine
Bonterra	New American
Carpe Diem	New American
Ethan's of Elizabeth	New American
ilios noche	Greek/Italian
McNinch House	Eclectic
Mickey & Mooch	Steakhouse
Palm	Steakhouse
Patou	French
Sonoma Modern American	Californian/New Amer.
Zebra Rest.	New French

F	D	S	C

BARRINGTON'S ☒ | 29 | 21 | 25 | $46 |

FoxCroft Shopping Ctr., 7822 Fairview Rd. (bet. Carmel & Colony Rds.), 704-364-5755; www.barringtonsrestaurant.com

No wonder it can be "impossible to get in to": No. 1 for Food and Popularity in Charlotte, this SouthPark New American "delights" and "surprises" fans with "memorable", "understated" creations from chef Bruce Moffett (whom the gods have blessed with the "most sophisticated palate" in the area) and service "as good as it gets"; if the "tiny" space feels "cramped" to some, scores side with the starry-eyed who say it's "intimate" – and the whole place "perfect."

BONTERRA DINING & WINE ROOM ☒ | 25 | 25 | 25 | $48 |

1829 Cleveland Ave. (E. Worthington Ave.), 704-333-9463; www.bonterradining.com

It's "only fitting to be served such heavenly food in a former church", proclaim patrons who sing the praises of this Dilworth New American that's akin to a "religious experience" considering the "imaginative" menu ("amazing" fried lobster tail) and a wine selection (including a "superb" by-the-glass lineup) with enough "breadth" to "astonish" oenophiles; the "considerate" staff "makes you want to say 'amen.'"

Carpe Diem ⊠   26 | 25 | 24 | $39
1535 Elizabeth Ave. (Travis Ave.), 704-377-7976;
www.carpediemrestaurant.com
"Everybody wins" at this New American "staple" in Elizabeth
impressing admirers with its winning combination of "artful",
"stellar" food (including a couple of "sophisticated" vegetarian
options) and "gorgeous" art nouveau–style decor; aiding and
abetting the "wow" factor is an "attentive" staff that adds to the
eatery's "eclectic" "charm"; P.S. though it's moved a few times,
this place is "fabulous no matter where it is."

Ethan's of Elizabeth   24 | 22 | 23 | $37
366 N. Caswell Rd. (7th St.), 704-375-3007
Comfort yourself at this "lovely" New American eatery in an old,
renovated house in Elizabeth whose "homey" ambiance belies
"consistently high-quality" cooking ("like having a great dinner
in a good friend's home") and a "fabulous" brunch that deserves
bragging rights; cosseting of clientele comes via an array of
"warm" and "unpretentious" servers.

ilios noche ⊠   24 | 19 | 21 | $26
11508 Providence Rd. (I-485), 704-814-9882;
www.iliosnoche.com
"If only they would take reservations" moan fans of this "unique"
Greek-Italian that "knows what it's doing" in light of its "excellent"
Mediterranean food that draws an "attractive clientele" to a
"suburban" spot in South Charlotte; if the "edgy", "funky" quarters
don't provide enough entertainment, the "loud, loud, loud" factor
may do the trick.

Luce ⊠   26 | 25 | 25 | $45
Hearst Tower, 214 N. Tryon St. (bet. 5th & 6th Sts.), 704-344-9222;
www.luceristorante.net
A "Tuscan oasis in a sea of barbecue", this "first-class" Uptown
Northern Italian shines with "luscious" food, a "wonderful" Boot-
centric wine list and "excellent" service; further enhancing the
"rich" experience is the "exquisite" decor that features Murano
glass and works by local artist Ben Long; all the above proves that
peripatetic restaurateur Augusto Conte's "done it again!"

MCINTOSH'S STEAKS & SEAFOOD ⊠ 27 | 22 | 25 | $53
1812 South Blvd. (East Blvd.), 704-342-1088; www.mcintoshs1.com
There's "no better steak in town", crow content constituents who
"don't leave a speck of food" on their plates at this "superb"
locally owned South End surf 'n' turfer, whose "impeccable"
service, dark-wood interior and basement humidors make it "feel
like a private club" – though "not a stuffy" one; it's "just what a
steakhouse should be", so who cares if you have to pack your
wallet, since it's "worth every penny."

McNinch House ⊠   25 | 26 | 27 | $95
511 N. Church St. (bet. 8th & 9th Sts.), 704-332-6159
Those looking to "score some points with that special somebody"
shouldn't overlook this "romantic", "special-occasion" Eclectic;
housed in a restored Victorian abode, it "treats you like royalty"
and turns out "wonderful" food; but prepare for a "whopper of a
tab", and a few grinches go even further, saying it's "overpriced";
N.B. jackets, and reservations, required.

MICKEY & MOOCH ◗   23 | 21 | 20 | $33
Arboretum, 8128 Providence Rd. (Hwy. 51), 704-752-8080
9723 Sam Furr Rd. (I-77), Huntersville, 704-895-6654
www.mickeyandmooch.com
"So low-key" yet "so well done", this pair of chophouses off
Highway 51 and in Huntersville wins kudos for "mammoth" portions
of consistently "excellent" offerings, "from sushi to steak"; the
settings, reminiscent of "a '50s New York supper club" (natch, since
"Frank's playing on the sound system"), are "always hopping",
so don't be taken aback by the "long waits" for a table or that
earplugs may be in order, since some swear the "noise level is off
the charts"; P.S. with "reasonable prices", you won't need to mooch
moola from family or friends.

NIKKO   26 | 18 | 22 | $30
Ballantyne Commons E., 15105 John J. Delaney Dr.
(Ballantyne Commons Pkwy.), 704-341-5550
1300 South Blvd. (Arlington Ave.), 704-370-0100
Charlotte can "thank God" that "superb" sushi's "finally come to
town": chef/co-owner Joanna Nix "proves" that "fabulous" raw
fare "doesn't require you to be near the water" at her pair of
Japanese eateries in Ballantyne and South End; P.S. they're
"the standard" for "fresh" fish, so don't be surprised if they can
get a little "disco"-like on weekend nights (i.e. "loud, like a
party's going on").

Noble's ⌂   26 | 26 | 25 | $45
3 Morrocroft Ctr. at SouthPark, 6801 Morrison Blvd.
(Cameron Valley Pkwy.), 704-367-9463;
www.noblesrestaurant.com
A "temple of gastronomic pleasure", this SouthPark "treasure"
delivers "spectacular" Continental-Italian creations from the
hands of chef-owner Jim Noble to fawning fans from far and
wide; the "elegant", "Tuscan-retreat" decor (rated No. 1 in
Charlotte) and ministrations of a "superb" floor crew enhance a
"magical" experience – albeit one that may require "saving your
pennies" to pay for.

ONEO   26 | 21 | 25 | $41
Colony Pl., 7725 Colony Rd. (Rea Rd.), 704-544-1170;
www.oneo-bistro.com
"Oh, yes!": the "fabulous wine list" and "spot-on flavors" of the
"outstanding" food via palate-in-chief and resident chef Chris
Zion (he can "even makes Brussels sprouts taste good") keep
delighted disciples coming back to this contemporary SouthPark
New American bistro; a "professional" staff deftly works the
"beautiful" dining space (featuring floor to ceiling windows) that
includes an outdoor patio for fresh-air addicts.

PALM   24 | 21 | 24 | $52
6705 Phillips Place Ct. (bet. Fairview & Sharon Rds.), 704-552-7256;
www.thepalm.com
In the steak sweepstakes, "consistency" gets you far decree
devotees of this Charlotte member of the national chophouse
chain, whose "tried-and-true" formula corrals herds into its
SouthPark digs to sample "serious", "well-prepared" cuts and
to find caricatures of "local personalities" on the walls and a
"buzzy" ("why pay the power bill when the noise alone could

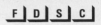
cook the food?"), "banker bar scene"; be prepared, however, since "you'll pay dearly" for the experience.

Patou ⊠
24 | 20 | 22 | $41

2400 Park Rd. (Ordermore Ave.), 704-376-2233; www.patoubistro.com
Don't expect a "see-and-be-seen" vibe at this "elegant" yet "unpretentious" bistro in Dilworth that's as "close to France as Charlotte gets", and where diners come "to enjoy great cooking" in the form of Classic Gallic specialties that, while "simple", "excel" nonetheless; all in all, it's a "find" that's "quality – all the way."

Sonoma Modern American ⊠
24 | 22 | 23 | $40

Founders Hall, 100 N. Tryon St. (Trade St.), 704-332-1132; www.sonomarestaurants.net
You'll "feel transported" to NYC at this "hot, hot, hot", "trendy" Uptown addition attracting acolytes with its "terrific", "innovative" Cal–New American food and "excellent wine list" in tow; owner Pierre Bader helps deliver a "great experience" to those who've entered the "modern", "minimalist" space that, depending on your point of view, is either "chic" or "cold"; P.S. checking out the "must-see bathrooms" is compulsory.

SULLIVAN'S STEAKHOUSE
27 | 24 | 25 | $48

1928 South Blvd. (Tremont Ave.), 704-335-8228; www.sullivansteakhouse.com
Bring "fellow carnivores" to this "classy" South End steakhouse that proffers "huge portions" ("wear elastic waistbands") of "consistently excellent" slabs of beef and "scrumptious" seafood amid a "swanky", "boxing-themed" setting; the "great bar scene" and live jazz pep up the overall "happenin'" vibe; and while it may be "pricey", for a "high-end" celebration, it "can't be beat."

Toscana ⊠
26 | 23 | 25 | $42

Specialty Shops on the Park, 6401 Morrison Blvd. (Roxborough Rd.), 704-367-1808
Try if you can, but you "won't be able to go wrong" at serial restaurateur Augusto Conte's standby in SouthPark that "deserves" and gets high marks for "insanely good" Northern Italian specialties ("bravo!" to the "wonderful" white bean and olive oil overture) and "cordial", "attentive" service; P.S. opt for the "lovely patio" if weather permits.

UPSTREAM
26 | 25 | 24 | $46

Phillips Pl., 6902 Phillips Place Ct. (bet. Colony & Sharon Rds.), 704-556-7730; www.upstreamit.com
Surveyors swim from all corners to sup on "outrageously good" seafood at this "chic" SouthPark eatery where chef Tom Condron's "exotic", "outside-the-box" cooking "amazes", and the "attentive", "enthusiastic" staff "pampers" both the "ladies who lunch and chaps who cut deals"; it manages to be "upscale" and "not uptight", and if some balk at the prices, far more maintain it's "worth every dime."

VOLARE ⊠
28 | 22 | 26 | $43

545B Providence Rd. (Laurel Ave.), 704-370-0208
So "very small but so romantic" that dinner here "can qualify as foreplay", this "hidden" "gem" in Myers Park scores with "serious", "heavenly" Italian food that's "magic" to the eyes and "perfection" to the palate; "passionate" service and a "charming"

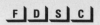
owner produce "pampering done right", so "reserve early" and get ready for a "splurge" that's a "must."

Zebra Restaurant & Wine Bar ☒   25 | 24 | 22 | $50
4521 Sharon Rd. (bet. Fairview Rd. & Morrison Blvd.), 704-442-9525;
www.zebrarestaurant.com
"Attention to detail" abounds at this SouthPark New French, from the "fantastic" fare whose "superb flavors are exceeded by the visual appeal" of the dishes to "unobtrusive" service to an "impressive" 800-label wine list; they keep the "noise level well under control", which suits those interested in business or romance just fine; P.S. you may wish to "pack your platinum card" for dinner, though "lunch is a steal."

Chicago

TOP FOOD RANKING

	Restaurant	Cuisine
28	Tallgrass	New French
	Carlos'	New French
	Tru	New French
	Ambria	New French
	Mirai Sushi	Japanese
	Seasons	New American
27	Charlie Trotter's	New American
	Le Titi de Paris	New French/New Amer.
	302 West	New American
	Everest	New French
	mk	New American
	Arun's	Thai
	Topolobampo	Mexican
	Le Vichyssois	French
	Bistro Banlieue	French
	Oceanique*	New French/New Amer.
	Kevin	New French/New Amer.
26	Avec	Mediterranean
	Eclectic	Eclectic
	Spiaggia	Italian

OTHER NOTEWORTHY PLACES

Restaurant	Cuisine
Alinea	New American
Avenues	Eclectic
Blackbird	New American
Chicago Chop Hse.	Steakhouse
Frontera Grill	Mexican
Gibsons	Steakhouse
Green Zebra	Vegetarian/New Amer.
Hot Doug's	Hot Dogs
Japonais	Japanese
Le Français	French
Les Nomades	New French
Lou Malnati's	Pizza
Morton's	Steakhouse
Naha	Med./New American
NoMI	New French
North Pond	New American
one sixtyblue	New American
Ritz-Carlton Dining Room	New French
Shanghai Terrace	Pan-Asian
Spring	Seafood/New Amer.

---

* Indicates a tie with restaurant above

Alinea
▽ 26 | 28 | 28 | $192

1723 N. Halsted St. (bet. North Ave. & Willow St.), 312-867-0110; www.alinearestaurant.com

"Believe the hype" about this "breathtakingly good" Lincoln Park newcomer: "devoted chef" Grant "Achatz is simply brilliant", and his "vision and attention to detail" render "a dazzling array" of "mind-blowing experimental" New American "food-as-fine-art", offered by an "exquisitely informative, warm staff" in an "elegantly appointed space"; a few find the "over-the-top" creations "a tad weird", but most report an "unforgettable" "nth-degree dining experience" that's "worth the significant investment."

AMBRIA ⊠
28 | 26 | 27 | $72

Belden-Stratford Hotel, 2300 N. Lincoln Park W. (Belden Ave.), 773-472-5959; www.leye.com

"A gem for years", this "culinary delight" "in a top-end Lincoln Park residential hotel" has created "many wonderful memories" with its "unbelievably delicious" Spanish-influenced New French cuisine served by a "battalion of waiters" who "make you feel like royalty" within a "quiet, wood-paneled room that speaks of old money"; a few find the "jackets-required" policy "stuffy", but most say this is "what a restaurant should be"; P.S. sommelier Bob Bansberg is a "guru – trust him."

Arun's
27 | 23 | 26 | $86

4156 N. Kedzie Ave. (bet. Belle Plaine & Berteau Aves.), 773-539-1909; www.arunsthai.com

Chef-owner Arun Sampanthavivat "brings you to a unique and enchanting world" with his "ultimate Thai food" at this "refined" Northwest Side Siamese; "plan to spend a few hours" "blowing the budget" on the tasting menu (no à la carte), each "exquisitely prepared course" "customized to your tastes"; the "smooth" staff is "accommodating", the "vast wine list has unexpected choices" and the "quiet" space with "gorgeous artwork" has "nice niches for conversation" – in short, "these folks got it" right.

Avec ☽
26 | 19 | 23 | $37

615 W. Randolph St. (Jefferson St.), 312-377-2002; www.avecrestaurant.com

Foodies feel that Koren Grieveson's "profound" "merry-go-round of Med" small plates "blows the competition away" at this West Loop wunderkind (spin-off of Blackbird), where oenophiles enjoy "lovely big pours" of "unusual" wines and service is "energetic" and "attentive"; "you have to like minimalism to get" the "stark", "sauna" decor, and the "elbow-to-elbow" "communal" "table setup" isn't for introverts, but it does "enable" social-ists "to meet sexy, interesting and sophisticated people."

Avenues
25 | 24 | 23 | $71

Peninsula Hotel, 108 E. Superior St. (bet. Michigan Ave. & Rush St.), 312-573-6754; www.peninsula.com

The "civilized, quiet" space studded with "comfortable chairs" and agreeably "far-apart tables" (some of which boast "wonderful views of Water Tower") sets the stage at this River North "gourmet" Eclectic; enthusiasts eat up the "exquisite service", even if critics decry the "expense-account" prices and "attitude" (jackets are suggested); N.B. the Food rating may not reflect the post-*Survey* arrival of chef Graham Elliot Bowles.

Bistro Banlieue
27 | 21 | 24 | $40

*44 Yorktown Convenience Ctr. (bet. Butterfield Rd. & Highland Ave.),
Lombard, 630-629-6560; www.bistrobanlieue.com*

Fans find this "lovely" West Suburban bistro offering "outstanding",
"innovative French cuisine" is just "getting better with age"; expect
"an impeccable dining experience" with "attentive, friendly
service" and "reasonable prices" (especially since they "offer half
portions – a great idea"), but be sure to allow yourself plenty of time
to find its "hidden strip-mall location."

Blackbird ⊠
26 | 20 | 22 | $53

*619 W. Randolph St. (bet. Desplaines & Jefferson Sts.), 312-715-0708;
www.blackbirdrestaurant.com*

Faithful fans "flock" to this "absolute pinnacle of hip" in the West
Loop where Paul Kahan's "outstanding" "seasonal" New American
fare "will knock your socks off", "service is unexpectedly friendly"
and the "modern, austere" digs are part of the "high concept";
contrarily, critics crow that the "cold", "sterile decor", noise and
"too-close tables" "detract from the food."

CARLOS'
28 | 24 | 27 | $80

*429 Temple Ave. (Waukegan Ave.), Highland Park, 847-432-0770;
www.carlos-restaurant.com*

"Bring a Polaroid camera" (and gentlemen, wear a jacket) to Carlos
and Debbie Nieto's "beautiful" North Shore "temple" of "exciting,
inspired" "New French cuisine" to capture the "meticulous
presentation" of its "fabulous food"; also expect "personalized
service" from a "courteous staff" that's "knowledgeable about"
the "outstanding list" of "amazing wines", but be warned that
"high prices" make this "a special-occasion favorite."

CHARLIE TROTTER'S ⊠
27 | 25 | 27 | $119

*816 W. Armitage Ave. (Halsted St.), 773-248-6228;
www.charlietrotters.com*

"If food can be poetic, orgasmic or intoxicating", you'll find it at
this "benchmark" New American in Lincoln Park, where "master"
chef and owner Charlie Trotter "still reigns", creating cuisine that
"can change your life"; believers "bow down before" the "perfect
harmony" of "sublime" "food-as-art", a "wonderful wine list" "as
thick as a phone book" and "unbelievably attentive", "top-tier
service" – even if a few infidels insinuate it's "a bit full of itself" and
are "not sure it's worth the price."

Chicago Chop House
25 | 19 | 22 | $49

*60 W. Ontario St. (bet. Clark & Dearborn Sts.), 312-787-7100;
www.chicagochophouse.com*

"Mainline" and "testosterone-laced" (though you may see "women
smoking cigars"), this "old-school" River North steakhouse with
piano bar rouses raves from red-meat eaters for its "superb beef"
selections – such as char-grilled prime rib – accompanied by sides
that, contrary to tradition, are "not à la carte"; kudos, too, for
servers with "lotsa hustle" "who remember what being a waiter
is all about"; still, unkind cattlemen call it "touristy" and "cramped."

Eclectic ⊠
26 | 18 | 23 | $42

117 E. North Ave. (Lake Cook Rd.), Barrington, 847-277-7300

"They take their name so seriously that each dish seems to draw
upon four or five continents for its inspiration" at "fantastically

creative" chef-owner Patrick Cassata's Northwest Suburban Eclectic, an "intimate" "find" set in a "charming historic old schoolhouse" whose atmosphere gives the impression of "dining in someone's private home"; add in "excellent service" by a "hip, knowledgeable staff" and it's one "terrific package for a night out."

EVEREST ⬛ 27 | 26 | 27 | $86

One Financial Pl., 440 S. La Salle Blvd. (Congress Pkwy.), 312-663-8920; www.leye.com

High-minded Francophiles seeking "the summit of Chicago dining" say "chef Jean Joho continues to weave magic" with his "world-class", Alsatian-accented New French cuisine at this "special place" with a "million-dollar view" above the Loop; "noble service", a "posh setting" and sommelier Alpana Singh, a "wonderful guide" to the "extraordinary wine list", also help justify the "steep prices", though skeptics say the "polished staff" can be "stiff" and the "room needs updating"; N.B. jacket suggested.

FRONTERA GRILL ⬛ 26 | 21 | 22 | $37

445 N. Clark St. (bet. Hubbard & Illinois Sts.), 312-661-1434; www.fronterakitchens.com

"Genius" Rick Bayless' "more casual alternative to its swankier [sibling] Topolobampo" "remains spirited, fresh and fun" for "amazing" "non-gringo" regional Mexican cooking "that lives up to the hype" and "changes with the seasons" (and oh, "those incomparable margaritas" and that "wide variety of tequila"), all in a "boisterous" setting filled with "festive art"; a soupçon of spoilsports submits that "service can vary greatly" when it's "crowded", while "long waits" sadden even some supporters.

GIBSONS STEAKHOUSE ◑ 25 | 19 | 23 | $54

1028 N. Rush St. (Bellevue Pl.), 312-266-8999
Doubletree Hotel, 5464 N. River Rd. (bet. Balmoral & Bryn Mawr Aves.), Rosemont, 847-928-9900
www.gibsonssteakhouse.com

This "A-list" Gold Coast steakhouse "is da place" for "pretty people" (including those "looking for a mistress" or a "sugar daddy") who hanker for "a hunka hunka burnin'" prime-aged beef in a "high-energy" "boys'-club" atmosphere (the "bar scene is jumping"); those who eschew this "expense-account" meetery say "service suffers" from "crowding" and "reservations are rarely on schedule" ("it helps to be the mayor"); P.S. the O'Hare area spin-off is "a nice sibling."

Green Zebra – | – | – | E

1460 W. Chicago Ave. (Greenview Ave.), 312-243-7100; www.greenzebrachicago.com

Spring chef-partner Shawn McClain gives his upscale New American cuisine a vegetarian slant at this Wicker Park encore named for an heirloom tomato variety; the menu showcases organic and locally raised produce (with a few fish and poultry items), the wine list emphasizes artisanal producers and the soothing, harvest-hued space (a former hat shop) is accented with stainless steel and live greenery.

Hot Doug's ⬛⇗ – | – | – | I

3324 N. California Ave. (Roscoe Blvd.), 773-279-9550; www.hotdougs.com

Gourmet sausage addicts rejoice: Doug Sohn's encased-meats mecca has reopened a half-mile west of its original Northwest Side location; the new incarnation offers plenty of street parking, more seating (plus outdoor tables), the chef's trademark duck-fat french fries on Fridays and Saturdays, and a full lineup of unusual, high-quality dogs – but, alas, it still closes at 4 PM.

Japonais

24 | 27 | 19 | $56

600 W. Chicago Ave. (Larrabee St.), 312-822-9600;
www.japonaischicago.com
Superlatives surrounding this "ultrachic" Near West Japanese, "one of the brightest lights on the local dining scene", cover the "drop-dead gorgeous" decor that "transports" "the 'it'-crowd" patrons "out of Chicago", the "amazing sushi and innovative menu items" and the "Indochine-sexy" "bar"-cum-"patio that opens up to the river"; still, unswayed raters report that all that "style comes at a high price" and the "service is not the best."

Kevin ⑤

27 | 23 | 24 | $55

9 W. Hubbard St. (State St.), 312-595-0055; www.kevinrestaurant.com
Kindred spirits contribute copious kudos for Kevin Shikami's "beautifully prepared", "inventive" New American–New French "fusion cuisine with definite Asian overtones", the foundation of a "superb dining experience" at his "high-power" River North namesake where the "spare and elegant" surroundings glow in "flattering low lighting"; still, skeptical scribes suggest it's "pricey" and pick up a whiff of "attitude."

Le Français ⑤

– | 23 | 26 | $89

269 S. Milwaukee Ave. (Dundee Rd.), Wheeling, 847-541-7470;
www.lefrancaisrestaurant.com
Hope springs anew at this North Suburban "classic" that keeps cycling through chefs, as Roland Liccioni, one of the venerable restaurant's reputation-building originals – appointed the first time around by founding chef Jean Banchet – returns, bringing some contemporary twists to his new Classic French menu (à la carte or dégustation) and bargain-priced prix fixe lunch; the "beautiful room" with plush booths and tastefully placed mirrors is also home to "impeccable" service and a "fantastic wine list."

Les Nomades ⑤

– | 26 | 28 | $89

222 E. Ontario St. (bet. Fairbanks Ct. & St. Clair St.), 312-649-9010;
www.lesnomades.net
Nomads come and go, and chefs have been doing the same at this "sophisticated", sedate former "private dining club" in a "civilized" Streeterville townhouse: the post-*Survey* departure of Roland Liccioni has led to the arrival of Chris Nugent, whose pricey New French prix fixe fare partners well with a "top-notch wine list", all presented by a "personable", "solicitous" staff that "unobtrusively" provides "impeccable service."

Le Titi de Paris

27 | 24 | 25 | $64

1015 W. Dundee Rd. (Kennicott Ave.), Arlington Heights, 847-506-0222;
www.letitideparis.com
A "rare find in the Northwest Suburbs", this "treasure" "maintains its excellence year after year" – even after the 2004 retirement of former chef-owner Pierre Pollin – due to longtime collaborator Michael Maddox, whose "outstanding" New American–influenced New French fare is offered "at a fair" price by an "exceptional" staff within a "quiet", "intimate" setting; P.S. the wine list is as "fantastic" as it is "extensive."

Le Vichyssois 27 | 21 | 21 | $48
220 W. Rte. 120 (2 mi. west of Rte. 12), Lakemoor, 815-385-8221;
www.levichyssois.com
"If you want to understand the way French food was intended to
be", head for the Northwest Suburbs to this "true family-run"
"favorite" that's "still excellent after all these years" thanks to
new and "classic cuisine prepared by a real pro", chef-owner
Bernard Cretier; throw in "good service", a "quaint" ambiance
and "great prices" that make it "a nice value", and you'll see why
most contributors proclaim it's "worth the drive."

Lou Malnati's Pizzeria 23 | 12 | 16 | $18
439 N. Wells St. (Hubbard St.), 312-828-9800
3859 W. Ogden Ave. (Cermak Rd.), 773-762-0800
958 W. Wrightwood Ave. (Lincoln Ave.), 773-832-4030
85 S. Buffalo Grove Rd. (Lake Cook Rd.), Buffalo Grove, 847-215-7100
1050 E. Higgins Rd. (bet. Arlington Heights & Busse Rds.),
Elk Grove Village, 847-439-2000
1850 Sherman Ave. (University Pl.), Evanston, 847-328-5400
6649 N. Lincoln Ave. (bet. Devon & Pratt Aves.), Lincolnwood,
847-673-0800
131 W. Jefferson Ave. (Washington St.), Naperville, 630-717-0700
1 S. Roselle Rd. (Schaumburg Rd.), Schaumburg, 847-985-1525
www.loumalnatis.com
Chi-town pizza fanaticism is alive and well, with delirious devotees
dubbing this "enduring" "A-list" "institution's" "dangerously
addictive deep-dish" pies the "only Chicago-style 'za worth
eating" ("you won't be disappointed" by the "fantastic thin
crust", either); whether it's the "just-right mix of ingredients" or
the optional "butter crust to die for", fans are "sure that if there's
a heaven, they serve Lou's there"; P.S. it "ships well, too."

MIRAI SUSHI 28 | 21 | 20 | $45
2020 W. Division St. (Damen Ave.), 773-862-8500;
www.miraisushi.com
"The fish swim down Division to get" to this "always amazing"
"trendy Japanese", the "best in Chicago" thanks to its "fresh",
"creative" and "adventurous sushi" ("love the rare varieties they
have") and "cool" "scene" (especially the "great bar upstairs");
nonconformists nag that they "need to work on the service" and
pout about the "premium price" you'll pony up for the "edible art",
though ayes aver "you get what you pay for."

mk 27 | 24 | 24 | $56
868 N. Franklin St. (bet. Chestnut & Locust Sts.), 312-482-9179;
www.mkchicago.com
"Long adored" and "still among the best", this River North New
American proffers chef-owner Michael Kornick's "creative menu",
which "delivers on the promise" of "subtle", "sophisticated"
cuisine "with minimal pretension" (it "looks simple, but a lot of work
went into these dishes") accompanied by "stupendous desserts"
and "wonderful wines"; "service is stellar", and the "sleek",
"swanky" space is "elegant in that urban-warehouse-loft kind of
way", even if "a bit noisy."

Morton's, The Steakhouse 26 | 21 | 24 | $56
Newberry Plaza, 1050 N. State St. (Maple St.), 312-266-4820
9525 W. Bryn Mawr Ave. (River Rd.), Rosemont, 847-678-5155

(continued)

Morton's, The Steakhouse

1470 McConnor Pkwy. (Meacham Rd.), Schaumburg, 847-413-8771
1 Westbrook Corporate Ctr. (22nd St.), Westchester, 708-562-7000
www.mortons.com

Still beating the competition in its carnivorous category, "Chicago's original" "genteel" "king of the steakhouse chains" "continues to reign supreme" "in a town famous for steak", with the "best" "prime beef", "clubby" digs and "service as crisp as the hash browns" ("save room for" the "must-have" hot Godiva cake); a note to wallet-watchers, though: everything's "huge", including the "big prices"; N.B. the Loop location opened post-*Survey*.

Naha ⊠　　　　　　　　26 | 24 | 24 | $57

500 N. Clark St. (Illinois St.), 312-321-6242;
www.naha-chicago.com

"Creative" chef-partner Carrie Nahabedian's "amazing" seasonal New American "dining with daring Mediterranean touches" tempts travelers to her "flat-out superb" River North "keeper" where "the *Queer Eye* guys would be proud" of the "streamlined", "simple" "Zen-like" decor; sure, her "food is pricey" but most meditate it's "worth the splurge" – though what's a "great buzz" to some is just plain "noisy" to others.

NoMI ❂　　　　　　　　26 | 27 | 24 | $66

Park Hyatt Chicago, 800 N. Michigan Ave. (Chicago Ave.), 312-239-4030;
www.nomirestaurant.com

Beguiled boulevardiers believe "they built the Park Hyatt hotel around this" "fabulous" "first-class" "favorite" where a table by the window offers a "celestial" Gold Coast view and the "stunning modernist decor" sets the stage for "superb", "innovative" New French fare and selections from the "top-notch sommelier"; still, those who aren't "loaded" lament the "inflated prices" and say "the staff needs to loosen up"; N.B. the Food rating may not reflect the post-*Survey* departure of chef Sandro Gamba.

North Pond　　　　　　　25 | 27 | 21 | $53

2610 N. Cannon Dr. (bet. Diversey & Fullerton Pkwys.), 773-477-5845;
www.northpondrestaurant.com

"Nestled" "lagoon-side" in a "breathtaking" Lincoln Park locale, this "beautiful", historic ice-skating shelter features a "fantastic" "Prairie School interior", a suitable setting for "gifted chef" Bruce Sherman's "phenomenal seasonal" New American fare employing "local artisan ingredients", paired with a "unique wine selection"; still, perfectionists point out that the "stiff staff" is "not always as attentive" as you'd expect given the "top-of-the-line prices."

Oceanique ⊠　　　　　　　27 | 20 | 23 | $51

505 Main St. (bet. Chicago & Hinman Aves.), Evanston, 847-864-3435;
www.oceanique.com

Putting his "creativity on display nightly", "personable" "chef-owner Mark Grosz continues to amaze" at this "unpretentious" but "absolutely fabulous" North Suburban New French–New American "favorite" serving seafood so "inventive and outstanding" it "should be illegal"; kudos, too, for the "understated storefront" space with "fabric-draped ceiling" and a "knowledgeable staff" "attuned to the needs of the diner"; P.S. the three-course $35 menu is a "great deal."

one sixtyblue ☒
| 25 | 24 | 23 | $58 |

1400 W. Randolph St. (Ogden Ave.), 312-850-0303;
www.onesixtyblue.com

"There's a modern freshness to both the food and decor" at "Michael Jordan's" "out-of-the-way" Market District "jewel" where chef Martial Noguier's "phenomenal" New American cooking "is an object lesson in perfect simplicity", the wine list is "eclectic but appropriate" and the "civilized" setting with a "huge" open kitchen is "cosmopolitan" yet "comfortable"; no wonder most say it's "worth every penny", even if a few fans call a financial foul ("I enjoyed my meal until I got the check").

Ritz-Carlton Dining Room
| – | 28 | 28 | $79 |

Ritz-Carlton Hotel, 160 E. Pearson St. (Michigan Ave.), 312-573-5223;
www.fourseasons.com

This top-scoring, "tony" Streeterville spot recently saw the departure of its champion chef team, followed by the arrival of toque Kevin Hickey; a skew toward imaginative New American cuisine takes it in a fresh direction, though patrons still "put on the Ritz", being "treated like royalty" by a "solicitous" staff within the "luxurious", "old-world setting"; N.B. rolling dim sum and sushi have been added to the lavish brunch.

Seasons
| 28 | 27 | 27 | $77 |

Four Seasons Hotel, 120 E. Delaware Pl. (bet. Michigan Ave. &
Rush St.), 312-649-2349; www.fourseasons.com

"Top-flight" seasonal New American cuisine "is always refined but has an edge" at this "formal-dining" "power scene" in the Gold Coast's Four Seasons Hotel, a "haven of culinary delights" where devotees declare the "expense is worth it" thanks to not only the "outstanding food" (especially the "incredible brunch" on Sundays) but "exceptional atmosphere" (the decor "defines elegance") and the "sensitive", "unobtrusive" staff's "superb timing"; N.B. the Food score does not reflect the post-*Survey* departure of chef Robert Sulatycky.

Shanghai Terrace ☒
| 26 | 26 | 26 | $54 |

Peninsula Hotel, 108 E. Superior St. (bet. Michigan Ave. & Rush St.),
312-573-6744; www.chicago.peninsula.com

Survey says this "very special", "sophisticated" "jewel within the magnificent Peninsula" in River North serves "the highest available caliber of inventive Pan-Asian cuisine" going, with "clean, fresh, delicate" flavors featured in its "pricey but perfect" provender, "impeccably" "presented" with "flawless service" in a "posh" "little lacquered jewel-box of a room"(or "outdoors on the rooftop in summer"); N.B. the Decor rating may not reflect a post-*Survey* redo.

Spiaggia
| 26 | 26 | 25 | $72 |

One Magnificent Mile Bldg., 980 N. Michigan Ave. (Oak St.),
312-280-2750; www.spiaggiarestaurant.com

Patrons say "pinch me" about this "epitome of sophisticated dining" and "special place for special times" that "serves its fair share of glitterati" on the Gold Coast; chef Tony Mantuano's "heavenly, luxurious" Italian cuisine deserves its "stunning setting" with a "view of the lake", and a "knowledgeable" staff "anticipates any need" (in particular, "sommelier Henry Bishop is first rate"); N.B. jackets are required.

Spring　　　　　　　　　26 | 24 | 24 | $55
2039 W. North Ave. (Damen Ave.), 773-395-7100;
www.springrestaurant.net
A "multi-sensory experience" that's "everything a gourmet" eatery
should be, this Wicker Park New American seafood "standout" has
surveyors swooning over chef-partner Shawn McClain's "subtle,
savory" and "sublime" dishes offered with "high-class service" in
an "über-cool", "Zen" "converted bathhouse"; a few rain on this
parade, though, calling the "austere" setting "cold" and "noisy"
and the experience "a bit overpriced."

TALLGRASS　　　　　　28 | 22 | 25 | $62
1006 S. State St. (10th St.), Lockport, 815-838-5566;
www.tallgrassrestaurant.com
Grateful gastronomes "thank goodness there's a real restaurant"
gracing the Southwest Suburbs – especially considering that it's
this "intimate" example of the genre, where "creative chef" and
partner Robert Burcenski's "memorable" New French fare is simply
"out of this world" and No. 1 in the Chicago area; the "fantastic
wine list" is "extensive" and the "staff is very knowledgeable";
N.B. both jackets and reservations are de rigueur.

302 West ⊠　　　　　　27 | 26 | 26 | $49
302 W. State St. (3rd St.), Geneva, 630-232-9302; www.302west.net
Superlatives abound for this "romantic" New American "dining
treasure" where "terrific, modern city fare" from a "creative" daily
changing menu belies the "far-outpost" setting of its "unique",
"elegant-yet-casual" "old bank building" within a "postcard-
perfect" West Suburban town; there's also a "great wine list", and
the "yummy", "homemade desserts" alone "are well worth the
trip"; N.B. after the untimely passing of chef-owner Joel Findlay
in 2004, his protégé, Jeremy Lycan, continues his tradition.

Topolobampo ⊠　　　　27 | 23 | 25 | $53
445 N. Clark St. (bet. Hubbard & Illinois Sts.), 312-661-1434;
www.fronterakitchens.com
"Master chef" Rick Bayless' "upscale" regional Mexican in
River North ("Frontera's higher-end partner") is nothing short of
a "national treasure" that "expands eaters' horizons" with "a
parade of tastes" exhibiting "creativity and respect for ingredients"
("do they do it this well in Mexico?"); plus, "they've achieved
margarita perfection", the "savvy sommelier" picks "wonderful
wine pairings", the staff is "informative and unassuming" and the
ambiance is "festive" yet "elegant."

TRU ⊠　　　　　　　　28 | 27 | 27 | $107
676 N. St. Clair St. (bet. Erie & Huron Sts.), 312-202-0001;
www.trurestaurant.com
"Talented [toque] Rick Tramonto and [pastry chef] Gale Gand's
one-two punch" has grateful gastronomes gushing about their
"extraordinary" New French "event-dining" "extravaganza", the
Most Popular restaurant in Chicago; from the "serene, minimalist
decor" and "choreographed service" to the "knowledgeable
sommelier" Scott Tyree, it's a "seamless" Streeterville "food-as-
theater" "spectacle", and if a few "nitpickers" find it "over the
top" ("you can easily spend four hours at dinner") and beyond
"expensive", the majority nevertheless advises you to just "spend
the money and do it."

Cincinnati

TOP FOOD RANKING

	Restaurant	Cuisine
29	Jean-Robert at Pigall's	New French
28	Daveed's at 934	Eclectic
27	Boca	Italian
	BonBonerie	Bakery
	Palace, The	Continental/New Amer.
26	Precinct	Steakhouse
	Sturkey's	Eclectic
	Jeff Ruby's	Steakhouse
25	Morton's	Steakhouse
	South Beach Grill	Seafood/Steakhouse

OTHER NOTEWORTHY PLACES

Aioli	Eclectic
Beluga	Asian Fusion
China Gourmet	Chinese
Cumin	Indian
Dewey's	Pizza
JeanRo	French
Montgomery Inn	Barbecue
Nicola's	Northern Italian
Palomino	Med./New American
Pho Paris	French/Vietnamese

F	D	S	C

Aioli 🅿
23 | 20 | 19 | $36

700 Elm St. (7th St.), 513-929-0525; www.aiolibistro.com
"Unpretentious" and "relaxed", this Downtown Eclectic eatery
is an "every-night kind of place", smile supporters of chef-owner
Julie Francis, saying the "forward-thinking" toque deserves
props for her "wonderful, inventive" and "always unexpected"
Southwestern- and Asian-inspired cuisine, paired with European
and California vintages; its convenient corner location draws a
standing ovation from theatergoers, but be advised that you may
have to goose the somewhat "slow" staff in order to make
your curtain time.

Beluga ●🅿
25 | 23 | 20 | $42

3520 Edwards Rd. (Erie Ave.), 513-533-4444
A whale of a nightspot, this "as-hip-as-it-gets" Asian fusion fave
in monied Hyde Park serves up "amazing sushi" and much more
during dinner hours, then "shifts into high gear" when the house
DJ starts spinning house and hip-hop tunes and the famed
martinis start flowing; a "delightfully meandering floor plan"
and "minimalist" white rooms puts the focus on the "gorgeous
clientele", while "accommodating" service helps compensate
for the Tokyo-esque prices.

BOCA ☒

27 | – | 24 | $48

3200 Madison Rd. (between Ridge Rd. and Braizee St.), 513-542-2022;
www.boca-restaurant.com

'Boca, right on!' cheers the "impassioned local following" of
gregarious chef/co-owner David Falk, whose "utter devotion to
sharp, distinctive flavors" gives rise to "contemporary Italian
cuisine" with the "perfect balance of color, taste and texture";
new, customized digs in hipster enclave Oakley bring this "foodie
mecca" more attention, especially for sommelier Paul Ortiz's
"excellent" wine pairings on the six to eight-course Chef's Grand
Tasting Menu; diners are divided on service, though — some call
it "superb", others "spotty."

BONBONERIE ☒

27 | 17 | 18 | $14

2030 Madison Rd. (Grandin Rd.), 513-321-3399;
www.thebonbon.com

"They could charge just for the aroma" of the "decadent desserts"
in this East Side "sweet-tooth heaven", coo carbophiles who claim
the cakes constitute a "reason to look forward to your birthday";
what's more, the bakery's "quirky" tearoom offers light breakfasts
and lunches, and an "excellent selection" of leaves "from
jasmine green to cherry sencha" plus the "world's best scones"
make it a "great place to meet a friend" for a cuppa (reserve 24
hours in advance).

China Gourmet ☒

24 | 17 | 23 | $37

3340 Erie Ave. (Marburg Ave.), 513-871-6612

Sino-style specialties (whole steamed fish, "five-spice oysters"
in season) are prepared and served "with flair and uncommon
elegance" at this Hyde Park "fixture" beloved by an "upscale
crowd"; proprietors from the Moy family dynasty "are always
present and it shows": "they know you by name" and "make you
feel right at home", while the "accommodating" staff "will adapt a
dish to any desire"; a small minority calls prices "inscrutably high",
but most feel the "total experience justifies the cost."

Cumin

25 | 17 | 19 | $27

3514 Erie Ave. (Pinehurst St.), 513-871-8714

Cumin and sit down at this Hyde Park "nouveau" Indian bistro to
savor "lots of unusual taste mixtures" from chef-owner Yajan
Upadhyaya, whose "superlative", "cutting-edge" subcontinental
dishes ("delicious dosas") demonstrate his "creativity and flair";
with portions "on the small side", you can "try a bit of many things";
however, the "minimalist, Ikea-like" space is diminutive as well,
which makes claustrophobes feel "cramped" and "crowded", and
the "service needs a bit of help."

DAVEED'S AT 934 ☒

28 | 20 | 24 | $58

934 Hatch St. (Louden St.), 513-721-2665

At this "romantic, inventive and intimate" 65-seat "hideaway"
in trendy Mt. Adams, chef/co-owner David Cook lives up to his
name, creating an Eclectic menu that "mixes the familiar and the
innovative" to create an "adventure for the palate"; wife Liz
"lovingly" manages the "comfortable", colorful dining rooms, a
"delightful back patio under the trees" and a crew of "considerate"
servers (though a few foes find them "condescending" to non-
"connoisseurs"); as a result, respondents report it's a "terrific
choice for special occasions."

Dewey's Pizza
23 | 16 | 20 | $17

265 Hosea Rd. (Clifton Ave.), 513-221-0400
Oakley Sq., 3014 Madison Rd. (bet. Markbreit Ave. & Romana Pl.),
513-731-7755
Newport on the Levee Mall, 1 Levee Way (Monmouth St.), Newport,
859-431-9700
Shops at Harper's Point, 11338 Montgomery Rd. (bet. E Kemper Rd. &
Harpers Point Dr.), Symmes, 513-247-9955
www.deweyspizza.com
"Why can't all pizza be this good?" wonder 'za zealots who zip
over to this local chain of pie palaces for the "perfect formula" of
"great crust", "top-notch toppings and good value" rolled into
"exotic", "garlic-laden" combinations (e.g. the "incredible Bronx
Bomber"); you can also opt to "build your own" or dig into "very
shareable salads"; staffers are "friendly" and "lively", and "kids
love watching" the "chefs toss and top" the dough in the open-
windowed kitchen, while parents appreciate the "terrific wines"
and "good beers on tap."

JeanRo ⊠
25 | 24 | 23 | $36

413 Vine St. (bet. 4th & 5th Sts.), 513-621-1465;
www.bistrojeanro.com
"Like everything else Jean-Robert de Cavel touches", this Gallic
is "golden", report city "power brokers" who peg this "low-cost
offspring of [Jean-Robert at] Pigall's" as a Downtown "star"; at
the "chummy yet sophisticated" bistro, "casual but not lax" servers
proffer "authentic", "not over-fussy" "French comfort foods" and
a "wine list full of values"; the deep and narrow room has walls
of "Provençal yellow" with "cafe-style posters" of old Paris, plus
a copper bar ideal for "meeting friends" and pretending "you've
escaped" to the City of Light.

JEAN-ROBERT AT PIGALL'S ⊠
29 | 28 | 29 | $83

127 W. Fourth St. (bet. Elm & Race Sts.), 513-721-1345;
www.pigalls.com
"Alain Ducasse, look out for Jean-Robert" de Cavel (ex the
late Maisonette), whose Downtown New French, Cincinnati's
Most Popular restaurant, was also voted its No. 1 for Food;
demonstrating "impeccable taste", the maestro's "ethereal"
cuisine (offered only as a three-course prix fixe or a five-course
tasting menu) "stimulates the eye as much as it does the palate"
against the backdrop of an "elegant but understated" room where
the "welcoming" servers "read your mind"; according to the
"upper-crust" "society-crowd" clientele, the whole experience
is simply "world-class."

JEFF RUBY'S ⊠
26 | 22 | 24 | $59

700 Walnut St. (7th St.), 513-784-1200; www.jeffruby.com
Living large is the motif at this Downtown meatery, a "celebrity
hot spot" where "everything is supersized" from the "great
martinis" and "deep wine list" to the "shrimp on steroids" and
"aged-on-the-premises" "roasts disguised as steaks" that will
"fill you up with beef happiness"; meanwhile, the "well-done" art
deco–influenced interiors are "flashy" but "not over-the-top
gaudy", and servers "never miss a beat"; all agree you'll need a
"fat wallet" or an "expense account" to dine here, though the
unimpressed couldn't care less: "overrated, overpriced, overdone –
I'm over it."

MONTGOMERY INN   22 | 19 | 20 | $31
925 Eastern Ave. (Pete Rose Way), 513-721-7427
9440 Montgomery Rd. (bet. Cooper & Remington Rds.), Montgomery,
513-791-3482
400 Buttermilk Pike (I-75), Ft. Mitchell, 859-344-5333
www.montgomeryinn.com
"I'd like to be committed into this local institution", pun pork-loving
partisans of this "venerable" BBQ mini-chain known for "steamed,
not smoked, ribs"; they praise "melt-in-your-mouth" meat ("no
gnawing necessary") and "sauce so good you won't mind wearing
it" as you perch in the "crowded" dining rooms (the Boathouse
location offers "nice evening views of the Ohio River"); however, the
reluctant rib "it's living on its rep" and reject the "factory" feel, the
"ordeal" of "long waits" and the "fatty, greasy", "heavy" eats.

Morton's, The Steakhouse   25 | 20 | 24 | $59
Tower Place Mall, 28 W. Fourth St. (Race St.), 513-241-4104
"Expense-accounters" know there are "mountains of meat" and
"Paul Bunyanesque" vegetables to be had at this "very reliable"
Downtown chainster, a "traditional steakhouse" that's always
"good for business" bread-breaking; the dining room is "big, open
and bright", and staffers exhibit the amiability that earned "the
Midwest its friendly reputation", but the restaurants' standard
pre-meal display of ingredients leaves some wondering "who
wants to meet their dinner before they eat it?"

Nicola's ⚅   25 | 21 | 22 | $44
1420 Sycamore St. (Liberty St.), 513-721-6200
"You may stay" in "Porkopolis", but "your taste buds leave for
Firenze" when you dine Downtown at this Tuscan with its "expertly
crafted food", "strong" 1,200-label Italian wine list and "marvelous
sauces" ("you'll never want to touch another jar of Ragu"); what's
more, the tasting menus of chef Christian Pietoso (son of Nicola)
"add contemporary flair"; meanwhile, the spacious setting, a
"transformed old trolley barn" with a "pleasant patio", provides
a "nice atmosphere", but the "friendly" service can sometimes
be "painfully slow."

PALACE, THE ⚅   27 | 25 | 25 | $63
Cincinnatian Hotel, 601 Vine St. (6th St.), 513-381-6006;
www.palacecincinnati.com
"Attention to detail" is the hallmark of this "first-rate" longtimer in
Downtown's Cincinnatian Hotel, where "talented" toque Guy Hulin
turns out "extraordinary", "artfully presented" Continental–New
American cuisine, complemented by a cellar that boasts some
"truly wonderful gems"; meanwhile, even commoners feel like
"royalty" here thanks to "exquisite service", live music and a stately
dining room that's an "oasis of civility", "elegance and style."

PALOMINO   22 | 23 | 20 | $36
Lazarus Ctr., 505 Vine St. (5th St.), 513-381-1300; www.palomino.com
Its "primo location" ensures quick access to the Convention Center
and the Aronoff Center for the Arts plus "excellent views" of
"Fountain Square skaters" at holiday time – but that's hardly the
only reason "beautiful people" "abound" at this "slick" Downtown
chain link; a "piece of Seattle in Cincy", it turns out "extraordinarily
consistent" Mediterranean–New American fare served by a
"courteous and professional staff"; the "lively", "loud" atmosphere

is generally a plus, though occasionally the "din" makes it hard to "enjoy your dinner."

Pho Paris ⑤   – | – | – | M |

3235A Madison Rd. (bet. Brazee St. & Ridge Ave.), 513-871-1234; www.phoparis.com

Star restaurateur-chef Jean-Robert de Cavel (Jean-Robert at Pigall's) has scored another hit with this French-Vietnamese, a duet with the Lê family (owners of a local Asian eatery, Song Long); though the exterior is more strip mall than sleek, the black stone-topped bar within makes a great cocktail hour perch for hipsters, while suburban couples throng the dining room with its collection of Eiffel Towers and silver-leafed walls, ordering up such fusion fare as mussels steamed in coconut milk and five-spices salmon with shallot compote.

PRECINCT   26 | 21 | 24 | $52 |

311 Delta Ave. (Columbia Pkwy.), 513-321-5454; www.jeffruby.com

Carnivores (including "local celebs" and professional ballplayers) cop to craving the "mammoth portions" of "aged-to-perfection" steak dispatched at Jeff Ruby's "white-tablecloth" Columbia-Tusculum beefhouse, once a district police station; also singing a siren song are the raw bar, "fabulous cellar" and "outstanding service", all fit for "boys' night out" or to "impress a date"; however, a uniform complaint is that "tables are too close together" ("busy nights can be ear-shattering"), leaving even loyalists a little blue.

South Beach Grill at the Waterfront ⑤   25 | 22 | 24 | $49 |

14 Pete Rose Pier, Covington, 859-581-1414; www.jeffruby.com

It "feels like you are walking into a cruise ship" when you board this surf 'n' turf riverboat – now, once again, being helmed by Jimmy Gibson – moored in Covington; surveyors state it's a "great place for a special occasion" and "worth" the "steep" prices, thanks to "excellent" steaks, the "freshest seafood outside of the ocean" and "sharp" service; the "view of Downtown is hard to beat" and makes up for somewhat "tired" decor.

Sturkey's   26 | 19 | 23 | $41 |

400 Wyoming Ave. (Oak St.), Wyoming, 513-821-9200; www.sturkeys.com

"Personable" proprietors "Pam and Paul" perennially please patrons of their popular eponymous Eclectic, located in the suburban, historic village of Wyoming; the "innovative", "fabulous food" is "beautifully presented" ("desserts are works of art in their own right" and "even the house salad is magnificent"), "friendly" staffers foster a "very pleasant" atmosphere, and the decor is colorful and uncluttered – even if a few aesthetes assess it as a little too "South Florida."

Cleveland

TOP FOOD RANKING

Restaurant	Cuisine
28 Johnny's Bar	Continental/N. Italian
27 Chez François	French
Phnom Penh	Cambodian
Lolita	Med./New American
Blue Point Grille	Seafood
Giovanni's Ristorante	Northern Italian
Flying Fig	Eclectic/American
26 Battuto	Italian
Classics	French
Sans Souci	French/Mediterranean

OTHER NOTEWORTHY PLACES

Baricelli Inn	Continental
Century	New American
fire	New American
Fulton Bar & Grill	Eclectic
Ginza Sushi House	Japanese
Grovewood Tavern	Eclectic
Hyde Park Prime	Steakhouse
Parallax Restaurant	Seafood
Red the Steakhouse	Steakhouse
Three Birds	New American

F	D	S	C

BARICELLI INN ⊠
26 | 25 | 25 | $57

Baricelli Inn, 2203 Cornell Rd. (Murray Hill Rd.), 216-791-6500; www.baricelli.com

Fromage fanatics smile and "say cheese" when focusing on the "exceptional" artisanal wedges paired with pours from a "great" 400-label wine list at this "elegant" East Side Continental where Paul Minnillo's cuisine is "creative and ever-changing" yet "consistently excellent"; diners also deem the "comfortable, quiet" setting in a "gracious" mansion-turned-B&B "conducive to talking, meeting or celebrating occasions" with the help of "impeccably" "attentive" staffers; some shudder at "the size of the check", but others regard rates as "reasonable" for a "very special" evening.

Battuto Restaurant ⊠
26 | 20 | 23 | $43

12405 Mayfield Rd. (125th St.), 216-707-1055

At this East Side "oasis on a street of ketchup and egg noodles", chef-owners Mark and Giovanna Daverio conjure up "incredible", "inventive" variations on Italian classics that servers present with "style and panache"; another "nice change" from nearby eateries is a "cozy" interior tinged with "modern-Euro coolness" instead of Little Italy kitsch; as a result, pleased patrons are prone to pick this "relaxing place" when they aim to "linger over dinner with friends."

BLUE POINT GRILLE　　　27 | 25 | 24 | $47
700 W. Saint Clair Ave. (6th St.), 216-875-7827; www.hrcleveland.com
Fin fans have a merry time at this maritimer in the Warehouse
District, voted Cleveland's Most Popular; all this "terrific fresh
seafood" ("so many oysters, my wife found me attractive") in such
a landlocked locale is a "rare treat", the nautical-themed, lofty
room with floor-to-ceiling windows is "stunning" for "special
celebrations", and the ministrations of "attentive" servers fall "just
short of palm-frond fans and hand-fed grapes" – so surveyors
simply tune out or tolerate noise from an often-"boisterous"
business-class crowd.

Century　　　　　　　　　26 | 26 | 25 | $51
Ritz-Carlton Hotel, 1515 W. Third St. (Huron Rd.), 216-902-5255
Call it the "the Orient Express on the Cuyahoga": the Ritz-Carlton's
"spectacular" yet "comfortable" railroad-style New American
recalls the "days of luxury train travel" – complete with attendants
who provide "stellar" "white-glove service with a smile" – so
reviewers make tracks Downtown for its "Asian-inspired" fin fare
("superb, fresh sushi") and post-prandial bowl of cotton candy;
since the fare is "pricey", the cash-crunched come for lunch,
confiding "there's no cheaper way to feel like a million bucks."

CHEZ FRANÇOIS　　　　　27 | 26 | 28 | $63
555 Main St. (Liberty Ave.), Vermilion, 440-967-0630;
www.chezfrancois.com
"Exemplary" service from an "experienced staff" and "the best
French food within 100 miles" ("foie gras to die for") make this
"high-end special-occasion eatery" about 40 minutes west of
Downtown "worth the hike"; the converted sailmakers' loft on the
Vermilion River boasts a "charming" exposed-brick interior and a
patio for "great alfresco dining", and provides docking to those
who barge in – but even the yachtsmen who weigh anchor here
admit it's "kinda pricey"; N.B. jacket required.

Classics ⊠　　　　　　　26 | 28 | 26 | $67
InterContinental Hotel & Conference Ctr., 9801 Carnegie Ave.
(E. 100th St.), 216-707-4157; www.classicsrestaurant.com
Revived in early 2003, this "incarnation" of a "special-occasion"
culinary classic resides east of Downtown; "wowed" admirers
attest to "first-class" "fairy-tale evenings" that are "worth the
splurge", citing an "opulent" atmosphere that's "polished in every
way", "fanciful" yet "exacting" French dishes and "impeccable
service" ("so many servers, you wonder who gets the tip") – yet to
the less impressed it "lacks the excitement of its predecessor" and
sometimes even "borders on the pretentious"; N.B. gentlemen,
please don a jacket – and leave children under 10 at home.

fire　　　　　　　　　　25 | 21 | 22 | $42
13220 Shaker Sq. (N. Moreland Blvd.), 216-921-3473;
www.firefoodanddrink.com
Shaker Square's flickering fortunes notwithstanding, "talented
chef" Doug Katz's "lively" New American is still hot; foodies are
fired up about his "simply prepared" but "imaginative" seasonal
cuisine cooked in brick ovens and tandoors ("phenomenal pork
chops") and servers who are "usually" "downright charming";
meanwhile, the exposed-brick, open-kitchen environs spark
heated debate – some term them "upscale" and "chic", others

"noisy" and "cramped" (with chairs so "uncomfortable" they "should be burned"); regardless, elbow-roomers will appreciate alfresco patio dining in summer.

Flying Fig　　　　　　　　　27 | 21 | 24 | $40
2523 Market Ave. (W. 25th St.), 216-241-4243
Foodies give far more than a flying fig for this "undiscovered gem" in trendy Ohio City; in fact, they lick their chops over chef-owner Karen Small's "brilliant", "unconventional" and "thoroughly satisfying" Eclectic-American concoctions, presented by servers "as entertaining as the menu"; though it's set on "one of the coziest streets in Cleveland", the dining room's sleek, minimalist decor "captures the feel of a Lower Manhattan eatery" – complete with "reverberating acoustics", so silence-seekers may want to sup "out on the streetside patio."

Fulton Bar & Grill　　　　　　22 | 20 | 20 | $37
1835 Fulton Rd. (Bridge Ave.), 216-694-2122
Though it's no longer the "chef-driven spot it once was", this "great neighborhood bar" in Ohio City still delivers "inventive" Eclectic eats from a "kitchen that is open late"; the "cozy" space, adorned with murals by a local artist and housed in a historic 1880 building, has a "warm", "fun" vibe and "friendly servers", making it a "perfect place to take a date", "hang out with pals" or just "grab a cocktail" – especially on the candlelit patio.

Ginza Sushi House 🚭　　　　24 | 16 | 21 | $30
1105 Carnegie Ave. (E. 9th St.), 216-589-8503; www.ginzasushi.com
When they want "the most authentic Japanese in town with the least Midwestern flair", aficionados angle to attend this "best value" sushi specialist situated "close to Jacobs Field" Downtown; they savor its "amazing", "fresh" fin fare and say "personable proprietors" provide a "true Tokyo experience" within a simple setting (larger parties can even choose "traditional" sunken seating); the "quality-rather-than-flash" philosophy makes for a "pleasant" meal "without too much fuss"; N.B. wine and beer only.

Giovanni's Ristorante 🚭　　　27 | 24 | 27 | $62
25550 Chagrin Blvd. (Richmond Rd.), Beachwood, 216-831-8625; www.giovanniscleveland.com
"Don't be fooled by the location" in a suburban office building – this "expensive" Beachwood "grande dame" is one of "Cleveland's classiest places", where "traditional" Tuscan dishes are "prepared to perfection" and paired with any of 700 wines; within the "lush" paneled main room, a "skilled" "black-tie" staff provides "superb" "old-school service"; cutting-edgers call the place a "throwback" that's "formal to the point of distraction", but well-wishers willing to "wear a jacket" (not required, but preferred) deem it "divine."

Grovewood Tavern and Wine Bar　22 | 12 | 17 | $30
17105 Grovewood Ave. (E. 172nd St.), 216-531-4900; www.grovewoodtavern.com
Oenophiles especially enjoy this "funky and popular" East Side "neighborhood fave" because "staffers know their wine" and the "extensive" cellar contains some 150 vintages "in all categories", plus about 60 hard-to-find beers; even better, point out partisans, the "minuscule kitchen" turns out "innovative", "upscale" and "delicious" Eclectic eats in a "casual atmosphere" ("only the food here is snobby"); however, "unimpressed" customers

call the "bowling alley–like" tavern a "cavern" and caution of "alarmingly inconsistent service."

HYDE PARK PRIME STEAKHOUSE   25 | 22 | 24 | $49 |
123 W. Prospect Ave. (W. 2nd St.), 216-344-2444
26300 Chagrin Blvd. (Park East Dr.), Beachwood, 216-464-0688
Crocker Park Shopping Ctr., 21 Main St. (Crocker Rd.), Westlake, 440-892-4933
www.hydeparkrestaurants.com
The meat-eating elite take a seat at these outposts of the statewide chophouse chain where a menu of "delectable", "mouthwatering" steaks (some "named after Cleveland sports figures") accords with the "masculine" feel of handsome "wood-accented" rooms populated by a "business crowd" ("old guys with their trophy dates"); "superb service" from "personable" staffers makes patrons feel they "really count" – but some bean-counters have a beef with "lofty", "expense-account" prices; N.B. West Prospect serves lunch during the week.

JOHNNY'S BAR ⊠   28 | 22 | 25 | $51 |
3164 Fulton Rd. (Trent Ave.), 216-281-0055
No Johnny-come-lately, this "outstanding" 80-year-old patriarch just south of Downtown has once again been voted Cleveland's No. 1 for Food; the "sophisticated" Continental–Northern Italian cuisine provides so many "twists and surprises" "you'll never tire" of it, let alone the "high-end" 1,000-label wine list; paneled interiors with "faux-leopard carpets" give off a vintage vibe (as if you're "dining with the Great Gatsby") and "knowledgeable" staffers treat you "like a regular even if it's your first visit", so "dress up" and eat with the "'in' crowd"; N.B. lunch Tuesdays and Fridays only.

LOLITA   27 | 23 | 24 | $46 |
(fka Lola Bistro & Wine Bar)
900 Literary Rd. (Professor Ave.), 216-771-5652; www.lolabistro.com
"I would eat shoe leather if Michael Symon cooked it for me" vow votaries of the chef/co-owner's "fantastic", "inventive" Med–New American victuals (a "revelation" in a "pierogi and kielbasa town"), now offered in small-plate options, and 500 "well-valued" wines; meanwhile, his "cool-cat" Tremont 50-seater "pleases more than just your palate", since the "hip, chic" main room, all mocha walls and velvet furnishings, has "lots of energy" (read: "can get loud"), and the "professional service" is usually "excellent."

Parallax Restaurant & Lounge ⊠   – | – | – | E |
2179 W. 11th St., 216-583-9999; www.parallaxtremont.com
Zack Bruell and David Schneider, the chef-manager team behind Z Contemporary Cuisine (one of Cleveland's Tops in the mid-'90s), reunite with this Tremont trendster, which serves up seafood, sushi and – for the non-fin fans – grilled meats in a vaguely Asian, earth-toned setting; though already busy, the servers manage to be quite friendly.

PHNOM PENH ⊅   27 | 8 | 19 | $16 |
13124 Lorain Ave. (131st St.), 216-251-0210; www.ohiorestaurant.com
Ok, the "atmosphere is not luxurious" and it "looks like a dump from the outside", but this "quiet" West Side BYO delivers "tremendous value", turning out "exquisite" Cambodian rice and noodle dishes whose "brilliant flavors" put your "taste buds on sensory overload"; the "owners make you feel like family" and staffers "help you order"

so chances are "once you dine here, you'll join the cult" of fervent fans frequenting this phnom-enon; N.B. a branch at 1929 W. 25th Street is slated to open in October 2005.

Red the Steakhouse   – | – | – | E

3355 Richmond Rd. (bet. Chagrin Blvd. & Woodland Rd.), Beachwood, 216-831-2252; www.redthesteakhouse.com

Trendy to look at, be in and pay for, this big, airy steakhouse is sister to Moxie, just one strip-mall storefront away (they share kitchen space); within the modern, monochromatic interior, the meaty mains with Med touches are accompanied by a rich list of big fat ol' California reds, although the pomegranate martinis are a nice libation, too; service is good and professional.

Sans Souci   26 | 26 | 25 | $47

Renaissance Cleveland Hotel, 24 Public Sq. (bet. Superior Ave. & 3rd St.), 216-696-5600

A culinary "Old Faithful" just off the lobby of the Renaissance Cleveland Hotel, this "classy", "romantic" special-occasioner evokes a Provençal farmhouse via an enormous stone fireplace, beamed wooden ceiling and "murals with countryside themes"; "marvelous" French-Med fare shows the "kitchen's attention to detail", a "strong cellar" boasts 400 wines and "kind" staffers help create a "warm ambiance" where diners can usually "converse without shouting" – but "because this is a place where people go to celebrate", you may encounter "some noisy folks."

Three Birds   ⊠   25 | 24 | 22 | $47

18515 Detroit Ave. (Riverside Dr.), Lakewood, 216-221-3500; www.3birdsrestaurant.com

"Even East Siders will cross the Cuyahoga" to take a flyer on this Lakewood locale, which has feathered friends chirping about the "whimsical", "well-executed" New American entrees and what they call "Cleveland's prettiest garden patio" (with "fresh herbs grown" nearby); inside, big windows and brightly colored walls and booths add "energy to the room" where eagle-eyed eaters enjoy "people-watching" and "friendly", casually attired staffers flit to and fro; N.B. dinner only.

Connecticut

TOP FOOD RANKING

	Restaurant	Cuisine
28	Thomas Henkelmann	New French
	Le Petit Cafe	French Bistro
27	Ibiza	Spanish
	Jeffrey's	Continental/New Amer.
	Jean-Louis	French
	Union League	French Bistro
	Métro Bis	New American
	La Colline Verte	French
	Rest. du Village	French
	Cavey's	New French/N. Italian
	Max Downtown	Steakhouse/New Amer.
	Carole Peck's	New American
	Da Pietro's	French/N. Italian
	Frank Pepe	Pizza/S. Italian
26	Frank Pepe's Spot	Pizza
	Sally's Apizza	Pizza
	Coromandel	Indian
	Meigas	Spanish
	Cafe Routier	French Bistro
	Bernard's	French

OTHER NOTEWORTHY PLACES

Restaurant	Cuisine
Ann Howard	New American
Barcelona	Spanish
Bentara	Malaysian
Bravo Bravo	Italian
Bricco	New American
Ching's Table	Pan-Asian
City Limits	Diner
Il Palio	Northern Italian
L'Escale	French
Mako of Japan	Japanese
Max's Oyster Bar	Seafood
Mayflower Inn	New American
Ocean 211	Seafood
Ondine	French
Peppercorn's Grill	Italian
Piccolo Arancio	Italian
Rebeccas	New American
Relish	New American
Roomba	Nuevo Latino
Valbella	Northern Italian

Ann Howard Apricots   23 | 22 | 21 | $43

1593 Farmington Ave. (Highwood Rd.), Farmington, 860-673-5405
"It doesn't get more charming than" this "enduring" New American overlooking the "scenic Farmington River" that offers "heavenly" outdoor dining, a "special-occasion white-tablecloth restaurant upstairs" with "elegant food" and a "comfy downstairs pub" that's less pricey; add to that "outstanding service" and "excellent desserts" and you've got a perennial pleaser.

BARCELONA REST. & WINE BAR   22 | 20 | 18 | $39

4180 Black Rock Tpke. (Rte. 15, exit 44), Fairfield, 203-255-0800
18 W. Putnam Ave. (Greenwich Ave.), Greenwich, 203-983-6400
63 N. Main St. (bet. Ann & Marshall Sts.), Norwalk, 203-899-0088
971 Farmington Ave. (Main St.), West Hartford, 860-218-2100
www.barcelonawinebar.com
"Go with friends, because you'll be grazing your way from tapas to paella" at this quartet of "lively hangouts for trust-fund babies"; "unusual fare with Spanish flair", a "superb wine list" and bar scene pack in the crowds; but cons counter since "it's too popular for its own good", "the noise level can exceed Barcelona's airport"; N.B. the new West Hartford branch opened post-*Survey.*

Bentara   24 | 23 | 20 | $35

76 Orange St. (Center St.), New Haven, 203-562-2511; www.bentara.com
"You surely will find a dish to warm your soul" at this "top-notch" Malaysian in the "developing Ninth Square neighborhood" of New Haven; "spicy", "authentic roti appetizers, aromatic soups, lots of vegetarian options" and a straightforward signature filet of beef are complemented by an "award-winning wine list" and "stylish" atmosphere enhanced by "ethnic" artifacts.

Bernard's   26 | 23 | 25 | $60

20 West Ln./Rte. 35 (Rte. 33), Ridgefield, 203-438-8282;
www.bernardsridgefield.com
Chef-owner Bernard Bouissou "is a culinary genius and his wife, Sarah, must be his muse" at the "Frenchiest French restaurant" in Ridgefield, where "exceptional" cuisine, a "splendid prix fixe Sunday brunch" ($35), "refined service" and a "comfortable" setting are the order of the day; while detractors are disappointed in the "dated, drab decor", most maintain this is an "inviting", "top-tier" "destination."

Bravo Bravo   26 | 20 | 23 | $40

Whaler's Inn, 20 E. Main St./Rte. 1 (Holmes St.), Mystic, 860-536-3228;
www.whalersinnmystic.com
Boosters say "bravo to this pearl of a waterside dining spot" in Mystic; "robust, surprisingly elegant tastes" along with "excellent service" make this Italian a "favorite" and it's gotten even better now that "recent renovations" have improved comfort and noise levels; though "cram-packed on weekends", this is a "restaurant that could make it in NYC."

Bricco   24 | 20 | 20 | $37

78 LaSalle Rd. (Farmington Ave.), West Hartford, 860-233-0220;
www.restaurantbricco.com
"Expect to flash your bling" at the bar of this West Hartford New American – but "for once, it's not just the trendy atmosphere you're paying for", it's chef-owner Billy Grant's "consistently delicious"

cuisine; "the open kitchen is entertainment in itself", and there's "a great patio for people-watching in the summer"; sure, it can be "loud and crowded", but that doesn't keep loyalists from "wishing they took reservations."

Cafe Routier
26 | 22 | 24 | $43
1353 Boston Post Rd. (I-95, exit 65), Westbrook, 860-399-8700; www.caferoutier.com
"Definitely not for truckers, despite what the name says", this "awesome" spot gives Westbrookians "bragging rights" for having "the best restaurant on the shoreline" – chef Jeff Renkl's cooking "combines French Bistro classics with Yankee sensibility and NYC panache"; "good-hearted service" and "unstuffy" ambiance also "make it a regular hang for fine diners of all stripes."

Carole Peck's Good News Cafe
27 | 20 | 23 | $45
694 Main St. S./Rte. 6 (Rte. 64), Woodbury, 203-266-4663; www.good-news-cafe.com
"Always [featured] on the short list" for "discerning foodies" is this "adventuresome" New American whose namesake chef-owner is dubbed "the Alice Waters of the East" for her "creative but not coy" cuisine "prepared with local and organic ingredients"; the fact that this casual, "jeans-and-loafers" "modern landmark" is located in "the antique haven" of Woodbury makes dining here even better news.

Cavey's ⊠
27 | 24 | 26 | $51
45 E. Center St. (Main St.), Manchester, 860-643-2751
What "a pleasant surprise to find such a high-quality", two-in-one restaurant "off the beaten path in historic Manchester", offering "always phenomenal Northern Italian upstairs" and what some call even "more phenomenal New French downstairs"; throw in "impeccable service" and "a wine list that even makes guests from Napa and Florence drool" and no wonder surveyors concur "it's the place to celebrate a momentous occasion."

Ching's Table
26 | 17 | 18 | $35
64 Main St. (Locust Ave.), New Canaan, 203-972-8550; www.chingsrestaurant.com
"Buffy-and-Brooks-Brothers" types "with pastel cardigans draped around their necks" pack this "exceptional" Pan-Asian in New Canaan that "wakes up your taste buds" with "outstanding" dishes like "great duck" and "crispy snapper"; despite a "deafening noise level", it's "very popular" and "given how hard it is to get a reservation, Ching should add a few more seats at his table."

CITY LIMITS DINER
19 | 15 | 16 | $24
135 Harvard Ave. (I-95, exit 6), Stamford, 203-348-7000; www.citylimitsdiner.com
Stamford's "high-energy", "always-crowded" eatery remains a "favorite" for its "diverse menu" of "comfort food with flair"; if a few are fed up with "all the hype" (it's "better than a typical diner, but still a diner"), for most it is still a "tried-and-true everyday option."

Coromandel
26 | 16 | 21 | $31
Goodwives Shopping Ctr., 25-11 Old Kings Hwy. N. (Sedgewick Ave.), Darien, 203-662-1213; www.coromandelcuisine.com
"Long live India!" declare devotees of this "superb" subcontinental that serves "innovative" cuisine, providing patrons with the chance

to "discover taste buds they never knew they had"; with "service that could not be friendlier or faster" and a "bargain lunch buffet", you "feel like you could be in London, New Delhi or Midtown."

Da Pietro's ☒
| 27 | 18 | 25 | $62 |

36 Riverside Ave. (Boston Post Rd.), Westport, 203-454-1213
"Pietro Scotti is the Michael Jordan of chefs, so you may need an NBA salary to pay the bill" after a "truly great culinary experience" at his French–Northern Italian; "this is what happens when you do it because you love it", attest admirers who give A's to the "first-rate food and service" at "one of Westport's finest"; just note with "quarters this cramped, it's not the place to plot a bank heist."

Frank Pepe Pizzeria ⊘
| 27 | 11 | 14 | $18 |

157 Wooster St. (Brown St.), New Haven, 203-865-5762
"Pizza that will change your life" is the answer admirers give for why it's "worth standing in a blizzard for an hour" for the "perfect", "crispy, thin-crust" Neapolitan-style pies at this 80-year-old "New Haven institution" where "the poor service is part of the legendary charm"; surveyors swear "the clam pies are the eighth wonder of the world" and the chief reason why this "local treasure" "has a special place in the hearts and arteries of many."

Frank Pepe's The Spot ⊘
| 26 | 9 | 15 | $18 |

163 Wooster St. (Brown St.), New Haven, 203-865-7602
If you're "craving superior pizza and don't want to wait in big brother Pepe's longer lines, this spot fits the bill" with "great" pies; it's smaller and has a more "low-key vibe" than the original, but it's "like eating in the waiting room of a New Haven bus station" once you make it in.

IBIZA
| 27 | 23 | 26 | $49 |

39 High St. (bet. Chapel & Crown Sts.), New Haven, 203-865-1933
Executive chef Luis Bollo (also of Norwalk's Meigas) is at the "top of his game" at this "chic and unique" New Haven "showcase" for his "stunning", "cutting-edge" Spanish cuisine; "superior service", "eye-popping decor" and an "excellent wine list" add to the "fantastic", albeit "expensive", "world-class" experience.

Il Palio
| 24 | 25 | 21 | $45 |

5 Corporate Dr. (Bridgeport Ave.), Shelton, 203-944-0770; www.ilpalio.net
Foodies "finally have a reason to go to Shelton at night" – to dine at this "upscale", "surprisingly excellent" Northern Italian set in a "marble architectural masterpiece plopped in a corporate parking lot"; the "posh atmosphere" makes it a "a good place to impress" your guests, but some snipe the "slow" staff "could use some of the polish put into all that marble."

JEAN-LOUIS
| 27 | 22 | 26 | $71 |

61 Lewis St. (bet. Greenwich Ave. & Mason St.), Greenwich, 203-622-8450; www.restaurantjeanlouis.com
"Food that Eiffel-towers over other French restaurants in the area" is what supporters say about chef-owner Jean-Louis Gerin's "rarefied" cuisine; a "top-notch" staff presides over this "beautiful little island of grace and understated elegance in what is an increasingly flashy Greenwich scene"; while a few fume about the "claustrophobic" setting and "overpriced" tabs, more maintain it's "a great place to spend your year-end bonus – all of it"; N.B. a post-*Survey* renovation may outdate the above Decor score.

JEFFREY'S
27 | 23 | 24 | $46 |

501 New Haven Ave. (Old Gate Ln.), Milford, 203-878-1910
It's "small but it rocks" sums up Jeffrey Johnson's "classy" New
American–Continental overlooking the salt marshes in Milford;
"superb cuisine", "impeccable service" and a "lovely" candlelit
setting make for an "excellent all-around" experience; N.B. a
post-*Survey* redo and a new, more casual conceptual focus may
outdate the above scores.

La Colline Verte
27 | 24 | 27 | $57 |

*Greenfield Hill Shopping Ctr., 75 Hillside Rd. (Bronson Rd.),
Fairfield, 203-256-9242*
"You'll feel pampered and happy, but never part of a snobby crowd"
at this "refined" Fairfield French with the finesse to "make any meal
a celebration"; "you'll also pay credit-card-melting prices", but
"heavenly cuisine", a "beautiful" setting and "top-notch service"
are "worth it"; N.B. jackets for gents are recommended.

LE PETIT CAFE
28 | 20 | 25 | $45 |

*225 Montowese St. (Main St.), Branford, 203-483-9791;
www.lepetitcafe.net*
"Nice things do come in small packages", as this "impeccable"
Branford French bistro proves with its "deftly delivered" four-
course prix fixe menu served Wednesday–Sunday; chef-owner
"Roy Ip is a magician who never disappoints", the staffers are
"meticulous" and the setting is "warm" and "cozy"; quite simply:
"one of the best bargains on the shore."

L'Escale
23 | 24 | 20 | $59 |

*Delamar Hotel, 500 Steamboat Rd. (I-95, exit 3), Greenwich,
203-661-4600; www.lescalerestaurant.com*
"During the summer, watch the hedge-fund managers pull up in
their yachts" at this "posh" Greenwich Provençal attached to the
Delamar Hotel, where "celebrity faces abound", the "seafood is
fresh and well prepared" and dining at a terrace table overlooking
the water is a "treat"; detractors declare it's "pricey", "noisy",
service is "inept" and "divorcée seems to be the most popular
entree" at the "sexy bar", but it's made a big splash with the "big-
spender" set; N.B. a post-*Survey* chef change may outdate the
above Food score.

Mako of Japan
25 | 13 | 22 | $30 |

222 Post Rd. (Rte. 130), Fairfield, 203-259-5950
A "sushi bar where everybody knows your name" is how devotees
describe this family-run Fairfield favorite for its "extremely friendly
atmosphere" and "fabulous fresh food"; it's "small" and "not much
to look at", but finatics simply aren't fazed.

Max Downtown
27 | 25 | 24 | $48 |

*City Place, 185 Asylum St. (bet. Ann & Trumbull Sts.), Hartford,
860-522-2530; www.maxrestaurantgroup.com*
Highest-rated in the Max dining dynasty is this "first-class" New
American chophouse, "the epicenter of the Hartford power scene"
for "expense-accounters" or to "impress a date"; a "professional
staff" serves "awesome steaks" and "serious martinis", but the
bar action is "pretty good too" – "think polished, yet lively" with
"many beautiful young things" to ogle; the only "ouch" is when
the "wallet-wounding" bill arrives.

Max's Oyster Bar   26 | 24 | 23 | $43
*964 Farmington Ave. (S. Main St.), West Hartford, 860-236-6299;
www.maxrestaurantgroup.com*
"A seafood standout in the school of Max's restaurants" and the
hub of the "social universe in West Hartford", this "noisy" but
"festive" spot reels reviewers in with "amazingly fresh seafood"
and "awesome tiered raw appetizers"; despite the comfy burgundy
booths, movers prefer the "happening" bar "jammed with the
moneyed, the single, the divorced and the thirsty."

Mayflower Inn, The   23 | 27 | 25 | $60
*The Mayflower Inn, 118 Woodbury Rd./Rte. 47 (Rte. 109),
Washington, 860-868-9466; www.mayflowerinn.com*
This New American housed in a Relais & Châteaux Washington inn
that "oozes country charm with a soupçon of formality"; "great food
is flawlessly presented and served" against a backdrop of three
"gorgeous rooms and gardens"; while critics decry an "overpriced"
and "overrated" "place that's a little too pleased with itself", most
agree if you "dine on the terrace in summer with the one you love,
the check won't hurt so much."

Meigas   26 | 21 | 25 | $53
*10 Wall St. (bet. High & Knight Sts.), Norwalk, 203-866-8800;
www.meigasrestaurant.com*
"Aptly named (*meigas* means sorceresses)", Meson Galicia's
"worthy successor" "consistently performs magic" in serving
"sublime Spanish" spreads to "sophisticated clients"; "toque-of-
the-town" Luis Bollo's (also of New Haven's Ibiza) "creations are
truly a source of joy", and they're complemented by "owner Ignacio
Blanco's attentive, indulgent" staffers; this is "an occasion place,
to be sure" (read: "pricey"), but "still, one of the tops in Norwalk."

Métro Bis ⊠   27 | 19 | 24 | $46
*Simsburytown Shops, 928 Hopmeadow St./Rte. 10 (Rte. 44),
Simsbury, 860-651-1908; www.metrobis.com*
New American "culinary powerhouse" located in a Simsbury
shopping plaza, where "the food tastes like chef/co-owner Chris
Prosperi enjoys his craft" and every member of the "professional"
"staff can handle any question you can throw" at them about the
"delectable meals"; the "small" space gets "noisy", but few mind,
given the reasonable prices charged for the "creative" fare; Julia
Child is smiling down upon this gem" – and you will too.

Ocean 211 ⊠   24 | 20 | 21 | $46
*211 Summer St. (bet. Broad & Main Sts.), Stamford, 203-973-0494;
www.ocean211.com*
Though it's "near the movie theater", you'll want to "make an
evening out of your meal" at this ocean of "serenity in Downtown
Stamford", featuring "super-luxe seafood" ("the chef never met
a fish he didn't love to cook") and "a nice selection of oysters" (20
varieties); you can expect "fine service" and a "sophisticated
NYC-type" vibe – and, some say, "Manhattan prices" as well.

Ondine   26 | 24 | 25 | $57
69 Pembroke Rd./Rte. 37 (Wheeler Dr.), Danbury, 203-746-4900
"Use the smallest excuse to celebrate" at this "top-drawer"
Danbury French favorite where chef-owner Dieter Thiel's cuisine,
from the signature ebony-roasted duckling to the "marvelous

soufflés", is "elegant", the room is "romantic" and the service is "*très français*, but without the Parisian attitude"; P.S. the $55 five-course tasting menu is a model of "value gourmet dining."

Peppercorn's Grill 🅢   26 | 20 | 23 | $42
357 Main St. (bet. Buckingham St. & Capital Ave.), Hartford, 860-547-1714; www.piccoloarancio.com
"You can't go wrong" at this "consistent standout" whose "truly wonderful Italian fare" "makes going out in Hartford worthwhile again" "for anyone who appreciates a complete food-and-wine experience"; it's also "popular" with the "pre-theater crowd" because of its proximity to the Bushnell Center for the Performing Arts, and while some servers "could be friendlier", the "competent staff" "can be counted on to get you out in time" for the show.

Piccolo Arancio 🅢   25 | 20 | 22 | $41
819 Farmington Ave./Rte. 4 (Rte. 10), Farmington, 860-674-1224; www.piccoloarancio.com
"Try the signature ravioli *all'arancia*" "with orange sauce" and "you'll want to go back" to this "unassuming" but "excellent" Farmington Italian that's the "sister of Hartford's Peppercorn's Grill"; for culinary "imagination and exceptional ingredients, this is an easy choice as one of the area's better" places; now, if they could just "get rid of the noise, you'd have perfection."

Rebeccas 🅢   26 | 20 | 23 | $65
265 Glenville Rd. (Riversville Rd.), Greenwich, 203-532-9270
It's "no Sunnybrook Farm" (in fact, the "contemporary interior" is somewhat "spartan"), but this Greenwich grandee is a "gourmet mecca" for "pilgrims who park their limos out front" and enter to enjoy chef/co-owner Reza Khorshidi's "sublime" New American dishes; critics may call it "pompous" – "there's clearly an 'in' crowd feeling" – and "seriously overpriced", but it still remains "the place to be seen" (and to eat).

Relish   25 | 19 | 21 | $47
86 Washington St. (N. Main St.), Norwalk, 203-854-5300
"Be prepared to be awed, amused and delighted by chef-owner Bill Taibe's New American food at this small, hopping" ("earplugs would be helpful") "newcomer to SoNo's restaurant scene", a destination "for foodies who want to be blown away by new flavors" in old favorites that "they'll remember for days afterward"; it's "pricey" and some report service bumps, but most relish their experience here.

Restaurant du Village   27 | 23 | 26 | $57
59 Main St. (Maple St.), Chester, 860-526-5301; www.restaurantduvillage.com
You're actually in "charming little" Chester, but "the owners make you feel like you're in Alsace", "offering some of the most exquisite French cuisine" at this "classic"; the "expert preparations" are matched by "expert service", and you won't find a prettier spot "in the middle of nowhere"; in short, it's "still the best" and further "comments are not needed – though reservations are."

Roomba   25 | 23 | 21 | $43
1044 Chapel St. (bet. College & High Sts.), New Haven, 203-562-7666
"Hip, loud and vibrant", this "slice of Havana" "under the streets of Downtown New Haven" is "consistently abuzz" with diners

downing "wonderfully strong mojitos" and "exciting" Nuevo Latino eats from chef/co-owner Arturo Franco-Camacho, a "specialist in tall food"; it'd be "perfect for a celebration", except that it's "stuffed with a staff" "full of attitude."

Sally's Apizza ⌽   26 | 8 | 11 | $17
237 Wooster St. (Olive St.), New Haven, 203-624-5271
If there were a "secret password" to get into this "slice of heaven in New Haven's Little Italy" it would be "more coveted than the Hope diamond", for "the waits are excruciating"; "but when you sit down you're rewarded" with a "paper-thin crispy pizza crust" and "sauce so good even cheese is an unworthy topping"; few seem to mind the "spare" digs, but many warn it's "BYO service if you're not a regular."

THOMAS HENKELMANN ☒   28 | 27 | 27 | $74
Homestead Inn, 420 Field Point Rd. (Horseneck Ln.), Greenwich,
203-869-7500; www.thomashenkelmann.com
It's a clean sweep for "chef extraordinaire Thomas Henkelmann" and his wife, Theresa, whose "transporting" New French in a "charming" Greenwich inn was voted Most Popular and No. 1 for Food in CT; sure, "the size of the bill will stun you", but the "superb" cuisine, "lovely setting" with a view of "gorgeous gardens" and "enormously attentive service" set "the gold standard for fine dining in Fairfield County."

UNION LEAGUE CAFE ☒   27 | 26 | 26 | $51
1032 Chapel St. (bet. College & High Sts.), New Haven, 203-562-4299;
www.unionleaguecafe.com
A "genteel crowd of visiting parents, their Yalie offspring, tweedy professors and urbane foodies" flocks to this "constantly improving veteran" New Haven French bistro; "always exquisite", chef-owner Jean-Pierre Vuillermet's cuisine "respects and enhances the quality of seasonal ingredients", "the service is knowledgeable and, like the decor, is dignified without being stuffy."

Valbella ☒   25 | 24 | 24 | $62
1309 E. Putnam Ave./Rte. 1 (Sound Beach Ave.), Riverside, 203-637-1155
Oenophiles aim for "dining in the fabulous wine cellar" (which underwent a big-bucks renovation and holds 20,000 bottles) at this Riverside Northern Italian "place to see and be seen" where "fantastic seafood and pasta dishes" are served by a "superb staff" in a "romantic" setting; it's a "popular haven for venture capitalists and local royalty" who seem to simply shrug off the "extra-high prices."

Dallas

TOP FOOD RANKING

Restaurant	Cuisine
28 French Room	French/American
Lola	New American
27 York Street	New American
Teppo	Japanese
Café Pacific	Seafood
Abacus	Eclectic
Tei Tei Robata Bar	Japanese
Del Frisco's	Steakhouse
Café on the Green	New American
Mansion on Turtle Creek	Southwestern
26 Nana	New American
Green Room	New American
Bob's	Steakhouse
Hôtel St. Germain	Continental/French
Suze	Mediterranean
Al Biernat's	Steakhouse
25 Chamberlain's	Steakhouse
Tramontana	New American
Pappas Bros.	Steakhouse
Old Warsaw	Continental/French

OTHER NOTEWORTHY PLACES

Aurora	New American
Capital Grille	Steakhouse
Chow Thai	Thai
Fogo de Chão	Brazilian/Steakhouse
Grape, The	New American
Hibiscus	American
Il Mulino	Italian
Iris	New American
La Duni Latin Café	Pan-Latin
Lavendou	French Bistro
Local	New American
Mercury Grill	New American
Mi Piaci Ristorante	Northern Italian
Modo Mio Cucina	Italian
Nobu Dallas	Japanese/Peruvian
Oceanaire	Seafood
P.F. Chang's	Chinese
Roy's	Hawaii Regional
Steel	Japanese/SE Asian
2900	Eclectic/New American

ABACUS ☒　　　　　　　　27 ┃ 27 ┃ 26 ┃ $56 ┃

4511 McKinney Ave. (Armstrong Ave.), 214-559-3111;
www.abacus-restaurant.com

Chef Kent Rathbun "choreographs the perfect East-meets-West
dance" at this "trendy" Knox Henderson Eclectic where "exciting
specials" emerge from the open kitchen and the "hip-to-the-
max" decor is "an elegant version of *The Jetsons*"; factor in an
"exceptional wine list", "established movers and shakers" and
"attentive, down-to-earth" servers and you have the Most Popular
restaurant in Dallas.

Al Biernat's　　　　　　　　26 ┃ 24 ┃ 25 ┃ $53 ┃

4217 Oak Lawn Ave. (Herschel Ave.), 214-219-2201; www.albiernats.com

"Consummate host" Al Biernat "always remembers a repeat
customer" (not to mention the local business executives, socialites,
sports heroes and other headline grabbers sitting two tables
away) at this Oak Lawn steakhouse known for "fabulous salads", a
"killer rib-eye" and "surprisingly wonderful seafood"; an "artistic",
"contemporary" setting that's quite "pretty", a "cool bar scene"
and "snappy service" are other inducements.

Aurora ☒　　　　　　　　─ ┃ ─ ┃ ─ ┃ VE ┃

4216 Oak Lawn Ave. (Wycliff Ave.), 214-528-9400; www.auroradallas.com

At his Oak Lawn domain, chef/co-owner Avner Samuel constructs
intricate New American dishes with French inflections (the
adventurous opt for his 10- to 12-course tasting menu); fascinated
foodies can watch him – and vice versa – as he works in an
exposed stainless-steel kitchen, separated by an etched-glass
wall from the 56-seat ultrasuede-walled dining room hung with
Peter Max art; Limoges china, Christofle flatware and the cellar's
500 wines are all handled deftly by the staff; N.B. private dinners
for up to 10 can be held in the 3,000-bottle cellar.

BOB'S STEAK & CHOP HOUSE ☒　　26 ┃ 20 ┃ 24 ┃ $53 ┃

4300 Lemmon Ave. (Wycliff Ave.), 214-528-9446
The Shops at Legacy, 5760 Legacy Dr. (Dallas N. Tollway), Plano,
972-608-2627
www.bobssteakandchop.com

"Bring your hearing aid" to these "dark, clubby" "hangouts" on
Lemmon Avenue and in Plano, where a mix of celebrities, "real
Dallasites" and "conventioneering" "expense-account types"
begin meals over "the best blue-cheese salad" then segue to
"perfectly cooked steaks" ("the *côte de boeuf* is outstanding")
perhaps with an "oversized glazed carrot"; truth be told, they may
be "the city's best restaurants with TVs in the dining rooms."

Café on the Green　　　　　　27 ┃ 26 ┃ 26 ┃ $46 ┃

Four Seasons Resort & Club Dallas at Las Colinas,
4150 N. MacArthur Blvd. (Northgate Dr.), Irving, 972-717-2420;
www.fourseasons.com

"Quiet, calming" and "casually elegant", this New American
at the Four Seasons Las Colinas is lauded for an "impeccable"
staff that doesn't disturb the Zen-like setting, and, at dinner, a
"fabulous rotating menu" of "inventive" Asian-accented dishes
that is sure to "impress even the jaded"; in addition to being a
"wonderful venue for holidays and special events", it's also "one
of the most pleasant Sunday brunch experiences in existence";
N.B. child-care services are available while you dine.

CAFÉ PACIFIC ⊠   27 | 25 | 25 | $45

Highland Park Vlg., 24 Highland Park Vlg. (bet. Mockingbird Ln. & Preston Rd.), 214-526-1170

"If Dallas had an ocean this restaurant would be on the beach" avow admirers of this "swanky" seafood bistro in Highland Park, where patrons know to "dress the part" if they want to convincingly "rub elbows with the city's elite"; insiders insist "try the short-smoked salmon", the "unbelievable three-onion sea bass" and the "addictive sweet potato fries" and like to watch how "maitre d' Jean-Pierre Albertinetti runs the dining room in a no-nonsense, efficient Gallic manner" that ensures "polished service."

Capital Grille, The   25 | 25 | 25 | $53

Crescent Shops & Galleries, 500 Crescent Ct. (bet. Cedar Springs Rd. & Maple Ave.), 214-303-0500; www.thecapitalgrille.com

The opposite of a boring Texas-style meatery, this "masculine" Maple Avenue "power dining center" (part of a chain, but with only a "faint whiff" of one) is an "investment-banker heaven" for "top-quality beef", "wood-paneled" rooms that breathe "old-style class" and staffers who "know how to pace a great meal" with "fabulous wines" that are "properly served"; just "don't let your guest select unless you've struck oil, are celebrating" or have a "liberal expense account."

Chamberlain's Steak and Chop House   25 | 22 | 24 | $48

5330 Belt Line Rd. (Montfort Dr.), Addison, 972-934-2467; www.chamberlainsrestaurant.com

"Gracious" chef-owner Richard Chamberlain is both "wonderful cook and consummate host" ("he will prepare anything you request") at this "classy" Addison steakhouse that puts out "one of the best rib-eyes you will ever have" as well as "excellent" slow-roasted prime rib (in three portion sizes); "smooth, unobtrusive service", "heavy wood paneling" and handsome lithographs on the walls are other reasons some "enjoy giving gift certificates to this restaurant."

Chow Thai   24 | 21 | 20 | $28

5290 Belt Line Rd. (Montfort Dr.), Addison, 972-960-2999
3309 Dallas Pkwy. (Parker Rd.), Plano, 972-608-1883
www.chowthai.com

A family affair that "does Thai right" sums up reactions to these Addison and Plano sibs where "innovative" big bowls of noodles, "magnificent curries" and owner Vinnie Virasin's fusion specialties ("excellent tea-smoked pork chops") "have patrons running back for more"; the clan's recipes, moreover, are showcased in "upscale", "contemporary" settings that are thankfully "free of the usual Asian clichés."

Del Frisco's Double Eagle Steak House   27 | 25 | 26 | $58

5251 Spring Valley Rd. (N. Dallas Tollway), 972-490-9000; www.delfriscos.com

"That ultimate beef and lobster you promised your doctor you'd cut back on" is here at this two-story North Dallas "Mercedes of steakhouses", a "masculine" mecca with dark-wood paneling, fireplaces, eight dining rooms, a cozy downstairs lounge and a "wine cellar that's terrific for parties"; the "entire staff does a superb job" too – however, the à la carte menu means many can only go for "special occasions" or "on an expense account."

Fogo de Chão | 25 | 20 | 24 | $48 |
4300 Belt Line Rd. (Midway Rd.), Addison, 972-503-7300;
www.fogodechao.com
"Bring a huge appetite" to this expansive southern Brazilian
churrascaria in Addison, where meals begin with an "awe-
inspiring salad buffet" then segue into a "carnivore's orgy" of
traditional and exotic meats that are brought on skewers by
"charming", gaucho-wearing waiters and "carved tableside";
it's quite a show (especially the fire pit at the entrance) for
both locals and tourists – just remember to "pace yourself" at
this single-price extravaganza and try not to fill up on the
"wonderful" cheese bread.

FRENCH ROOM ⊠ | 28 | 29 | 28 | $77 |
Hotel Adolphus, 1321 Commerce St. (Field St.), 214-742-8200;
www.hoteladolphus.com
No. 1 for Food in Dallas, this "incomparable French-American" in a
"historic Downtown hotel" sets a "standard of excellence" with its
"outstanding" dishes; expect an "elegant experience from start
to finish" where gentlemen wear jackets, the staff "treats patrons
like royalty" and the "stunning", "romantic" interior includes
"exquisite frescoes" reminiscent of Versailles; "you will need to
sell family silver to pay the bill", but that's a small price given you're
dining at the "finest restaurant in town."

Grape, The | 25 | 22 | 23 | $35 |
2808 Greenville Ave. (Vickery Blvd.), 214-828-1981;
www.thegraperestaurant.com
"Always interesting, always good" wax loyal disciples of this
"longtime" Greenville Avenue New American located on a strip of
nightclubs and tequila bars; expect "outstanding" "seasonal
feasts" from a "creative", often-changing menu, as well as an
"awesome", "smart wine list"; as a "charming", "romantic"
"little nook" with "small tables", it's a "perfect first-date place"
so long as you're "prepared to get to know your neighbors" too.

Green Room | 26 | 20 | 23 | $44 |
2715 Elm St. (Crowdus St.), 214-748-7666; www.thegreenroom.com
"Hip" foodies wade through the "tattooed crowd" outside this
"dark", "funky" Deep Ellum venue to "have a drink on its rooftop
bar" and then sample "fabulous" New American cooking that
"works the outer edge of the envelope", particularly the "awesome
'Feed Me, Wine Me' multicourse menu" ("a great value"); "pierced"
servers, sometimes with "green hair", and "lots of rock 'n' roll
memorabilia" further fuel the "Hendrix-like haze of great food,
drink and music."

Hibiscus ⊠ | – | – | – | E |
2927 N. Henderson Ave. (Off Rte. 75), 214-827-2927;
www.consilientrestaurants.com
Perpetually packed with mixed-age hipsters, this American joins
a string of hit eateries and nightclubs from wiz kids Tristan Simon
and chef Nick Badovinus, who have staked their claim on the east
side of Knox Henderson; the dynamo Badovinus, looking more
rock star than culinary professional, expedites prime meats
and fin gems from an open kitchen in the heart of a series of
narrow, wood-trimmed rooms, all brimming with cheeky service
and high-decibel conversation.

Hôtel St. Germain ☒　　　26 | 27 | 26 | $72
2516 Maple Ave. (bet. Cedar Springs Rd. & McKinney Ave.),
214-871-2516; www.hotelstgermain.com
"Pack the kids off to grandma's", put on the heels or the jacket
and tie, then call a limousine to take you and the spouse to this
"romantic", "antique-filled", "neat old" mansion Uptown where
"white-gloved waiters" provide "silver service" as patrons
partake of "impeccable" seven-course French-Continental
meals in a "tiny", "extremely quiet" dining room overlooking
a courtyard; P.S. "top off the evening by staying in one of
the fabulous rooms."

Il Mulino ☒　　　– | – | – | VE
2408 Cedar Springs Rd. (Fairmont St.), 214-855-5511;
www.ilmulinodallas.com
An offshoot of NYC's perennially packed Italian institution, this
Uptown upper-cruster has created an uproar with its identical
menu of indulgently rich classic cuisine (served in stereotypically
enormous portions); a legion of suave white-tie waiters will
prepare pasta and debone fish tableside in a dimly lit old-world
dining room featuring oil paintings, draperies, chandeliers and
even marble-accented loos; given the hefty prices, it's especially
excellent for expense-accounters.

Iris ☒　　　– | – | – | E
5405 W. Lovers Ln. (Inwood Rd.), 214-352-2727; www.irisdallas.net
Owner Susie Priore (ex Suze) and her hand-picked partner, chef
Russell Hodges, lure the diva-designer-discerning-diner crowd to
this much-praised New American with creative, predominantly
organic eats like seared foie gras and pistachio-crusted rack
of lamb; meanwhile, the West Lovers site (which has seen a host
of eateries come and go) has undergone an extreme makeover
this time around, resulting in a serene scene of putty-colored
walls, dark-wood tables and iris-themed original works by
renowned Texas artists.

La Duni Latin Café　　　24 | 22 | 21 | $29
4620 McKinney Ave. (Knox St.), 214-520-7300
4264 Oak Lawn Ave. (Herschel Ave.), 214-520-6888 ☒
www.laduni.com
You "won't believe how little it costs to treat your taste buds" at
these "cute", "lively" Oak Lawn and Kox Henderson Pan-Latins
where the "super" dishes are complemented by "imaginative
cocktails" and "the best collection of South American wines in
the Metroplex", sometimes poured by "owners who hang around
and chat"; regulars rhapsodize about "first-rate", "lip-smacking
desserts" (particularly the "to-die-for" *cuatro leches* cake) and
the "novel Sunday brunch."

Lavendou ☒　　　24 | 23 | 23 | $40
19009 Preston Rd. (bet. Frankford Rd. & Pres. George Bush Tpke.),
972-248-1911; www.lavendou.com
The "next best thing to being in France" is a visit to this "unstuffy"
North Dallas bistro with a reputation for "reasonable prices" on
"first-rate" Gallic goodies ("don't-miss soufflés", "the best" roast
duck); so soak up the Provençal atmosphere, ask the "attentive",
"friendly" waiters to pour you a second glass of Burgundy and
savor another bite of crusty bread dipped in olive oil.

Local ☒
_ | _ | _ | E

2936 Elm St. (N. Walton St.), 214-752-7500

A modernist treatment of food and space creates a sensual New American experience at this Deep Ellum address; chef Tracy Miller's ever-changing, imaginative menu of small and large plates – including a not-to-be-missed array of artisanal breads and sorbets – is synched with wine notations from a tight boutique list; a passionate staff stands ready with lighted reading magnifiers, helping diners to deal with a dark converted space that updates rustic brick walls with commissioned art and Eames chairs.

LOLA ☒
28 | 24 | 27 | $51

2917 Fairmount St. (Cedar Springs Rd.), 214-855-0700;
www.lola4dinner.com

Dallas' "most creative bills of fare" await visitors to this "quaint, little cottage" Uptown, where the "deft culinarians" produce "amazing [two- to four-course] prix fixe" New American meals, complemented by an "incredible", 2,000-label, "fairly priced" wine list; a "uniformly knowledgeable" and "passionate front-of-the-house team" and a "charming patio" are added attractions; N.B. the adjacent 10-table Tasting Room offers "to-die-for" 10- and 14-course *petite*-portion menus that can be paired with wines.

MANSION ON TURTLE CREEK, THE RESTAURANT
27 | 27 | 27 | $70

2821 Turtle Creek Blvd. (Gillespie St.), 214-559-2100;
www.mansiononturtlecreek.com

Modern Southwestern "flavors you can't imagine anywhere else" are found at "Texas icon" and "master-inventor" chef Dean Fearing's "venerable" Uptown destination, an art- and antique-filled "grand place for a special occasion" where jacketed "old-money" "regulars" enjoy "sublime lobster tacos" and "must-try tortilla soup" brought by tuxedoed staffers, all part of a "well-orchestrated production"; quibblers say it's "no longer cutting-edge" and "you're paying for the reputation", but more love that "it just keeps rolling."

Mercury Grill, The
25 | 23 | 22 | $44

11909 Preston Rd. (Forest Ln.), 972-960-7774;
www.mcrowd.com

"Awesome food" (the "pepper-crusted seared ahi is as good as ever") from "a great menu" generates positive reviews for Chris Ward's "winning" New American, a "great find in a strip mall" in Preston Forest, below LBJ; with its "sleek", "sophisticated" vibe, it reminds Big Apple aficionados of "being in Manhattan" and draws a loyal crowd of local luminaries, especially now that there's a new lounge, Club 113.

Mi Piaci Ristorante
24 | 25 | 23 | $44

14854 Montfort Dr. (Belt Line Rd.), Addison, 972-934-8424;
www.mipiaci-dallas.com

"Ask for a patio table overlooking the pond" at this "sleekly serene" "Addison-meets–Northern Italy" classic where everything is "exceptional", from the "top-notch" staffers who could double as Armani models to the "fabulous" wine list and "handmade pastas with perfectly balanced sauces" ("the veal ragout was wonderful"); P.S. epicureans know to mark their calendar for truffle season, which brings the "best risotto in Texas."

Modo Mio Cucina Rustica Italiana 24 | 19 | 23 | $35

Frankford Crossing, 18352 Dallas Pkwy. (Frankford Rd.), 972-713-9559;
www.modomio.net
Dressy-casual patrons of this "small" North Dallas Italian know
to look for its camouflaged entrance within a bustling suburban
shopping center; the venue's "serious following" is attributable to
an "efficient staff" and "high-quality dishes" that are "a break from
the formulas used elsewhere"; while this is definitely "the place
for pasta", including a ravioli menu, the "sea bass is a standout"
too; N.B. the wine list has tripled in size over the last few years.

Nana 26 | 27 | 26 | $62

Wyndham Anatole Hotel, 2201 Stemmons Frwy., 27th fl.
(Market Center Blvd.), 214-761-7470; www.nanarestaurant.com
What a "calmly elegant", "romantic" room and "panoramic view",
declare diners dazzled by this "sky-high" Market Center dining
venue; "from its height you can look down at all the lesser
restaurants in town" while enjoying "scintillating" New American
fare (with some old-world influences) served on Versace place
settings; he-men hail it as a "place to make your woman happy",
and if you don't have one just swagger over to "the bar that swings
with jazz" nightly.

Nobu Dallas ☒ – | – | – | VE

Hotel Crescent Court, 400 Crescent Ct. (bet. Cedar Springs Rd. &
Maple Ave.), 214-252-7000; www.noburestaurants.com
Netting global kingfish Nobu Matsuhisa was the ultimate coup for
the Hotel Crescent Court; redesigned in brown hues, its dining room
hums with frenzied jet-setters and nomadic glitterati clicking their
stilettos and oxfords in appreciation of the Japanese-Peruvian
cuisine swept to the table by high-energy experts and partnered
with *masu* (square wooden cups) of aged sake; and even though the
tabs seem tied to the skyward prices of a barrel of West Texas
crude, already dinner requires booking weeks in advance.

Oceanaire Seafood Room 25 | 24 | 24 | $49

Westin Galleria Hotel, 13340 Dallas Tollway (LBJ Tollway), 972-759-2277;
www.theoceanaire.com
"Finally, great seafood comes to this landlocked town", declare
piscatorially partial partisans of this multilevel "upscale" chain link
located in the Westin Galleria; decorated with horseshoe-shaped,
fire-engine-red banquettes and a "nautical-but-nice" motif, it
makes patrons feel like they're "dining on a five-star liner" from
the '30s "with everyone at your service"; "crab cakes are a must",
as are the "incredible selection of oysters" from the raw bar.

Old Warsaw, The 25 | 24 | 25 | $57

2610 Maple Ave. (bet. Cedar Springs Rd. & McKinney Ave.),
214-528-0032; www.theoldwarsaw.com
"One hates to admit liking the same Uptown restaurant one's
parents did a generation ago, but it's hard not to enjoy a meal" at
this "elegant", "dress-up" Continental-French, which is "still a
grand dining venue" for a "well-heeled crowd" looking to celebrate
"special occasions" over "classic haute cuisine" ("wonderful
soufflés"); "personalized service" from tuxedoed waiters, a piano
player and "strolling violinist" add to the "charm", so when trendies
call it "tired" and "out of touch", defenders blithely boast that "it
will probably be open for another 100 years."

Pappas Bros. Steakhouse 🗷

| 25 | 24 | 24 | $55 |

10477 Lombardy Ln. (bet. I-35 & Northwest Hwy.), 214-366-2000;
www.pappasbros.com

Further evidence that "Texas is about 'big'" is this Love Field area
surf 'n' turf outpost, which is "not as much of a see-and-be-seen
steakhouse as other places in town" (though it does draw "famous
people") but boasts a "'40s-style art deco" interior with "great
private rooms", an "amazing wine cellar", the "largest rock lobster
tails you've ever seen" and "great steaks."

P.F. CHANG'S CHINA BISTRO

| 23 | 21 | 20 | $27 |

18323 N. Dallas Pkwy. (Frankford Rd.), 972-818-3336; www.pfchangs.com

"Addictive lettuce wraps", "to-die-for Mongolian beef" and "spicy
dishes galore" headline the "high-quality" Chinese menu at this
"expansive", "stylish" and "still wildly popular" North Dallas
upmarket chain outpost; true, it's "extremely noisy and crowded",
and you can "grow old waiting for a table" ("takeout is a brilliant
solution"); nevertheless, "it sure beats your local delivery place."

Roy's

| 24 | 23 | 22 | $45 |

2840 Dallas Pkwy. (bet. Park Blvd. & Parker Rd.), Plano, 972-473-6263;
www.roysrestaurant.com

"If I can't be in [the islands], at least I can come here", assert
admirers of Roy Yamaguchi's Hawaii Regional entry where the
"architectural", "zippy mixtures" from the huge open kitchen are
"something different and exotic"; some snipe that they get "a
little food for a lot of money", but hey, after one of the "fun", fruity
cocktails and a gander at the tropical plantation decor you'll think
"all that's missing is the Maui coast."

Steel ◗

| 24 | 26 | 20 | $48 |

Centrum Bldg., 3102 Oak Lawn Ave. (Cedar Springs Rd.), 214-219-9908;
www.steeldallas.com

With its "alluring", dark, "mysterious" interior, this Oak Lawn
Japanese–Southeast Asian showplace – a "see-and-be-seen
runway" for fashionistas, elite athletes and aspiring moguls – pairs
"delicious sushi" and "excellent cooked dishes" ("outstanding
sea bass") with an "unbelievable selection of wines and sakes"
(1,000 and 30, respectively); dissenters dis it as "flash and dash"
with a "condescending" staff and prices so "high" it's "a great
place to rack up frequent-flier miles."

Suze 🗷

| 26 | 17 | 24 | $36 |

4345 W. Northwest Hwy. (Midway Rd.), 214-350-6135

It's safe to say "you won't just stumble onto" Gilbert Garza's "cozy,
neighborhood" Mediterranean in an "out-of-the-way" strip center
near Love Field; but it's worth seeking out, since this "little gem"
exemplifies "all the quality and personal attention you'd expect
from a chef-owner" applied to dishes such as the signature veal
Bolognese and a "well-chosen wine list"; a recent, post-*Survey*
revamp may answer the prayers of patrons for a decor "upgrade",
including relief from the "cramped" seating.

Tei Tei Robata Bar

| 27 | 23 | 22 | $45 |

2906 N. Henderson Ave. (Willis Ave.), 214-828-2400;
www.teiteirobata.com

"If you've just gotten paid" and are seeking "out-of-this-world
sushi" ("including crazy stuff you can't get elsewhere"), "amazing

Kobe beef" and other "delicious grilled meat and fish", head to
this "unassuming" Knox Henderson "Japanese jewel box" where
owner Teiichi Sakurai is a "perfectionist" and "tables are a hot
commodity"; not surprisingly, "you'll see all the pretty people", as
well as DJs.

TEPPO YAKITORI AND SUSHI BAR | 27 | 24 | 23 | $39 |
2014 Greenville Ave. (Prospect Ave.), 214-826-8989; www.teppo.com
"Stylish" types who frequent this "small", "minimalist" Greenville
Avenue Japanese say the "hip" sushi ("great" "for pros and
amateurs") "might make you forget to order the grilled items",
which would be a shame since the "yakitori here is not to be
missed"; yes, many "wish the place were bigger" because "it's a
hassle to get a table", but it's "worth the wait."

Tramontana ⊠ | 25 | 19 | 23 | $39 |
*Preston Ctr. West, 8220B Westchester Dr. (bet. Luther & Sherry Lns.),
214-368-4188; www.mybistro.net*
"A neighborhood dining spot with an edge" sums up this Italian-
and Gallic-influenced New American where James Neel's large
menu (including a prix fixe option) of "distinctive", "creative"
cuisine is "consistently enjoyable"; surveyors say he and his staff
"go the extra mile" to ensure you get "personal attention",
and add that the space feels like a "charming bistro in Paris",
overcoming its location in the older part of Preston Center.

2900 ◑⊠ | 25 | 21 | 23 | $41 |
2900 Thomas Ave. (Allen St.), 214-303-0400; www.2900restaurant.com
Set in a former Uptown office space that's been converted to a
"sleek", "dark" and "romantic" eatery with black-and-white
photographs and a bar aglow with flickering candles, this "great
place to take a date" is a "hip, little neighborhood sleeper" that
serves "delicious", "innovative" Eclectic–New American fare
(grilled artichokes, stuffed tenderloin); P.S. the "live jazz band is a
nice touch" on Saturdays, so long as you're prepared to "yell at
your neighbor" to communicate.

YORK STREET RESTAURANT ⊠ | 27 | 22 | 28 | $54 |
6047 Lewis St. (Skillman St.), 214-826-0968
Chef-owner Sharon Hage "has more talent in one finger than the
rest of us have in 10", swear acolytes of this East Dallas New
American set in a tiny house in a "funky, old neighborhood", where
her "imaginative", "exciting", "market-driven" menu employs "the
freshest ingredients" and the staff "would rather help than hurry"
("they even gave my daughter a tour of the kitchen"); epicureans
beg "please don't tell anyone, it's already" too "crowded."

Denver Area & Mountain Resorts

TOP FOOD RANKING

	Restaurant	Cuisine
28	Mizuna	New American
27	Highlands Garden Cafe	New American
	Del Frisco's	Steakhouse
	L'Atelier	French
	Sweet Basil	New American
	Cafe Brazil	Brazilian/Colombian
	Sushi Den	Japanese
	Flagstaff House	Eclectic/New American
26	Six89 Kitchen/Wine	New American
	Matsuhisa	Japanese
	Keystone Ranch	New American
	John's	New American
	240 Union	Seafood/New American
	Montagna	New American
	Kevin Taylor	New American
	Alpenglow Stube	Bavarian/American
	Opus*	New American
	Capital Grille	Steakhouse
	Zengo	Asian/Nuevo Latino
	Grouse Mountain Grill	Regional American

OTHER NOTEWORTHY PLACES

Barolo Grill	Northern Italian
Emma's	New American
Frasca Food and Wine	Northern Italian
Full Moon Grill	Northern Italian
India's	Indian
Jax Fish House	Seafood
Kitchen, The	Eclectic
La Tour	New French
Left Bank	French
Luca d'Italia	Italian
Mel's Restaurant	New American
Morton's	Steakhouse
New Saigon	Vietnamese
Panzano	Northern Italian
Piñons	Regional American
Potager	New American
Q's	New American
Rioja	Mediterranean
Solera	New American
Syzygy	New American

---

* Indicates a tie with restaurant above

Alpenglow Stube   26 28 27 $73
Keystone Resort, 21996 Hwy. 6 (top of North Peak Mtn.), Keystone,
970-496-4386; www.keystone.snow.com
"Both the altitude and the food take your breath away" at this lodge
atop the North Peak of Keystone (elevation: 11,444 ft.) reachable
only by gondola; the "romantic" old-world aerie with roaring
fireplace boasts "exquisite panoramas", plus "outstanding"
staffers who provide "nice sheepskin slippers" and "wonderful,
creative" Bavarian-American cuisine; for this "peak experience",
"bring a fat wallet" and be sure to bundle up ("you freeze on the
way up and down"); N.B. limited hours in summer.

Barolo Grill ⌧   25 23 24 $48
3030 E. Sixth Ave. (bet. Milwaukee & St. Paul Sts.), 303-393-1040
"Warm and intimate" yet always "bustling", this Cherry Creek
dinner-only "class act" "could hold its own anywhere", thanks
to "consistently excellent", "belt-expanding" Northern Italian
favorites ("fabulous duck"), an "extensive", "expensive" list of
630 regional wines and an "attentive" staff that travels to The Boot
regularly for educational tastings; some surveyors find the "upsell,
upsell, upsell" approach too "pushy", yet happily take a "seat by
the fireplace" to "watch the sparks fly . . . literally."

Cafe Brazil ⌧   27 16 22 $32
4408 Lowell Blvd. (44th Ave.), 303-480-1877
Chef/co-owner Tony Zarlenga's "exciting", "exotic" Brazilian-
Colombian fare "astonishes the taste buds" at this "unpretentious",
"bright" 70-seater, in a "slightly folksy", "good-looking location"
in "not-quite-gentrified" Berkeley Park; "warm, friendly" and
"super laid-back" servers also add to the place's "personality";
regulars advise reservations, reporting "it's well worth the wait"
for such a "magical experience"; N.B. the Decor score may not
reflect the mid-*Survey* move.

Capital Grille, The   26 26 26 $50
1450 Larimer St. (15th St.), 303-539-2500; www.thecapitalgrille.com
A new soldier in "Denver's steakhouse wars", this "carnivore's-
dream" chain link in Larimer Square brings beef eaters "marvelous"
chops, "very good seafood" and more than 400 wines via the
ministrations of an "inspired" staff that "makes everyone feel like
a VIP"; "clubby" quarters are "chic, sleek and sophisticated"
"without the stuffiness" of some competitors, and the "see-and-
be-seen" "bar excels"; even those with expense accounts admit
that "your wallet will get a workout, but who cares when you're
treated like royalty?"; N.B. free valet parking.

DEL FRISCO'S DOUBLE EAGLE   27 25 26 $58
STEAK HOUSE
Denver Tech Ctr., 8100 E. Orchard Rd. (I-25), Greenwood Village,
303-796-0100; www.delfriscos.com
"Denver's elite" – including pro ballplayers (e.g. "the Broncos'
defensive unit") and other celebs – are among the "testosterone-
charged" "faithful" of this Greenwood Village chain meatery; they
consider it "well worth the coronary risk" to chow down on the
"succulent" "slabs of steer" and sides at this "clubby" "Western
parlor" where an "impeccable" staff is "out to please"; bellyachers
beef about a "loud crowd that likes to show off its money",
apparently preferring fellow diners to be seen and not herd.

Emma's ⊠   25 24 24 $41
603 E. Sixth Ave. (Pearl St.), 720-377-3662; www.emmasrestaurant.com
Habitués hail this "charming", "homey" New American 50-seater
in a Central Denver Victorian as "one of the friendliest places in
town", thanks to "delightful" owners Garen and Linda Austin and
their "accommodating" crew; what's more, the "ultra-competent
kitchen" turns out "terrific" seasonal entrees "rich with creative
sauces" and homegrown herbs yet "without pretension"; in short,
it's a "true find."

FLAGSTAFF HOUSE   27 26 27 $64
1138 Flagstaff Rd. (on Flagstaff Mtn.), Boulder, 303-442-4640;
www.flagstaffhouse.com
The "breathtaking views overlooking Boulder" from Flagstaff
Mountain are by themselves "worth the high price of admission" to
this "classic" hillside haven – but wait, there's more: loyalists laud
the "imaginative, delicious" "French- and Asian-accented" New
American–Eclectic fare, the "elegant", "romantic" dining room, the
"spectacular" 20,000-bottle wine cellar and the "white-glove"
service, though a miffed minority finds the "whole experience"
"hoity-toity" and "stuffy to the point of claustrophobia."

Frasca Food and Wine ⊠   – – – E
1738 Pearl St. (bet. 17th & 18th Sts.), Boulder, 303-442-6966;
www.frascafoodandwine.com
Giddy gastronaughts are arriving en masse to this lauded novice,
a Northeastern Italian noshery helmed by famed French Laundry
alums, including chef-owner Lachlan Mackinnon-Patterson and
master sommelier Bobby Stuckey; their efforts pack the subdued
dining room with bona fide foodophiles and oenophiles pining for
the revered handcut tagliatelle, prosciutto plate or pork leg paired
with one of the 200 varieties of vino from small producers; N.B. the
Monday night three-course tasting menu is one of Boulder's
best meal deals.

Full Moon Grill   25 19 23 $38
Village Shopping Ctr., 2525 Arapahoe Ave. (bet. Folsom & 28th Sts.),
Boulder, 303-938-8800; www.fullmoongrill.com
For a "guaranteed happy eating experience", Boulderites roll over
to this "cozy" shopping-center "gem" where the "consistently
excellent" seasonal Northern Italian cuisine ("try the pear-and-
polenta appetizer" and the "wonderful desserts") pleases both
neighbors and visiting "urbanites"; picky eaters appreciate
"knowledgeable" servers who "cheerfully honor custom requests",
while tipplers toast "spectacular monthly wine dinners"; a few
elbow-roomers sigh the "tables are uncomfortably close" and take
solace in patio seating.

Grouse Mountain Grill   26 25 25 $59
Beaver Creek Resort, 141 Scott Hill Rd. (Village Rd.), Beaver Creek,
970-949-0600; www.beavercreek.snow.com
When they want an "absolutely first-rate" "fine-dining" experience
the cognoscenti "come back" to this Beaver Creek stalwart for
"monstrous portions" of "creative", "outrageously delicious"
Regional American fare ("fantastic without being too fancy") and
450 vintages, all "wonderfully presented" by an "attentive and
professional" staff; the "elegant" yet "kid-friendly" setting offers
a fireplace, "gorgeous views" and the "most comfortable chairs

in the universe" from which to enjoy them; P.S. "ask for a table in the bar" near the jazz pianist.

HIGHLANDS GARDEN CAFE   27 | 27 | 25 | $43
3927 W. 32nd Ave. (bet. Osceola & Perry Sts.), 303-458-5920; www.highlandsgardencafe.com
The "quintessential place for ladies of a certain age" ("take your mom"), this "impeccable" North Denver "Victorian manor" is a "treat for all the senses"; chef-owner Patricia Perry proffers a "shockingly huge" New American menu of "creative", "challenging flavor combos" executed with "talent and style" plus 300 wines; "luscious flora" blooming in "charming" "courtyard gardens" make for a "lovely summer meal on the patio", especially when you're doted on by a "delightful staff."

India's   25 | 17 | 19 | $23
Tamarac Sq., 3333 S. Tamarac Dr. (Hampden Ave.), 303-755-4284
Still "the best Indian in town", this South Denver curry house has "regulars" raving about its "titillating", "flavorful and aromatic" food, including "impressive lamb vindaloo" ("every pore on your body will sweat"), "great vegetarian dishes" and a "value-priced" ($6.95) lunch buffet; yes, the "somber" staff has "a lot of rules" (e.g. "no shorts!") and the "colorful" room looks like "something out of a bad Bollywood movie", but satisfied spice cadets stay loyal "no matter how many [competitors] come and go."

Jax Fish House   24 | 18 | 20 | $34
1539 17th St. (Wazee St.), 303-292-5767; www.jaxfishhousedenver.com
928 Pearl St. (bet. 9th & 10th Sts.), Boulder, 303-444-1811; www.jaxfishhouseboulder.com
Everyone agrees the quarters are "tight" and the noise level is "way over the top" ("you'll need to use the crayons on the table to communicate"), but even so, most are swept away by the "lively" "party atmosphere" at these "happening" LoDo and Boulder "cult fish houses for locals"; finatics file in to feast on "scrumptious seafood" (the "oysters rock") that's ferried to the table by "hotties" who navigate the "cool" environs swimmingly; P.S. the hooked beseech "please start taking reservations" on weekends.

John's ⊠   26 | 19 | 25 | $46
2328 Pearl St. (bet. 23rd & 24th Sts.), Boulder, 303-444-5232; www.johnsrestaurantboulder.com
For an "intimate respite" from Boulder's "hectic Pearl Street Mall", epicures opt for this New American "classic charmer" set in a "delightfully quiet" cottage; they love "longtime faves" ("incredible Stilton filet mignon") combined with "inventive" and "eclectic" "new offerings", all of which is served "gracefully" and with "professional" aplomb; a 2003 "ownership change" for this "standby" has apparently "kept things going well" — though to some, that means decor is "dated" and the menu "stale."

Kevin Taylor ⊠   26 | 25 | 25 | $60
Hotel Teatro, 1106 14th St. (Arapahoe St.), 303-820-2600; www.hotelteatro.com
Downtown Denver's Hotel Teatro is the stage for this "posh" Parisian-style haute house, an "elegant" and "rather formal" "special-occasion place"; foodies effervesce over chef-owner Kevin Taylor's "delicately balanced" and "innovatively presented" New American cuisine ("perfection on a plate"), the "great"

1,000-label cellar and "truly dedicated" staffers who "cater to your every need" -- even if naysayers nitpick that prices are "ridiculous" and the scene "pretentious."

Keystone Ranch Restaurant   26 | 25 | 25 | $70 |
Keystone Ranch Golf Course, 1437 Summit County Rd. 150 (Rd. D), Keystone, 970-496-4386
Keystone cognoscenti crow about this "consistently exceptional" lodge embellished with an "elegant" "Western ambiance" ("your own cabin in the hills, if your name happens to be Trump"); its "first-class" Colorado-style New American fare (bison, rack of lamb, wild game) is complemented by some 500 "interesting wines"; afterwards, in a "sitting room" complete with "roaring fireplace", the "tremendous" crew serves "wonderful desserts" and coffee; sure, it's "expensive", but just "bring a fat wallet", "forget about" the cost and enjoy a "true mountain experience."

Kitchen, The   – | – | – | E |
1039 Pearl St., Boulder, 303-544-5973; www.thekitchencafe.com
Proving that the most convivial room in the house is, indeed, the kitchen, this chic Boulder bistro – a magnet for enthusiastic chowhounds and wine geeks – is known for its 12-ft. community table (made from century-old Douglas fir), commitment to organic, local ingredients and eco-conscious sensibilities (the restaurant is completely wind-powered); it all translates into a jubilant dining experience, staffed by servers who are knowledgeable about the Eclectic, daily changing menu and 450-label wine list.

L'ATELIER   27 | 23 | 23 | $44 |
1739 Pearl St. (18th St.), Boulder, 303-442-7233; www.latelierboulder.com
Chef-owner Radek Cerny is once again a culinary "artiste-in-residence", "cooking up French-inspired eats" for "NY-wannabes" at his "charming" three-year-old Boulder cafe; well-wishers wallow in the "dazzling", "imaginative" and "exquisitely presented" fare ("colorful essences and reductions") served on "beautiful art-glass dishes" in "good-size portions" that make for "outstanding value"; however, claustrophobes cluck this site has "tables too close together", resulting in "too many people in too small a space."

La Tour   – | – | – | E |
122 E. Meadow Dr. (I-70), Vail, 970-476-4403; www.latour-vail.com
At this Vail Contemporary French, chef-owner Paul Ferzacca turns out a slew of Gallic goodies (sole meunière, sweetbreads) that skews toward seafood, while half a dozen sommeliers are on hand to help with the 350-label list of French and American wines (including 50 under $50); sleek, colorful and warm surroundings plus a convenient village location also help turn diners into Tour-ists.

Left Bank ⇗   25 | 21 | 24 | $62 |
Sitzmark Lodge, 183 Gore Creek Dr. (Bridge St.), Vail, 970-476-3696; www.leftbankvail.com
Gallic gourmet "classics" ("fantastic bouillabaisse", "don't-miss tomato soup", "sauces that make you want to lick your plate") without the "phony nouveau frills" make this "sophisticated" stop at Vail's Sitzmark Lodge a must for Francophiles (*"sans les enfants", s'il vous plait*) who also ooh-la-la over the "outstanding wine list" and "relaxed" but "meticulous" service; sure, the "old-fashioned" decor might be a mite "dated", and you'll need to "run to the ATM" beforehand (no cards) but "it's all worth it."

Luca d'Italia ☒ | 25 | 20 | 25 | $42 |
711 Grant St. (bet. 7th & 8th Aves.), 303-832-6600;
www.lucadenver.com
"Hey Dorothy, we're in Italy now", swear smitten surveyors who
swoon over this "high-on-the-buzz-chart" Capitol Hill spot from
chef-owner Frank Bonanno (Mizuna); foodies feast on "fabulous"
five-course tasting menus, crab gnocchi "to make your Italian
grandmother smile" and "wonderful 'rabbit three ways'", while
an "outstanding" staff that's "caring but not stuffy" traverses the
"upscale", "minimalist", modern dining room; though a few fret
that the menu's "quirky" and "confusing", most maintain the
experience is "hip, happening and heavenly."

Matsuhisa | 26 | 21 | 21 | $64 |
303 E. Main St. (Monarch St.), Aspen, 970-544-6628;
www.nobumatsuhisa.com
"Omakase . . . oh my goshe", gasp gourmets who gather at this
Aspen outpost of the "Nobu empire", where "refined Japanese
chow" and "world-class sushi" constitute a "culinary experience
not to be missed"; decor is comparatively "down-home" vis à vis
the coastal siblings, comprising a "tastefully decorated" basement
dining room and a "swanky" upstairs lounge for sipping "tasty
saketinis"; though there's a groundswell of grumbling about
"indifferent service", overall the cognoscenti consider a dinner
here "worth the wound" on your "bleeding wallet."

Mel's Restaurant & Bar | 24 | 20 | 23 | $40 |
235 Fillmore St. (bet. 2nd & 3rd Aves.), 303-333-3979;
www.melsbarandgrill.com
The "mature 'in' crowd" hangs in and "hangs out" at this Cherry
Creek "hardy perennial"; they report "kitchen magician" Tyler
Wiard "keeps reinventing the menu" with an "ever-changing"
roster of "delicious and satisfying" New American dishes, while
staffers who "take their jobs seriously" pour selections from a
"stellar" cellar, and live music at the "terrific bar" "brings in both
young city slickers and old-timers"; N.B. a recent fire mandated
a renovation, outdating the Decor score.

MIZUNA ☒ | 28 | 22 | 27 | $49 |
225 E. Seventh Ave. (bet. Grant & Sherman Sts.), 303-832-4778;
www.mizunadenver.com
"Let's be frank": Frank Bonanno's "exceptional" Capitol Hill New
American, rated No. 1 for Food in Colorado, is "best in breed, class
and show"; gourmets are "dizzy with glee" over the "globe-trotting"
goodies ("exquisite lobster mac 'n' cheese", "salads almost too
pretty to eat") and "stunning wine list" proffered by Denver's "most
polished kitchen", while the service is "not just responsive but
anticipatory"; a recent expansion of the "lovely and intimate
setting" to include a bar and private dining nook "means even more
happy diners" at this "winner."

Montagna | 26 | 26 | 27 | $66 |
The Little Nell Hotel, 675 E. Durant St. (Spring St.), Aspen, 970-920-6330;
www.thelittlenell.com
"Upscale, classy" and even a touch "formal" (you'll find "few
snowboarders here"), this "brightly shining star" at Aspen's Little
Nell Hotel is known for its "legendary service", "elegant outdoor
dining" and "unbelievably creative", "indescribably delicious" New

American cuisine (particularly "spectacular desserts"), bolstered by "treasured master sommelier" Richard Betts' perfect pairings; sure, "it's expensive, but worth it."

Morton's, The Steakhouse
`25` `22` `25` `$60`

1710 Wynkoop St. (17th St.), 303-825-3353
Denver Crescent Town Ctr., 8480 E. Belleview Ave. (DTC Blvd.), Englewood, 303-409-1177
www.mortons.com

"Chockablock" with "devoted carnivores" and "local celebrities" who store "their own personal wine collections", these "old-school, clubby" cow palace chainsters in LoDo and Englewood bring in beef eaters for "dinner and a show": an "impeccable" "tag-team" staff presents a "food tour" of "plump and juicy" slabs later "seared to perfection" and served with "diabolically rich sides"; of course, as the "sizzling" meat "melts in your mouth", "funds in the wallet melt at a similar pace", so "cash in a bond before you go" or "enjoy it on a corporate expense account."

New Saigon
`26` `11` `17` `$21`

630 S. Federal Blvd. (bet. Center & Exposition Aves.), 303-936-4954; www.newsaigon.com

With an "enormous" menu the "size of a Tolstoy novel" (there's "an entire section devoted to frogs' legs"), this "awesome", "authentic" "old-timer" in a South Denver strip mall remains an "inexpensive" way to "take your tongue on a trip to Vietnam"; "attentive" if sometimes "surly" servers will "guide you" to a "truly wonderful" meal (the "best spring rolls", "outrageous noodle soups", "fantastic smoothies"), and though "fancy folk" fret the "nothing-special" interiors are "starting to fray around the edges", the "food makes up for it."

Opus
`26` `23` `25` `$44`

2575 W. Main St. (Curtice St.), Littleton, 303-703-6787

"Yes, Virginia, there really is great" fare in the "land of the bland chain restaurants" announce "pleasantly surprised" diners who've found this "quaint" "storefront in Downtown Littleton"; they talk up its "adventuresome", "exciting" and "wonderful" New American entrees presented with "panache" by "professional" servers in an "urban-chic" setting some call "stark"; a vocal minority maintains the place "still feels like a work in progress", but all admit this "up-and-comer" is "trying hard."

Panzano
`25` `23` `22` `$41`

Hotel Monaco, 909 17th St. (Champa St.), 303-296-3525; www.panzano-denver.com

"Even with the loss of chef Jennifer Jasinski", this sunny, "centrally located" Downtown "hotel restaurant" has "kept its status as a great Northern Italian bastion"; the "awesome" "open kitchen makes it fun to watch the action" as new top toque Elise Wiggins creates her "hearty yet sophisticated" and "delicious" cuisine (Sunday brunch is "unusual and terrific") for "power-lunchers", "special visitors" and "relatives from New York"; still, some say it's been "hit-or-miss lately", with service that can be "slow."

Piñons
`25` `24` `25` `$62`

105 S. Mill St. (E. Main St.), Aspen, 970-920-2021

"No Aspen trip is complete" without dining at this "always excellent and reliable" Regional American "classic"; in a "comfortable" room that feels like a "Southwestern art gallery", "cordial" staffers extend a "wonderful welcome" before "knowledgeably" describing chef Rob Mobilian's "Colorado cuisine" for the "gourmet Western palate" and "superb wines"; granted, the "off-the-charts" tabs have a few foes grumbling it's "overrated and overpriced", but converts counter "even if the total bill comes to $5 per bite, it's worth every penny."

Potager ⊠   24 | 20 | 22 | $40

1109 Ogden St. (bet. 11th & 12th Aves.), 303-832-5788
Clearly a "Chez Panisse devotee", chef Terry Rippeto fashions her "eclectic, seasonal" New American fare from "sublime", "freshest-of-the-fresh" ingredients at this "funky" Capitol Hill "charmer"; add in a "breezy", "bohemian", "Euro-distressed" dining room and a "delightful garden" conducive to "romantic interludes" and a "friendly", "wine-savvy staff" that's up on the "thoughtful" "boutique" list and you get a Berkeley-style "bistro that could – and does"; still, some sticklers' "high expectations" are "disappointed" by "loud acoustics" and "indifference" from the crew; N.B. no reservations.

Q's   25 | 23 | 23 | $42

Boulderado Hotel, 2115 13th St. (Spruce St.), Boulder, 303-442-4880;
www.qsboulder.com
An "oasis within the People's Republic of Boulder" that's "far from the tree-hugging crowd", this "classy", "historic" New American in the Boulderado Hotel is a "great place to take your parents or have a business dinner"; servers "really care" and "outstanding" chef John Platt's "inspiring" seasonal menu is "heavenly" (though acrophobes assert his "artistic presentations" are "a little heavy on the towers"); "breakfast is awesome" too, especially if you sit on the "nice porch" overlooking the Pearl Street pedestrian mall.

Rioja   – | – | – | E

1431 Larimer St. (bet. 14th & 15th Sts.), 303-820-2282;
www.riojadenver.com
The name refers not only to the provenance of the winsome wines dotting the eclectic, moderately priced roster, but also to the province inspiring chef/co-owner Jennifer Jasinski's (ex Panzano) Med menu at this stylish new hot spot on trendy Larimer Square; already, a mix of locals and tourists is rhapsodizing about such dishes as the artichoke mousse-filled tortelloni and goat cheese and fig beignets, while swank singles belly up to the lively copper-topped bar for sangria and small plates.

Six89 Kitchen & Wine Bar   26 | 22 | 24 | $45

689 Main St. (7th St.), Carbondale, 970-963-6890;
www.six89.com
Tight-lipped tastemakers "hate to share the secret" of iconoclastic chef-owner Mark Fischer's Carbondale New American, but admit they "owe it" to him to spill the beans; in fact, his "passionate", "creative" "culinary artistry" ("each dish is more delicious than the last") has won over flocks of foodies willing to journey "from Denver just for the meal and then home the same night"; "genius sommelier" Bill Bentley's "stellar cellar" and "hospitable", "well-trained" servers who make everything "look effortless" also contribute to this "uplifting" "down-valley" experience.

Solera Restaurant and Wine Bar ⊠   25   22   23 $45
5410 E. Colfax Ave. (Grape St.), 303-388-8429; www.solerarestaurant.com
"Rising star" Goose Sorensen took a "tough location" on a "seedy strip" in East Denver and elevated it to a "superb neighborhood eatery" with his "innovative, playful" and "utterly fantastic" New American fare bolstered by an "incredible selection" of "reasonably priced wines"; thanks to "snappy service", a "quiet and calming" atmosphere and a "beautifully appointed patio" perfect for "starlit summer nights", it's "a delicious experience" for those "interested in food, not scenes"; P.S. "Wednesday wine tastings are a treat."

Sushi Den   27   23   20 $39
1487 S. Pearl St. (E. Florida Ave.), 303-777-0827;
www.sushiden.net
"Beverly Hills meets the Rockies" at this "sleek", "modern" sushi specialist in Washington Park, where "beautiful people galore" gather for "artful and inventive" "ultra fresh" fare ("creative rolls", "must-eat" sashimi) made from fish that's "flown in from Japan daily", along with "amazing banana cream pie"; some snipe that "service is pompous and pretentious" but admit the "food is worth the 'tude – barely" ("I wish it weren't so good, so I could stop going"); P.S. no reservations, so "be prepared" for "long waits" during prime time.

SWEET BASIL   27   22   24 $51
193 E. Gore Creek Dr. (Bridge St.), Vail, 970-476-0125;
www.sweetbasil-vail.com
"After so many [28] years", this "super place" still "satisfies and stimulates", declare devotees of this "dynamic" Vail Village "landmark", voted Colorado's Most Popular; respondents "never tire" of Bruce Yim's "clever, innovative" New American cuisine "with Asian touches" ("lamb that's better than you thought possible"), the "caring" staff, "great après-ski scene" or "beautiful views" of Gore Creek; regrettably, the reservation list fills "months in advance", and you might have to "sell your seat at the bar" to "help defray the cost", but the place's "energy and verve" endures; P.S. "insider's tip: go for lunch."

Syzygy   25   23   23 $58
520 E. Hyman Ave. (bet. Galena & Hunter Sts.), Aspen,
970-925-3700
"Syzygy – a word constructed from sizzle and energy?" wonder wordsmiths who in any event agree this "great Aspen secret" "has both"; "wild-game master" Martin Oswald conjures up "terrific" New American dishes that aren't "drenched in sauces" for pairing with bottles from a "superb wine list"; the setting "has it all", with an "elegant", "tastefully simple" dining room and a lively bar offering "jumping jazz" on weekends; it may be "expensive", yet most feel this "hip", "happening place" is "worth every dollar."

240 UNION   26   20   24 $36
240 Union Blvd. (bet. W. Alameda Pkwy. & 6th Avenue Frwy.),
Lakewood, 303-989-3562; www.240union.com
This "beacon of exciting food in the culinary desert" of the Western suburbs is "alive, exciting and always busy" boast boosters who believe it's "a bargain for the quality of food you get"; the "modern" dining room is overseen by "superb" servers, and chef Matt

Franklin's "a genius with seafood", creating "bright, innovative" and "consistently excellent" New American fin fare and "seasonal menus" whose "flavors sing on the plate"; perhaps that's one reason the sound-sensitive snipe it's "too darn loud."

Zengo   26 | 27 | 24 | $44
1610 Little Raven St. (15th St.), 720-904-0965; www.modernmexican.com
Whether or not it's actually "the coolest-looking eatery in the West", it's certainly "unlike any other restaurant in Denver", rave respondents about Richard Sandoval's new "sassy", "bodaciously" "sexy" "urban hot spot" in River Park; take in the loungey lair's vibrant colors and textures or "snatch a seat at the chef's counter" to watch the busy kitchen concoct "exotic", "bizarre" and "deliciously unique" Asian–Nuevo Latino concoctions, complemented by "sublime drinks" and "smooth service"; still, a few grumblers growl that "deafening noise" deters "dinner conversation."

Detroit

TOP FOOD RANKING

	Restaurant	Cuisine
28	Rugby Grille	Continental/American
	Lark, The	Continental
	Emily's	Med./New French
27	Zingerman's	Deli
	Tribute	French
	Bacco	Italian
	Common Grill	Seafood
26	Five Lakes Grill	New American
	West End Grill	New American
	Il Posto Ristorante	Italian

OTHER NOTEWORTHY PLACES

Beverly Hills Grill	New American
Cafe Bon Homme	New French
Grill at the Ritz-Carlton	New American
No. VI Chop House	Seafood/Steakhouse
Opus One	Continental/American
Oslo Sushi Bar & Lounge	Japanese/American
Ristorante Café Cortina	Italian
Steve's Deli	Deli
Sweet Georgia Brown	American
Traffic Jam & Snug	Eclectic

F	D	S	C

Bacco ☒ | 27 | 25 | 25 | $52 |
29410 Northwestern Hwy. (W. 12 Mile Rd.), Southfield, 248-356-6600; www.baccoristorante.com
"Delectable food" with "wonderful flavors" from a "pure-Italian" kitchen that pays "attention to detail" has regulars ranking this "rather elegant", "pricey", "upscale" Southfield spot among the "best in Detroit"; there's also "top-notch service" from a "knowledgeable and friendly staff", as well as "great people-watching" at the bar and a "gorgeous", "contemporary" interior, all of which makes it "a place to be seen with the 'in' crowd."

Beverly Hills Grill | 26 | 19 | 23 | $33 |
31471 Southfield Rd. (W. 13 Mile Rd.), Beverly Hills, 248-642-2355
"Always reliable", this "lively" Beverly Hills New American "favorite" "never disappoints" with its "amazing breakfasts", but it also gets "raves" for its "creative brunches", "delicious lunches" and "outstanding dinners" thanks to a "consistently stellar" kitchen and an "expertly trained staff"; true, the "casual" space is "crowded, small and noisy", but most admirers insist the "quality" "makes up for" the "drawbacks" – now "if only they would take reservations."

Cafe Bon Homme ⑤   26 | 20 | 23 | $55
844 Penniman Ave. (bet. Harvey & Main Sts.), Plymouth, 734-453-6260
"Lovely, welcoming experiences" await at this "charming" New French "in the great little town of Plymouth", where "superb food" (including "sensational desserts") is paired with a "great wine list" and served by an "outstanding" staff in a "cozy", "quiet" setting; a few feel the "outdated decor" "is tired", but more maintain that the "quaint", "intimate atmosphere" helps "make every dinner there a special occasion."

COMMON GRILL, THE   27 | 20 | 24 | $34
112 S. Main St. (bet. Middle & South Sts.), Chelsea, 734-475-0470; www.thecommongrill.com
It's "worth the trip" to this "off-the-beaten-path" storefront spot "in the wonderful town of Chelsea", an "hour's drive" from Detroit, thanks to "great chef" and owner Craig Common's "excellent seafood" menu, which offers "variety, freshness" and fish "as good as at an East Coast restaurant"; a "fun, bistro-like bustle" pervades the "always-crowded" dining room, but be warned that the atmosphere is decidedly "high decibel" (and "expect to wait to be seated").

EMILY'S ⑤   28 | 22 | 27 | $63
505 N. Center St. (8 Mile Rd.), Northville, 248-349-0505; www.emilysrestaurant.com
"A cute house in Northville" is the setting of this "charming" 50-seater, an "absolute gem" where chef Gabe Lacouture creates a "seasonal" menu of "fresh, imaginative" New French–Med dishes, which "warm and welcoming" owner Rick Halberg "exceptionally matches" with "an excellent wine list"; the "outstanding service" and "unpretentious", "intimate atmosphere" also contribute to "a thoroughly enjoyable experience" that epitomizes "fine dining at its best."

Five Lakes Grill ⑤   26 | 20 | 23 | $42
424 N. Main St. (Commerce St.), Milford, 248-684-7455; www.fivelakesgrill.com
Fans feel they've "died and gone to heaven" after a visit to this "fairly priced" New American where "excellent chef"-owner Brian Polcyn's "innovative" menu emphasizes "fresh, fresh, fresh" Michigan ingredients and includes "delightful twists on old favorites"; it's "food you'll find nowhere else", and the storefront space offers a surprisingly "urbane atmosphere" given its location "in the quaint old town" of Milford, 40 minutes north of Detroit.

Grill at the Ritz-Carlton, The   26 | 26 | 27 | $57
Ritz-Carlton Dearborn, 300 Town Center Dr. (bet. Hubbard Dr. & Southfield Frwy.), Dearborn, 313-441-2100; www.ritzcarlton.com
A "gracious", "attentive" staff provides "refined", "first-class service" at this "top-notch" Dearborn hotel near Ford's world headquarters, a "special-occasion" favorite that's "guaranteed to impress" with an "amazing" New American menu of "wonderful food" made from the "highest-quality ingredients"; P.S. a "recent renovation" has rendered the "beautiful, elegant room" "even more luxurious", and the Food rating may not reflect the post-*Survey* arrival of chef Robert Wilson.

Il Posto Ristorante 🖫   26 24 24 $51
29110 Franklin Rd. (Northwestern Hwy.), Southfield, 248-827-8070;
www.il-posto.com
"When you want to splurge", "dress up" and dash to this "elegant,
expensive Italian" in Southfield, where "classic" cuisine that
"never disappoints" is "prepared flawlessly" from "the noblest of
ingredients", accompanied by a "great wine list" and "formally"
served by "bona fide waiters from [The Boot]" in a "fabulous
room"; some purport it's "pretentious", saying certain staffers are
"supercilious", but more maintain it's a must for "memorable meals"
of the "highest quality."

LARK, THE 🖫   28 26 28 $81
6430 Farmington Rd. (W. Maple Rd.), West Bloomfield, 248-661-4466;
www.thelark.com
"Romance abounds" at this "still-superb" West Bloomfield
"legend" "modeled after a Portuguese country inn" that remains
the Most Popular of Detroit-area restaurants; "consummate
hosts" and owners "Jim and Mary Lark treat you like guests in
their home", while their "educated, professional staff" supplies
"superior service"; in the kitchen, chef Kyle Ketchum "provides
freshness to the outstanding menu" of "divine" Continental fare,
"adding to an already fabulous dining experience."

No. VI Chop House & Lobster Bar   26 24 25 $56
27790 Novi Rd. (12 Mile Rd.), Novi, 248-305-5210;
www.mattprenticerg.com
"Fantastic food" is featured at this "first-class" surf 'n' turfer that
has fans "salivating" with "some of the best steaks going", "divine
morel bisque" and "wonderful" "sautéed lobster tails with whipped
potatoes", plus "top-notch service to match"; some find the "dark
wood" environs too "dimly lit" and the "manly prices" "sinful",
but most feel this "favorite" is "worth the drive" to its "far-out"
location; P.S. the "catchy name is actually" a play on the town's
moniker – "get it?"

Opus One 🖫   26 25 25 $53
565 E. Larned St. (Beaubien St.), 313-961-7766; www.opus-one.com
"Still a favorite" with "business- and theater-crowd" "movers
and shakers", this "Downtown institution" "delivers on all levels"
thanks to chef-partner Tim Giznsky's "interesting, varied menu"
offering "a mix of traditional American" and Continental dishes,
"owner Jim Kokas' superb wine list", a "professional staff" that
"makes every guest feel special" and recently "updated decor"
with "a refreshing, modern look"; a few feel "there are better
values", but more insist it's "fine dining the way it was meant to be."

Oslo Sushi Bar and Lounge 🖫   – – – I
1456 Woodward Ave. (John R St.), 313-963-0300; www.osloworld.com
Located at the intersection of sushi and American sensibility, this
stylish, skinny (20 x 80 ft.) space Downtown creates a buzz with
its striking wood-and-brass interior, laid-back ambiance and super-
fresh, scandalously low-priced morsels from the quick fingers of
Tokyo-born chef Kaku Usui; it's frequented by a mix of foreign auto
execs and locals upstairs and a younger crowd in the downstairs
lounge, who savor the 12 different kinds of sake and know to order
the chef's choice combination plate – thus reaping the best of a
menu that, like the tides, changes twice a day.

Ristorante Café Cortina ⊠　　　26 | 24 | 24 | $53
30715 W. 10 Mile Rd. (Orchard Lake Rd.), Farmington Hills, 248-474-3033;
www.cafecortina.com
"When you crave" "true Italian flavor", find your way to this
"fabulous" Farmington Hills "favorite", a "beautiful cafe" where
the "classic" cuisine (including "superb pastas") is "wonderfully
prepared" using vegetables and "herbs grown in an [on-site]
garden", and the "attentive", "smartly dressed" staff "makes you
feel like family"; some fault the "high prices" and feel "the food
and service can be a bit uneven at times", but a majority is won
over by the "insanely romantic" ambiance.

RUGBY GRILLE　　　　　　28 | 26 | 28 | $60
Townsend Hotel, 100 Townsend St. (Pierre St.), Birmingham,
248-642-5999; www.townsendhotel.com
"You may have to mortgage your house, but it's worth it" for the
"old-fashioned dining experience" at this "classy", "clubby"
Continental-American that's rated No. 1 for Food in Detroit;
"housed in the Townsend Hotel" ("where out-of-town celebs",
"stars and musicians stay"), it's "reminiscent of the best intimate
European restaurants", and its "exceptional" fare and "elegant
service" are "worth every penny" according to "everyone who's
anyone in Birmingham"; P.S. "you'll want to be seated inside"
"the tiny grille" "rather than the hallway outside."

Steve's Deli　　　　　　　25 | 11 | 18 | $17
Bloomfield Plaza, 6646 Telegraph Rd. (Maple Rd.), Bloomfield Hills,
248-932-0800; www.stevesdeli.com
"As close to a New York deli as you can get", this "wonderful
delicatessen" "in a strip mall" in Bloomfield Hills "turns out" a
"phenomenal selection" of "consistently good", "fast eats",
including "the best chicken noodle soup in town" and "fabulous
corned beef"; some advise you "avoid the seating experience",
though, claiming the "cramped, crowded", "unappealing room"
and "perennial wait for tables at prime times" "make carryout
a better choice."

Sweet Georgia Brown　　　　– | – | – | VE
1045 Brush St. (Monroe St.), 313-965-1245; www.sweetgb.com
Local movers and shakers, policy makers and visiting celebrities
enjoy this Greektowner's American way with comfort foods taken
to their deluxe utmost, in dishes like fried lobster, crabmeat-
topped rib-eye and desserts that look southward (bourbon pecan
torte, berries with mint julep cream); the richly textured setting
swings on weekends with jazz trios and at Sunday brunch with
saxophonist Herbie Ross.

Traffic Jam & Snug　　　　　– | – | – | M
511 W. Canfield St. (2nd Ave.), 313-831-9470;
www.traffic-jam.com
Detroit's first brewpub, this Cultural Center institution makes
cheeses and European-style beers in the same giant vats, all the
better to anchor an Eclectic menu that ranges from inventive
sandwiches to meatloaf to spinach lasagna (just save room for the
over-the-top desserts, many made with the house's own dense ice
cream); the culinary mélange is just right for its mixed clientele
augmented by pre- and post-theatergoers, who enjoy the eccentric
decor that features farm implements hanging from the ceiling.

TRIBUTE 🗷
27 | 27 | 25 | $76

31425 W. 12 Mile Rd. (Orchard Lake Rd.), Farmington Hills, 248-848-9393;
www.tributerestaurant.com

Acolytes just "cannot say enough about" the "one-of-a-kind",
"remarkable experience" at this "shining star" in Farmington Hills
that "deserves all of its acclaim"; "everything is impeccable",
from the "innovative menu" of "delicious", "decadent Classic
French" fare with global accents to the "phenomenal ambiance"
of its "breathtakingly" "beautiful" space to the "wonderfully
attentive staff" – even if "small portions", "over-the-top" prices
and certain "haughty staffers" have some saving this "culinary
masterpiece" for "a special-occasion" "splurge."

West End Grill 🗷
26 | 23 | 26 | $47

120 W. Liberty St. (Ashley St.), Ann Arbor, 734-747-6260

"Make reservations well in advance" for a spot within the "quiet,
candlelit setting" of this "romantic, intimate", "white-tablecloth"
65-seater located in the "heart of the action" in Downtown Ann
Arbor; reviewers call it "a jewel" for "exquisitely prepared" New
American cuisine "impeccably served" by a "solidly trained",
"knowledgeable staff" and accompanied by a "fantastic wine list";
true, it's "always crowded" and "occasionally noisy", but you'll
be "treated as if you're the only ones dining at the restaurant."

ZINGERMAN'S DELI
27 | 16 | 21 | $17

422 Detroit St. (Kingsley St.), Ann Arbor, 734-663-3354;
www.zingermans.com

"Long lines" "out the door" mark this "legendary" Ann Arbor
"institution", "a national treasure" that locals laud as the "best
deli in America"; don't be dismayed by the "dizzying array of
sandwiches", as the "knowledgeable", "personable staff" will
"guide you through the huge selection" (though you may also
need "help" handling the "humongous proportions" and "high
prices"), or by "the dreary sit-down area" "where your meal is
brought to you", as you can always "carry out."

Ft. Lauderdale

TOP FOOD RANKING

Restaurant	Cuisine
28 Sunfish Grill	Seafood/New American
27 La Brochette	Mediterranean
Cafe Maxx	Eclectic/New American
26 Canyon	Southwestern
Cafe Martorano	Italian
Casa D'Angelo	Northern Italian
Eduardo de San Angel	Mexican
Mark's Las Olas	Floribbean
Galanga	Japanese/Thai
Silver Pond	Chinese

OTHER NOTEWORTHY PLACES

Anthony's	Pizza/American
Café Vico/Vico's Downtown	Italian
Cheesecake Factory	American
Chima	Brazilian/Steakhouse
Hi-Life Café	New American
Houston's	American
Johnny V's	Floribbean
Josef's	Northern Italian
Ruth's Chris	Steakhouse
3030 Ocean	Seafood/New American

F	D	S	C

Anthony's Coal-Fired Pizza   25 | 14 | 20 | $20
2203 S. Federal Hwy. (SE 22nd St.), 954-462-5555
Even those demanding "NY pizza perfection" beat a path to this small Ft. Lauderdale storefront for "fantastic" pies such as the "one-of-a-kind" eggplant Marino (named for the football Hall of Famer), a "meatball" version that's a "must" and other goodies including "excellent chicken wings"; waist-watchers weigh in and say this "gem" provides "the best excuse to cheat on a diet."

CAFE MARTORANO ⌧   26 | 18 | 20 | $61
3343 E. Oakland Park Blvd. (N. Ocean Blvd.), 954-561-2554
"Fast for a week" before going to this "small" no-menu, no-reserve Ft. Lauderdale Italian serving "huge portions" of "fantastic" fare to patient patrons who endure "painful waits", staff "attitude" and enough "ear-cleaning noise" to make "Q-Tips unnecessary"; though it's "like dining in the middle of a dance floor" "after the disco ball descends", regulars say this "crazy scene" "is worth it."

CAFE MAXX   27 | 20 | 25 | $56
2601 E. Atlantic Blvd. (NE 26th Ave.), Pompano Beach, 954-782-0606;
www.cafemaxx.com
This Pompano Beach "stalwart" still "amazes" after 20 years; the "dining adventure" features "incredible" Eclectic–New American

food including "outstanding seafood" and an "excellent" wine list that includes a "large selection by the glass"; while some scoff it's "a bit pricey", regulars rave it's a "special-occasion place that should be your any-occasion place" – especially given the "newly decorated" digs; N.B. with a liquor license pending, look for cocktails this winter.

Cafe Vico/Vico's Downtown   23 | 20 | 23 | $38
1 E. Broward Blvd. (NE 1st St.), 954-463-4414 ⊠
IHOP Plaza, 1125 N. Federal Hwy. (NE 11th Ave.), 954-565-9681
www.cafovico.com
Admirers appreciate the "winning" formula of "wonderful" Italian cooking, "reasonable prices", Marcos Vico Rodrigues' "charm" (he "greets everyone like family") and a "friendly staff" at this "pretty" Lauderdale "favorite" in a shopping center; the majority "counts on it" since it "never disappoints"; N.B. the Downtown satellite now serves lunch only (dinner for private parties).

CANYON   26 | 23 | 23 | $44
1818 E. Sunrise Blvd. (N. Federal Hwy.), 954-765-1950; www.canyonfl.com
While it may be hard to resist "the best prickly pear margaritas on the planet", the "sensational" Southwestern fare also stands tall in the opinion of many at this "hip", "high-energy" Ft. Lauderdale "treasure"; the "worth-every-calorie desserts" are the crowning touch, and the service is "top-notch" (yet sometimes "rushed"), but be aware that the "small" digs and no-reservations policy mean you're headed for "too-long" waits at peak times; P.S. ask for a "quiet booth" "away from the racket."

CASA D'ANGELO   26 | 20 | 24 | $49
Sunrise Square Plaza, 1201 N. Federal Hwy. (bet. E. Sunrise Blvd. & NE 13th St.), 954-564-1234; www.casa-d-angelo.com
It's "as good as it gets", say legions of loyalists who line up for "celebrity chef" Angelo Elia's Tuscan treat in Lauderdale, where the toque turns out "beautiful" Italian fare with a "superb wine list" in tow; it's "jam-packed with folks ready to spend the cash", so it helps that the "attentive" staff's at the ready to calm rattled nerves unnerved by the "long waits."

CHEESECAKE FACTORY ◐   20 | 18 | 19 | $26
600 E. Las Olas Blvd. (S. Federal Hwy.), 954-463-1999
Sawgrass Mills Oasis, 2612 Sawgrass Mills Circle (Flamingo Rd.), Sunrise, 954-835-0966
www.thecheesecakefactory.com
The "best chain – ever", aver acolytes of these South Florida Americans whose "encyclopedic" menus feature "giant-sized portions" of everything, from "burgers to Thai", and the "unbelievable", "ultrarich" namesake desserts, all served by a "cheerful", "efficient" staff; sure, "the line goes all the way to I-95" and it's so loud you'll want to "bring your megaphone", but the "consistent", reasonably priced fare and "kid-friendly" credo make them Ft. Lauderdale's Most Popular.

Chima Brazilian Steakhouse   25 | 25 | 24 | $52
2400 E. Las Olas Blvd. (SE 25th Ave.), 954-712-0580; www.chima.cc
Round up your "hungry" pals for this "festive", all-you-can-eat Ft. Lauderdale rodizio, a "carnivore's dream" where waiters dressed in full gaucho regalia roam the "beautiful", Brazilian-themed dining room and bring "skewer after skewer" bearing over

a dozen kinds of "first-rate" meats; though the big meal ends with a "big tab", it's "worth the money"; P.S. the "outstanding" salad bar completes the feast.

Eduardo de San Angel ⊠
26 | 22 | 25 | $50

2822 E. Commercial Blvd. (bet. Bayview Dr. & 28th Ave.), 954-772-4731; www.eduardodesanangel.com

Venturing beyond "chips and salsa" is this "exemplary" Mexican in Lauderdale, whose kitchen "magician", chef-owner Eduardo Pria, cooks food "so good you'll want to order everything"; the "warm", "unobtrusive" service and "romantic" setting cap "memorable" meals that make "return visits" a no-brainer; N.B. reservations a must during season.

Galanga
26 | 24 | 22 | $35

2389 Wilton Dr. (NE 8th Ave.), Wilton Manors, 954-202-0000

Winning over seasoned surveyors is this "stylish" Wilton Manors Asian offering "knockout" cuisine that fuses Thai and Japanese elements to "superb" effect, "helpful service" and "gorgeous" "Zen-like" atmosphere; that it's "great" for "world-class people-watching" is another reason it's a "treat for the senses."

Hi-Life Café
25 | 21 | 25 | $38

Plaza 3000, 3000 N. Federal Hwy. (south of Oakland Park Blvd.), 954-563-1395; www.hilifecafe.com

Mixing "Southern charm and urban sophistication", this "romantic" New American in a Ft. Lauderdale shopping center shines, thanks to "delicious" savory fare, "awesome desserts" and the "warmth" of owners Carlos Fernandez and Chuck Smith, who make people of all persuasions "feel welcome"; if partiers pout "no liquor license", more toast a "wonderful wine list" and "bargain" pre-theater menu.

HOUSTON'S
21 | 20 | 21 | $32

1451 N. Federal Hwy. (13th St.), 954-563-2226
2821 E. Atlantic Blvd. (Federal Hwy.), Pompano Beach, 954-783-9499
www.houstons.com

Floridians fare well at these South Florida chain links known for "rock-solid" American food, especially "great burgers" and the now legendary "fabulous" spinach dip; the "comfortable", "clubby" setting, "consistent service" and "active bar scene" is a testament to their popularity and reason for many to endure "long waits."

Johnny V's
25 | 22 | 23 | $50

625 E. Las Olas Blvd. (Federal Hwy.), 954-761-7920

"It's the best thing to happen to Las Olas", say surveyors smitten about this "trendy", "top-tier" Lauderdale venture from chef Johnny Vinczencz, whose "sumptuous" Spanish-Med influenced Floribbean cuisine draws "diehard foodies", while grazers go for the "creative" tapas bar menu and oenophiles revel in an "excellent wine list"; the "sleek" setting complements the "beautiful" crowd.

Josef's ⊠
25 | 22 | 25 | $43

Central Park Pl., 9763 W. Broward Blvd. (Nob Hill Rd.), Plantation, 954-473-0000

A "gourmet oasis" "in suburbia", this "worthwhile" enterprise in Plantation "delights" with chef-owner Josef Schibanetz's "delicious", "interesting" slate of Northern Italian fare backed by a compact, yet "interesting wine selection"; the "hospitality" is courtesy of the "attentive" staff.

LA BROCHETTE BISTRO ⌷

| 27 | 18 | 25 | $42 |

Embassy Lakes Plaza, 2635 N. Hiatus Rd. (Sheridan St.), Cooper City, 954-435-9090

This "winner" in a Cooper City strip mall "exceeds expectations" with "beautifully presented", "first-rate" Med fare featuring "great seafood", rack of lamb and "excellent" grilled meats brought to table by a "sharp" staff; though "tucked away" in a strip mall, it manages to be "romantic", and an experience "you won't regret."

MARK'S LAS OLAS

| 26 | 23 | 23 | $56 |

1032 E. Las Olas Blvd. (SE 11th Ave.), 954 463-1000; www.chefmark.com

When "you want to impress or be impressed", this Lauderdale "triumph" from Mark Militello fits the bill with "glorious" Floribbean dishes that "taste as good as they look", a "professional staff" and a "modern" (albeit, "loud") setting; the few infidels who intimate it's "lost its edge" are roundly outvoted by those who still consider it at the "acme of South Florida's dining scene."

RUTH'S CHRIS STEAK HOUSE

| 25 | 21 | 23 | $56 |

2525 N. Federal Hwy. (bet. Oakland Park & Sunrise Blvds.), 954-565-2338; www.ruthschris.com

Carnivores chris-ten this national chain's Lauderdale link a "consistent" performer, considering its "tender", "tasty", butter-bedecked beef ("the best way to eat a steak") accompanied by "attentive service" that "comes with a smile"; many stake their claim that the "clubby" confines are perfect for "impressing a client", even if the "high prices" are "out of line."

Silver Pond

| 26 | 11 | 17 | $24 |

4285 N. State Rd. 7 (south of Commercial Blvd.), Lauderdale Lakes, 954 486-0885

Sinophiles swear by this "bustling" strip-maller in Lauderdale Lakes, whose "unremarkable decor and service" are besides the point to "adventurous" diners who aver the spot serves "real Chinese food" that includes "fresh fish" "plucked out of the tank"; its "favorite" status is confirmed by "lines during season."

SUNFISH GRILL ⌷

| 28 | 15 | 23 | $51 |

2771 E. Atlantic Blvd. (Intracoastal Waterway), Pompano Beach, 954-788-2434; www.sunfishgrill.com

You'll be in "fish heaven" at this "outstanding" Pompano Beach New American ranked No. 1 for Food in Ft. Lauderdale thanks to chef-owner Anthony Sindaco's "out-of-this-world" (if "pricey") seafood creations abetted by wife Erika's "delicious desserts" and a "crisp" staff; despite its "tiny" strip-mall locale, devotees deem it a "diamond in the rough" that's "too good to miss" and advise to "reserve way ahead."

3030 Ocean

| 25 | 23 | 23 | $50 |

Marriott Harbor Beach Resort & Spa, 3030 Holiday Dr. (Seabreeze Blvd.), 954-765-3030; www.3030ocean.com

Patrons "almost forget they're in a hotel" when dining at this "sophisticated" New American seafood specialist in the Marriott, where the kitchen (under the direction of chef Dean Max) nets locals and tourists hooked on the "delectable", "beautifully plated" food served by a "superb" staff; a "lively" setting featuring a "great bar" makes it one of Ft. Lauderdale's "best-kept secrets."

Ft. Worth

TOP FOOD RANKING

	Restaurant	Cuisine
28	Lonesome Dove	Regional American
27	Saint-Emilion	French
	La Piazza	Italian
26	Boi NA Braza	Brazilian
	Kincaid's	Burgers
25	Del Frisco's	Steakhouse
	Classic Cafe	American
	Pegasus	Eclectic/Med.
	Cacharel	French/American
	Bistro Louise	Med./New American

OTHER NOTEWORTHY PLACES

Restaurant	Cuisine
Angelo's	Barbecue
Babe's Chicken	American
Bonnell's	SW/American
Cafe Aspen	New American
Chop House	Steakhouse
Joe T. Garcia's	Mexican
Piccolo Mondo	Italian
Reata	Southwestern
62 Main Restaurant	New American
Texas de Brazil	Brazilian

	F	D	S	C

Angelo's Barbecue ☒⊘
24 | 13 | 16 | $13

2533 White Settlement Rd. (University Dr.), 817-332-0357;
www.angelosbbq.com

The "sound of a knife chopping beef and the girl behind the counter yelling for beer" is music to the ears of patrons of this legendary "rustic" Westsider, a "cheap date heaven" whose management "doesn't worry about decor, service" or atmosphere that "reeks of smoke" because they serve "the best BBQ on earth", including ribs and brisket with "lots of napkins"; P.S. lunch on Saturdays, when the lines are shorter, is "a tradition among the well-heeled crowd."

Babe's Chicken Dinner House
24 | 14 | 22 | $13

104 N. Oak St. (Main St.), Roanoke, 817-491-2900

"Loosen your belt" and prepare for "the best darn fried chicken in the Metroplex" at this Roanoke clucker specialist; sure, there's "not a lot of selection" (poultry pooh-poohers can opt only for chicken-fried steak), but there are "bottomless bowls" of sides and buttermilk biscuits, all "perfect comfort food" served family-style and at a "great food-dollar ratio"; just be prepared for a "long, long wait", and remember to BYO if iced tea and soft drinks are not your thing.

BISTRO LOUISE　　　　　　25 | 23 | 23 | $39 |
Stonegate Commons, 2900 S. Hulen St. (Oak Park Ln.), 817-922-9244;
www.bistrolouise.com
You'll "feel like you've wandered into Provence" upon entering
Louise Lamensdorf's New American–influenced Mediterranean
on the southwest side of town, where she "strolls through the
aisles soliciting opinions" while delighted diners compliment her
on the "attentive service" and "consistently excellent" food –
"no matter what [they] order" from the menu ("we could live on
her gazpacho"); it's also endorsed as a "ladies' lunch" spot, and
the "Sunday brunch is simply the best."

BOI NA BRAZA　　　　　　26 | 23 | 26 | $50 |
4025 William D. Tate Ave. (Hall Johnson Rd.), Grapevine, 817-329-5514;
www.boinabraza.com
Bring your appetite, drop off the Hummer with the valet and prepare
for an all-you-can-eat spectacle of "expertly prepared" tare
(meaning "meat, meat and more meat") at this warmly atmospheric
Grapevine Brazilian churrascaria where "roving", "friendly"
gaucho-clad waiters ferrying giant skewers sometimes make you
forget there's also a "wonderful salad bar"; tip: "come at lunch
when virtually the same offerings are available at a lower price."

Bonnell's ⊠　　　　　　23 | 21 | 24 | $39 |
4259 Bryant Irvin Rd. (Southwest Blvd.), 817-738-5489;
www.bonnellsrestaurant.com
The "fabulous gourmet game selections" will "bring out the wild in
you" at chef-owner Jon Bonnell's "Texas-chic" gathering spot for
"suits and spurs" on the southwest side of town, where the "great
Southwestern"- and Creole-influenced American menu also
includes "interesting twists on familiar standards" (the "superb
quail and grits appetizer" is an "epicurean delight"); "nice
atmosphere", a "knowledgeable staff" and an "extensive wine
list" also help "make the dining experience memorable."

Cacharel ⊠　　　　　　25 | 22 | 25 | $46 |
Brookhollow Tower Two, 2221 E. Lamar Blvd. (Ballpark Way),
Arlington, 817-640-9981; www.cacharel.net
Reviewers report this "quiet, low-key" French-American veteran
atop a nondescript Arlington office tower works both for "a bad
week, because it's the place to go for an attitude adjustment", and
"for a good week, to celebrate" "special occasions"; an "absolute
culinary delight" (featuring a separate steak menu and the "best
soufflés around") with "attentive and courteous" staffers, this is
"by far the classiest and most romantic dining spot in town";
P.S. "ask for a window table with great views."

Cafe Aspen ⊠　　　　　　24 | 18 | 23 | $33 |
6103 Camp Bowie Blvd. (Bryant Irvin Rd.), 817-738-0838;
www.cafeaspen.com
This "sparsely decorated" but "cozy" Westsider has a split
personality: by day it's a "fast" unfussy lunch outlet, where
"pumpkin-seed–crusted catfish is a favorite" and the dessert
display is "fabulous" ("it's impossible to pass without making a
selection"), while at night it morphs into a "romantic", candlelit
New American where live jazz is featured in the back room; at
either time, voters applaud the "reasonable prices", "delicious"
food and "top-quality service"; N.B. there's now a breezy patio.

Classic Cafe at Roanoke, The ⊠　25　20　25　$39
504 N. Oak St. (Denton St.), Roanoke, 817-430-8185;
www.theclassiccafe.com
"A culinary oasis in a sea of burger joints", this "classy" Roanoke
American is a rare "white-linen gourmet" experience in the
suburbs, complete with "personalized service" and an "intimate",
"relaxing" interior; it's ideal for businessmen and "ladies who
lunch" on "unusual salads and sandwiches" or dine on dishes
both traditional and "creative"; N.B. a slate of special steaks
includes free-range options enhanced with chimichurri, Stilton
cheese and more.

DEL FRISCO'S DOUBLE EAGLE　25　22　24　$56
STEAK HOUSE
812 Main St. (8th St.), 817-877-3999; www.delfriscos.com
"Wonderful", "enormous steaks and prices to match" are the rule
at this "loud", "cavernous", "definitive" Downtown beefhouse,
which has a "classy men's club" look that attracts "power diners"
wearing "boots and creased jeans" (hang your cowboy hat at the
entrance) and conventioneers willing to drop big bucks on the
"comprehensive wine list"; since it's the Most Popular in Ft. Worth,
expect "waits, even with reservations."

Ft. Worth Chop House　24　22　23　$43
301 Main St. (2nd St.), 817-336-4129; www.mcrowd.com
A menu overhaul by chef Chris Ward has spiffed up the selections
at this "comfortable", brick-walled steakhouse near Sundance
Square's epicenter; the "great steaks", veal chops and seafood
here are presented with flavorful *jus,* rich reductions and elegant
garni, and "wonderful treatment" from the staff confirms this is
"no hurry-up-and-eat place."

JOE T. GARCIA'S ⇗　20　20　20　$20
2201 N. Commerce St. (22nd St.), 817-626-4356; www.joets.com
Amigos shout "*olé*" for this "not-to-be-missed", cash-only
Northside Mexican "institution" where they take "out-of-town
guests" for enchiladas, fajitas and margaritas that "knock their
socks off"; "on a warm summer night" its lush 600-seat "tropical
garden" with pool makes for fine "people-watching" too, though
critics insist the place is "overrated" and strictly "for drinks."

KINCAID'S HAMBURGERS ⊠⇗　26　15　17　$10
4901 Camp Bowie Blvd. (Eldridge St.), 817-732-2881
100 N. Kimball Ave. (Southlake Dr.), Southlake, 817-416-2573
Those people pining for patties "rearrange their schedules" to
accommodate the "limited hours" (till 6 PM) of this West End
mecca because they adore its "fantastic", "big", "juicy" burgers
served in paper bags; a "legend" in the state since 1946, its
"communal" tables are often so crowded many have to "stand
up to eat" at "countertops", a small price to pay for "the best
hamburger anywhere"; N.B. the new Southlake branch is unrated.

LA PIAZZA　27　24　22　$44
University Park Vlg., 1600 S. University Dr. (I-30), 817-334-0000
Owner Vito Ciraci has "mellowed" some but still "serves up one
heck of a true Italian meal" (especially the "definitive veal") – plus
he occasionally sings opera – at this University mainstay that's a
"class act from beginning to end"; since the soft-hued rooms are

the "place to rub shoulders with Ft. Worth's upper crust" and spot celebs like Van Cliburn, remember to "dress properly" ("it's the perfect spot to air out your mink on a cold day") or you may get snubbed by a "snooty" waiter.

LONESOME DOVE   28 | 23 | 25 | $43
WESTERN BISTRO ⊠
2406 N. Main St. (24th St.), 817-740-8810; www.lonesomedovebistro.com
Don't be afraid to "wear your cowboy boots" as you "step from the Old West stockyards into the tasteful New West atmosphere" of this "comfortable" Northside Regional American (rated No. 1 for Food among Ft. Worth restaurants); working out of a "tiny open kitchen", chef Tim Love and his "warm" staffers create "innovative" Western dishes "emphasizing beef and game" that are an "adventure in upscale dining"; P.S. if you have to wait for a table, lean against the "rustic bar" and order a glass from the small, "carefully chosen" wine list.

Pegasus, The   25 | 21 | 24 | $41
2443 Forest Park Blvd. (Park Hill Dr.), 817-922-0808
"One could live on the meze menu alone" at this "sophisticated", "family-run" Forest Park Mediterranean, but doing so would preclude your trying other items on the "extensive" Eclectic menu like "crab cakes, any number of phyllo-wrapped goodies" and a signature baklava ice cream sandwich; while its "off-street" location may be a tad hard to find, the place itself is "great for de-stressing" because of its clean lines and oversized windows looking out onto treetops.

Piccolo Mondo   24 | 18 | 23 | $32
829 Lamar Blvd. E. (Collins St.), Arlington, 817-265-9174;
www.piccolomondo.com
Loyalists of this Arlington Italian ("one of the best-kept secrets" around, despite being in the neighborhood for more than 20 years) advise that you don't let the "strip-center location keep you away"; environs notwithstanding, this "steady-in-all-things" "gem" is a "friendly, romantic oasis" where the "food delights the mouth", particularly such specialties as eggplant parmigiana and scaloppine al lemon.

REATA RESTAURANT   24 | 26 | 24 | $40
Sundance Sq., 310 Houston St. (3rd St.), 817-336-1009; www.reata.net
It may be "billed as cowboy cuisine, but cowboys never ate so well" as they do at this Southwestern "reincarnation of an old favorite", which may have "lost its view" in the move to Downtown digs "but not its style" ("lots of Western memorabilia, but done with decorum"); since "they put enough on the plate for two ranch hands", go with a "big appetite", or just kick back with a longneck and appetizers in the "rooftop dining area."

SAINT-EMILION ⊠   27 | 24 | 27 | $46
3617 W. Seventh St. (Montgomery St.), 817-737-2781
The "crème de la crème" of French dining in town is Bernard Tronche's Cultural District "cottage" "hideaway" where you'll "feel like you've been transported" to an "intimate" "country farmhouse" in Provence as "timely" servers deliver "divine" food and "superb wines" from a list that's strong on Bordeaux; in sum, it's a "leisurely" "escape for a few hours" and an "ideal spot for a romantic tryst."

62 Main Restaurant ⊠   – | – | – | E
62 Main St. (bet. Hwy. 26 & Pleasant Run Rd.), Colleyville, 817-605-0858;
www.62mainrestaurant.com
His high-profile reign above the Dallas skyline at Nana prepped
chef David McMillan for a roost of his own in the newly minted
Colleyville Towne Center, where his vibrant New American
cuisine finesses flavors from a cured Texas oak-fired oven; the
four-course tasting menu (Tuesdays–Thursdays) and seating at
the chef's bar endear the culinary curious to the gently lit faux
Tuscan interior, staffed by seemingly stress-free servers; N.B. he's
planning to expand soon with a seafooder in the building's
lower-level space.

TEXAS DE BRAZIL   23 | 22 | 23 | $46
101 N. Houston St. (Weatherford St.), 817-882-9500;
www.texasdebrazil.com
While "not as well known as the competition", this "dark", "cool"-
looking Brazilian churrascaria chainster Downtown is a "place to
take out-of-town guests" ("you'll never have to feed them again"
during their stay) for "lots of" "well-seasoned" meat of "fine
quality" (especially "for the money") served on "big skewers" by
a "very accommodating staff"; as befits examples of this genre,
"excellent salad bars" are also available.

TOP FOOD RANKING

	Restaurant	Cuisine
28	Alan Wong's	Hawaii Regional
27	La Mer	New French
26	Hoku's	Pacific Rim
	Roy's	Hawaii Regional
	Chef Mavro	Hawaii Reg./New French
	Roy's Ko Olina	Hawaii Regional
	Orchids	American
	3660 on the Rise	Pacific Rim
	Hy's Steak House	Steakhouse
25	Ruth's Chris	Steakhouse

OTHER NOTEWORTHY PLACES

Restaurant	Cuisine
Bali by the Sea	Pacific Rim
Duke's Canoe Club	Seafood
Hiroshi Eurasian	European Fusion
Indigo	Asian/Eclectic
L'Uraku	Pacific Rim
Michel's	French
Nick's Fishmarket	Seafood
Olive Tree Café	Greek/Mediterranean
Pineapple Room	Hawaii Regional
Sansei	Japanese/Pacific Rim

F	D	S	C

ALAN WONG'S 28 | 20 | 26 | $58

McCully Ct., 1857 S. King St. (bet. Hauoli & Pumehana Sts.), 808-949-2526; www.alanwongs.com

Rated the islands' Most Popular and No.1 for Food, this Hawaii Regional "away from the tourist fray" "never ceases to amaze" fans of chef Alan Wong's "creative brilliance"; with dishes like the "heavenly ginger-crusted onaga", "amazing" tasting menus and "stealthlike", "unobtrusive service", it's the "Pacific meets perfection", despite the second-floor "nondescript" space and "limited street parking"; P.S. make reservations "well in advance."

Bali By The Sea ⊠ 24 | 26 | 24 | $55

Hilton Hawaiian Vlg., 2005 Kalia Rd. (Ala Moana Blvd.), 808-941-2254; www.hiltonhawaiianvillage.com

The "expertly prepared seafood" that's "so fresh" "you swear it was just caught" and the "arty" chocolate replica of Diamond Head (it "smokes" thanks to dry ice) delight diners at this Hilton Hawaiian Village Pacific Rim restaurant with an "idyllic" location that's "really by the sea"; you may have to book a few days in advance for the most "dramatic views", but with such a "warm and welcoming" atmosphere, you'll "dream about coming back."

CHEF MAVRO
| 26 | 23 | 26 | $72 |

1969 S. King St. (McCully St.), 808-944-4714; www.chefmavro.com
"From the moment you enter until the end of your meal", dinner here is an "experience for all the senses", say fans of the "inspired" New French–meets–Hawaii Regional cuisine of chef George Mavrothalassitis, who "often greets guests himself"; service is very "knowledgeable", the "wine pairings are outstanding" and the interior is "beautiful", so even if "the neighborhood leaves a bit to be desired" and "portions are tiny", most take one bite of the "homemade malasada" dessert and declare it all "fabulomavrous!"

DUKE'S CANOE CLUB
| 17 | 22 | 17 | $31 |

Outrigger Waikiki on the Beach, 2335 Kalakaua Ave. (bet. Kaiulani Ave. & Dukes Ln.), 808-922-2268; www.hulapie.com
"Wild, wacky" and "tons of fun", this "always packed" open-air, oceanfront seafooder in the Outrigger Waikiki is a "tourist mecca" with a "great" breakfast buffet, "classic mahi sandwiches", "kitschy Hawaiian cocktails" and a "famous hula pie", all delivered with "a smile"; there's lots of "memorabilia" honoring the "great surfing legend" Duke Kahanamoku, and after sunset, when the "hotties" show up for live music, it becomes "*the* happening place."

Hiroshi Eurasian Tapas
| 24 | 20 | 23 | $46 |

Restaurant Row, 500 Ala Moana Blvd. (Punchbowl St.), 808-533-4476
The tapas concept comes to Hawaii with this "innovative" Eurasian on Restaurant Row, where the "classic techniques" of chef Hiroshi Fukui (formerly of L'Uraku) are coupled with the talents of master sommelier Chuck Furuya, who offers "interesting wine flights"; "every plate is a piece of art" (too bad the same can't be said of the "drab" decor) and the staff serves it amiably, but hungry wallet-watchers wail all those "too tiny" portions add up to a big bill.

HOKU'S
| 26 | 26 | 26 | $60 |

Kahala Mandarin Oriental Hotel, 5000 Kahala Ave. (Kealaolu Ave.), 808-739-8780; www.mandarinoriental.com
For "sublime dining" with a "beautiful view of the ocean", this Pacific Rimmer in the Kahala Mandarin Oriental is a "stunning" choice; feast on "creative", "phenomenal" fare among the "movers and shakers", revel in the "gracious" service and soak up the "romantic" ambiance "at sunset" with the one you love; sure it may "break the bank", but it leaves you "happy to pay"; N.B. no shorts, of course.

Hy's Steak House
| 26 | 23 | 25 | $56 |

Waikiki Park Heights Hotel, 2440 Kuhio Ave. (Uluniu Ave.), 808-922-5555; www.hyshawaii.com
"Excellent" slabs of beef grilled "exactly how you ordered" right "before your eyes" on an open kiawe-wood fire make this "superb" steakhouse a "throwback to the '60s or '70s", with a dimly lit, "muted", "old-world" setting complete with "curved booths for cuddling" and "impeccable" service; meat mavens maintain it's so "consistent", they'd "eat there nightly" if they could; N.B. live guitar music Wednesday–Saturday.

Indigo
| 23 | 23 | 21 | $38 |

1121 Nuuanu Ave. (Hotel St.), 808-521-2900; www.indigo-hawaii.com
"Wow your taste buds" with the "irresistible" Asian-Eclectic eats of chef Glenn Chu, who "blends unique flavors for a multicultural

feast" at his "exotic" "Sex-and-the-City-meets-South-Pacific" Chinatown "hipster"; it's a "favorite for the Downtown lunch crowd" and "trendy twenty- and thirtysomethings" seeking a "killer happy hour" full of "eclectic pupus" and "fantastic martinis" at the "grass shack bar"; sure, it can get "noisy", but it's also one of the most "provocative" settings you've seen in a while; P.S. "valet parking is available and recommended."

LA MER

27 | 28 | 27 | $78

Halekulani Hotel, 2199 Kalia Rd. (Lewers St.), 808-923-2311; www.halekulani.com

The "breathtaking" location overlooking "seductive" ocean waves and the royal service are nothing short of "unforgettable" at this "landmark" in the Halekulani Hotel; not to be outdone, "each bite" of chef Yves Garnier's "delectable" New French "with an island touch" "is a taste of heaven", so even if you need to wear a jacket and the "cost rivals that of NY's" top spots, it's the "ultimate special date" choice.

L'Uraku

24 | 23 | 23 | $42

Uraku Tower, 1341 Kapiolani Blvd. (Piikoi St.), 808-955-0552; www.luraku.com

"Even with chef Hiroshi's departure", the quality of his "somewhat eclectic menu", along with "his unique presentations" of Pacific Rim "fusion food that works" has remained "excellent" at this "whimsical" Ala Moana eatery where "upside-down", colorful, "hand-painted" umbrellas "hang from the ceiling" and "attentive service" continues to draw fans back; for a "real bargain", try the "tasty" three-course weekend lunch for $17.

Michel's

25 | 26 | 25 | $64

Colony Surf Hotel, 2895 Kalakaua Ave. (Poni Moi Rd.), 808-923-6552; www.michelshawaii.com

It's "the place to go if you're in love", sigh smitten sorts who relish the "fantastic sunsets" and the "music of the surf caressing the shore" at this Classic French with "an island touch" at the foot of Diamond Head; it's "a bit dressy by Waikiki standards" with an "impeccable" "tuxedoed staff" (jackets for men are "requested but not required"), and some say since it "costs a bundle", it's "only worth it if you have the view", but others happily return to feast on "sumptuous" lobster bisque and "steak Diane done tableside."

Nick's Fishmarket

23 | 19 | 22 | $52

Waikiki Gateway Hotel, 2070 Kalakaua Ave. (Olohanna St.), 808-955-6333; www.nicksfishmarket.com

A "Honolulu institution", this seafooder still dazzles fans with "amazingly delicious", "innovative" fresh fish presentations; the curved booths are "romantic" and the service "efficient" ; but foes complain the decor "could use a little injection of creativity" (looks like "the '80s"), but "all in all, it's a grand dining experience."

Olive Tree Café ▱

23 | 10 | 15 | $17

4614 Kilauea Ave. (Pahoa Ave.), 808-737-0303

For "fabulous", "authentic" Greek-Med fare, such as "phenomenal fish souvlaki", head to this "popular neighborhood hangout" in Kahala, where "the counter service" and BYO policy keep the "prices low"; "parking and seating can be hard" and there's no decor, but it's "definitely worth" waiting amid the "madhouse crowds" to sample this "hidden treasure."

Orchids
26 | 27 | 26 | $57

Halekulani Hotel, 2199 Kalia Rd. (Lewers St.), 808-923-2311;
www.halekulani.com

With "amazing breakfasts", "fantastic Sunday brunch" and a
"view over the water at sunset that couldn't be any better", this
open-air, beachside American in the Halekulani (just downstairs
from La Mer) is a "relaxing" choice; "sip the most fabulous mai tai",
feast on "superb" fare served by an "impeccable" staff, listen to
the "lapping waves" and be "transported."

Pineapple Room
24 | 18 | 21 | $35

Macy's, Ala Moana Shopping Ctr., 1450 Ala Moana Blvd. (Atkinson Dr.),
808-945-6573; www.alanwongs.com

This "little-known outpost" of the "mega-talented" chef Alan Wong
is "oddly located" in the Ala Moana Shopping Center Macy's ("a
gift to the ladies who lunch"); the prices "will leave some padding
in your wallet" compared to his namesake King Street location,
and the "master's touch" is discernible in the "excellent" Hawaii
Regional fare, especially the "to-die-for Kahlua pig BLT", but some
snipe at "inconsistent service" and a "view of the rooftop mall
parking" lot; P.S. "reservations are a must."

ROY'S
26 | 21 | 24 | $50

6600 Kalanianaole Hwy. (Keahole St.), 808-396-7697;
www.roysrestaurant.com

The "original" Hawaii Kai "flagship" (of a two-dozen-location
chain) that "put Hawaii Regional cuisine on the culinary map"
continues to thrill with its "unpretentious, eye-appealing and
always delicious" offerings and seemingly "choreographed"
service; while some suggest dining in the "quieter" downstairs
portion, others say "come early", head upstairs and "watch
the beautiful sunset."

Roy's Ko Olina
26 | 23 | 25 | $47

Ko Olina Resort, 92-1220 Aliinui Dr. (Kamoana Pl.), Kapolei, 808-676-7697;
www.roysrestaurant.com

"There's a reason Roy has become so ubiquitous" in the islands,
the Mainland and abroad – "fabulous" Hawaii Regional fare with
"twists" and "creativity"; some like this Kapolei outpost "better than
the original" for its "beautiful setting overlooking the Ko Olina Golf
Course", its aloha "hospitality" and its "fabulous" fare (especially
the signature macadamia-encrusted mahi mahi); so even if it's far
away, most find it "well worth the drive"; N.B. also open for lunch.

Ruth's Chris Steak House
25 | 21 | 23 | $55

Restaurant Row, 500 Ala Moana Blvd. (bet. Punchbowl & South Sts.),
808-599-3860; www.ruthschris.com

"If you want a good steak" served "exactly how you like it", this
chainster is "the place to go"; with dishes "generous enough for the
local army", a "comfortable" "clubby" atmosphere on Restaurant
Row and a "courteous" staff, it attracts locals as well as expense-
accounters for a "very urban" yet "genteel" dining experience.

Sansei Seafood Restaurant & Sushi Bar
24 | 18 | 21 | $41

Waikiki Beach Marriott Resort, 2552 Kalakaua Ave. (Kapahulu Ave.),
808-931-6286; www.sanseihawaii.com

For "a bit of sushi heaven" in the islands, head to this "innovative"
Japanese–Pacific Rimmer, with everything from crispy Asian

seafood ravioli to "fresh, fresh, fresh" sashimi prepared by chef D.K. Kodoma and his mom, who started the chain on Maui; despite a recent move from Restaurant Row to the Waikiki Beach Marriott, the "cool and mod" joint is still crowded with "locals lining up for early-bird specials" and visitors digging into those "generous portions"; N.B. call for half-price happy-hour and late-night bargains.

3660 on the Rise

26 20 24 $50

3660 Waialae Ave. (Wilhelmina Rise), 808-737-1177; www.3660.com
The "innovative" Pacific Rim cuisine of chef Russell Sui, a "master of food and wine", "amazes" diners at this Kaimuki "favorite" where the menu includes an "ahi katsu appetizer that will melt in your mouth", a "to-die-for bread pudding" and a "delicious" lychee martini brought to table by an "engaging", "informal" staff; there's "no view" and the interior "looks like a coffee shop" to some, but others answer "who cares?" – this one "rises" higher than most.

Houston

TOP FOOD RANKING

Restaurant	Cuisine
28 Mark's	New American
Chez Nous	French
27 Pappas Bros.	Steakhouse
26 Cafe Annie	Southwestern
Indika	Indian
Quattro	Italian/New American
Da Marco	Italian
Brennan's	Creole/French
Churrascos	S. American/Steakhouse
25 Ashiana	Indian
Damian's Cucina Italiana	Italian
Ruth's Chris	Steakhouse
Aries	New American
Tony's	Continental
Américas	South American
Simposio	Northern Italian
Capital Grille	Steakhouse
Kubo's	Japanese
24 Artista	New American
23 Goode Co. Texas BBQ	Barbecue

OTHER NOTEWORTHY PLACES

Azuma	Japanese
benjy's	New American
Charivari	European
Daily Review Café	New American
Fleming's Prime	Steakhouse
Fogo de Chão	Brazilian/Steakhouse
Goode Co. Texas Seafood	Seafood
Hugo's	Mexico
Julia's Bistro	Pan-Latin
La Griglia	Italian
La Mora Cucina Toscana	Northern Italian
Mama Ninfa's	Tex-Mex
Mockingbird Bistro	New American
Pesce	Seafood
Rainbow Lodge	Gulf Coast
Ruggles	New American
Shade	Eclectic/New Amer.
t'afia	Mediterranean
Tony Mandola's	Cajun/Italian
Zula	New American

AMÉRICAS ☒　　　　　　　25 | 26 | 22 | $40 |
The Pavilion, 1800 Post Oak Blvd. (bet. San Felipe St. & Westheimer Rd.), 713-961-1492; www.cordua.com

The South American menu at Michael Cordua's Galleria-area "crown jewel" has much in common with its "less pricey cousin, Churrascos" (including the "mouthwatering" steaks), but this is the "place to take out-of-town guests for the wow factor" of its "amazing decor" (like a "tree house in the middle" of a "rainforest on acid"); other attributes include "superior service" and "solid seafood" options (the "corn-crusted snapper is a must").

Aries ☒　　　　　　　　　25 | 21 | 23 | $54 |
4315 Montrose Blvd. (Richmond Ave.), 713-526-4404; www.ariesrestaurant.com

For four years now, Scott Tycer's Montrose hot spot has won over Houston foodies with an "adventurous" New American menu featuring "exotic combinations of ingredients and cooking styles" and a "unique wine list"; his "clever and creative kitchen" produces "food that entrances", including "seafood so good" fans feel the place "should have been called Pisces", and though the "well-mannered" staff is "often busy", service "doesn't suffer for it."

Artista　　　　　　　　　24 | 26 | 21 | $42 |
Hobby Ctr. for the Performing Arts, 800 Bagby St. (Walker St.), 713-278-4782; www.cordua.com

Set in Hobby Center, this venue has been "well received" thanks to its "dramatic decor" and "intriguing" New American menu "that lets you pick and choose among meats, accompaniments and sauces" (don't miss the "crunchy, smoky crawfish taquito appetizer"); looky-loos like to "sit on the balcony for great people-watching" and a "marvelous view of Downtown", while theatergoers appreciate the "quick", "outstanding" service "that doesn't leave you nervous you're going to miss the first act."

Ashiana　　　　　　　　　25 | 20 | 22 | $29 |
12610 Briar Forest Dr. (Dairy Ashford Rd.), 281-679-5555; www.ashiana.cc

The "very good (but not very expensive) lunch buffet" at this "upscale" Memorial Indian "gives the novice the opportunity to try something new in a posh environment", but subcontinental sophisticates savor its "more formal dinners" as "epic, sumptuous dining events"; with a list boasting 300 labels, it's no wonder the venue also hosts a monthly wine meal.

Azuma　　　　　　　　　　23 | 23 | 18 | $33 |
5600 Kirby Dr. (Nottingham St.), 713-432-9649
Azuma Rice
909 Texas St. (Travis St.), 713-223-0909
Azuma Sushi
1709 Dryden Rd. (Main St.), 713-790-9997
www.azumajapanese.com

This Japanese trio is "the place to go" for "hyper-fresh, delicious raw fish", "inventive rolls" and "authentic" robata dishes cooked over an open-fire grill; don't miss "their specialty, the hot-rock beef" (Kobe steak that "you cook" yourself "on what looks like a heated pet rock"); while the atmosphere within the "Asian-chic interior" is "fun", some surveyors complain that "the service lags behind the food."

benjy's   24 | 20 | 21 | $33
2424 Dunstan St. (Kelvin Dr.), 713-522-7602; www.benjys.com
Owner Benjy Levit keeps his Rice Village New American the "hip and happening spot for Houston's trendy set" with "wonderful" cuisine ("out-of-this-world salads", "stunning desserts") featuring Asian influences and "adventurous combinations of flavors"; "the only thing hotter" than the "modern", "minimalist decor" is the "attentive", "well-trained staff"; and the "slick upstairs bar" and lounge "is a destination in itself"; P.S. "don't miss" the "fabulous weekend brunch", which fans feel "is one of the best in Houston."

BRENNAN'S OF HOUSTON   26 | 25 | 26 | $49
3300 Smith St. (Stuart St.), 713-522-9711; www.brennanshouston.com
With "French Quarter–inspired interiors", a "stunning" courtyard for "romantic alfresco dining" and a gracious staff that "exemplifies Southern hospitality", this self-styled Texas-Creole "institution" in Midtown "brings the best of New Orleans to Houston"; go for the "wonderful jazz brunch" on Sunday, and "try the turtle soup" as well as the "classic bananas Foster", but "don't leave without your complimentary homemade praline."

CAFE ANNIE ⌷   26 | 25 | 26 | $56
1728 Post Oak Blvd. (San Felipe St.), 713-840-1111; www.cafe-annie.com
The place that "put Southwestern food on the map", this "first-tier restaurant" known for its "unfussy elegance", "unmatched wine selection" and "consistently outstanding" and "innovative" cuisine is a "perennial" favorite in the Galleria area; popular with "the beautiful people and businessmen alike", it's "the best thing to come out of Houston since oil", say most surveyors; N.B. there's a separate, more casual menu in the Bar Annie space.

Capital Grille, The   25 | 24 | 24 | $52
5365 Westheimer Rd. (Yorktown St.), 713-623-4600;
www.thecapitalgrille.com
"True carnivores" covet this "traditional steakhouse" – part of "a national chain, [but] without the chain feel" – for its "ab-fab" "dry-aged steaks" and servers who "go out of their way to make you feel special"; with a "lively bar scene" and a "men's club"–meets–"library atmosphere", it's "great for entertaining clients as well as having fun with friends", though some sensitive snouts are "turned off" by the cigar bar and the "stench of smoke" that "permeates" the dining room at times.

Charivari ⌷   24 | 19 | 23 | $39
2521 Bagby St. (McGowen St.), 713-521-7231; www.charivarirest.com
"Hands-on owner" and "European-trained chef" Johann Schuster, along with Irmgard-Maria, "his wife, are charming hosts" and offer up "amazing Transylvanian" and "Bavarian-style food" at this "hidden gem in Midtown", where it feels "like dining in a four-star European hotel"; "the service is attentive and paced", and "the atmosphere is such that you can actually hear the conversation"; P.S. "they go nuts when white asparagus is in season."

CHEZ NOUS ⌷   28 | 22 | 26 | $50
217 S. Ave. G (Staitti St.), Humble, 281-446-6717;
www.cheznousfrenchrestaurant.com
"Far off the beaten path" from Houston proper, this "charming" "treasure" set "in an old church" "hidden in Downtown Humble" is

a French "gastronomic oasis in the middle of a dining desert"; "for special occasions", foodies flock northward for its "fine cuisine" (including "excellent duck" and "sinful desserts"), not to mention "friendly, low-key service and quaint ambiance."

CHURRASCOS   26 | 21 | 23 | $36
Shepherd Sq., 2055 Westheimer Rd. (S. Shepherd Dr.), 713-527-8300
9705 Westheimer Rd. (Gessner Rd.), 713-952-1988
www.cordua.com
Michael Cordua's Shepherd Square and Galleria-area duo of "comfortable, casual" South American steakhouses is known for "sublime churrasco steaks" served with "addictive chimichurri sauce"; but this is "not just another big-hunk-of-meat restaurant" – the "hefty portions" of "fabulous beef" come with an "unusual grilled veggie assortment" (plus "crispy plantain" chips to start), and be sure to save room for the "amazing *tres leches*" for dessert; N.B. the Decor rating may not reflect a post-*Survey* remodeling of the 9705 Westheimer Road location.

Daily Review Café   23 | 16 | 20 | $29
3412 W. Lamar St. (Dunlavy St.), 713-520-9217; www.dailyreviewcafe.com
"Hidden away on a River Oaks side street", this "stylish and clever" New American "gem" may be "hard to find", but "in-the-know" folks feel it's "worth the search" for its "creative", "ever-changing menu" of "chicken-pot-pie comfort food" "taken up a notch"; an "interesting wine list", a "pretty patio" and a "friendly staff" also help make it "a staple" for "brunch, lunch or a quiet dinner for two."

Da Marco ✉   26 | 20 | 23 | $49
1520 Westheimer Rd. (Mulberry St.), 713-807-8857;
www.damarcohouston.com
"Excellent chef" and owner Marco Wiles "dares to differ" from the Italian restaurant formula at this "cozy" Montrose spot with "superb" cuisine "steeped in tradition (but always inventive)", plus a "good wine selection" and a "friendly staff" that "never rushes you"; the "romantic" and "charming interior space" "seems bathed in a golden glow", but the "pretty patio" might be better "if you have a hearing problem."

Damian's Cucina Italiana ✉   25 | 21 | 25 | $41
3011 Smith St. (Rosalie St.), 713-522-0439; www.damians.com
Overflowing with "old-world charm", this "classic" "white-tablecloth" Midtown Italian is "the kind of place you'd expect Frank and Dean to roll into", and savoring "top-notch food" and "impeccable service" with the local Rat Pack may make you feel like a "Houston insider" ("something about the cozy interior makes people divulge their secrets"); P.S. its "close-to-Downtown" site makes it "great for a business luncheon or a pre-theater meal."

Fleming's Prime Steakhouse & Wine Bar   24 | 23 | 23 | $52
The Woodlands Mall, 1201 Lake Woodland Dr. (I-45), The Woodlands,
281-362-0103
River Oaks Ctr., 2405 W. Alabama St. (Kirby Dr.), 713-520-5959
www.flemingssteakhouse.com
"A regular haunt of the Houston power-broker set", this "'in' place" (the River Oaks outlet of a national chain) with a "knowledgeable" staff is "giving [its competitors] a run for their money" thanks to "wonderful steaks" that are "crispy outside", "rare inside" and

accompanied by "zillions of wines by the glass"; there's also a "hopping bar scene on the weekends" – and the "deafening noise" that goes with it; N.B. Woodlands Mall opened post-*Survey*.

Fogo de Chão
24 | 20 | 24 | $48

8250 Westheimer Rd. (Dunvale Rd.), 713-978-6500; www.fogodechao.com

With a "dizzying flock" of "gaucho"-style waiters using "swords to slice a huge variety" of "tender", "tasty", "high-quality meats" "off of steaming skewers" and "right onto your plate" "till you beg them to stop", this "authentic Brazilian steakhouse" in the Galleria area is definitely a "carnivore's paradise"; the "impressive salad bar" "is also exceptional", but consider it "your enemy" if you want to "eat your money's worth" of "quite-good animal flesh."

Goode Co. Texas BBQ
25 | 16 | 18 | $15

8911 Katy Frwy. (Campbell Rd.), 713-464-1901
5109 Kirby Dr. (bet. Bissonnet St. & Westpark Dr.), 713-522-2530
www.goodecompany.com

"Visitors and locals alike" love to "get their fingers dirty" at Jim Goode's pair of "funky Texana" BBQ smokehouses in Hadwick and West U., where the food is served "cafeteria-style" but the "tender and meaty ribs", "first-class brisket", "homemade jalapeño cheese bread" and "killer pecan pie" are "worth every stand-in-line minute"; there's "limited indoor seating", but with an "icy cold beer", even "dining on the long picnic tables outside" (at the Kirby Drive branch) seems like "heaven on earth."

Goode Co. Texas Seafood
23 | 17 | 20 | $25

10211 Katy Frwy./I-10 W. (Gessner Dr.), 713-464-7933
2621 Westpark Dr. (Kirby Dr.), 713-523-7154; www.goodecompany.com

Jim Goode's seafood "masterpieces" offer "a truly unique taste of the Gulf Coast" "served with a sparkle" ("don't miss" the "worth-a-special-journey campechana seafood cocktail" or the "perfect mesquite-grilled" fish); partially housed in an old "railroad boxcar", the Upper Kirby District branch has a "fun, funky" "down-home" atmosphere, while the Memorial address is a little more "uptown."

Hugo's
22 | 22 | 19 | $35

1600 Westheimer Rd. (Mandell St.), 713-524-7744;
www.hugosrestaurant.net

Chef-owner Hugo Ortega offers "an excellent, high-end, truly authentic experience" at his "lively" Montrose establishment that's "not your typical chips-and-salsa place" – instead, you'll find "out-of-this-world squash blossom appetizers", "meats with the flavor of Mexico", "great Spanish wines and powerful Grand Marnier margaritas" on the menu; still, those "underwhelmed" by certain "indifferent" staffers say the "somewhat lacking service" "could use some improvement."

INDIKA ☒
26 | 21 | 21 | $36

12665 Memorial Dr. (Gessner St.), 713-984-1725;
www.indikausa.com

"East meets West" at this "upscale", "gourmet" eatery set in a "cozy house in Memorial"; "inspired chef" and owner Anita Jaisinghani "takes Indian to a new level" by using "Western influences" to create an "adventurous" menu of "inventive and delicious" dishes that are "pleasing to the eye and the palate"; needless to say, this is "not the same old saag panir"; N.B. a move to the Montrose neighborhood is scheduled for late 2005.

Julia's Bistro ☒
– | – | – | M

3722 Main St. (W. Alabama St.), 713-807-0090; www.juliasbistro.com
Located just off the brand-new light rail in Midtown, this up-and-comer is fast becoming the see-and-be-seen site in a booming neighborhood; snow-white tablecloths stand out against the brightly colored walls in a contemporary chic space where chef Jose Garcia (ex Artista) makes his mark with Latino dishes that bridge the Old and New Worlds, from Spain to South America: pumpkin seed–crusted snapper, grilled pork tenderloin and a sinful *torta de coco* (layered white cake laced with sweet coconut milk).

Kubo's
25 | 19 | 18 | $34

2414 University Blvd. (Morningside Dr.), 713-528-7878;
www.kubos-sushi.com
"Regular sushi eaters" claim this "comfortable and serene" Rice Village favorite serves the "freshest in the city", and with fish flown in from California and Japan daily, then fashioned into "creative, large portions", they just might be right; some say the experience may be a little "highly priced", but considering the "vivacious service", "elegant, subdued decor" and "convenient location with lots of parking", most maintain it's "worth every penny."

La Griglia
23 | 22 | 22 | $37

River Oaks Ctr., 2002 W. Gray St. (bet. McDuffie St. & Shephard Dr.),
713-526-4700; www.lagrigliarestaurant.com
This River Oaks Italian is a "fun favorite" for the "chichi crowd" thanks to "excellent food" and "bend-over-backward" service; with a "party atmosphere" and "lively bar crowd", it "can be a little noisy on weekends", but there's always "great people-watching" to "replace conversation" – or try the "quieter and more intimate" outdoor patio; N.B. the ratings may not reflect a post-*Survey* change in ownership.

La Mora Cucina Toscana ☒
24 | 22 | 23 | $38

912 Lovett Blvd. (Montrose Blvd.), 713-522-7412; www.lamora.net
A "hideaway in the heart of the city", this Montrose Northern Italian is "one of Houston's best-kept secrets" for "authentic Tuscan fare" such as "*molto bene* risotto" and "outstanding gnocchi", not to mention a "superb wine list" and "knowledgeable", "attentive" servers; lovers laud the "cozy" "villa-like surroundings" as perfect for a "romantic date" – and "especially charming at night."

Mama Ninfa's
24 | 16 | 20 | $21

463 Bay Area Blvd. (Galveston Rd.), 281-480-4090
8353 Gulf Frwy. (Howard Dr.), 713-943-3183
9333 Katy Frwy. (Echo Ln.), 713-932-8760
3601 Kirby Dr. (Southwest Frwy.), 713-520-0203
2704 Navigation Blvd. (bet. Delano & Nagle Sts.), 713-228-1175
600 Travis St. (Texas St.), 713-228-6200 ☒
6154 Westheimer Rd. (Briarhurst Dr.), 713-781-2740
www.mamaninfas.com
There's "nothing like the original", declare die-hard devotees who delight in the "out-of-this-world fajitas", "fresh tortillas" and "powerful margaritas" at the "fantastic and funky" flagship location (on Navigation, in the Second Ward) of this sprawling family of "Tex-Mex shrines"; a "legend in its own time", it's "almost a tourist attraction" but still popular with "all walks" of locals, including "some of Houston's most powerful political and business figures."

MARK'S AMERICAN CUISINE ◑ 28 | 25 | 26 | $52 |
1658 Westheimer Rd. (bet. Dunlavy & Ralph Sts.), 713-523-3800;
www.marks1658.com
Surveyors "sing hallelujah" for this "heavenly" Montrose venue
in a "charming converted church building" blessed with "vaulted
ceilings" and a "wine 'cellar' in the choir loft", voting it No. 1 for
Food and Popularity among Houston restaurants; "innovative chef"-
owner Mark Cox's "extraordinary New American fare" is supported
by a "superb wine list" and served by a "knowledgeable" and
"genuinely helpful staff", so followers gladly put up with "closely
packed tables" and "nearly impossible reservations."

Mockingbird Bistro 23 | 20 | 22 | $40 |
1985 Welch St. (bet. Hazard & McDuffie Sts.), 713-533-0200;
www.mockingbirdbistro.com
John Sheely's "crowded neighborhood hangout", "tucked away"
in a residential area just south of the River Oaks Shopping Center,
offers "simple but modern" New American "bistro fare" (you "gotta
have the frites!") and a "very good and reasonably priced wine list"
in a "quirky", "Gothic" setting; regulars report the "enthusiastic"
staff "always knows your name and favorite glass" of vino.

PAPPAS BROS. STEAKHOUSE ⌧ 27 | 24 | 25 | $54 |
5839 Westheimer Rd. (Fountain View Dr.), 713-780-7352;
www.pappasbros.com
When on "someone else's expense account", head to this "manly-
man" Galleria-area steakhouse for "melt-in-your-mouth beef",
"wonderful à la carte sides", "a wine list about as big as *War and
Peace*", "desserts grandma wishes she could make" and a "clubby
atmosphere" reminiscent of "an old-style New York dining room"
("be careful if you're sensitive to smoke"); "expect to see ladies in
cocktail dresses and gentlemen in sport coats."

Pesce ⌧ 24 | 24 | 22 | $50 |
3029 Kirby Dr. (W. Alabama St.), 713-522-4858; www.pescehouston.com
"See and be seen" at this "glitzy" Upper Kirby District *mer*-fare
"destination" that benefits from "electric atmosphere", a "nice bar
scene", "first-class service" and a "great selection" of "excellently
cooked and seasoned fish" dishes; "don't miss the seafood martini"
or the "sublime Dover sole (when available)", "but first see your
loan officer" as this "posh" place can be "extremely pricey."

Quattro 26 | 26 | 25 | $48 |
Four Seasons Hotel, 1300 Lamar St. (Austin St.), 713-276-4700;
www.fourseasons.com
The former site of the stuffy old Deville in Downtown's Four Seasons
Hotel was "reincarnated" as this "sleek", "chic" "cosmopolitan"
address that's popular for "great power lunches", "excellent
dinners" and "incredible Sunday brunches"; the Italian–New
American menu features the "freshest" and "finest ingredients"
combined in "familiar" yet "creative" ways ("try the french fries
with truffle oil", "an addiction unto themselves"), presented
by "spectacular service."

Rainbow Lodge 23 | 27 | 23 | $45 |
1 Birdsall St. (Memorial Dr.), 713-861-8666; www.rainbow-lodge.com
"A wilderness oasis" within the "concrete jungle", this "hunting
lodge"–inspired Regional American on the edge of River Oaks

offers "amazing game dishes", including "unusual entrees such as ostrich and wild boar"; the "romantic setting" features "beautiful grounds" for a stroll before dinner and "scenic views of the tree-lined bayou" during your meal, making it a "great place to take a date" or "pop the question" – "as long as she's a carnivore"; N.B. the Food rating may not reflect a post-*Survey* chef change.

Ruggles　　　　　　　　　| 24 | 19 | 18 | $37 |
Saks Fifth Avenue, The Galleria, 5115 Westheimer Rd. (bet. Post Oak Blvd. & Sage Rd.), 713-963-8067 🗷
903 Westheimer Rd. (Montrose Blvd.), 713-524-3839
www.rugglesgrill.com
Of husband-and-wife team Bruce and Susan Molzan's pair of "great New American" grills, the Montrose original, an "institution", remains a "fun", "happening" place where "people-watching" and "huge portions" of "original" Southwestern-influenced cuisine add up to "loud" "crowds on weekends"; its more "sleek" and "chic" Galleria sibling is popular with "well-dressed" "beautiful people" for its "beautifully presented and perfectly prepared" French-accented fare, "prettier dining room" and "shorter wait."

Ruth's Chris Steak House　　| 25 | 19 | 23 | $50 |
6213 Richmond Ave. (bet. Fountain View & Hillcroft Aves.), 713-789-2333;
www.ruthschris.com
"Yes, it's a chain", but this Galleria "gold-standard" steakhouse is "still a gem" thanks to its "clubby", "quiet environment", "polite" and "welcoming" staffers and, most of all, "thick and juicy" cuts of "first-class" beef (committed carnivores claim that the "portly portions" of "butter-soaked steaks" are "fit to tempt vegetarians").

Shade　　　　　　　　　　| – | – | – | E |
250 W. 19th St. (Rutland St.), 713-863-7500;
www.shadeheights.com
Much-loved chef Claire Smith returns to Houston with this venture located in the city's quaint Heights neighborhood; the minimalist space designed by Carl Eaves is the perfect complement for her and co-chef Jeb Stuart's Eclectic–New American cuisine, which incorporates influences from across the globe; favorites such as wasabi-and-cucumber-encrusted grouper and chocolate cherry croissant bread pudding can be enjoyed inside or on the patio.

Simposio 🗷　　　　　　　| 25 | 16 | 22 | $40 |
5591 Richmond Ave. (Chimney Rock Rd.), 713-532-0550;
www.simposiorestaurant.com
"Don't let the strip mall fool you" – the exterior "does not do justice to the kitchen" at this Galleria-area "Northern Italian gem", where "remarkable chef" and owner Alberto Baffoni creates "serious food", including a selection of "lovely pastas" and "fantastic osso buco" "to suck marrow for"; combine that with "proper service" and a "well-thought-out wine list" and you've got a "warm, satisfying dining experience" that transcends its "plain location."

t'afia 🗷　　　　　　　　　| – | – | – | E |
3701 Travis St. (bet. W. Alabama & Winbern Sts.), 713-524-6922;
www.tafia.com
Already one of the booming lower Midtown district's biggest draws, this venue is helmed by chef-owner Monica Pope, who makes every effort to incorporate locally grown, organic ingredients into her coastal Mediterranean fare, turning out such memorable dishes

as pistachio-crusted salmon; be warned, though, that one trip is not enough – the adventurous menu changes almost daily.

Tony Mandola's Gulf Coast Kitchen   23 | 18 | 22 | $32

River Oaks Ctr., 1962 W. Gray St. (McDuffie St.), 713-528-3474;
www.tonymandolas.com

A "neighborhood favorite", this "casual, comfortable", "convivial Cajun-Italian" seafooder in River Oaks "inspires loyalty" with "incredibly fresh and beautifully prepared fish", "lovely oysters", "delicious crab" and "New Orleans–style po' boys" served by "attentive" and "knowledgeable" waiters who treat everyone like "a member of the extended Mandola family"; in short, it's a "real Gulf Coast experience."

Tony's   25 | – | 25 | $64

3755 Richmond Ave. (Timmons Ln.), 713-622-6778;
www.tonyshouston.com

"Hurray for Tony" Vallone – he "knows how to run a restaurant" say fans of this Continental, now ensconced in contemporary, cinnamon-colored digs on Richmond Avenue; after 40 years, this "Houston institution" is still "the place to see celebrities and social climbers", especially on weekends (jacket suggested on Saturday nights), and while some call it a "faded rose", "many older Houstonians" stand by the "classic" menu, the "exquisite details" and the "fawning", "over-the-top" service.

Zula ☒   23 | 25 | 21 | $42

705 Main St. (Capitol St.), 713-227-7052; www.zulahouston.com

This "fashionable" New American is owned by chef Lance Fegan, whose "creative, well-executed menu" of "flashy food" includes "absolutely fantastic crab cakes and river trout" (the latter at lunch only); "consistently excellent service", "spectacular" "Las Vegas"–style decor and a crowd that includes "local professional athletes" combine to give this "upscale place" "the cool factor."

Kansas City

TOP FOOD RANKING

Restaurant	Cuisine
27 Bluestem	New American
26 Stroud's	American
Oklahoma Joe's	Barbecue
Le Fou Frog	French Bistro
American Rest.	New American
Fiorella's Jack Stack	Barbecue
Tatsu's	French
Starker's Reserve	New American
Danny Edwards'	Barbecue
25 Plaza III	Steakhouse

OTHER NOTEWORTHY PLACES

Café Sebastienne	New American
Circe	New American
d' Bronx	Deli/Pizza
40 Sardines	New American
Grand St. Cafe	Eclectic
Lidia's	Northern Italian
McCormick & Schmick's	Seafood
1924 Main	New American
Room 39	American
zin	New American

F	D	S	C

AMERICAN RESTAURANT ☒ | 26 | 25 | 27 | $52 |

Crown Ctr., 200 E. 25th St. (Grand Ave.), 816-545-8000;
www.theamericanrestaurantkc.com
With "superb service" and "magnificent" views, this "showpiece" at Hallmark's Crown Center is a "KC institution" and a "favorite of professionals and gourmet diners alike" – especially now that "imaginative" toque Celina Tio has "invigorated" the New American menu ("lots of game") to go with the "excellent" 1,500-label wine list; "you feel grand gliding down the staircase" into the "cathedral-like" dining room, though more than a few snipe the "'80s decor" needs a "major face-lift"; P.S. the "prix fixe lunch is a steal."

BLUESTEM | 27 | 23 | 23 | $41 |

900 Westport Rd. (Roanoke Rd.), 816-561-1101;
www.kansascitymenus.com
Voted KC's No. 1 for Food, this "sophisticated" New American named after a variety of prairie grass offers grazers an "eclectic, adventurous menu" that "balances the flavors" of "local seasonal items" to "sublime" effect; admirers also appreciate the "simple, clean" "urban comfort" of the "intimate" Westport space; however, with meals being so "expensive", habitués hope it will soon get over its "growing pains."

Café Sebastienne   25   25   23 $31
Kemper Museum of Contemporary Art, 4420 Warwick Blvd. (45th St.),
816-561-7740; www.kemperart.org
At this "striking" yet "serene" "urban escape", an "airy", mural-
bedecked venue at the Kemper Museum, chef Jennifer Maloney
pleases palates with "creative" New American cuisine (the "food
they probably serve in heaven"); patrons praise "relaxed" servers
too, while pointing out to partiers that "nighttime hours are limited"
(Friday–Saturday only, till 9:30 PM).

Circe   –   –   –   M
1715 W. 39th St. (Bell St.), 816-931-0596; www.circekc.com
Schoolmates Nathan Feldmiller and Jonathan Phillips have come
full circle with their return to Kansas City (after stints in other
places, like NYC's Bouley Bakery) and the opening of this upscale
New American on 39th Street's Restaurant Row; they're enchanting
diners with such straightforward but luxurious dishes as duck club
sandwiches and Kobe beef burgers, served in a yellow-toned
space; the wine list is ripe with pickings from small vintners.

Danny Edwards' Famous   26   9   17 $14
Kansas City Barbecue ⊠
1227 Grand Blvd. (E. 13th St.), 816-283-0880
"Don't dress up" for lunch at second-generation pitmeister Danny
Edwards' "funky", "git-down" "dump of a place" Downtown, but
do be prepared to eat some of the "best 'cue in the rib capital of
the world"; factor in a "friendly staff" and "price-is-right" tabs
and it's obvious why BBQ buffs "wish they were open more";
N.B. kitchen closes at 2:30 PM.

d'Bronx   25   14   16 $12
Crown Ctr., 2450 Grand Blvd. (25th St.), 816-842-2211
3904 Bell St. (39th St.), 816-531-0550 ⊠
"A slice of the Big Apple in the heart of Cowtown", this fave in
the 39th Street area draws "customers from all over" for "deli
sandwiches so big and real they could fool a lifelong New Yorker"
and the "best damn pizza in KC"; "nobody seems to mind" the
"rustic", "no-frills" setting, but those who give a Bronx cheer to the
"long lines and noise" may prefer the take-out outpost at Crown
Center; P.S. "the only beer here is root beer."

FIORELLA'S JACK STACK   26   22   22 $22
13441 Holmes Rd. (135th St.), 816-942-9141
101 W. 22nd St. (Wyandotte St.), 816-472-7427
9520 Metcalf Ave. (95th St.), Overland Park, 913-385-7427
www.jackstackbbq.com
"Who says authentic BBQ has to come from a greasy joint with
Formica tables?" ask aficionados of this "high-toned" trio where
the "posh" interiors perplex pit purists ("'cue with white linen
napkins?") even as the "fork-tender brisket" and the city's "best
sides" prove "addictive"; everyone agrees "it's worth the wait" –
and what with the no-reservations policy, "wait you will."

40 Sardines   24   21   22 $40
11942 Roe Ave. (W. 119th St.), Leawood, 913-451-1040;
www.40sardines.com
"Enterprising" "husband-wife chef team" Michael Smith and
Debbie Gold "wow" "epicurean adventurers" at their "refreshing"

New American in suburban Leawood, whipping up "imaginative and flavorful meals" and offering a "budget-friendly list of great $20 wines" with the assistance of "engaging and thoughtful servers"; the "industrial but not hip" room can be "abominably noisy when crowded", but reviewers report that recent changes "have improved acoustics dramatically."

GRAND ST. CAFE　　　24　22　24　$32
4740 Grand St. (47th St.), 816-561-8000; www.eatpbj.com
"Everything from burgers to steak and seafood" is served by a "friendly" and "efficient" staff at this "upscale", "upbeat" Eclectic eatery near the Plaza that remains a "lively" "lunch venue for business or pleasure" and a "classic standby" for dinner; "try to sit outside" on the "best patio in town", suggest sound-sensitive surveyors who blame "hard surfaces" for indoor "noise", while others wonder "is the decor getting tired – or does it just seem that way because we go there so often?"

LE FOU FROG　　　26　19　22　$38
400 E. Fifth St. (Oak St.), 816-474-6060; www.lefoufrog.com
Francophiles are *fou* for this "little bit of Paris" in the River Market area, a "charming", "funky" bistro where chef-owner Mano Rafael serves up "Midwestern portions" of Gallic "*gastronomie*", plus "unusual" entrees like elk; meanwhile, a "skillful" staff helps the con*fou*sed peruse chalkboard menus that change daily and "one of KC's finest wine lists" – so though foes fret about the "gritty" neighborhood, "tough-to-find" location and "elbow-to-elbow seating", most maintain the "wonderful meal" is "well worth it all."

LIDIA'S　　　24　27　23　$33
101 W. 22nd St. (Baltimore Ave.), 816-221-3722; www.lidiasitaly.com
TV chef and NYC culinary matriarch Lidia Bastianich is the force behind this "spectacular" showplace, a "rehabbed" "brick station house" (note the "breathtaking" Dale Chihuly chandeliers) in the "revitalizing" Crossroads arts district; *amici* assert the "delicious" Northern Italian eats (e.g. the prix fixe pasta trio) "sometimes achieve the sublime" and "value-priced" vinos are a boon for the "wine-challenged"; but the "disappointed" declare the place "has lost some of its spark."

MCCORMICK & SCHMICK'S　　　25　25　23　$36
448 W. 47th St. (Pennsylvania Ave.), 816-531-6800;
www.mcormickandschmicks.com
"Seafood lovers" stranded "1,000 miles from an ocean" are "delighted" by the "staggering array" of "exceptional" fin fare at this chainster, voted the area's Most Popular site; a "happening place" for "movers and shakers" at lunch and "lively fun" after work ("top-notch" "happy-hour eats"), this "yuppie" magnet provides "prompt service" and a "pleasant ambiance", with a "beautiful stained-glass rotunda" and "patio overlooking the Country Club Plaza"; even if curmudgeons carp it can be "packed" and "pricey for KC", hooked habitués hail it as "worth every dollar."

1924 Main　　　–　–　–　M
1924 Main St. (19th St.), 816-472-1924; www.1924main.com
Chef-owner Rob Dalzell brings prix fixe to the Crossroads – for a set $30 ($15 at lunch), diners compile their own three-course meal, choosing from several selections at each stage – with this New American, housed in the lovingly renovated Rieger Building

(the original tiled floors remain); the weekly changing menu offers optional wine pairings, while hard-liquor sippers can savor the serious selection of single malt scotch.

OKLAHOMA JOE'S　　　　　26 | 9 | 16 | $12
BARBECUE & CATERING

Shamrock Gas Station, 3002 W. 47th Ave. (Mission Rd.), 913-722-3366 ⊠
11950 South Strang Line Rd. (119th St.), Olathe, 913-782-6858
www.oklahomajoesbbq.com

"Winners of umpteen contests", the "smoked-arts" practitioners at this Roeland Park fave turn out "moist", "tender, lean" KC-style meats and "fabulous" signature Carolina-style pulled pork; its "down 'n' dirty" gas station location means there's "limited seating" for the "unlimited line" of folks waiting to fill up; N.B. there's a new 'cue branch in Olathe.

PLAZA III THE STEAKHOUSE　　25 | 21 | 25 | $43

4749 Pennsylvania Ave. (Ward Pkwy.), 816-753-0000;
www.plazaiiisteakhouse.com

"Great beef and this establishment both prove some things do get better with aging", laud loyalists of this "old-line" "mainstay" on the Country Club Plaza; it's an "earthy", "dark-wood" den where "any CEO would feel comfortable" thanks to "perfect" porterhouses, a "fabulous" 350-label cellar and the ministrations of an "elegant, charming staff"; still, critics counter this "tired" place may now be "past its prime"; P.S. the bar downstairs offers "access to the full menu" plus "outstanding" live jazz four nights a week.

Room 39 ⊠　　　　　　　– | – | – | I

1719 W. 39th St. (Bell St.), 816-753-3939

Every day is a daily special at this small American, a kind of classy coffee shop where chef-owners Ted Habiger and Andrew Sloan put a stylized spin on standards (e.g. bacon, egg and cheese panini, crispy root-vegetable fries) for breakfast and lunch; if the custom-blended coffee and chai (sweetened with jaggery, boiled Indian sugar cane) don't wake you up, the colorful walls, floors and gilded mirrors surely will.

Starker's Reserve ⊠　　　　26 | 24 | 25 | $45

201 W. 47th St. (Wyandotte St.), 816-753-3565; www.starkersreserve.com

"Often overlooked" and "underpatronized", this second-story, "top-notch" New American on the Country Club Plaza is an "exquisite" "treasure" say surveyors who savor the "feeling of exclusivity" inside the "romantic", "casual French" room while "looking out on the activity" below; owner "Cliff Bath's attention to detail" comes through in "outstanding food" and an "incomparable" cellar of more than 1,500 wines, and a "wonderful staff" that's "unobtrusive but available" helps make "special occasions" celebrated here "elegant, intimate" and "memorable".

STROUD'S　　　　　　　26 | 14 | 22 | $19

1015 E. 85th St. (Troost Ave.), 816-333-2132
5410 NE Oak Ridge Dr. (Vivion Rd.), 816-454-9600
www.stroudsrestaurants.com

"Legendary fried chicken that deserves the rep", served with "otherworldly cream gravy", "extraordinary cinnamon rolls" and other traditional American favorites "worth traveling long distances for" are the draw at these "living memorials" to "grandma's farm cookin'"; the South KC original, dating from 1933, is a "warped" yet

"homey" "roadhouse", while the larger 19th-century homestead
north of the river offers "country atmosphere", antique furniture
and a live piano player; in both places, staffers are "very friendly",
which helps keep patrons' spirits up during the "horrific waits";
N.B. no reservations.

Tatsu's   26 | 19 | 24 | $37 |

4603 W. 90th St. (Roe Ave.), Prairie Village, 913-383-9801; www.tatsus.com
"Consistency, thy name is Tatsu", declare denizens of this Prairie
Village "perennial" who note that its menu "changes very slowly –
thank God"; chef-owner Tatsu Arai continues to create "old-style"
"haute" "French cuisine of the first order" ("poached fish done
perfectly", "outstanding Grand Marnier soufflé") in his "civilized"
restaurant, assisted by an "exemplary" staff; however, cutting-edge
types crack the "place and its clientele have aged together" and
claim the "outdated" decor is in "dire need of a face-lift."

zin   25 | 22 | 24 | $40 |

1900 Main St. (19th St.), 816-527-0120; www.zinkc.com
Located in the "blossoming" Crossroads arts district, this "sexy",
"stunning", stripped-down New American with a "cool urban feel"
"attracts a cultured crowd", especially on "First Fridays when the
galleries are open late"; hipsters hoover up "innovative" and
"delicious" seasonal specialties (including a "worth-it" $60 tasting
menu) and appreciate the "charming", "attentive" staffers'
"impeccable advice" about the "excellent wine list", though a few
critics cluck it's all too "trendy with a capital T."

Las Vegas

TOP FOOD RANKING

	Restaurant	Cuisine
28	Nobu	Japanese/Peruvian
27	Picasso	New French
	Malibu Chan's	Asian/Pacific Rim
	Le Cirque	New French
	Rosemary's	New American
	Michael Mina	Seafood
	Bradley Ogden	New American
	Lotus of Siam*	Northern Thai
	Prime	Steakhouse
26	Andre's	French
	NOBHILL	Californian
	Delmonico	Steakhouse
	Del Frisco's	Steakhouse
	Roy's	Hawaii Regional
	Mayflower Cuisinier	Chinese/French
	Sterling Brunch	New American
	Michael's	Continental
	Steak House	Steakhouse
	Shintaro	Japanese
25	Hyakumi	Japanese

OTHER NOTEWORTHY PLACES

Restaurant	Cuisine
Alex	French
Alizé	New French
Aureole	New American
Bellagio Buffet	Eclectic
Bouchon	French Bistro
Commander's Palace	Cajun-Creole
Craftsteak	Seafood/Steakhouse
Daniel Boulud	French
Eiffel Tower	French
Emeril's New Orleans	Cajun-Creole/Seafood
Firefly	Spanish/Tapas
Gaetano's	Northern Italian
Medici Café	New American
Mix	Eclectic/French
Osteria del Circo	Northern Italian
Pamplemousse	French
Piero's	Northern Italian
Seablue	Seafood
3950	Continental
Valentino	Northern Italian

* Indicates a tie with restaurant above

subscribe to zagat.com

Alex
    – | – | – | VE

Wynn Las Vegas, 3131 Las Vegas Blvd. S. (Desert Inn Rd.), 702-770-9966;
www.wynnlasvegas.com

Chef Alex Stratta, who found fame at Renoir and at Mary Elaine's in
Phoenix, returns with this elegant, eponymous address anchored
by a *Hello, Dolly*-esque staircase in the Wynn Las Vegas; his fans
can sample his southern French favorites (turbot with chanterelles,
peach napoleon with sangria sorbet); and while the wine cellar
boasts 950 labels, you're also welcome to bring your own.

Alizé
    25 | 28 | 25 | $64

Palms Casino Hotel, 4321 W. Flamingo Rd. (Arville St.), 702-942-7777;
www.alizelv.com

Dine on a "decadent meal in the sky" at "great" chef-proprietor
Andre Rochat's "romantic", "fancy-schmancy" New French set
"56 stories up" atop the Palms, one of "Vegas' hippest resorts"; it
flaunts the city's "best view of the Strip" "through glass on three
sides", but there's lots to appreciate in the foreground, as well, as
when the "discreet, professional staff" sets down the plates and
"removes the silver lids in unison – ta-da!" – they reveal "truly
superb" culinary treasures.

Andre's
    26 | 25 | 26 | $61

Monte Carlo Resort & Casino, 3770 Las Vegas Blvd. S. (bet. Harmon &
Tropicana Aves.), 702-798-7151
401 S. Sixth St. (bet. Bonneville St. & Bridger Ave.), 702-385-5016
www.andrelv.com

Francophilic fans of "hometown celebrity chef" Andre Rochat's
"tooo romantic" eateries (a "cozy" "French-countryside auberge"
transported to Downtown, and its sibling, a "peaceful respite" "a
world away" from, and yet within, the Monte Carlo casino) "would
eat here every night"; "prepare to be pampered" with "superb"
fare ferried by "attentive, well-informed, entertaining" servers at
this "Vegas tradition."

AUREOLE
    25 | 27 | 24 | $69

Mandalay Bay Hotel, 3950 Las Vegas Blvd. S. (Hacienda Ave.),
702-632-7401; www.charliepalmer.com

"Excellent entertainment" awaits at this "happening" Mandalay
Bay "outpost of the NYC original", where it's "fun watching" the
"flying" "goddesses" of the grape as they're "lifted on cables to
retrieve your selection" from the many-thousand-bottle "tower
of power", the centerpiece of the "stunning interior"; "wowed
crowds" of "glitterati" report that the "outstanding" New American
fare is "divine" and the "sommeliers are helpful" in navigating the
"cool, computerized wine list", though some say the rest of the
"snotty" staff "needs to cork its attitude."

BELLAGIO BUFFET, THE
    24 | 19 | 19 | $29

Bellagio Hotel, 3600 Las Vegas Blvd. S. (Flamingo Rd.), 702-693-8255;
www.bellagio.com

Next to a royal flush, the best spread at the Bellagio is this Eclectic
"buffet for people who would otherwise not be caught dead at
one"; an "embarrassment of riches" including "orgasmic" Kobe
beef (holidays only), "mountains of excellent king crab legs" (at
dinner) and "bottomless" bubbly (at weekend brunch), this "feast"
might be "higher priced" than other smorgasbords, but "never has
quality matched quantity like this."

Bouchon
− − − E

*Venetian Hotel, 3355 Las Vegas Blvd. S. (bet. Flamingo &
Spring Mountain Rds.), 702-414-6200; www.bouchonbistro.com*

Foodies are flocking to this notable newcomer, a French bistro from
renowned restaurateur Thomas Keller (of SF's French Laundry)
done on the larger-than-life scale of the Venetian's Venezia Tower;
breakfasts offer such classics as coddled eggs with toasted
brioche, while dinners feature favorites like steak frites and
seasonal boudins, served in Adam Tihany's Francophile-friendly
interior (complete with metallic-topped bar) or on the patio
overlooking the garden ponds.

Bradley Ogden
27 25 26 $72

*Caesars Palace, 3570 Las Vegas Blvd. S. (Flamingo Rd.), 702-731-7731;
www.caesars.com*

Connoisseurs come to Caesars Palace not to bury chef Bradley
Ogden but to praise him for his "extravagant, outstanding" New
American menu featuring "superb" organic dishes made from
"farm-fresh" ingredients (such as a "Maytag blue cheese soufflé
that'll make you think you died and went to foodie heaven"),
accompanied with "serious china and linens" and presented by
an "engaging" staff; such a "sublime experience" "doesn't come
cheap", though, so you'd "better win big or you'll leave hungry."

Commander's Palace
25 23 25 $55

*Desert Passage at Aladdin, 3663 Las Vegas Blvd. S. (Harmon Ave.),
702-892-8272; www.commanderspalace.com*

A "worthy offspring of the great New Orleans" Brennan-family
institution, this Strip spot in the Aladdin is "a bastion of civilization
in a sea of sweatpants and spandex", where "excellent Creole
and Cajun" such as "out-of-this-world pecan-encrusted fish" and
"bread pudding from heaven" are ferried by a "knowledgeable",
"gracious" staff amid "gorgeous" "reminders of the Vieux Carré";
"it ain't the original (what in Vegas is?)", but it's "tons" of "top-
drawer" "fun", especially during the "transporting jazz brunch."

Craftsteak
24 23 23 $68

*MGM Grand Hotel, 3799 Las Vegas Blvd. S. (Tropicana Ave.),
702-891-7318; www.mgmgrand.com*

"Craft your own meal" at this "gorgeous" "high roller", a surf 'n'
turfer in the MGM from Manhattan chef Tom Colicchio, whose menu
is a virtual "primer on artisanal and organic foods" ("incredible
vegetables", "moo-velous" beef from corn- and "grass-fed" cattle)
that allows guests to "graze on" "pure", "unique flavors"; the
"family-style" feasting means the "fun" just "gets better the larger
your group" is, but be sure to leave folks who "don't like to serve
themselves" back in the hotel room.

Daniel Boulud Brasserie
− − − E

*Wynn Las Vegas, 3131 Las Vegas Blvd. S. (Desert Inn Rd.), 702-770-9966;
www.wynnlasvegas.com*

A rip-tide of foodies floods in for such Daniel Boulud specialties as
a short rib- and foie gras–filled burger, plus other Gallic goodies
whipped up by executive chef Philippe Rispoli, at this Wynn Las
Vegas brasserie with a view of the resort's forest-edged lake; it's
all served in a French-styled bastion of etched glass, mosaic tile
and leather banquettes that, despite the bustle, provides a serene
respite from the northern Strip scene.

Del Frisco's Double Eagle Steak House   26 | 23 | 24 | $63 |
3925 Paradise Rd. (Corporate Dr.), 702-796-0063; www.delfriscos.com
The "attentive servers treat everyone like a whale" (in Vegas parlance, a high roller) at this "excellent", "high-end" beef palace east of the Strip that offers an "elegant break from the tables"; its "savory steaks" – "juicy, delicious" and "perfectly done" – are served with "fabulous" sides, "fantastic" wines and "hot, messy bread brought right away", and the "polished atmosphere" of its "clubby" environs comes complete with a "cigar bar" and a Tuesday–Saturday pianist.

DELMONICO STEAKHOUSE   26 | 24 | 25 | $63 |
Venetian Hotel, 3355 Las Vegas Blvd. S. (bet. Flamingo & Spring Mountain Rds.), 702-414-3737; www.emerils.com
Food Network chef "Emeril [Lagasse] knows how to keep it real" at this "modern and uncluttered" Venetian "meat lover's dream", where he "kicks steaks up a notch", making them so tender that "you don't need a knife"; an "(almost overly) attentive staff" ensures a "special experience", delivering the "spicy, juicy", "decadent comfort foods" via their "signature synchronized service"; in short, "your wallet and cardiologist will be mad, but your stomach will thank you."

Eiffel Tower   22 | 26 | 22 | $69 |
Paris Las Vegas, 3655 Las Vegas Blvd. S. (bet. Flamingo Rd. & Harmon Ave.), 702-948-6937; www.eiffeltowerrestaurant.com
"Look down your nose at the people on the Strip" from this "marvelous place" located atop a "half-size re-creation" of the eponymous City of Light landmark at the Paris Las Vegas where the "fabulous view of the Bellagio fountains" complements a "superb menu" of "fine French cuisine" and "reserve wines"; conversely, critics complain that "the bill is as high as the elevator takes you", the "food is phony as the tower" and the "pretentious servers" "treat you like you just parked your mobile home" outside.

Emeril's New Orleans Fish House   24 | 19 | 22 | $51 |
(fka Emeril's)
MGM Grand Hotel, 3799 Las Vegas Blvd. S. (Tropicana Ave.), 702-891-7374; www.emerils.com
"Bam!"-boosters swear "you can almost smell the Mississippi" at this "fantastic fish house" in the MGM Grand, a "charming N'Awlins bistro" where "ragin' Cajun" and Creole are presented by "smart" synchronized servers; "you gotta like noise", though, since the joint's "usually packed to the gills", or you can "grab a bowl of gumbo at the bar" to "avoid the long lines" and "large crowds"; still, the "underenthused" imply that "Emeril needs to go back in the kitchen and out of the limelight"; N.B. the Decor score may not reflect a recent remodel.

Firefly ☽   – | – | – | M |
3900 Paradise Rd. (bet. Flamingo Rd. & Twain Ave.), 702-369-3971; www.fireflylv.com
Tapas-style dining finally alights in this buffet-heavy town via this bright, new Spaniard, a late-night, indoor-outdoor nosh spot just east of the Strip near Restaurant Row that's helmed by chef John Simmons; fans flit through favorites from artichoke toasts and mango babyback ribs to paella and Parmesan frites while getting lit on pitchers of the housemade sangria.

Gaetano's   24   22   22 $35
*Siena Promenade, 10271 S. Eastern Ave. (Siena Heights Dr.),
Henderson, 702-361-1661; www.gaetanoslasvegas.com*
Rory and Gaetano Palmeri are "owners who care about their
customers", keeping their "personal attention" "on premises"
"to ensure your dining experience" at their "warm", "wonderful"
Northern Italian in Henderson; with "delicious" menu items such
as "incredible gnocchi and butternut squash ravioli", 10 to 15
"tempting specials" per night and those "pleasant" proprietors
prompting you to eat, "no one goes hungry here."

Hyakumi   25   20   22 $44
*Caesars Palace, 3570 Las Vegas Blvd. S. (Flamingo Rd.), 702-731-7110;
www.caesars.com*
"Within the tumult of a large casino, this lovely oasis" with
"nice lighting and bamboo" is "one of the best places" on the
Strip for "gorgeous appetizers" followed by "deftly prepared"
sushi and "delicious" teppanyaki cooked at table "with flair" by
"charming chefs"; the guys with ginsus "flipping shrimp tails
into diners' shirt pockets are as entertaining as the Nemo exhibit
down the hall."

LE CIRQUE   27   27   26 $78
*Bellagio Hotel, 3600 Las Vegas Blvd. S. (Flamingo Rd.), 702-693-8100;
www.bellagio.com*
Move over Cirque du Soleil – "the best circus in town" is this French
"powerhouse" helmed by "real pros" Sirio Maccioni and family;
you'll feel "like you're eating under the big top" thanks to its "fun,
flamboyant decor" (featuring "colorful" "fabric hanging from
the ceiling"), which is "as rich as" the "luxurious", classic-with-
contemporary-influences fare and "first-class wines"; some say
"you don't have much privacy" at the "crowded" tables and claim
the staff is "uptight", but most maintain this "spectacular" is still
"worth the splurge" – and worth donning a long-sleeved shirt for.

Lotus of Siam   27   10   21 $21
*Commercial Ctr., 953 E. Sahara Ave. (bet. Maryland Pkwy. &
Paradise Rd.), 702-735-3033; www.saipinchutima.com*
"As soon as the first bite enters your mouth", you'll sigh "wonderful,
wonderful, wonderful" at this "hole-in-the-wall" "jewel" east of the
Strip, where the "plentiful" portions of "flavorful" Southern and
"ethereal" Northern Thai cuisine include "addictive, delicious"
"whole sizzling catfish" and "fabulous mango and sticky rice", all
complemented by an "excellent list of German wines" and offered
at "ridiculously low prices"; with so much to "win you over", smitten
surveyors are happy to "put the decor and location aside."

MALIBU CHAN'S ◐   27   21   23 $31
*W. Sahara Promenade, 8125 W. Sahara Ave. (Cimarron Rd.),
702-312-4267; www.malibuchans.com*
Visit this "great local joint" on the West Side for an "innovative"
"menu of Pacific Rim"–Asian fare, including the "best squid
appetizer in Vegas" and a "mouthwatering" selection of "incredible
sushi"; "early-birds" love landing for its "excellent", "special-
value" entrees, while the "beautiful people" flock to its 10 PM–
2 AM "reverse happy hour" ("it's all about the tapas, baby"), making
this "absolutely fabulous" favorite "worth the drive" anytime;
P.S. "the banana Chan dessert is delicious."

Mayflower Cuisinier 🗷　　26 | 20 | 23 | $34
Sahara Pavilion, 4750 W. Sahara Ave. (Decatur Blvd.), 702-870-8432;
www.mayflowercuisinier.com
Set sail for the west-of-Strip Sahara Pavilion shopping center, and
"you won't feel your time was wasted" when you land at this
"creative Chinese-French fusion" "gem", a "longtime favorite of
locals"; you'll get "hooked on" the "beautiful presentation" and
"great flavors" of "wonderful appetizers" and "interesting" entrees
such as "Hong Kong chow mein filled with scallops" – no wonder
"surprised" first-timers are "delighted" "to discover" it.

Medici Café　　　▽ 23 | 25 | 24 | $34
Ritz-Carlton, Lake Las Vegas, 1610 Lake Las Vegas Pkwy.
(Grand Mediterra Blvd.), Henderson, 702-567-4700; www.ritz-carlton.com
Though few have managed the "getaway" to this "relaxing",
"outstanding" Henderson youngling, intrepid aficionados predict
you'll "return often" after visiting its "impressive" site overlooking
the Florentine Gardens and sampling its "well-presented" New
American dishes, ferried by "friendly" staffers as "graceful" and
"attentive" as "you would expect from the Ritz"; P.S. sweet-toothed
surveyors advise saving room for the "phenomenal desserts."

Michael Mina　　　27 | 25 | 25 | $67
(fka Aqua)
Bellagio Hotel, 3600 Las Vegas Blvd. S. (Flamingo Rd.), 702-693-8255;
www.michaelmina.net
"Stunning attention to detail" is the hallmark of this "swimmingly
wonderful" Bellagio seafood "beauty" whose "imaginative chef"
and co-owner Michael Mina brings "delish" fish to "the middle of
the desert", offering "high rollers" "exquisite" items ("especially
a lobster pot pie" that's "all it's cracked up to be") and three
"outstanding tasting menus"; the service is "like a ballet", as
waiters move "gracefully" through the "posh" room, making for
an "upscale experience" that's "worth the home equity loan."

Michael's　　　26 | 22 | 26 | $76
Barbary Coast Hotel & Casino, 3595 Las Vegas Blvd. S. (Flamingo Rd.),
702-737-7111; www.barbarycoastcasino.com
It might be "hard to believe that this long-running gourmet is still
better than most of the new designer" haunts, but the "venerable"
Barbary Coast "institution" remains "out of this world" for "classy"
Continental (including an "always-good Dover sole"); "high rollers"
"love" to slip into an "old-time red booth" surrounded by "romantic"
decor "right out of Bugsy's days" and nibble at the "special pre-
meal crudité" while "treated like royalty" by the "attentive staff."

Mix　　　– | – | – | VE
Mandalay Bay Hotel, 3950 Las Vegas Blvd. S., 64th fl. (Hacienda Ave.),
702-632-9500; www.chinagrillmgt.com
A 24-ft. chandelier of 15,000 glass balls designed to resemble
champagne bubbles greets guests entering this high-rise
newcomer, a Strip scenester co-owned by Alain Ducasse and
restaurateur Jeffrey Chodorow; as they consume Eclectic-
French entrees prepared by chef de cuisine Bruno Davaillon
(including such pricey trendies as lobster au curry or bison
tenderloin) and whimsical desserts, they can drink in the view
from the 64th-floor terrace; another option is just to gather for
cocktails and light bites in the black leather-clad bar.

NOBHILL | 26 || 25 || 25 || $63 |

MGM Grand Hotel, 3799 Las Vegas Blvd. S. (Tropicana Ave.),
702-891-7337; www.mgmgrand.com

Though the atmosphere is "serene", chef Michael Mina's "roll-your-eyes-to-the-back-of-your-head good" Californian cuisine is likely to "knock your socks off" at this Strip spot; the "exquisite variety" of "addictive" dishes made from organic ingredients includes "sublime lobster pot pie", and the "professional" staff provides service as "polished" as the "stylin'", "minimalist decor", which features "glass-enclosed booths" in which you can cry "wow!" without bothering your neighbors.

NOBU ● | 28 || 23 || 24 || $69 |

Hard Rock Hotel & Casino, 4455 Paradise Rd. (bet. Flamingo Rd. &
Harmon Ave.), 702-693-5090; www.nobumatsuhisa.com

"Master/showman" Nobu Matsuhisa's "magnificent", "mind-blowingly" "artful" creations are "so beautiful you hate to eat them", but they're also "simply" "sublime" ("whether cooked or raw"), "amazing taste buds" and earning this "trendy" east-of-Strip Japanese-Peruvian the No. 1 rating for Food in Vegas; "crowded" with the "young and hip" having "noisy" "fun", it's "not a great place for the rookie", and you'll definitely need to "bring your yen" (or "your banker"), but rest assured it does "live up to the hype."

Osteria del Circo | 25 || 26 || 24 || $59 |

Bellagio Hotel, 3600 Las Vegas Blvd. S. (Flamingo Rd.), 702-693-8150;
www.bellagio.com

Le Cirque's "ringmasters", the Maccionis, crack the whip at this "epicurean" extravaganza of Northern Italian "delights" in the Bellagio, where a "formal" staff "elegantly" juggles "exquisitely prepared" plates and flagons of "fantastic wines" in a "chic, playful" "fantasy-room" setting; it's a "noisy", "non-stuffy" place that has barkers bellowing "run, don't walk, in your Manolo Blahniks" for a "memorable experience"; still, others opine that the "ridiculously priced", "overhyped" fare takes "second" billing to the "awesome view of the water show."

Pamplemousse | 25 || 21 || 26 || $50 |

400 E. Sahara Ave. (bet. Joe W. Brown Dr. & Paradise Rd.), 702-733-2066;
www.pamplemousserestaurant.com

"Old-time Vegas is brought to life" at chef Georges LaForge's "quaint" east-of-Strip French, "an institution" "for more than 30 years" that "never loses its magic", in part due to the incantatory powers of its "impeccable" servers who "recite the menu every night", describing the "excellent, garlicky escargot" and rack of lamb with pistachio crust while guests "pick at" "the huge basket of crudité" brought gratis to the table; no wonder "romantics" rate it "perfect" for "a great meal with someone you love."

PICASSO | 27 || 29 || 27 || $91 |

Bellagio Hotel, 3600 Las Vegas Blvd. S. (Flamingo Rd.), 702-693-8255;
www.bellagio.com

"If you had a choice for your last meal on earth", this "fancy", Spanish-influenced New French in the Bellagio Hotel offers just the "sensual experience to savor" in your final moments; garnering Most Popular and Top Decor rankings in Las Vegas, this prix fixe "theater" is home to "genius" Julian Serrano, whose "artfully crafted" and "exquisitely served" dishes complement the mastery

of the "walls of Picassos"; it may be "ridiculously expensive", but
this "over-the-top" experience is also "ridiculously good."

Piero's Italian Cuisine   23 21 23 $53
*355 Convention Center Dr. (bet. Las Vegas Blvd. & Paradise Rd.),
702-369-2305; www.pieroscuisine.com*
Like something "out of *Casino*" (a scene was filmed here), this
"longtime" "local hangout" east of the Strip is as "famous" for its
"people-watching" as for the kitchen's "outstanding" Northern
Italian specialties and "excellent" seafood, including "stone crabs
from Florida"; it can be "expensive just to see and be seen", but
"dress in black and fit right in" with the town's "old guard", who
know that "gracious owner/host" Freddy Glusman will "treat you
right" in a setting that's "truly old Vegas", "baby."

PRIME STEAKHOUSE   27 27 26 $72
*Bellagio Hotel, 3600 Las Vegas Blvd. S. (Flamingo Rd.), 702-693-8255;
www.bellagio.com*
"What all steakhouses hope they grow up to be", this "classic,
classy" chophouse in the Bellagio is a "carnivore's delight" sporting
chef-partner Jean-Georges Vongerichten's "signature panache";
"rich" is how "satisfied meat eaters" sum up its "sumptuous" decor,
"great martinis" and "superb" cuisine, which includes "fabulous
appetizers" and, of course, "perfectly prepared" beef; besides,
the "beautiful fountain views" and "knowledgeable", "gracious
service" are themselves "worth the hefty prices."

ROSEMARY'S   27 21 25 $53
*W. Sahara Promenade, 8125 W. Sahara Ave. (bet. Buffalo Dr. &
Cimarron Rd.), 702-869-2251; www.rosemarysrestaurant.com*
"Locals love" "former Emeril protégé" Michael Jordan and his wife
Wendy's "wonderful" French-influenced New American on the
West Side; the couple cooks up "musts" such as BBQ shrimp with
Maytag blue cheese, as well as "terrific prix fixe" meals, enticing
with "spectacular food in a lovely, unpretentious setting" that's
"definitely worth the cab ride" to their "strip-mall" location.

Roy's   26 24 25 $47
*8701 W. Charleston Blvd. (bet. Durango Dr. & Rampart Blvd.), 702-838-3620
620 E. Flamingo Rd. (Palo Verdes St.), 702-691-2053
www.roysrestaurant.com*
"Roy Yamaguchi is the Wolfgang" Puck of the Islands, overseeing
these east-of-Strip and West Side "fine-dining" favorites that
feature "creative, colorful" Hawaii Regional cooking and a vibe as
"comfortably unpretentious" as a "honeymoon in Kauai"; "even
though they're part of a chain", they'll "send your taste buds to
heaven" with dishes that "delight all the senses" – from the "sticky,
flavorful" ribs to the "incredible fish" (e.g. "wonderful" blackened
ahi) to the "oozing chocolate soufflé" that'll leave you "raving."

Seablue   – – – E
*MGM Grand Hotel, 3799 Las Vegas Blvd. S. (Tropicana Ave.),
702-891-3486; www.michaelmina.net*
Set on the Strip, chef Michael Mina's seafooder is a hot spot for
celeb watching, including the Mr. Limpets in the round aquarium;
stone waterwalls and a central raw bar add to the panache of a
place where ocean offerings are charred on an open wood-fired
grill, with some finished in Moroccan clay pots, while the tapas-
style menu encourages something that's rare in this town: sharing.

Shintaro
26｜25｜22｜$59

Bellagio Hotel, 3600 Las Vegas Blvd. S. (Flamingo Rd.), 702-693-8255;
www.bellagio.com

"Whether you're at" the sushi bar backed by a "colorful jellyfish tank", at "the hibachi tables" or in the "dining room with a view of the Bellagio water displays", you can always expect a feast for your eyes" and "your mouth" at this "superb Japanese" triple threat; "after a hard day of gambling", the "luxurious surroundings" are "wonderfully relaxing" for "unwinding" with plates of "toro like butter" and "tender" Kobe beef, or with the chef's "amazing" tasting menu, though some suggest that "overpricing" makes it strictly the "rich man's Benihana."

Steak House
26｜21｜23｜$44

Circus Circus Hotel, 2880 Las Vegas Blvd. S. (Riviera Blvd.), 702-794-3767;
www.circuscircus.com

"Once you" "fight your way through the sea of parents and sticky, screaming children" in the lobby of the "not-so-classy" Circus Circus, you'll find this "surprisingly good steakhouse" "crowded" with "locals" scarfing down "huge", "brilliantly prepared" slabs; as you might expect from the "unlikely setting", there's "a nice bit of theatrics" (abetted by an "open kitchen"), and the "reasonable prices" make it one of the "best deals in Vegas, baby."

Sterling Brunch
26｜20｜23｜$60

Bally's Las Vegas Hotel, 3645 Las Vegas Blvd. S. (Flamingo Rd.),
702-739-4111

"A little bit of heaven in Sin City", this "luxurious" New American Bally's brunch lets you "gorge on unlimited" "delicacies such as lobster, caviar, rack of lamb" and "bottomless glasses of fine French champagne", starting at 9:30 AM on Sundays; overseen by "a perfect, old-school" maitre d', it's the "only" spread "where you don't have to fight your way through" "using your fork as a defensive weapon", and the "orgasmic" offerings make it just about the "finest" morning meal "in the United States."

3950
23｜24｜23｜$55

Mandalay Bay Hotel, 3950 Las Vegas Blvd. S. (Hacienda Ave.),
702-632-7414; www.mandalaybay.com

"Traditional classics" such as "excellent" bisque and steaks are "finely prepared" with "flair" to match the "colorful", "hi-tech room" at this Mandalay Bay Continental, and the "attentive service" is just as "snappy" as the "modern" decor; still, conservatives complain that the "pricey" place is "trying really hard to be trendy", with "too-loud music" and a "dressed-to-thrill" "young crowd" that can make the dining room "quite noisy."

Valentino Las Vegas
24｜22｜23｜$66

Venetian Hotel, 3355 Las Vegas Blvd. S. (bet. Flamingo &
Spring Mountain Rds.), 702-414-3000; www.welovewine.com

Scale the heights of the "*alta cucina*" for a "culinary adventure" at this "classy" Venetian cousin of "maestro" Piero Selvaggio's Santa Monica original; chef Luciano Pellegrini offers "remarkable" Northern dishes and "a wine list envied by Bacchus himself", all proffered by a "smooth" staff in an "elegant" room; still, some call the cuisine "not up to the standards in CA", suggesting you try a less "pricey" lunch at their grill.

Long Island

TOP FOOD RANKING

Restaurant	Cuisine
28 Kotobuki	Japanese
Polo	New American
27 Kitchen a Bistro	French Bistro
Peter Luger	Steakhouse
Mill River Inn	Eclectic/New American
La Plage	Eclectic
Chachama Grill	New American
Maroni Cuisine	Eclectic/Italian
Le Soir	French
26 Mirabelle	French
Dario	Northern Italian
Orient, The	Chinese
Panama Hatties	New American
On 3	New American
Siam Lotus Thai	Thai
La Piccola Liguria	Northern Italian
Il Mulino	Northern Italian
Barney's	French/New American
Piccolo	Italian/New American
Da Ugo	Northern Italian

OTHER NOTEWORTHY PLACES

American Hotel	French/American
Bryant & Cooper	Steakhouse
Cheesecake Factory	American
Coolfish	Seafood/New American
Della Femina	New American
Frisky Oyster	Eclectic/Seafood
Harvest on Fort Pond	Mediterranean/N. Italian
Jimmy Hay's	Steakhouse
La Pace Tuscan Grill	Northern Italian
Louis XVI	New French
Mio	Northern Italian
Mirko's	Eclectic
Nick & Toni's	Mediterranean
Plaza Cafe	New American
Rialto	Northern Italian
Robert's	Italian
Starr Boggs	New American
Stone Creek Inn	French/Mediterranean
Tellers Chophouse	Steakhouse
Trattoria Diane	Northern Italian

American Hotel
25 | 23 | 23 | $59

*The American Hotel, 49 Main St. (bet. Bay & Washington Sts.),
Sag Harbor, 631-725-3535; www.theamericanhotel.com*
A combo of "19th-century charm and Hamptons chic", this
"classic" Sag Harbor hotel garners garlands for "top-flight"
French-American cuisine and a "fabulous" 2,500-label wine list
that's "thicker than a phone book" ("you have to be in good shape
just to lift it"); "attentive but not fawning" servers "meet every
need" in the antique-filled dining rooms or on the "perfect"
porch, so though a few grumble it's "stuffy", "snooty" and
"pricey", admirers assert they "never regret paying the bill."

Barney's
26 | 23 | 24 | $59

*315 Buckram Rd. (Bayville Rd.), Locust Valley, 516-671-6300;
www.barneyslocustvalley.com*
"Don't wait for a special occasion" to "search out" this "hidden
gem" in Locust Valley, urge surveyors who swoon over its
"sensational", "inventive and mouthwatering" French–New
American cuisine and "excellent" 250-label wine list; the
"charming" space feels "like a country inn" ("try to get the
table by the fireplace") and "impeccably" "professional"
staffers make visitors "feel like royalty" – so though it's
indubitably "expensive", all agree that the experience is
"worth every penny."

BRYANT & COOPER STEAKHOUSE
25 | 19 | 21 | $58

*2 Middle Neck Rd. (Northern Blvd.), Roslyn, 516-627-7270;
www.bryantandcooper.com*
"Pack your appetite and your wallet" and go to this "meat
lovers' paradise" in Roslyn for "colossal", "outrageous steaks"
("melt-in-your-mouth filets"), "wonderful" seafood and "great
sides" in a decidedly "masculine" setting; the tables are so close
together some feel "packed in like cattle" and you can expect
long waits even if you've booked a table, but the service is
"friendly and accommodating."

Chachama Grill
27 | 14 | 23 | $43

*Swan Lake Nursery Commons, 655-8 Montauk Hwy. (S. Country Rd.),
East Patchogue, 631-758-7640; www.chachamagrill.com*
"The secret's out": at this "quiet", simple, "family-run" sophomore
set in a "dreary" East Patchogue storefront, "every bite is a
taste sensation"; an "unexpected" "gem", it serves "excellent"
New American specialties "beautifully prepared" and "uniquely
presented", and delighted diners declare they "don't know
what's better, the staff or the food"; P.S. the three-course early-
bird is "a steal."

CHEESECAKE FACTORY ◑
21 | 18 | 17 | $28

*Mall at the Source, 1504 Old Country Rd. (Merchants Concourse),
Westbury, 516-222-5500; www.thecheesecakefactory.com*
"They have a winning formula", calculate consumers who
commend this Westbury chain link "based on price/value ratio"
alone; "humongous portions" of "delicious" American eats plus
"incredible" cheesecake and a "cavernous" yet "comfortable"
space equal "everyone's favorite"; servers are "usually friendly"
but "not always on the ball", and amid the "noisy", "chaotic"
conditions you can "grow old waiting" – fortunately, more seating
upstairs "has helped reduce the time."

COOLFISH 24 22 21 $47

North Shore Atrium, 6800 Jericho Tpke. (Michael Dr.), Syosset, 516-921-3250; www.tomschaudel.com

"Off the beaten path" in a Syosset office park ("who knew?"), this "hard-to-find" New American seafooder is worth the search considering its, yes, "cool fish" and equally "cool vibe"; it's known for "creative", "classy" dishes served by an "accommodating" crew in quarters that have "verve", and though it's "a little pricey", the "early-bird special is a terrific deal."

Dario ⌧ 26 18 24 $52

13 N. Village Ave. (bet. Merrick Rd. & Sunrise Hwy.), Rockville Centre, 516-255-0535

This "simply wonderful" family-owned Rockville Centre special-occasioner, one of "the best on Long Island", provides a culinary experience "of the highest degree"; "excellent", "sophisticated" Northern Italian cuisine that's "worth the splurge" brought to table by a "friendly" and "utterly professional" staff that "knows how to take care of people"; the room may be "small" and "nondescript" but overall delighted diners declare Dario "da bomb."

Da Ugo ⌧ 26 18 23 $48

509 Merrick Rd. (Long Beach Rd.), Rockville Centre, 516-764-1900

"For that special occasion", reviewers recommend this Rockville Centre "hideaway" serving "top-notch" Northern Italian fare in a "charming", "romantic setting" where kids are scarce ("don't go without an AARP card"); the food is "worth sitting on your neighbor's lap for" – a good thing since "quarters are tight" – but service can be an issue ("regulars get the royal treatment" but "infrequent visitors are often disappointed"); nevertheless, this "class act" remains a "tough reservation."

Della Femina 24 22 21 $58

99 N. Main St. (Cedar St.), East Hampton, 631-329-6666; www.dellafemina.com

A "true Hamptons experience" can be had at this East Hampton New American, a "perennial favorite" for "delicious" meals in a "lively" (read: "crowded, noisy") "see-and-be-seen" atmosphere that provides "neck-craners" with choice "celebrity-spotting" opportunities; pleasingly "professional" service and "classy" "California-casual" decor are further reasons that it "matches the hype" and is "well worth" prices "as high as the quality."

Frisky Oyster 25 21 20 $51

27 Front St. (bet. Main & 2nd Sts.), Greenport, 631-477-4265; www.thefriskyoyster.com

"NYC hits the North Fork" at this "fantastic" "hot spot" in Greenport, where "imaginative" Eclectic seafood dishes "emphasizing local ingredients" present a "superb blend of flavors"; given that the "owner is super-accommodating", the "service professional" and the atmosphere "sophisticated", no wonder it's "easier to get a reservation at the White House on a Saturday night."

Harvest on Fort Pond 26 22 22 $46

11 S. Emery St. (S. Euclid Ave.), Montauk, 631-668-5574; www.harvest2000.com

The "bountiful portions" of "rustic" Mediterranean–Northern Italian cuisine are "meant to be shared" at this Montauk "jewel", which has rapt reviewers raving that the "food is incredible", the "helpful" staffers are "professional" and the "serene setting" with "amazing sunset views" across Fort Pond is ever so "romantic" – but "go with a group" if you hope to finish the "humongous" servings; "reservations are a must", and if possible, insiders advise "snagging a seat in the Tuscan-style garden."

Il Mulino

26 | 22 | 22 | $80

1042 Northern Blvd. (bet. Old Northern Blvd. & Searingtown Rd), Roslyn, 516-621-1870
"Primo" Northern Italian cuisine in "copious quantities" "comes to Roslyn", crow cognoscenti who cheer for the "outstanding" food served in a "beautiful room" at this new "hot spot"; despite service that can be "inconsistent", even "pretentious", and "outrageous" prices that warrant "bringing your banker along", a reservation here is still "just as hard to get" as at its Manhattan cousin.

Jimmy Hay's

25 | 21 | 22 | $51

4310 Austin Blvd. (Kingston Blvd.), Island Park, 516-432-5155
Reviewers rave "the beef is tops" at this Island Park meatery that "deserves its popularity" for serving some of "the best steak on the South Shore"; not only is the filet mignon "outstanding", the "fish is excellent" as well, and an "efficient" staff keeps things moving; after a "much-needed face-lift", the decor finally comes close to matching the first-rate food, so it's now "a good experience all around" – just beware the "heart-attack prices."

KITCHEN A BISTRO ⊘

27 | 9 | 21 | $35

532 N. Country Rd. (Lake Ave.), St. James, 631-862-0151
"For people who care more for food than ambiance", this "superb" St. James French bistro delivers "fabulous value" in the form of "spectacular", "cutting-edge" cuisine ("outstanding seafood", desserts "straight from heaven") at "rock-bottom prices" plus a "satisfying" BYO policy; "young, energetic" staffers "love what they do", and although the "lilliputian" 25-seat room is "cramped" and "lacks atmosphere", nobody seems to mind much – almost all avow they're happy to "take whatever reservations are available."

KOTOBUKI

28 | 16 | 21 | $33

86 Deer Park Ave. (Main St.), Babylon, 631-321-8387
377 Nesconset Hwy. (Rtes. 111 & 347), Hauppauge, 631-360-3969
"Plain and simple" sushi "so fresh it's still swimming" explains why this Babylon and Hauppauge Japanese duo has been voted No. 1 for Food in LI; "the wait is insufferable at peak times" ("reservations would be nice"), "the tables are too close for comfort" and there's "no ambiance" to speak of, but finatics agree "it's all worth it" because the food is "heaven to the taste buds" and the "kind" staffers are "helpful to first-timers"; N.B. post-*Survey* renovations at the Babylon branch, which is slated to reopen in fall 2005, may outdate the above Decor score.

La Pace Tuscan Grill

25 | 21 | 24 | $52

51 Cedar Swamp Rd. (bet. 2nd St. & 3rd Sts.), Glen Cove, 516-671-2970
"Still a standout after all these years", this "exquisite" Glen Cove Northern Italian with "impeccable" service continues to set the pace for "superb" gourmet dining that's "high-class" "all the way"; the 200-bottle wine list, "classic" cuisine and "formal setting" all "contribute to the longevity" of this "fine old-timer" that's a "no-brainer for a special occasion."

La Piccola Liguria   26 | 19 | 25 | $52
47 Shore Rd. (bet. Mill Pond & Old Shore Rds.), Port Washington, 516-767-6490
Don't bother "looking at the menu" – at this "stellar" Northern Italian in Port Washington, the servers memorize an "array of specials" so "extensive" it "almost takes your breath away"; once you choose, the result is a "meal to remember", with the "owner and his fine staff" "treating you like a king"; seating is "cozy" (some say "tight") and getting a reservation is "tough", but it's worth whatever it takes for one of the Island's "best" dinners.

La Plage   27 | 20 | 23 | $52
131 Creek Rd. (Sound Rd.), Wading River, 631-744-9200; www.laplagerestaurant.com
Serving the kind of "spectacularly creative" fare "you'd expect at a NYC place *du jour*", this "hideaway" in Wading River is an "absolute gem"; the "artistically plated" Eclectic cuisine "sparkles" and the "wonderful staff" helps maintain a "laid-back atmosphere"; some say the "beach-house setting" is a bit too "rustic", but supporters who savor the "black-tie food in a khaki-pants ambiance" sigh "thank God it's hard to find" – or else, "we'd never get in."

Le Soir   27 | 20 | 23 | $45
825 Montauk Hwy. (Bayport Ave.), Bayport, 631-472-9090
Chef-owner Michael Kaziewicz "gets better every year" rave "regulars" of this "very special" Bayport French; they swear by his "consistently excellent", "complex" cuisine (a "gastronomic delight") and appreciate the "lovely", "attentive" service and "unpretentious" country feel – all of which has surveyors sighing "if only there were one of these in every town"; since there isn't, the weekday all-inclusive dinner special, "one of the best values on the Island", is definitely "worth the trip."

Louis XVI   26 | 27 | 25 | $72
600 S. Ocean Ave. (Masket Dock), Patchogue, 631-654-8970; www.louisxvi.org
A "magnificent experience" awaits at this "opulent" waterfront château in Patchogue, where the "elaborately decorated", "gorgeous" environs are "enhanced" by "drop-dead ocean views"; "spectacular" New French cuisine comes in a "top-notch" tasting menu or a prix fixe that "offers great variety", and service is "impeccable"; it's a "must-see at least once in a lifetime" – just be sure to "bring your best plastic."

Maroni Cuisine ⌿   27 | 14 | 22 | $43
18 Woodbine Ave. (bet. Main St. & Scudder Ave.), Northport, 631-757-4500
Michael Maroni is a "fabulous chef" "worthy of NYC", rave reviewers who've squeezed into this "lilliputian" 20-seat hideaway in Northport; order his tasting menu and you'll savor "a hundred bits of heaven" (well, 12 or 13 courses anyway); the food is Eclectic with an Italian bent, and while it can be "pricey", it's all "of delectable quality", whether you dine in this "itty-bitty space" or "take out."

MILL RIVER INN   27 | 22 | 26 | $68
160 Mill River Rd. (bet. Lexington Ave. & Oyster Bay-Glen Cove Rd.), Oyster Bay, 516-922-7768; www.millriverinn.com
Year after year one of Long Island's top-rated restaurants, this tiny Oyster Bay New American–Eclectic "hideaway" continues to turn

out "sterling" cuisine that, matched with an "excellent wine list", "impeccable service" and a "warm", "romantic" setting, makes for a perfect "special-occasion" meal; "first-class" credentials notwithstanding, the experience feels more like "going to a friend's house for dinner" – albeit a "wealthy friend" who has hired a "legendary chef" like Nick Molfetta.

Mio　　　　　　　　　　　　26 | 20 | 22 | $53
1363 Old Northern Blvd. (bet. Bryant Ave. & Main St.), Roslyn, 516-625-4223; www.mio-restaurant.com

"You won't be singing solo" at this Roslyn Northern Italian now that it has been "discovered" and is drawing diners in droves with its "innovative", "superbly prepared" fresh pastas and other classic dishes, personal attention from chef-owner Dino Vlacich and "hip" setting "reminiscent of" The Boot; there are a few grumbles about "noisy" acoustics and "pricey" tabs, but most don't notice much once they've taken a bite of the "melt-in-your-mouth" edibles.

Mirabelle　　　　　　　　　　26 | 22 | 25 | $66
404 N. Country Rd. (Edgewood Ave.), St. James, 631-584-5999; www.restaurantmirabelle.com

"*C'est magnifique*", enthuse epicures about this St. James "treasure" where "masterful" chef-owner Guy Reuge "never fails to surprise and thrill" with "amazing" French fare that "sings", the wine list is "exquisite" and service is "always gracious" and "civilized"; some find the "subtle" space a bit "plain" for such an "extravagant experience", but others appreciate the "cozy" ambiance; P.S. the $25 prix fixe lunch is the "best deal in town."

Mirko's　　　　　　　　　　　25 | 21 | 23 | $63
Water Mill Sq., 670 Montauk Hwy. (bet. Old Mill & Station Rds.), Water Mill, 631-726-4444

One of "the best in the Hamptons", this "wonderful" Water Mill legend dwells in a "strange location" that's worth seeking out for "tip-top" Eclectic cuisine enjoyed in "pretty and romantic" (if "cramped") quarters; it's "hard to get a reservation in season" and the greetings here range from "the warmest" and "most gracious" to "snobby" depending on whom you ask (insiders advise "only go if you are known to them"), but "once inside" the "swell crowd" and "culinary magic" are truly "memorable."

Nick & Toni's　　　　　　　　24 | 20 | 21 | $60
136 N. Main St. (bet. Cedar St. & Miller Terrace), East Hampton, 631-324-3550

"Still great after all these years", this "rustic" East Hampton Med retains an army of admirers thanks to "sophisticated" seasonal menus that emphasize "outstanding" organic ingredients and an "excellent" staff that helps sustain a "warm and friendly" atmosphere; by now, however, everyone knows it's "a hit with all the celebs", so in season it's almost "impossible to get in" without offering "your first-born" or having "the Spielbergs in your party."

On 3　　　　　　　　　　　　26 | 21 | 24 | $56
32 Railroad Ave. (bet. Prospect & School Sts.), Glen Head, 516-656-3266

Reviewers rhapsodize that "all the elements work" at this "first-rate" Glen Head sophomore; the "innovative" New American cuisine is "excellent" "down to the smallest detail" and matched by "impeccable" service from a "very professional" crew; though the "tiny" room is sometimes loud, its "upscale", "upbeat" decor lends it a "movie-set feel", and "outdoor seating in the new bungalow" can even "make you forget you're on Long Island"; N.B. bringing kids is not encouraged.

Orient, The   26 | 11 | 19 | $21
623 Hicksville Rd. (Central Ave.), Bethpage, 516-822-1010
"You'll think you're in Chinatown" at this "excellent" Bethpage Chinese offering a "tremendous selection" of "authentic", "unusual dishes and old favorites" plus a "super" weekend dim sum that "rivals favorites in Flushing"; owner Tommy Tan is a "gracious host" who's "always willing to recommend the best dishes" and "make anything you ask for, any way you like it."

Panama Hatties   26 | 23 | 25 | $69
Post Plaza, 872 E. Jericho Tpke. (2 mi. east of Rte. 110), Huntington Station, 631-351-1727; www.panamahatties.com
At this Huntington Station "gourmet's delight" owned by exec chef Matthew Hisiger, connoisseurs are "continually amazed" by the "excitingly creative" and "artistically presented" New American cuisine, and find the personnel even "friendlier since Hisiger bought the place"; the "bundles-of-bucks" prices and "sophisticated atmosphere" seem to some a "surreal" mix with the "strip-mall setting", but most figure that's the flip side of having "upper-echelon NYC quality in your own neighborhood."

PETER LUGER ⊅   27 | 16 | 21 | $60
255 Northern Blvd. (Tain Dr.), Great Neck, 516-487-8800; www.peterluger.com
"Incredibly" "succulent" steaks that are "the best of the best" have made this Great Neck "classic" Long Island's No. 1 for Popularity for the 12th straight year; yes, the decor could use "a peppy marinade" and the "curt" "old-time waiters" can exhibit "attitude", but it's "worth every penny (and you'll need quite a few)" – put simply, this "king of steakhouses" "beats them all for beef"; P.S. "no vegetarians and no Visa" (cash, debit or Peter Luger cards only).

Piccolo   26 | 21 | 24 | $53
Southdown Shopping Ctr., 215 Wall St. (bet. Mill Ln. & Southdown Rd.), Huntington, 631-424-5592
Admirers "can't say enough" about the "amazing" New American–Italian fare, particularly the extensive list of "innovative specials", at this "fabulous" Huntington haunt; the "knowledgeable waiters" "treat you as an honored guest", and the "enchanting" ambiance with "delightful piano players" helps make it a "perfect place to celebrate romance"; add a 400-bottle wine list, and "no wonder the crowds keep coming" – it's "first-class all the way."

Plaza Cafe   25 | 21 | 24 | $51
61 Hill St. (bet. First Neck & Windmill Lns.), Southampton, 631-283-9323; www.plazacafe.us
"Brilliant" chef Doug Gulija creates "incredible" New American cuisine (he has seafood "down to a science"), and when you combine it with "one of the most interesting wine lists on Long Island", "dining doesn't get much better than this"; add a "top-notch staff" (without "that frenetic Hamptons attitude") and a "romantic" room with a big stone fireplace, and this Southampton "gem" delivers a "true NYC-quality eating experience."

POLO
28 | 27 | 26 | $64

Garden City Hotel, 45 Seventh St. (bet. Cathedral & Hilton Aves.), Garden City, 516-877-9353; www.gchotel.com

This "class act" in the Garden City Hotel earns "high marks" all around from pleased patrons, who praise the "outstanding", "knowledgeable" staff, the recently refurbished "formal" decor and the "spectacular" New American cuisine "of the highest quality"; everything combines to create an "indulgent" dining experience "right out of *The Great Gatsby*" – "it breaks the bank", but it's "almost perfect."

Rialto
26 | 18 | 23 | $49

588 Westbury Ave. (bet. Glen Cove Rd. & Post Ave.), Carle Place, 516-997-5283

The "top-notch" Northern Italian fare is "among the finest Long Island has to offer", avow *amici* of this "quiet" "old-world" Carle Place "gem" where the "tuxedoed waiters" "fawn on you" and the welcoming owner "makes you feel like you're a special guest in his home"; sure, it's "expensive" (the penny-wise protest that "the price of the fish might drown you."), but it's a "lovely place."

Robert's
25 | 21 | 21 | $56

755 Montauk Hwy. (Water Mill traffic light), Water Mill, 631-726-7171

With "unbelievable" Italian cuisine and "accommodating" service in an "intimate" "country-house" setting, this Water Mill destination has its clientele cheering; the kitchen creates "fabulous blends of taste and texture", and the "grown-up atmosphere" feels "more like New England than the Hamptons"; sure, pettifoggers pout about staffers who can be "arrogant" and "pushy", and it's "pricey", too, but enthusiasts insist it's "worth every penny."

Siam Lotus Thai
26 | 16 | 23 | $31

1664 Union Blvd. (bet. 4th & Park Aves.), Bay Shore, 631-968-8196; www.siamlotus.info

Flower power is evident at this "affordable" Bay Shore Thai, decorated in pink and green to evoke the eponymous blossom; the "sublime" food is "so full of flavor" ("ask for the heat and you'll get it") that a meal is "great from start to finish"; add in "personalized" service from owner Danny Poom and his "gracious" staff, and the combo is "worth the trip from anywhere" laud locals – who nevertheless admit they're "glad" they "don't have to drive far."

Starr Boggs
25 | 24 | 20 | $56

6 Parlato Dr. (Library Ave.), Westhampton Beach, 631-288-3500

We "call him Four-Star Boggs" and we "thank heaven he's back" swoon Starr-gazers smitten with this "legendary" East End chef; "he's done it again" at his newest outpost in Westhampton Beach, where everything on the "memorable" seafood-centric New American menu is "imaginative" and you dine in "gorgeous rooms" decorated with Warhol prints or in the "breathtaking back garden"; "the only thing prettier and richer than the food is the crowd", so it's too bad the "young" servers are sometimes so "unprofessional."

Stone Creek Inn
26 | 24 | 24 | $57

405 Montauk Hwy. (bet. Carter Ln. & Wedgewood Harbor), East Quogue, 631-653-6770; www.stonecreekinn.com

"Chef-owner Christian Mir continues to impress year after year", and his talent is "showcased" in his "imaginative" and "perfectly prepared" French-Mediterranean "haute cuisine", well matched with the "varied wine list" and "professionally" served in this "elegant" "historic house"; it's "everything a great night out should be" and "well worth a trip" to East Quogue from anywhere; P.S. "the prix fixe menu is a steal."

Tellers American Chophouse   25 | 26 | 22 | $61 |
605 Main St. (Rte. 111), Islip, 631-277-7070; www.tellerschophouse.com
"Soaring ceilings and huge windows" distinguish this Islip surf 'n' turfer named for its "spectacular" setting in a 1927 bank building; the "brontosaurus-size" rib-eyes and the "extra dividends" of "tasty sides" captivate carnivores, as do servers who remain "gracious" "no matter how busy"; some happily exchange the "noisy" main dining room for the "intimate" upstairs Gallery, while others warn "you'll be ignored" up there "like a counterfeit $20 bill"; still, most maintain a meal at this meatery is "worth every cent."

Trattoria Diane   25 | 21 | 22 | $52 |
21 Bryant Ave. (bet. Roosevelt Ave. & Skillman St.), Roslyn, 516-621-2591
"Inspired food" in an "intimate" setting makes for an "elegant evening", enthuse epicures who've dined at this "sophisticated" yet "charming" trattoria in Roslyn; the "imaginative Tuscan menu" "changes with the seasons" and the quality is always "outstanding" ("you can't resist" the housemade "wonderful breads" and the "even better desserts"); the staff is "accommodating" as well, and the $29.95 Sunday prix fixe may be "the deal of the decade."

Los Angeles

TOP FOOD RANKING

Restaurant	Cuisine
28 Mélisse	French/New Amer.
Matsuhisa	Japanese
Katsu-ya	Japanese
27 Brandywine	Continental
Nobu Malibu	Japanese
Water Grill	Seafood
Sushi Sasabune	Japanese
Maison Akira	French/Japanese
Hamasaku	Japanese
Angelini Osteria	Italian
Sona	New French
Derek's	Californian/French
La Cachette	New French
Josie	New American
Brent's Deli	Deli
Frenchy's Bistro	French Bistro
Giorgio Baldi	Italian
Joe's	Cal./New French
26 Saddle Peak	New American
Shiro	Asian Fusion/Cal.

OTHER NOTEWORTHY PLACES

A.O.C.	Cal./Mediterranean
Belvedere, The	New American
Café Bizou	Californian/French
Campanile	Californian/Med.
Capo	Italian
Chaya Brasserie	Asian/Eclectic
Cheesecake Factory	American
Chinois on Main	Asian/French
Christine	Med./Pacific Rim
Depot, The	Eclectic
Grace	New American
Grill on the Alley	American
Hotel Bel-Air	Californian/French
JiRaffe	Californian
L'Orangerie	French
Mimosa	French Bistro
Mori Sushi	Japanese
Providence	Seafood
Spago	Californian
Valentino	Italian

Angelini Osteria
27 | 17 | 22 | $46

7313 Beverly Blvd. (Poinsettia Pl.), 323-297-0070

At his "wildly popular" Beverly Boulevard osteria, "hospitable" chef-owner Gino Angelini of La Terza proffers a "fantastic" Italian "feast for the senses" that "puts you back in Rome"; dishes like the "perfectly prepared" lasagna are so "splendid" "you'll remember your meal long after you dine" – "if only Mama's cooking was as good"; sure, it's a "sardinelike" scenario, but that just enhances the "noisy, alive" "authentic feel."

A.O.C.
26 | 22 | 23 | $50

8022 W. Third St. (Crescent Heights Blvd.), 323-653-6359;
www.aocwinebar.com

"Eat slowly and share everything", surveyors suggest, to "enjoy the abundance" of "unexpected" French, Cal and Med flavors "executed with perfection" at Suzanne Goin and Caroline Styne's "hip" Third Street "foodie heaven", rated LA's Most Popular; from the "delicious" tapas to "esoteric yet sublime" vinos to the "informed staff", it's "impressive beyond belief", offering the "best grazing in town"; sure, it's "cramped", but that just "fuels the friendly feeding frenzy" and you can always "try to snag a seat" at the wine bar.

Belvedere, The
26 | 28 | 27 | $66

The Peninsula Beverly Hills, 9882 Little Santa Monica Blvd.
(Wilshire Blvd.), Beverly Hills, 310-788-2306;
www.peninsula.com

Offering "an elegant setting for stargazing" over "power breakfasts and lunches" or "outstanding dinners", this "prime spot" in the Peninsula Beverly Hills is a "true destination" that's "pricey but worth every penny"; give in to the "gorgeous setting", "magnificent service" from a "top-notch staff" and "exemplary" New American "cuisine that's fit for a king"; P.S. though every meal is a "near-perfect experience", the cognoscenti confide that the "lovely Sunday brunch", with its rounds of "endless champagne", is an especially "wonderful" "winner."

BRANDYWINE ⊠
27 | 21 | 26 | $53

22757 Ventura Blvd. (Fallbrook Ave.), Woodland Hills,
818-225-9114

Locals laud this "lovely" Woodland Hills Continental as a "flashback to another time", and just the thing "for a night of indulgence", thanks to "superb" offerings like "exquisite" lobster medallions and "incredibly fresh" vegetables; factor in "personal service" in an "intimate" space, and you have a "gourmet experience" "to impress a date or reignite a flame"; still, a handful find it "rather pricey for the neighborhood."

Brent's Deli & Restaurant
27 | 12 | 21 | $18

19565 Parthenia St. (bet. Corbin & Shirely Aves.), Northridge,
818-886-5679; www.brentsdeli.com

"Packed to the gills", this family-run "gold standard" of Jewish delis brings culinary fame to Northridge with "gargantuan" portions of "great" chopped liver and "to-die-for" blintzes; even East Coast "transplants" moon over the "mouthwatering" meats, and endure "long" waits, the sometimes-"sassy" waitstaff and the "kitsch comfort" decor of this "hamish" "pastrami heaven" to eat at the "best delicatessen west of NYC."

CAFÉ BIZOU 22 | 19 | 20 | $30 |
91 N. Raymond Ave. (Holly St.), Pasadena, 626-792-9923
14016 Ventura Blvd. (bet. Costello & Murietta Aves.), Sherman Oaks,
818-788-3536
www.cafebizou.com
Serving "fine" Cal-French cuisine "at bargain prices" – "a formula
that will allow them to take over the world" – these "perennially
popular" "neighborhood bistros" in Pasadena and Sherman Oaks
captivate Angelenos with an "innovative menu that's always being
tweaked"; it's constantly "crowded", and "deservedly" so what
with "$1 daily soups" and salads and "$2 corkage" ("yes, two").

CAMPANILE 26 | 24 | 24 | $51 |
624 S. La Brea Ave. (bet. W. 6th St. & Wilshire Blvd.), 323-938-1447;
www.campanilerestaurant.com
"First choice" for even the pickiest palates, this "gourmand's
institution" turns out "terrific" Cal-Med "food that only gets
better", thanks to "flawless" chef-owner Mark Peel who's
"always at the helm", and his "ever-so-attentive" staff; with a
"delightful" "architectural space" built by Charlie Chaplin, the
experience is "worth every Benjamin", declare disciples, who
predict that you'll remember your meal here "for the next 20 years";
N.B. co-founder Nancy Silverton is no longer involved.

Capo ⊠ 26 | 24 | 23 | $71 |
1810 Ocean Ave. (Pico Blvd.), Santa Monica, 310-394-5550
"Sell your first son into slavery" if you must, but don't miss chef/
co-owner Bruce Marder's "exquisite" Italian masterpieces at this
Santa Monica *ne plus ultra* where "cool art" and a wood-burning
fireplace set the scene for regular "celebrity sightings"; sure the
"extensive wine list" created by partner Steve Wallace of Wally's
Wine Shop fame is "stellar", and "more exorbitant than Westside
real estate", but for most, it's "worth every extravagant dollar" –
"if you're signing that two-picture deal and the studio is paying."

Chaya Brasserie 24 | 23 | 21 | $45 |
8741 Alden Dr. (bet. Beverly Blvd. & 3rd St.), West Hollywood,
310-859-8833; www.thechaya.com
"Consistently wonderful for more than 20 years", this "old standby"
in West Hollywood serves "dreamy" Asian-Eclectic dishes paired
with "fun cocktails" (like raspberry or litchi martinis) to diners more
concerned with "creative" cuisine than a "roaring scene"; while
the room is "a tad too noisy", the "friendly" staff and the "very LA
stargazing" make this a "still hot" "place where you don't have to
wait a month to get in."

CHEESECAKE FACTORY 20 | 18 | 18 | $24 |
364 N. Beverly Dr. (Brighton Way), Beverly Hills, 310-278-7270
11647 San Vicente Blvd. (bet. Barrington Ave. & Wilshire Blvd.),
Brentwood, 310-826-7111
4142 Via Marina St. (Admiralty Way), Marina del Rey,
310-306-3344
2 W. Colorado Blvd. (Fair Oaks Ave.), Pasadena, 626-584-6000
605 N. Harbor Dr. (190th St.), Redondo Beach, 310-376-0466
Sherman Oaks Galleria, 15301 Ventura Blvd. (Sepulveda Blvd.),
Sherman Oaks, 818-906-0700
Thousand Oaks Mall, 442 W. Hillcrest Dr. (Lynn Rd.), Thousand Oaks,
805-371-9705

(continued)

CHEESECAKE FACTORY

Warner Center Trillium, 6324 Canoga Ave. (Victory Blvd.), Woodland Hills, 818-883-9900

www.thecheesecakefactory.com

Even die-hard chain-haters confess to periodic "gorge-athons" at this "solid" American chain where the menu "goes on for miles" and the "gargantuan portions" could "feed a small army"; it's a good "value", but the trade-off lies in "hit-or-miss" service, "noisy" atmosphere (it's "always a mob scene") and the "painful" wait for a table – a "purgatory" that can last "two or three eternities."

Chinois on Main   26 | 20 | 22 | $55

2709 Main St. (bet. Ashland Ave. & Ocean Park Blvd.), Santa Monica, 310-392-9025; www.wolfgangpuck.com

The "original gem of the Wolfgang Puck empire", Santa Monica's two-decade-old "epicurean's delight" – aka the "granddaddy of French-Asian dining" – "continues to shine", groupies gush, through its "transcendent" cuisine that "will never go out of style"; even if a few pucker at the "intolerable" noise level in the packed-"like-sardines" space – and declare the whole experience is "not all it's cracked up to be" – supporters swear it's "where to go for your last meal."

Christine   25 | 19 | 23 | $39

Hillside Vlg., 24530 Hawthorne Blvd. (Via Valmonte), Torrance, 310-373-1952; www.restaurantchristine.com

With a "creative" menu that "beckons for multiple visits", and "congenial" service from the "knowledgeable foodie staff", "true gourmet" chef-owner Christine Brown "packs them in year after year" at this South Bay "rarity" for "delicious and artful" Med–Pacific Rim fare; the "imaginative" dishes take advantage of "the freshest seasonal produce", so admirers' only objection is that the "cozy" space in a mini-mall could be "a little bigger."

Depot, The ⊠   24 | 22 | 22 | $38

1250 Cabrillo Ave. (Torrance Blvd.), Torrance, 310-787-7501; www.depotrestaurant.com

Auto execs and "all those who love" "innovative" food board the chew-chew train for this "terrific" "destination" housed in an Old Torrance railroad station, an "always packed" whistle-stop thanks to the "superb" Eclectic cuisine from "gracious" chef-owner Michael Shafer's "creative" kitchen; the "outstanding" service and free valet parking help make this "gem of the South Bay" just the ticket for everything from "business lunches" to "special events."

Derek's ⊠   27 | 22 | 25 | $54

181 E. Glenarm St. (Marengo Ave.), Pasadena, 626-799-5252; www.dereks.com

"Great host" Derek Dickenson titillates "serious food lovers" with "innovative" Cal-French cuisine full of "beautiful, balanced flavors" and paired with "outstanding" wines at his "homey", "romantic" bistro set in an "unlikely location" "in a Pasadena strip mall"; sit near the "inviting fireplace" and indulge in "quiet conversation" – it's a "classy adult dining experience", enhanced all the more by the "tremendously knowledgeable staff"; N.B. wear a jacket and leave the kids at home.

Frenchy's Bistro
27 | 16 | 24 | $42

4137 E. Anaheim St. (bet. Termino & Ximeno Aves.), Long Beach, 562-494-8787; www.frenchysbistro.com

"Don't let the drab exterior" or "off-the-beaten path" neighborhood "put you off" because this "charming little" French "bistro is among the best tables in town" – in fact, "everything changes once you're inside", with "Parisian husband-and-wife" team Andre and Valerie Angles offering "seriously good, seriously authentic" Gallic cuisine", "carefully selected wines" and live music on weekends; if a few whiners "wish it would move", others realize a "nicer location" would mean "higher prices."

Giorgio Baldi
27 | 17 | 21 | $60

114 W. Channel Rd. (PCH), Santa Monica, 310-573-1660; www.giorgiobaldi.com

"Don't let the stars distract you" from the "delicious authentic food" at this namesake chef-owner's "perfect beachy neighborhood" Italian; the "crowded", "noisy" Santa Monica digs are filled with "show-biz" types savoring a "stellar wine list" and pasta so "sublime" "you almost cry when finished"; but service turns some surveyors snarky: it's "great if you're famous", but it can be "too cool for mere mortals"; P.S. DIYers "buy the house sauce" en route "out the door."

Grace
26 | 25 | 25 | $58

7360 Beverly Blvd. (Fuller Ave.), 323-934-4400; www.gracerestaurant.com

Still "excellent in every way", this Beverly Boulevard standout from chef-owner and "talented fella" Neal Fraser is a "lovely experience" thanks to "adventurous" New American cuisine, "stellar service" (even if you're not "Ashton or Leo") and Michael Berman's "soothing, contemporary" interior; if a few are put off by presentation that's "too fussy" and atmosphere that's "a tad sceney", for most this "smashing" place remains an "icon."

Grill on the Alley, The
24 | 21 | 23 | $52

(aka The Grill)
9560 Dayton Way (Wilshire Blvd.), Beverly Hills, 310-276-0615; www.thegrill.com

Serving up "down-to-earth", yet "gourmet" American food and "hard-to-pass-up martinis" to an "abundance of agents" and "power brokers", this "clubby" Beverly Hills "standby" still gets nods for "excellent" steaks, "off-the-hook" burgers and "hearty" "comfort food", all served "professionally"; the "great old-style" setting makes you "feel like a player", especially at "lunch, when everyone who's anyone is here" – but "forget the [green leather] booths", because they're "for the real" heavy "hitters."

Hamasaku ☒
27 | 18 | 23 | $49

11043 Santa Monica Blvd. (Sepulveda Blvd.), West LA, 310-479-7636; www.hamasakula.com

"Oh, my! I've died and gone to sushi heaven", sigh Japanese junkies enamored by this West LA hot spot, where "you're sure to see one celebrity or another" – and pay "insane" prices for some of the "most creative rolls in town" and "great cuts of fish"; it helps that owner Toshi Kihara "makes it an incredible, personal experience" even for the non-famous, but "don't bother without reservations."

Hotel Bel-Air Restaurant | 25 | 28 | 27 | $67 |

Hotel Bel-Air, 701 Stone Canyon Rd. (Sunset Blvd.), Bel Air, 310-472-1211;
www.hotelbelair.com

"Heaven on earth" is how hedonists hail this haute "hideaway" in
the "charming" Hotel Bel-Air, a "breathtaking" oasis that "wows"
the "rich" and "famous" with its "sublimely romantic" setting,
"delightful garden patio", "superlative service" from an "attentive",
"pampering" staff and "exceptional" Cal-French fare; be warned,
though, that this "top-of-the-line" experience comes at a "top
price", and "try not to stare at the star or starlet at the next table";
P.S. word is that "Nancy Reagan loves this place."

JiRaffe | 26 | 22 | 24 | $49 |

502 Santa Monica Blvd. (5th St.), Santa Monica, 310-917-6671;
www.jirafferestaurant.com

Chef-owner Raphael Lunetta's "exquisite" Californian cuisine made
with "fresh, seasonal ingredients" attains "understated perfection"
at this "perennial favorite" with "staying power" in Santa Monica;
"sophisticated without being stuffy", it "feels like a slice" of New
York City "on the left coast" with "extremely cordial service"; if
rubberneckers find the noise level "overbearing", others suggest
it's "quieter" upstairs and just right for "that special occasion
like selling your script"; P.S. the prix fixe "Monday night bistro
dinners are a delicious bargain."

Joe's | 27 | 21 | 23 | $48 |

1023 Abbot Kinney Blvd. (bet. Main St. & Westminster Ave.),
Venice, 310-399-5811; www.joesrestaurant.com

"Eat at Joe's", as in Joe Miller's, and "you won't be disappointed",
intone fans of this "crowded" Venice "gem" where the "genius"
chef-owner "works the room" – actually a "mad labyrinth" of
"unpretentious", recently refurbished rooms, plus a "neat" patio –
and "makes you feel like he cooked" the "magnificently executed"
Cal–New French cuisine "just for you"; if a few have "no clue why
it's so beloved", no sleuthing is necessary for loyalists who deem
the prix fixe lunch "dollar for dollar, bite for bite, the best value
in the city."

Josie Restaurant | 27 | 23 | 25 | $55 |

2424 Pico Blvd. (25th St.), Santa Monica, 310-581-9888;
www.josierestaurant.com

"Gastronomic delight", "culinary bliss" – surveyors run out of
supper-latives to describe chef Josie Le Balch's "flawless"
French-accented New American cuisine at this Santa Monica
"gem"; enthusiasts "embrace" the "imaginative but comforting"
dishes, including "earthy truffle fries" and the "best game in
town", cradled by "seamless" service in a "classy" setting, with
"soft lighting and a glowing fireplace"; if a few whine the "excellent
wine list" is "pricey", most reveal "as you leave, you're already
planning your return."

KATSU-YA | 28 | 14 | 20 | $37 |

16542 Ventura Blvd. (Hayvenhurst Ave.), Encino, 818-788-2396
11680 Ventura Blvd. (Colfax Ave.), Studio City, 818-985-6976

Cloaked in a mini-mall and packed with "incognito starlets",
this "noisy" Encino "heaven" and Studio City "industry fave"
serve sushi that's "as good as sushi gets"; "don't go without a
reservation", but do "order everything from the specials board",

and be ready to "tolerate the crowds"; finally, eat your "sublime", "extremely fresh" fish quickly because "they're always rushing to get you out."

La Cachette   27 | 25 | 24 | $58
10506 Little Santa Monica Blvd. (Thayer Ave.), Century City, 310-470-4992; www.lacachetterestaurant.com
"Expect graciousness at every turn" at this "delicious bit of France" in Century City, attest *amis* who agree that "brilliant" chef-owner Jean Francois Meteigner is "doing brilliant things" with "modern French" fare at this recently refurbished "hideaway" "for grown-ups"; join the "great mix of blue-haired ladies" and "high-powered" "sunglass-wearing Hollywood producers" and you'll be rewarded with "creative cuisine" that's lavished with "Gallic flavor" yet "appropriately light" "for the California palate."

L'Orangerie ⌧   25 | 28 | 26 | $84
903 N. La Cienega Blvd. (Willoughby Ave.), West Hollywood, 310-652-9770; www.lorangerie.com
"Old Hollywood glamour" lives on at this "timeless", "tip-top" special-occasion spot on La Cienega that's "magnificent, every step of the way, and terribly romantic" too ("Brad and Jennifer spent one of their last nights together here"), with a "sublime", "fresh flower"–bedecked setting, "outstanding" French food and "service a king would be proud of"; "dress up", "go early, have a glass of champagne in the lounge and listen to the piano" and presto, "you feel like you're in Paris."

Maison Akira   27 | 21 | 24 | $51
713 E. Green St. (bet. El Molino & Oak Knoll Aves.), Pasadena, 626-796-9501; www.maisonakira.com
You might "feel like you're eating dishes from the *Iron Chef*" when you dine at this "intimate", "posh" Franco-Japanese "destination" near the Pasadena Playhouse Theatre where "it's so quiet, you can hear a pin drop" and the "accommodating staff" "never makes you feel rushed"; "lunchtime bento boxes are a bargain", but expect to "fork over a wad of cash" for "very impressive" "big nights" out.

MATSUHISA   28 | 16 | 23 | $74
129 N. La Cienega Blvd. (bet. Clifton Way & Wilshire Blvd.), Beverly Hills, 310-659-9639; www.nobumatsuhisa.com
You're "almost certain to see a celebrity" at this "unassuming" Beverly Hills Japanese on La Cienega, "where the worldwide Nobu empire began" back in 1987; most surveyors are still left "speechless" by the "inspired" "edible art" produced by this "temple of sushi" and cooked fare (the much-"copied" "miso cod still rocks"); "the secret is knowing what to order", so either "go with someone [savvy] or let the staff direct the show"; otherwise, "you'll be horrified" by the seemingly "overhyped" eats at "insanely expensive" prices.

MÉLISSE ⌧   28 | 26 | 26 | $78
1104 Wilshire Blvd. (11th St.), Santa Monica, 310-395-0881; www.melisse.com
"Dress your best" – you're about to "embark on a fabulous journey" to "nirvana" when you visit this "swanky" Santa Monica destination, rated No. 1 for Food in the Los Angeles area for its "brilliant" French–New American fare; chef-owner Josiah Citrin's near-"perfect" creations (tip: "the tasting menu with wine pairings

is the way to go") are "the culinary equivalent of the Louvre" – "this isn't food, it's art" – and in addition, these treasures are "deftly" presented by a "formal", but "superlative" staff; it all adds up to a "memorable splurge", so "save up for the pleasure of eating here."

Mimosa ⊠　　　24　18　22　$43
8009 Beverly Blvd. (bet. N. Edinburgh & N. Laurel Aves.), 323-655-8895; www.mimosarestaurant.com
"*Fantastique* chef"-owner "Jean Pierre Bosc does great things" with "satisfying", "superb", yet "simple dishes like cassoulet" boasting "complex flavors" at his "little find" on Beverly that feels like "France, without all the frills"; "charming" and "intimate", it's the "perfect place to take your sweetheart on Valentine's Day" for "timeless bistro fare" "at its best."

Mori Sushi ⊠　　　26　18　21　$62
11500 W. Pico Blvd. (Gateway Blvd.), West LA, 310-479-3939
"Indulge in the" "transcendental omakase" at this "sublime" West LA Japanese and let "perfectionist" master chef Mori Onodera concoct an "astounding" array of "fresh and delicate" raw fish creations, "which he serves on ceramic plates he also makes"; even in this "minimalist" setting, worshipers at the shrine of Mori-san (he's "our hero") swear it's "worth the splurge" to dine at "one of the best sushi bars in" the city.

NOBU MALIBU　　　27　20　23　$66
3835 Cross Creek Rd. (PCH), Malibu, 310-317-9140; www.nobumatsuhisa.com
It may be "Malibu-casual but an extraordinary dining" experience still awaits at this "unbelievably inviting", "lively scene" that "has Nobu magic" aplenty; follow the "knowledgeable" servers' advice" and order "astonishing" dishes along with the "perfect sushi" –"every bite is worth every dollar" – then "star gaze" as you "graze" (there are so many celebs it's "distracting"); if a few find the "drive a drawback" and the "decor nondescript", most "would go every night" if they could.

Providence　　　▽　25　25　27　$92
5955 Melrose Ave. (Cole Ave.), 323-460-4170; www.providencela.com
Chef/co-owner Michael Cimarusti is "the anointed Neptune of California" – he's even "surpassed" the "high bar he set for himself at the Water Grill" at this "outstanding" new seafooder in the "spiffed-up" former Patina space near Paramount Studios where frontman/partner Donato Poto also oversees the "superb service"; early-comers enthuse it's the "best fish-centered menu in LA" – we "didn't know that it could be fixed in so many creative ways" – plus the "wine pairings are astounding."

Saddle Peak Lodge　　　26　27　25　$58
419 Cold Canyon Rd. (Piuma Rd.), Calabasas, 818-222-3888; www.saddlepeaklodge.com
Whether you park yourself "by the fireplace and wallow in rustic elegance" or sit "outside and listen to the brook", you're in for an "epicurean escape" at this "hunting lodge"–themed New American steakhouse, a "wilderness retreat" set in a former Pony Express station in Calabasas; while the menu is more streamlined under chef Mark Murillo, it's "still the place to go" "if you're game for

game, have the bucks" and lust for farm-raised "meats you only see on *Animal Planet*"; it's all served by a "superb staff" with a "terrific wine list to boot."

Shiro   26 | 18 | 24 | $44 |
1505 Mission St. (Fair Oaks Ave.), South Pasadena, 626-799-4774; www.restaurantshiro.com
Definitely a "delight, year in and year out", this "perennial favorite" in South Pasadena is "worth the trip" for "lovely presentations" of "inventive" seafood-centric Asian fusion cuisine "done with finesse", including the "amazing" fried catfish in ponzu sauce; a "wonderful" staff makes you "feel welcome" and the setting is an "oasis of relaxation", making it a "great date place", especially "if you want to impress a foodie."

Sona ⑤   27 | 23 | 26 | $77 |
401 N. La Cienega Blvd. (bet. Beverly Blvd. & Melrose Ave.), West Hollywood, 310-659-7708; www.sonarestaurant.com
"Simply the best husband-wife team cooking and baking in LA", David and Michelle Myers are "visionaries" who "always take risks" in their freestyle approach to modern French cuisine, adding "subtle twists" and "unexpected ingredients" that result in an "astonishingly good" "dining experience" on La Cienega; the "staff bends over backwards" to assure that you have a "memorable culinary adventure", and the 1,300-selection wine list "boggles the mind" – just "make sure you're sitting down when you get the bill."

SPAGO   26 | 25 | 24 | $66 |
176 N. Cañon Dr. (Wilshire Blvd.), Beverly Hills, 310-385-0880; www.wolfgangpuck.com
Wolfgang Puck's "incomparable" Beverly Hills flagship "lives up to its impossible reputation" and provides a refresher course on what a "premier dining" establishment can be; it's still the "center of the universe" for foodies who treat themselves to Lee Hefter's "unforgettable" Californian cuisine (including the "ever-famous pizza") and Sherry Yard's "incredible desserts" served by a staff "that treats you like a star" in a "celeb"-filled room; so, while the tabs may be "sky high", it remains "unforgettable."

Sushi Sasabune ⑤   27 | 7 | 18 | $56 |
11300 Nebraska Ave. (Sawtelle Blvd.), West LA, 310-268-8380
"Go with the flow" and put yourself "at the mercy of the chef" at this West LA Japanese where even patrons who object to omakase on principle bow down before "transcendental", "bliss-inducing" sushi packed with "fascinating flavors and textures"; it's a "unique experience", and most take a tip from devotees who forget about the "shabby decor" and sit back and eat up till either their stomachs or "pocketbooks call it quits."

Valentino ⑤   26 | 23 | 25 | $65 |
3115 Pico Blvd. (bet. 31st & 32nd Sts.), Santa Monica, 310-829-4313; www.welovewine.com
After over 30 years, "consummate host"-owner "Piero Selvaggio still deserves his reputation as an innovator" offering "world-class Italian" cuisine at SM's "chic", "ultimate date spot"; the "truly memorable experience" begins "the instant you walk in the door" and continues with "so many beautiful moments", from dining on "superb" dishes to choosing a bottle from the "extraordinary wine

list" comparable to "Webster's dictionary"; if a few feel it's "coasting on past reputation", for most it "never disappoints."

Water Grill 27 | 24 | 25 | $58
544 S. Grand Ave. (bet. 5th & 6th Sts.), 213-891-0900; www.watergrill.com
"If the fish were any fresher, it would be on the end of your rod and reel", proclaim patrons of this "clubby", "classy" "splurge"-worthy Downtown seafooder that's "perfect for that special occasion", "pre-theater treat" or "power business dinner"; if a few feel that new chef David LeFevre "needs time to catch up", most "enjoy every morsel" of the "exotic, flavorful fin-fare, exquisitely presented by a down-to-earth staff" and "worth the dent to your wallet."

Miami

TOP FOOD RANKING

Restaurant	Cuisine
28 Francesco	Peruvian
27 Romeo's Cafe	Northern Italian
Nobu Miami Beach	Japanese/Peruvian
Chef Allen's	Eclectic
Matsuri	Japanese
26 Ortanique on the Mile	Caribbean
Prime One Twelve	Seafood/Steakhouse
Azul	Asian/Med.
Mark's South Beach	New American
Norman's	New World
Joe's Stone Crab	Seafood
Osteria del Teatro	Northern Italian
Shoji	Japanese
Pascal's on Ponce	New French
Talula	New American
AltaMar	Seafood
Toni's Sushi Bar	Japanese
25 Capital Grille	Steakhouse
La Dorada	Seafood/Spanish
Palme d'Or	New French

OTHER NOTEWORTHY PLACES

Bond St.	Japanese
Cacao	Nuevo Latino
Carmen the Restaurant	New American
Cheesecake Factory	American
Graziano's Parilla	Argentinian/Steakhouse
Houston's	American
Lan	Pan-Asian
La Sandwicherie	French
Mosaico/Salero	Spanish/Tapas
Nemo	New American
Porcão	Brazilian/Steakhouse
Restaurant at the Setai	Eclectic
River Oyster Bar	Seafood
Tamarind	Thai
TapTap	Haitian
Timo	Italian/Mediterranean
Tropical Chinese	Chinese
Versailles	Cuban
Vix	Eclectic
Wish	New American

AltaMar
26 | 15 | 21 | $41

1223 Lincoln Rd. (Alton Rd.), Miami Beach, 305-532-3061
You may "have passed it a hundred times" and never noticed this "low-key" "neighborhood gem" on the "quiet end of Lincoln Road"; finatics swear it is one of the "best on South Beach" for chef-owner Claudio Giordano's "exquisitely prepared" Med-inspired seafood and for daily specials that are "the stars of the show"; it's a "rare find" that comes with "modest prices" and, blessedly, "no attitude."

Azul
26 | 27 | 25 | $66

Mandarin Oriental Hotel, 500 Brickell Key Dr. (8th St.), 305-913-8358;
www.mandarinoriental.com
The Mandarin Oriental's "cool", "sublime" eatery soars with "the best" combination in the city: "spectacular", swoon-worthy Asian-accented Mediterranean food, a "gorgeous" room, "breathtaking views" of Downtown and "polished" service; though it may be "pricey", and many "miss" chef Michelle Bernstein (who left well over a year ago), in the minds of the majority, this "class act" continues to thrive "at the top."

Bond St. Lounge ◗
25 | 21 | 19 | $48

Townhouse Hotel, 150 20th St. (Collins Ave.), Miami Beach, 305-398-1806;
www.townhousehotel.com
"Beautiful people" populate this "small" subterranean Japanese (a relative of the NYC original) in SoBe's "chic" Townhouse Hotel; a "dark", "sexy" scene that's a cross between "*Miami Vice* and *Nip/Tuck*" is the backdrop for "incredible sushi" and other "fabulous" offerings; the "mini-marshmallow ottomans" may be "uncomfortable" for some, but many know you're virtually guaranteed to "impress a date" here.

Cacao ⊠
25 | 24 | 23 | $51

141 Giralda Ave. (bet. Galiano St. & Ponce de Leon Blvd.), Coral Gables,
305-445-1001; www.cacaorestaurant.com
"Ca-wow!" exclaim admirers of this "amazing" Coral Gables Nuevo Latino, where you can indulge in "exotic", "extraordinary" fare from the "incredible" Edgar Leal in a "pretty", "jewel-box" setting enhanced by "lighting that makes everyone look gorgeous", an "excellent staff" and a "knowledgeable" sommelier; sure, it's "expensive", but the "spectacular desserts" help to make it "worth every penny."

Capital Grille, The
25 | 24 | 25 | $57

444 Brickell Ave. (SE 5th St.), 305-374-4500; www.thecapitalgrille.com
Lobbyists laud this "high-class" DC-based steakhouse as "the best of the big-name [chophouse] chains"; the "beautiful", "clubby" confines come complete with the requisite "dark wood" accents, cigar storage rooms and "extensive" wine list and an "exceptional staff" serves "flawless" steaks and seafood, and "great sides"; just remember to "raise capital" before you go.

Carmen the Restaurant
24 | 20 | 22 | $57

David William Hotel, 700 Biltmore Way (Cardena St.), Coral Gables,
305-913-1944; www.carmentherestaurant.com
Chef-owner Carmen Gonzales "hits her stride" and "makes the rounds" in the dining room at this "elegant" eatery in the David William Hotel; the Latin-influenced New American fare and "innovative" Puerto Rican specialties are "big on flavor", so if

detractors detect off notes in "uneven service", far more maintain this "gem" provides a "wonderful experience"

CHEESECAKE FACTORY

20 | 18 | 19 | $26

Aventura Mall, 19501 Biscayne Blvd. (NE 195th St.), Aventura, 305-792-9696
CocoWalk, 3015 Grand Ave. (Virginia St.), Coconut Grove, 305-447-9898 ●
Dadeland Mall, 7497 N. Kendall Dr. (88th St.), Kendall, 305-665-5400
www.thecheesecakefactory.com

The "best chain – ever", aver acolytes of these South Florida Americans whose "encyclopedic" menus feature "giant-sized portions" of everything – from "burgers to Thai" – and the "ultrarich", "unbelievable" namesake desserts, served by a "cheerful", "efficient" staff; sure, "the line goes all the way to I-95" and it's so loud you may want to "bring your megaphone", but the "consistent" reasonably priced fare and "kid-friendly" credo make it a "winner."

CHEF ALLEN'S

27 | 22 | 25 | $65

19088 NE 29th Ave. (bet. 28th Ave. & NE 191st St.), Aventura, 305-935-2900; www.chefallens.com

The "genius" evident in "inimitable" chef-owner Allen Susser's "top-notch" fare has earned him his "well-deserved reputation" and puts his "high-end" Aventura Eclectic into the "classic" category in the hearts of admirers; "every bite" of food ferried by a "polished staff" (you'll "feel like royalty") is a "sheer delight", even though a few fuss that the decor "could use an upgrade."

FRANCESCO ☒

28 | 17 | 24 | $43

325 Alcazar Ave. (bet. Le Jeune Rd. & Salzedo St.), Coral Gables, 305-446-1600; www.francescorestaurant.com

Nabbing the No.1 ranking for Food in Miami is this *pequeña* Peruvian on Coral Gables' Restaurant Row, whose "efficient" staff serves "tiraditos that melt in your mouth", "out-of-this-world squid ink pasta" and "amazing seviche", as well as a "value wine" list that's "ripe for the picking"; no wonder savvy surveyors smile that, even if the "formal" "decor is unspectacular", this experience is "as close as it gets to being in Lima."

Graziano's Parrilla Argentina

25 | 20 | 20 | $41

9227 SW 40th St./Bird Rd. (92nd Ave.), Westchester, 305-225-0008; www.parrilla.com

True-blue beef eaters say "if you can't make it to Argentina", then head to Westchester for this "perennially packed" strip-mall steakhouse where you'll find "massive portions" of "superb" grilled meats accompanied by "service that's "friendly", but "slow"; P.S. bring "your wine mag", as the "impressive" list bulges with "great South American selections."

HOUSTON'S

21 | 20 | 21 | $32

201 Miracle Mile (Ponce de Leon Blvd.), Coral Gables, 305-529-0141
17355 Biscayne Blvd. (NE 172nd St.), North Miami Beach, 305-947-2000
www.houstons.com

Floridians fare well at this national chain known for "rock-solid" American food, especially "great burgers" and the now legendary "fabulous" spinach dip; the "comfortable", "clubby" setting, "consistently good service" and "active bar scene" is a testament to their popularity and reason for many to endure "long waits."

JOE'S STONE CRAB
26 | 19 | 22 | $58

11 Washington Ave. (1st St.), Miami Beach, 305-673-0365;
www.joesstonecrab.com

A "treasured institution" and Miami's Most Popular spot for the fifth straight year, this 1913 South Beacher "lives up to the hype" with "the best stone crabs on earth" accompanied by "great" hash browns and an obligatory "killer Key lime pie" served by legions of "wholly professional" veterans in a setting akin to a "glorified diner"; whether you "claw your way in" or endure the "hellish" wait, be ready to "shell out" a lot of cash; N.B. this trap's shut from August till mid-October.

La Dorada ◑
25 | 19 | 23 | $60

177 Giralda Ave. (Ponce de Leon Blvd.), Coral Gables,
305-446-2002

Coral Gables' "elegant" Spanish "sleeper" offers "exceptional" seafood (with fresh catch flown in daily) that's brought to table by "flawless servers"; it's a "memorable" experience to many, even if some aver that given the "shocking prices", the fish "should be made out of 18 karats."

Lan
23 | 11 | 20 | $23

Dadeland Station, 8332 S. Dixie Hwy. (84th St.), Kendall,
305-661-8141

Overlook the "odd" shopping-mall locale and "simple decor" at suburbia's "best-kept secret", a Pan-Asian "jewel" in Kendall capturing kudos for its "tasty" fare including "fresh sushi", "yummy noodles" and an "amazing lunch special"; the "friendly" staff and "reasonable prices" keep it "popular."

La Sandwicherie ◑
25 | 10 | 19 | $12

229 14th St. (bet. Collins & Washington Aves.), Miami Beach,
305-532-8934; www.lasandwicherie.com

The ultimate "French fast food" can be found at this "tiny" SoBe counter serving the "best sandwiches you can get your hands on" (including "fab" pâté and Camembert versions), "outstanding smoothies" and "amazing salads"; that it's "near a gas station" and a "tattoo parlor" ensures "interesting people-watching"; N.B. open 9 AM to 5 AM.

Mark's South Beach
26 | 22 | 24 | $63

Hotel Nash, 1120 Collins Ave. (bet. 11th & 12th Sts.), Miami Beach,
305-604-9050; www.chefmark.com

"Break out the Gucci" and "head to the hull" of the Hotel Nash, where "celebrity chef"-owner Mark Militello "elevates" palates by turning out "trendy, yet tremendous" New American creations that continue to "break new ground" "without being weird"; the "welcoming, knowledgeable staff" makes their mark, too; but while the "gorgeous" decor may evoke "the '30s", the prices are strictly "21st century."

MATSURI
27 | 14 | 21 | $28

5759 Bird Rd. (Red Rd.), South Miami, 305-663-1615

The "best sushi in town", an "extensive", "authentic" menu and "fair prices" account for the acclaim of this "unassuming" South Miami strip-maller that "mustn't be overlooked"; it's the standby for many (especially for "lots of Japanese patrons"), so don't be surprised if the staff's stymied "when it gets busy."

Mosaico/Salero ⊠   24 | 24 | 24 | $54
1000 S. Miami Ave. (10th St.), 305-371-3473;
www.mosaicorestaurant.com
This bi-level Spanish set in a 1923 firehouse mesmerizes devotees
with Jordi Valles' "spectacular presentations" of "transcendent",
"new wave" cooking that "pushes the envelope"; the "formal"
upstairs features a "beautiful" room and rooftop area displaying
"spectacular views"; the more casual downstairs serves tapas.

Nemo   25 | 22 | 22 | $54
100 Collins Ave. (1st St.), Miami Beach, 305-532-4550;
www.nemorestaurant.com
Superlatives stream in for this "low-key" New American that
charms with "fabulous" fare, "stellar fish" dishes, a "great raw bar"
and a Sunday brunch that ranks among "the greatest around";
the "light-hearted, terrific staff" helps make for an "unbeatable",
though "pricey", time; P.S. snare a seat in the "beautiful" courtyard
or patio for a uniquely "SoBe experience."

NOBU MIAMI BEACH ◗   27 | 23 | 23 | $71
The Shore Club, 1901 Collins Ave. (20th St.), Miami Beach, 305-695-3232;
www.noburestaurants.com
Nobu Matsuhisa's "chichi" South Beach branch of his NYC flagship
"shines as brightly as the trendy, flashy crowd" ready for "mind-
blowing" Japanese-Peruvian cuisine (the black cod miso is
"an undisputed classic"), "remarkably un-SoBe service" and the
inevitable "killer waits" in an "ultramod" blue-tiled setting; do
yourself a favor, though, and "bring your Amex Black card" and
"make sure your date's worth it"; N.B. takes reservations only for
parties of six or more.

NORMAN'S ⊠   26 | 23 | 25 | $66
21 Almeria Ave. (Douglas Rd.), Coral Gables, 305-446-6767;
www.normans.com
After more than a decade atop the Miami dining scene, "master"
chef-owner Norman Van Aken's "world-class", eponymous eatery
in Coral Gables remains the benchmark for "original", "seductively
delicious" New World fare served in a "classy" setting by a staff
that "makes you feel important"; though you'll "pay top dollar" for
the privilege of dining here, it's "worth whatever it costs."

Ortanique on the Mile   26 | 23 | 23 | $51
278 Miracle Mile (Le Jeune Rd.), Coral Gables, 305-446-7710;
www.cindyhutsoncuisine.com
It may be tough to "combine fine dining with Caribbean influences",
but chef-owner Cindy Hutson "pulls it off" with her "exciting" New
World fare that's "a party for the palate" at this "paradise" on
Miracle Mile in Coral Gables; though the space is "tight", the staff
does an "incredible job", and the "beautiful", tropical-themed
setting puts this "gem" "at the top of everyone's list."

Osteria del Teatro ⊠   26 | 15 | 24 | $54
1443 Washington Ave. (Española Way), Miami Beach, 305-538-7850
"You can't go wrong" at this SoBe standby where the quarters are
"tight" and the loyal audience applauds the "excellent" Northern
Italian standards, "attentive service" and "window seating" that
allows you to "watch the world go by"; if the hostile hiss the "high"
tabs, others offer that it "would be a bargain at twice the price";

F	D	S	C

N.B after 10 PM, night-owls can get the $18 'twilight special' that includes wine, salad and pasta.

Palme d'Or ☒

25	25	25	$70

Biltmore Hotel, 1200 Anastasia Ave. (Granada Blvd.), Coral Gables, 305-445-1926; www.biltmorehotel.com
For a taste of "five-star hotel dining found only in Europe", this "elegant" New French in Coral Gables' historic Biltmore Hotel ranks among the "best in South Florida" thanks to the "astonishing" small-plates menu devised by chef Philippe Ruiz, "superb service" and "romantic" environs; it's there "when you want to splurge" for a trip to "gastronomic heaven"; N.B. closed Sundays and Mondays.

Pascal's on Ponce ☒

26	19	23	$53

2611 Ponce de Leon Blvd. (bet. Almeria & Valencia Aves.), Coral Gables, 305-444-2024; www.pascalmiami.com
"Thank goodness" for this Coral Gables "gem" where the kitchen turns out "standout" New French food under the direction of chef Pascal Oudin, while wife Ann-Louise oversees a floor crew that "makes everyone feel important"; the "charming", though "tight", quarters recently received a "face-lift", and a new liquor license may make it even more of a "must."

Porcão ●

21	17	21	$47

801 Brickell Bay Dr. (SE 8th St.), 305-373-2777; www.rodizioplace.com
Meat mavens find it hard to be un-moo-ved at this "eat-till-you-drop" Downtown Brazilian rodizio, whose "friendly", skewer-bearing servers carry "fantastic churrascaria" fleshed out by an "excellent salad bar" to patrons prepared to "pork out"; it all makes for an "entertaining meal", as long as you're not done in by the pre-supper cocktails.

Prime One Twelve ●

26	24	22	$70

112 Ocean Dr. (1st St.), Miami Beach, 305-532-8112; www.prime112.com
It's always prime time at this "sceney" SoBe steakhouse/seafooder that "blows its competitors away" with "perfect" (and "pricey") oversized steaks, "delicious seviches" and desserts that induce "outer body experiences"; you may have to wait "forever" – "even with a reservation" – but at least the "hot bar" area offers complimentary chow and "celeb sightings."

Restaurant at the Setai, The

–	–	–	VE

The Setai, 2001 Collins Ave. (20th St.), Miami Beach, 305-520-6000; www.setai.com
A host of chefs from around the globe labor in the sprawling exhibition kitchen of this new eatery in South Beach's über-luxe Setai Hotel; a young staff delivers pristine samplings of Eclectic, multinational fare to patrons for whom price is no object; the sleek, elegant teak- and stone-laden dining rooms and sunken pods that dot the courtyard's shallow pools and pergolas are sure to wow the jet-set clientele.

River Oyster Bar, The ☒

24	22	22	$40

650 S. Miami Ave. (SW 7th St.), 305-530-1915; www.therivermiami.com
There's more than just the "amazing oysters" at this "civilized" "winner", an "upscale", yet "comfortable" seafooder near the Miami River that attracts fans with "the best seviche in town", "heavenly calamari" and other "superb" items; the "trendy crowd" fishes for catch over drinks at the "inviting" mahogany bar.

ROMEO'S CAFE
27 | 19 | 27 | $69

2257 SW 22nd St./Coral Way (bet. 22nd & 23rd Aves.), 305-859-2228;
www.romeoscafe.com

"Give yourself over to Romeo" Majano's "creativity" at his "small"
Coral Gables Northern Italian where the "exquisitely planned"
(there's "no printed menu"), "magnificent" six-course meals are
"prepared to your taste" and where the "charming" service makes
you feel "like you're the only one there"; "romantics" report that
the "dimly lit" setting means "your date won't see your tears when
the check arrives."

Shoji ●
26 | 20 | 21 | $49

100 Collins Ave. (bet. 1st & 2nd Sts.), Miami Beach, 305-532-4245;
www.shojisushi.com

South Beach sushiphiles sign on to this "top-flight" Japanese
using "impeccably fresh" fish in "fantastic" fare that goes "far
beyond" the norm; "attentive service" and a "romantic garden"
make it a neighborhood "favorite", and though tabs run high, it's
still "cheaper" than others in its league; N.B. the loss of chef
Shingo Inoue may affect the Food score.

Talula
26 | 20 | 22 | $52

210 23rd St. (bet. Collins Ave. & Dade Blvd.), Miami Beach, 305-672-0778;
www.talulaonline.com

Situated on an "unassuming corner" of South Beach is this
"outstanding" New American bistro created by the "talented",
married team of Andrea Curto-Randazzo and Frank Randazzo; their
"fine-dining oasis" provides a "serious gastronomic experience"
with food that "sings" in a town where it's often "all about
looks"; praise extends to the "comfortable", brick-walled setting
and "friendly servers."

TAMARIND
▽ 24 | 16 | 22 | $26

946 Normandy Dr. (71st St.), Miami Beach, 305-861-6222

Chef-owner (and cookbook author) Vatcharin Bhumichitr's art-filled
"sleeper" in Miami Beach's Normandy Isle proffers "beautiful
presentations" of "excellent" Thai fare that combines classic
dishes with street-food specialties; prices that are "a steal" and
"welcoming staff" turn it into an "unexpected treasure."

TapTap Haitian
21 | 21 | 17 | $28

819 Fifth St. (bet. Jefferson & Meridian Aves.), Miami Beach,
305-672-2898

For some "Haitian flavor with SoBe flair", consider this "funky"
"off-the-beaten-path" standby where you can wash down
the "delicious", "authentic" cooking with "awesome drinks";
though naysayers knockknock the "slow service", "colorful"
decor and "excellent music" (Thursdays–Saturdays) help
atone for it.

Timo
23 | 20 | 21 | $45

17624 Collins Ave. (bet. 175th Terr. & 178th St.), Sunny Isles Beach,
305-936-1008; www.timorestaurant.com

Grab a seat and join the "good-looking crowd" at this Sunny Isles
Italian-Med in a strip mall; it's a "terrific find", thanks to chef Tim
Andriola's "sensuous" cuisine and a "hip" environment overseen
by a "solid", "accommodating" front of the house; devotees declare
it's now officially "on the North Miami radar."

Toni's Sushi Bar ◑   26 | 17 | 22 | $41
1208 Washington Ave. (12th St.), Miami Beach, 305-673-9368
The fish's "always fresh" and the room's "always packed" at this
South Beach sushi "institution" whose "ultratasty" Japanese fare
coupled with an "interesting sake list" has helped win over fans;
one caveat: some say the seats are "tiny", so come early for a
spot at the bar where the "accommodating" chefs and "friendly"
servers make you feel "relaxed."

Tropical Chinese   25 | 17 | 18 | $28
Tropical Park Plaza, 7991 SW 40th St./Bird Rd. (SW 79th Ave.),
Westchester, 305-262-7576
Orient yourself toward this "strip-mall" Westchester Chinese,
whose open kitchen dispenses "incomparable" fare and some of
the "best dim sum east of Hong Kong"; though Sundays mean "long
lines", and surveyors hold a dim view of service ("impersonal"),
the majority maintains the food "makes it worth it."

Versailles ◑   21 | 15 | 18 | $22
3555 SW Eighth St. (SW 35th Ave.), 305-444-0240
"Everyone from high-society types to drag queens" makes a
pilgrimage to this "lively" late-night Little Havana "landmark" to
"rub elbows with politicians", chow down "cheap" Cuban eats or
simply "discover the wonders of café con leche" in a "huge",
"kitschy" complex; even those who quip "it's a tourist trap" (with so
much "gold and mirrors" "you ought to be wearing sunglasses")
agree that "everybody should eat here at least once."

Vix ◑   ∇ 25 | 29 | 21 | $80
Hotel Victor, 1144 Ocean Dr. (bet. 11th & 12th Sts.), Miami Beach,
305-428-1234; www.hotelvictorsouthbeach.com
New and "ultrachic", this South Beach hot spot in the "posh" Hotel
Victor entrances enthusiasts with its "incredible", Jacques Garcia–
designed, jellyfish-themed decor and "spectacular" Eclectic food
that makes you feel like you're taking a culinary trip "around the
world"; though, it's "pricey", it's still "phenomenal" and "worth
all the hype."

Wish   24 | 25 | 22 | $61
The Hotel, 801 Collins Ave. (8th St.), Miami Beach, 305-674-9474;
www.wishrestaurant.com
Romantics retreat to this "serene" South Beach "favorite" where
the "superb", "playful" Asian-influenced New American creations
coupled with a "fabulous" Todd Oldham–designed space featuring
an "enchanting" tropical garden make believers out of many;
while prices are "stiff", come once, many insist, and your "only
compulsion will be to return."

Milwaukee

TOP FOOD RANKING

	Restaurant	Cuisine
29	Sanford	New American
27	Dream Dance	New American
	Ristorante Bartolotta	Northen Italian
26	Immigrant Room/Winery	Eclectic
	Heaven City	New American
	Three Brothers	Serbian
	Eddie Martini's	Steakhouse
	Riversite, The	American
25	Coquette Cafe	French Bistro
	Lake Park Bistro	French Bistro

OTHER NOTEWORTHY PLACES

Restaurant	Cuisine
Bacchus	New American
Dancing Ganesha	Indian
Maggiano's	Southern Italian
Moceans	Seafood
Mr. B's	Steakhouse
Osteria del Mondo	Northern Italian
P.F. Chang's	Chinese
River Lane Inn	Cajun-Creole
Roots	Asian Fusion/Californian
Singha	Thai

F | D | S | C |

Bacchus   − | − | − | E |
Cudahy Towers, 925 E. Wells St. (Prospect Ave.), 414-765-1166;
www.bacchusmke.com
Joe Bartolotta (Lake Park Bistro, Ristorante Bartolotta) breathes
new life into the Downtown space that once housed the Boulevard
Inn, transforming it into a big-city New American with mirrors,
square lampshades and brown-leather banquettes; chef Brandon
Wolff (ex Dream Dance) mans the high-profile kitchen, turning out
trademarks such as braised beef short ribs, day-boat scallops with
parsnip puree and Australian rack of lamb, all confidently served
by a knowledgeable staff.

Coquette Cafe ⊠   25 | 22 | 23 | $33 |
316 N. Milwaukee St. (St. Paul Ave.), 414-291-2655;
www.coquettecafe.com
"Tucked away" in the "trendy" Third Ward, this "charming bistro"
(the "more casual" and "affordable" French "little sister" of award-
winning chef Sandy D'Amato's "renowned Sanford") features
"homey" yet "nuanced" selections (folks "love" the "excellent
hanger steak") "served with a Midwestern lack of pretension" "in a
warm setting"; P.S. proximity to a plethora of playhouses makes it
a "great" "place for pre- or post-theater dining."

Dancing Ganesha `22 | 20 | 20 | $27`
1692-94 N. Van Buren St. (Brady St.), 414-220-0202;
www.dancingganesha.com
When you "want something a little different", try this "inventive"
East Side Indian that "puts a unique twist on" subcontinental fare
via a "creative menu" marked by "deep, rich flavors"; perhaps it's
"not the most authentic", but most say it's "a sure bet", especially if
you "order the edgier" dishes – "they'll make you dance!"

DREAM DANCE 🖾 `27 | 23 | 26 | $53`
Potawatomi Bingo Casino, 1721 W. Canal St. (16th St.), 414-847-7883;
www.paysbig.com
"Hidden away" in Downtown's Potawatomi Bingo Casino is this
"classy" "special-occasion" venue, a "little pot of dining gold"
featuring a "fantastic", "innovative New American" menu that
"showcases local specialties" and is "superbly served" by
"outstanding" staffers who go "above and beyond"; still, it's "not
a dream for" those who "can't get past" its "incongruous setting"
upstairs from a "smoke-filled" "gambling hall"; N.B. the Food rating
may not reflect a post-*Survey* chef change.

EDDIE MARTINI'S `26 | 24 | 26 | $51`
8612 Watertown Plank Rd. (84th St.), 414-771-6680
Diners "step back in time" at this "crowded", "clubby" steakhouse,
a West Side mainstay for "mouthwatering" meat and "delicious
seafood"; "personable" team "servers in white coats" "make you
feel like a favorite", though some say service "can get overdone" –
and you'd better "plan on spending a boatload of money"; N.B. a
post-*Survey* chef change may outdate the Food score.

HEAVEN CITY `26 | 25 | 23 | $40`
S91 W27850 National Ave./Hwy. ES (Edgewood Ave.), Mukwonago,
262-363-5191; www.heavencity.com
"Knowing the history" of this "worth-a-drive" New American set "in
an old house" "hidden" in Mukwonago "is half the fun"; reportedly
a "former" "gangster hideout", "religious retreat and house of
ill repute" (at different times), it's now a "fun, funky place" with
"many theme nights" (folks "love May Mushroom Madness")
and "a maze of small, romantic rooms"; N.B. new owners took
over post-*Survey*.

IMMIGRANT ROOM & WINERY, THE 🖾 `26 | 26 | 27 | $60`
American Club, 419 Highland Dr. (School St.), Kohler, 920-457-8888;
www.destinationkohler.com
"Top-notch service", "superb food" and "an incredible setting"
inside a Kohler resort have diners immigrating to this "ultimate"
Eclectic, a "wonderful" (if "pricey") place that leaves "every
sense satisfied"; its "lovely", "old European-style" dining room is
"a treat for a special occasion" or to signal "a spectacular end to
a day on the golf course or at the spa"; P.S. the separate Winery
Bar offers "unique appetizers", "outstanding wines" and a "cheese
selection that's the best" around.

LAKE PARK BISTRO `25 | 26 | 24 | $45`
Lake Park Pavilion, 3133 E. Newberry Blvd. (Lake Park Rd.),
414-962-6300; www.lakeparkbistro.com
With this East Side "French jewel", restaurateur Joe Bartolotta
"has created a masterpiece" inside a "perfect setting" – Frederick

Law Olmsted–designed Lake Park ("romantics" recommend that you "ask for a table by the window with a view of Lake Michigan"); fans exclaim "Seine-sational!" about the "top-shelf", "consistently wonderful" "classic and modern bistro fare", but even devotees deride the "unacceptable noise level."

MAGGIANO'S LITTLE ITALY   20 | 18 | 19 | $28

Mayfair Mall, 2500 N. Mayfair Rd. (W. North Ave.), Wauwatosa, 414-978-1000; www.maggianos.com
Big appetites are appeased at this Wauwatosa link in a chain of "great family-style places" that's "still going strong" with its "abundant" "red-sauce" Southern "Italian comfort-food" concept and "vibrant atmosphere" that's "a touch old Italy, a touch Rat Pack"; the jaded jeer that "it's not worth the wait" to tolerate the "forgettable food", "overcrowded" conditions and merely "competent service"; but it's voted the Milwaukee area's Most Popular, so they must be doing something right.

Moceans ⊠   – | – | – | E

747 N. Broadway (bet. Mason St. & Wisconsin Ave.), 414-272-7470; www.moceans.com
Bringing energy and spunk to the staid dining digs of the defunct Grenadier's, this Downtown seafood hot spot is the domain of chefs Karla Fischer (late of River Lane Inn) and Eric Vollman, who take a minimalist approach in preparing large portions of fresh seafood such as hash brown–crusted halibut; there's also a raw oyster selection ranging from Bluepoints to Belons, and the white linen–topped tables are patrolled by poised tag-team servers.

Mr. B's: A Bartolotta Steakhouse   25 | 21 | 23 | $45

17700 W. Capitol Dr. (Calhoun Rd.), Brookfield, 262-790-7005; www.mrbssteakhouse.com
The "flavor of real fire" from "a wood-burning oven" infuses the "tender, melt-in-your-mouth" filets ("including Kobe beef") plus "great sides and desserts" at this "high-end" (e.g. "expensive") Brookfield steakhouse, part of the Joe Bartolotta empire; the "warm colors" and "cozy" feel of its "charming", "rustic" setting are also favored, but the kitchen takes licks from some who say it yields "uneven experiences."

Osteria del Mondo   25 | 23 | 23 | $43

1028 E. Juneau Ave. (N. Astor St.), 414-291-3770; www.osteria.com
"Take someone you want to impress" to chef-owner Marc Bianchini's "elegant", "special date" place, a "nice surprise for Downtown Milwaukee" that satisfied supporters say shines like a "supernova" (though, unlike such celestial phenomena, it has lasted for more than a decade); with its "authentic" Northern Italian cuisine, "good wine selection" and "charming" front patio, it "stacks up against any other for quality", even if the "crowds and critics tend to overlook" it.

P.F. CHANG'S CHINA BISTRO   20 | 19 | 18 | $26

Mayfair Mall, 2500 N. Mayfair Rd. (W. North Ave.), Wauwatosa, 414-607-1029; www.pfchangs.com
Champions of this "Chinese chain" gang with a national presence cheer that they're a "consistent", "good choice" for "great", "upscale" "Americanized food" ("everyone loves the lettuce wraps") in a "fun", "noisy and crowded" atmosphere staffed by "upbeat servers"; the quality of the latter's efforts appears to vary

by location, and detractors who find the chow "derivative" grunt "go to Chinatown."

RISTORANTE BARTOLOTTA   27 | 23 | 23 | $41

2625 N. Downer Ave. (Belleview Pl.), 414-962-7910
7616 W. State St. (Harwood Ave.), Wauwatosa, 414-771-7910
www.bartolottaristorante.com

"Anything Joe Bartolotta touches is great", so it's no surprise followers brave a "high noise level" and "on-top-of-each-other" tables to get a piece of this West Side "favorite" where "dreamy" Northern Italian fare and "gracious service" find a "comfortable", "rustic" yet "classy" home; remember, though, that "reservations are a must", since "crowds" of "smiling people" mean it's "still hard to get into after all these years"; perhaps his new (unrated) branch on North Downer Avenue will help ease the squeeze.

River Lane Inn 🖾   24 | 17 | 21 | $35

4313 W. River Ln. (Brown Deer Rd.), 414-354-1995

"Wonderful opportunities to try" "great seafood" (including some Cajun-Creole specialties such as the "best blackened fish around") abound at this "off-the-beaten-path" North Shore spot, the casual counterpart to The Riversite; "popular with locals", it's a "fantastic place" that fans feel is "like an old friend or a favorite sweater", though a few naysayers negate the menus as "a little tired."

Riversite, The 🖾   26 | 25 | 24 | $43

11120 N. Cedarburg Rd. (Mequon Rd.), Mequon, 262-242-6050

"A beautiful view of the Milwaukee River", "exceptional wines" and the skills of "creative" chef Tom Peschong keep this "reliable", "upscale" North Shore American on its audience's A-list; "superbly hospitable" owner Jim Marks is often "present and will guide you through the myriad choices", which include "extraordinary appetizers" and "excellent seafood" selections; P.S. the "nice setting" is "especially lovely when the snow flies."

Roots Restaurant and Cellar   – | – | – | E

1818 N. Hubbard St. (Vine St.), 414-374-8480; www.rootsmilwaukee.com

Putting down roots in the up-and-coming Brewers Hill area, this dramatic venue with beautiful city views features two spaces – an upscale upper level serving seasonally changing Californian-Asian fusion fare and a more casual cellar with a sandwich-and-salad focus; N.B. both menus use ingredients grown on the restaurant's proprietary farm.

SANFORD 🖾   29 | 26 | 29 | $66

1547 N. Jackson St. (Pleasant St.), 414-276-9608;
www.sanfordrestaurant.com

"If I only had one meal left, I would have it here", attest acolytes "astounded" by this "intimate", "elegant" East Side New American mecca that "defines gourmet in Milwaukee", setting "the standard" by scoring the town's top honors for Food; "genius" co-owner and "chef Sanford D'Amato amazes with his spectacular cooking" and "adventurous menu", while the staff offers "outstanding service", ensuring that this "true culinary experience" is "worth the splurge."

Singha Thai   25 | 16 | 19 | $19

2237 S. 108th St. (Lincoln Ave.), 414-541-1234; www.singhathai.com

Though "any of the curries are great", regulars of this "awesome" West Side Thai know to "go to the back page" of its "expansive menu" "for house specialties", including Singha beef, charcoal chicken, crispy shrimp and spicy noodles; "don't expect to be wowed" by "its typical strip-mall" location, "but at least you aren't paying for frills."

Three Brothers 🚭　　　　　　26 17 22 $27
2414 S. St. Clair (Russell Ave.), 414-481-7530
Owners Branko and Patricia Radicevic "treat you like family the minute you walk in the door" of their "one-of-a-kind" Serbian set in an old South Side Schlitz tavern that oozes "simple", "old-world charm"; ranging from "well-dressed businessmen to everyday anarchists", the "crowd" "spends hours" at this "authentic" "fixture" sampling the likes of burek, chicken paprikash and goulash – all foods that "warm your heart."

Minneapolis/St. Paul

TOP FOOD RANKING

	Restaurant	Cuisine
28	Bayport Cookery	New American
	La Belle Vie	Med./New French
27	D'Amico Cucina	Northern Italian
	Vincent	French Bistro
	Manny's	Steakhouse
	Levain	New American
	Alma	New American
26	Oceanaire	Seafood
	Lucia's	New American
	Ristorante Luci	Italian

OTHER NOTEWORTHY PLACES

Restaurant	Cuisine
Bakery on Grand	French Bistro
Cosmos	Eclectic
Dakota Jazz	Regional American
Heartland	Regional American
Origami	Japanese
Solera	Spanish
St. Paul Grill	American
20.21	New American
Zander Cafe	New American
Zelo	Italian

F	D	S	C

Alma ⊠
27 | 21 | 24 | $39

*528 University Ave. SE (6th Ave.), Minneapolis, 612-379-4909;
www.restaurantalma.com*
"A treasure", this Dinkytown "destination" "near the University" of
Minnesota is "always packed" thanks to a "constantly changing
menu" of "astonishing" New American cuisine "meticulously
prepared" by "creative chef" Alex Roberts, who is "dedicated to
fresh local ingredients" and "sustainable" farming; the "spruced-
up storefront" space is "beautiful" yet "homey", and the "attentive"
staff provides "welcoming service", making it "a class act all the
way" – though some sigh "if [only] it were a little cheaper."

Bakery on Grand
25 | 15 | 20 | $32

3804 Grand Ave. S. (38th St.), Minneapolis, 612-822-8260
"Much more than a bakery", this "bustling" South Minneapolis
storefront with owner and "majordomo Doug Anderson at the
helm" is "simultaneously a neighborhood restaurant and a
destination for the entire metro area" thanks to "inventive",
"hearty" French Bistro fare; the "spartan setting" may be a bit
"bare-bones", but the staff is "unpretentious" and the "prices are
reasonable", especially for the "excellent lunch" and "Sunday
night prix fixe special."

BAYPORT COOKERY
28 | 20 | 25 | $51

328 Fifth Ave. N. (Rte. 95), Bayport, 651-430-1066;
www.bayportcookery.com
"A pleasant 30-minute drive from Downtown" through the "beauty
of the St. Croix River area", this "small storefront" spot "wows"
with "amazing" New American fare (voted No. 1 in the region)
offered via "excellent", "ever-changing and imaginative" prix fixe
or à la carte meals; it's a "lovely place for a romantic dinner", so
"get reservations well in advance"; P.S. "the annual springtime
morel festival is not to be missed."

Cosmos
25 | 26 | 24 | $55

Graves 601 Hotel, 601 First Ave. N. (6th St.), Minneapolis, 612-677-1100;
www.cosmosrestaurant.com
"Exquisite" Eclectic cuisine is "exceptionally served" by a
"top-notch" staff within a "sophisticated setting" at this "sleek
dining room" located in the Warehouse District's "über-hip"
Graves 601 Hotel; "the food tastes as good as it looks", and the
"beautiful-people" "clientele isn't far behind" in the appearance
department, making for a "super-chic" environment that seems
"far, far away from Minneapolis."

Dakota Jazz Club & Restaurant
– | – | – | E

1010 Nicollet Mall (10th St.), Minneapolis, 612-332-1010;
www.dakotacooks.com
It's about time, swear supporters who trumpet the move of the
metro area's best supper/jazz club from a moribund St. Paul
location to a snazzy David Shea–designed venue smack in the
middle of the high-traffic Nicollet Mall (all the better to lure out-
of-towners); local foodies and hepcats alike also hail the robustly
Regional American menu that, though now the domain of new
chef Jack Riebel (ex La Belle Vie), retains the legendary apple-
Brie soup and pecan-crusted walleye.

D'AMICO CUCINA ⊠
27 | 25 | 27 | $52

Butler Sq., 100 N. Sixth St. (2nd Ave.), Minneapolis, 612-338-2401;
www.damico.com
With "top-flight, creative Northern Italian cuisine" and a "superb
wine list", this "fancy standby" in the Warehouse District is "a
can't-miss choice" "for special nights out", and "still the one to
beat for entertaining clients" (regulars recommend you "try the
unparalleled and inventive tasting menu"); the "Tuscan"-like
"atmosphere is soothing", "the mood is formal but not uptight"
and the "attentive staff" "spoils you rotten" – but be sure to
"bring a well-stuffed wallet."

Heartland ⊠
25 | 21 | 23 | $45

1806 St. Clair Ave. (S. Fairview Ave.), St. Paul, 651-699-3536;
www.heartlandrestaurant.com
"Minnesota cuisine is no longer an oxymoron" thanks to this
Groveland "neighborhood jewel", "home" of "gifted chef"
Lenny Russo, whose "mission" is fashioning "fresh Midwestern
ingredients", "locally produced", into Regional American "food
worthy of a national reputation"; a few critics complain that
the "skimpy portions" are "not cheap", but sweeter hearts swear
that additional pluses such as "a strong wine list" and the
"comfortable" "Prairie School interior" make the overall
experience "worth it."

LA BELLE VIE
28 | – | 27 | $51

510 Groveland Ave. (Lyndale Ave.), Minneapolis, 612-874-6440;
www.labellevie.us

"There's not a bad choice on" the "imaginative Med"–New French menu at this "chef-owned" venue, recently relocated to the big city from small-town Stillwater, where partners Tim McKee and Josh Thoma's "care and attention is evident in the ingredient selection and preparation"; similarly, the "service is impeccable" and the "lovely wine list is well chosen and fairly priced", making the "experience worth every nickel"; N.B. it is scheduled to reopen in its new Loring Park home in October 2005.

Levain ⊠
27 | 17 | 22 | $50

4762 Chicago Ave. (48th St.), Minneapolis, 612-823-7111;
www.restaurantlevain.com

Hidden in "out-of-the-way" South Minneapolis, this New American can be nearly "impossible to spot", so look for the "little red door" behind which awaits "fabulous chef Steven Brown's" "trendy NY restaurant–style food (with NY prices)" complemented by an "exemplary wine list"; some decry the "noisy, noisy, noisy" atmosphere and quip that the fare's "as amazing as the decor is sparse", but most suggest you "do not miss" this "rare find."

Lucia's
26 | 20 | 24 | $35

1432 W. 31st St. (Hennepin Ave.), Minneapolis, 612-825-1572;
www.lucias.com

A "pioneer of nouvelle Minnesota cooking", this "upscale joint" "in the heart of Uptown" is "always a treat", offering a "small", "balanced" and "frequently changing menu" of New American food made from "fresh, locally produced" provender "cooked in creative ways" by chef-owner Lucia Watson; the "simple", "intimate environment" is further enhanced by a "friendly staff" that makes "excellent service" look "effortless"; P.S. check out her "good wine bar" and new bakery/flower shop next door, too.

MANNY'S STEAKHOUSE
27 | 20 | 25 | $53

Hyatt Regency, 1300 Nicollet Mall (Grant St.), Minneapolis, 612-339-9900;
www.mannyssteakhouse.com

"Still the benchmark" for local chophouses, this "meat eaters' nirvana" in Downtown's Hyatt Regency boasts an "accomplished staff" that serves "perfectly prepared, *Flintstones*-sized steaks" to a "fairly formal, business-oriented" crowd; some suggest the "old boys' club" decor is "a bit too male" ("women eat steak too!"), but most "satisfied carnivores" suggest you "save your pennies and appetite – you'll need both"; P.S. with its "photographs of past guests", "the bar is definitely the place to sit for ambiance."

OCEANAIRE SEAFOOD ROOM
26 | 23 | 25 | $51

Hyatt Regency, 1300 Nicollet Mall (Grant St.), Minneapolis,
612-333-2277; www.theoceanaire.com

The "fish is flown in fresh and tastes like it" at this "special-occasion" "seafood palace" Downtown, a "loud, crowded" outpost of a locally owned national chain that's the Most Popular restaurant "in landlocked Minneapolis"; the kitchen "doesn't miss a beat" in orchestrating an "amazing fish adventure" ("the old standbys are better than you remember, but try their more creative fare – it's excellent"), and the "elegant and attentive" service befits the "swank", "'30s-style" room reminiscent of a "grand ocean liner."

Origami
26 │ 18 │ 20 │ $35

30 N. First St. (1st Ave.), Minneapolis, 612-333-8430
Ridgedale Mall, 12305 Wayzata Blvd. (Ridgedale Dr.), Minnetonka,
952-746-3398
www.origamirestaurant.com

"Others may be cheaper, but nobody is fresher" than this "classy Japanese restaurant" in the "quiet Warehouse district", where it's "easy to binge on the fine, inventive" raw-fish fare ("the guys behind the bar really know how to take care of you"), not to mention the "nice selection" of "great cooked food"; the younger Ridgedale Mall branch splits surveyors, with some saying it "misses the mark" and others opining it serves "suburban sushi worth eating."

Ristorante Luci ⊠
26 │ 17 │ 24 │ $34

470 Cleveland Ave. S. (Randolph Ave.), St. Paul, 651-699-8258;
www.ristoranteluci.com

"Fine", "authentic Italian" fare "like your mamma would have cooked if she were a native" of The Boot is the forte of this "crowded but cozy" "neighborhood restaurant" in Highland Park, where "superb meals" that would be "a bargain at twice the price" are offered "in a pretension-free atmosphere"; P.S. it can be "hard to get a reservation", so regulars recommend you call "two weeks in advance – the food is worth" the extra effort.

Solera
24 │ 24 │ 21 │ $39

900 Hennepin Ave. (9th St.), Minneapolis, 612-338-0062;
www.solera-restaurant.com

"Colorful Gaudí-inspired decor" that's "sensual without being overwrought" evokes "sunny Spain" at this "new favorite" Downtown ("from the folks who brought us La Belle Vie") that "tantalizes" with "an unending list of tasty tapas" "made for sharing" and ferried by a "friendly, helpful" staff; it's not every "epicurean's dream come true", though, with some wondering "what all the hype's about" and warning that those "teeny-tiny" dishes "quickly add up, pricewise"; nevertheless, "the rooftop terrace is all the rage."

ST. PAUL GRILL
24 │ 24 │ 24 │ $43

St. Paul Hotel, 350 Market St. (5th St.), St. Paul, 651-224-7455;
www.stpaulgrill.com

"Grand dining in a grand room of a grand hotel" sums up the appeal of this "grande dame" in Downtown St. Paul that "continues to impress" with its "classy", "clubby atmosphere", "gorgeous mirrored bar" and "wonderful view of Rice Park"; it's where the "old-money" crowd meets for "true power lunches" and "excellent pre-theater" dinners of "well-done Traditional American" fare "graciously served" – no wonder well-wishers willingly "spend too much, eat too much and always adore it."

20.21
– │ – │ – │ E

Walker Art Center, 1750 Hennepin Ave. (Vineland Pl.), Minneapolis,
612-253-3410; www.wolfgangpuck.com

Seeking a name as famed as those of the Oldenburgs and Rothkos on its walls, the Walker Art Center has lured Wolfgang Puck to operate its new, finer-than-thou eatery; uniformly attired in determinedly upscale funk, the city's cognoscenti meet in the spare, classy digs to dine on the chef's signature Asian-influenced New American eats, peruse a wine list that incites sticker shock in moral Minnesotans and beg for a window seat to drink in the Downtown skyline view.

VINCENT　　　27 ▮ 23 ▮ 24 ▮ $48 ▮
1100 Nicollet Mall (11th St.), Minneapolis, 612-630-1189;
www.vincentarestaurant.com
"A welcome oasis", this Downtown "chef-owned gem" is helmed by "imaginative", "charismatic" toque Vincent Francoual, who "sincerely cares what his clients think" and garners *beaucoup de "mercis"* from them for giving his "high-end French Bistro" fare a "contemporary" American interpretation then pairing it with a "thoughtful wine list"; the "top-notch staff" and "elegant, minimal decor" with "hardwoods, high ceilings and loads of windows" for "people-watching on Nicollet Mall" "complete the package"; P.S. "try the chef's table" in the kitchen.

Zander Cafe　　　25 ▮ 18 ▮ 22 ▮ $35 ▮
525 Selby Ave. (bet. Kent & Mackubin Sts.), St. Paul, 651-222-5224;
www.zandercafe.com
"Thank goodness for a great neighborhood place we can afford" – so say Selby sorts smitten with this "warm and friendly" "jewel", the "signature restaurant" of chef-owner Alexander "Zander" Dixon ("the Zorro of gastronomy"), who concocts a "creative, inventive" New American menu; the "smart and casual staff", "a wine list to boggle the mind" and "live jazz some nights" are additional attributes that will "keep you coming back" to its "funky, hip" "storefront setting."

ZELO　　　23 ▮ 25 ▮ 22 ▮ $39 ▮
831 Nicollet Mall (9th St.), Minneapolis, 612-333-7000
"The best thing to happen to Minneapolis" next to "Jesse Ventura leaving the state" might be this "chic" Italian Downtown where "beautiful bankers" do that "single" "metrosexual thing"; "creative, modern cooking" and decor to match, featuring "dark wood and contemporary decorations galore" in a space staffed by "attentive" servers, make it "a good place to impress a date", or a "pickup" scored in the "happening" bar "where (old) boy meets (young) girl", if he's lucky.

New Jersey

TOP FOOD RANKING

Restaurant	Cuisine
28 Nicholas	New American
Ryland Inn	New French
27 DeLorenzo's	Pizza
Cafe Panache	Eclectic
Cafe Matisse	Eclectic
Scalini Fedeli	Northern Italian
Serenade	New French
Saddle River Inn	French/New Amer.
Augustino's	Southern Italian
Origin	French/Thai
Whispers	New American
Jocelyne's	French
Green Gables	Eclectic
Washington Inn	American
Dining Room	New American
La Isla	Cuban
26 Stage House	New French
Bernards Inn	New American
Chez Catherine	French
Latour	French/American

OTHER NOTEWORTHY PLACES

Amanda's	New American
Anthony David's	Eclectic/N. Italian
Bistro Olé	Portuguese/Spanish
Blue Point Grill	Seafood
Bobby Chez	Seafood
Cucharamama	South American
Daniel's on B'way	Seafood/New Amer.
Fascino	Italian
Frog and the Peach	New American
Giumarello's	Northern Italian
Hamilton's	Mediterranean
Ixora	French/Japanese
Mazi	Mediterranean
Perryville Inn	New American
Pluckemin Inn	New American
Rat's	New French
Sagami	Japanese
Siri's	French/Thai
Zafra	Pan-Latin
Zoe's by the Lake	French

AMANDA'S
26 | 25 | 24 | $43

908 Washington St. (bet. 9th & 10th Sts.), Hoboken, 201-798-0101;
www.amandasrestaurant.com
Still "elegant and wonderful", this "romantic" Hoboken "jewel" in
a "beautiful" restored brownstone is renowned for its "fabulous",
"creative" New American cuisine, a "thoughtfully" selected wine
list, "impeccable" service and "lovely" decor; "and how can
you beat their early-bird special?" – a "stupendous bargain" at
$12.50 per person.

Anthony David's
26 | 20 | 21 | $37

953 Bloomfield St. (10th St.), Hoboken, 201-222-8399
Admirers "love, love, love" chef-owner Anthony Pino's "tiny",
"first-class" Hoboken BYO where the "superb", "evolving"
Eclectic–Northern Italian fare is complemented by an "excellent
cheese selection"; fans are also quite fond of the "wonderful"
weekend brunch and "jazzy, casual" ambiance, so you better
"book a reservation in advance."

Augustino's ⌿
27 | 19 | 24 | $37

1104 Washington St. (bet. 11th & 12th Sts.), Hoboken, 201-420-0104
Expect a "treat" if you're "lucky enough" to score a reservation
at this "intimate" Hoboken Southern Italian, where the prize is
"glorious" "homespun" cooking, a "tiny", "cozy" brick-walled
dining room and "mouthy" but "ultrafriendly" waitresses who
"act like you're a regular"; be sure to call ahead – "unless
you know someone."

BERNARDS INN, THE
26 | 26 | 25 | VE

27 Mine Brook Rd. (Quimby Ln.), Bernardsville, 908-766-0002;
www.bernardsinn.com
The verdict's in: despite much talk about Ed Stone's departure last
year, chef Corey Heyer's tenure at the "grande dame" of "special-
occasion" dining in Bernardsville has been "exceptional", and the
"magic" of this "classic" in the land of "blue bloods" remains on all
fronts, from the "blue-ribbon" New American cuisine to "superb"
service to an "incredible wine list" backed by a "knowledgeable"
sommelier; while the prices may seem "exorbitant", the experience
here is likely to be "memorable."

Bistro Olé
26 | 19 | 23 | $36

230 Main St. (bet. Cookman & Mattison Aves.), Asbury Park,
732-897-0048; www.bistroole.com
Adding a second dining room has given more folks a chance to
check out chef Wil Vivas' "lively", "exceptional" cooking, a
"celeb"-worthy greeting from host-owner Rico Rivera and
"enthusiastic" service at this "swanky" Spanish-Portuguese
"pearl" in Asbury Park; "the waits to get in" can be "insane", but
be patient and you'll have an "amazing" time.

Blue Point Grill
26 | 15 | 21 | $34

258 Nassau St. (Pine St.), Princeton, 609-921-1211;
www.bluepointgrill.com
Scoring points for its "amazing" "variety" of "flawless", "super-
fresh" seafood preparations "kept simple" is this "casual"
Princeton BYO that's usually "packed to the gills"; the "great"
raw bar and "efficient" staff keep "hooking" 'em despite "long"
lines and noise.

Bobby Chez   26 | 10 | 17 | $20 |

Village Walk Shopping Ctr., 1990 Rte. 70 E. (bet. Old Orchard & Springdale Rds.), Cherry Hill, 856-751-7373 ☒

33 W. Collings Ave. (bet. Cove Rd. & Norwood Ave.), Collingswood, 856-869-8000 ☒

8007 Ventnor Ave. (S. Gladstone Ave.), Margate, 609-487-1922

Centerton Sq., Rte. 38 (Marter Ave.), Mount Laurel, 856-234-4146

Southgate Plaza, 1225 Haddonfield-Berlin Rd. (Lippard Ave.), Voorhees, 856-768-6660 ☒

www.bobbychezcrabcakes.com

"Crab cakes!" sums up the appeal of this South Jersey seafood chain that's primarily a take-out spot; loaded with "lump meat", the signature "hockey pucks" are the "best around", according to those advocates who can stand the "brutal" waits in the summer; the lobster mashed potatoes and "underrated" shrimp cakes collect kudos too.

CAFE MATISSE   27 | 26 | 26 | $60 |

167 Park Ave. (bet. E. Park Pl. & Highland Cross), Rutherford, 201-935-2995; www.cafematisse.com

A "go-to place" for a "special-occasion" "splurge", this "romantic" Rutherford BYO in a "charmingly decorated" renovated firehouse wows with a "consistently amazing" Eclectic menu, a "pastry chef who works wonders" and a "knowledgeable" staff that "pays attention to details"; the "velvet chairs" and "jeweled chandeliers" help create a "beautiful" environment even the artist would have approved; P.S. there's a wine shop up front – "how perfect is that?"

CAFE PANACHE ☒   27 | 21 | 25 | $52 |

130 E. Main St. (Rte. 17), Ramsey, 201-934-0030

It's no surprise that reservations are "hard to come by" at "one of Bergen's best", a Ramsey BYO via "magician" chef-owner Kevin Kohler that "delights" both palate and soul with an "ever-changing" menu of "terrific" Eclectic fare incorporating "fresh" ingredients "sourced from local farmers"; "impeccable" service and a recent "upgrade" of the decor adds to a "wonderful" experience.

Chez Catherine ☒   26 | 21 | 24 | $57 |

431 North Ave. (E. Broad St.), Westfield, 908-654-4011; www.chezcatherine.com

Edith and Didier Jouvenet are "doing a marvelous" job carrying on the tradition set by their predecessor; their "pink" and "cozy" French "landmark" in Westfield treats its audience to "beautiful" preparations of sometimes "otherworldly" cuisine and "first-class" service, making it a "superb" choice for a "special day or date"; N.B. closed Sundays and Mondays.

Cucharamama   25 | 27 | 22 | $41 |

233 Clinton St. (bet. 2nd & 3rd Sts.), Hoboken, 201-420-1700

Maricel Presilla's "amazing" Hoboken newcomer a block away from her sister restaurant, Zafra, "will delight your senses" with "powerful flavors" and an "ingenious use of ingredients" revealed in the "phenomenal" South American fare that's backed by "sexy", "swanky" sub-equatorial surroundings; "small" and sometimes "tough to get into", those who don't mind "waiting" are glad they did.

Daniel's on Broadway
25 | 24 | 24 | $51

416 S. Broadway (4th Ave.), West Cape May, 609-898-8770;
www.danielscapemay.com

The "elegant" country inn setting is a "perfect" complement to
the "sophisticated" New American menu featuring "unbelievable
seafood" and an "unbeatable" Sunday brunch at this "pearl" in
West Cape May; admirers sit back and watch a "staff that makes
every effort to please" and delight in a "romantic" experience that
some remark gets "better each time."

DELORENZO'S TOMATO PIES ⬆
27 | 8 | 15 | $15

530 Hudson St. (bet. Mott & Swann Sts.), Trenton,
609-695-9534

If all the universe were filled with competitors, this Trenton
"institution" with "zero" decor and no bathroom might still
"surpass" all others for its "thin-crust", "perfectly crisp" pies;
"join the line" "around the corner" to gain admission to this
pinnacle of pizza spots that offers up its "brilliant" creations to
legions of fawning followers.

Dining Room, The ⓩ
27 | 26 | 26 | $69

Hilton at Short Hills, 41 JFK Pkwy. (Rte. 24), Short Hills, 973-379-0100;
www.hiltonshorthills.com

Reserve this "elegant" and "formal" Hilton New American near
the Mall at Short Hills for those "momentous life events", or if
you're just in the mood to indulge in the "epitome of fine dining in
New Jersey"; it's "tops" in every way, from the "exquisitely
prepared" food, to the "romantic" ambiance to the "superb"
service – but remember to bring a "Brinks truck" to pay for it;
N.B. jacket suggested.

Fascino ⓩ
26 | 20 | 24 | $47

331 Bloomfield Ave. (bet. Grove & Willow Sts.), Montclair, 973-233-0350;
www.fascinorestaurant.com

A "top-notch" two-year-old, this "bustling" Montclair BYO run
by the "warm and talented" DePersio family has become "so
hot" that "reservations" are almost "impossible" to get since
there have been "nothing but raves" about its "outstanding"
"nouveau" Italian cuisine (be sure to save space for some "dreamy
desserts"), "superb" service and "cool", "sleek" decor; in simple
words, it's "fantastic."

FROG AND THE PEACH, THE
26 | 23 | 24 | $57

29 Dennis St. (Hiram Sq.), New Brunswick, 732-846-3216;
www.frogandpeach.com

An example of "excellence on all fronts" is New Brunswick's
"favorite" son, a New American that "continues to amaze"
repeat visitors with "innovative", "brilliantly executed" food,
"top-notch" service and a "superb" wine list; it's "still one of the
finest" and "most beautiful" restaurants in the state, but "oy! the
prices" are not for the faint of heart.

Giumarello's ⓩ
26 | 23 | 22 | $45

329 Haddon Ave. (bet. Cuthbert Blvd. & Kings Hwy.), Westmont,
856-858-9400; www.giumarellos.com

To its champions, "there's no mistaking it": this "high-class",
"romantic" Westmont Northern Italian is "one of, if not the best"
of its breed in South Jersey; the sense of "sensuality" in the

"fantastic" fare helps lure diners to its "upscale" quarters, and the "great martini list" is a further draw for those who settle in here for a few hours amid the "glitz and glam."

Green Gables 27 22 25 VE
Green Gables Inn, 212 Center St. (bet. Bay & Beach Aves.), Beach Haven, 609-492-3553
Though it may be hard to find a menu here, acolytes who deem this Victorian Beach Haven BYO "wonderful" don't seem to mind, since the Eclectic food on the five-course prix fixe menu is "phenomenal"; it's true, "you never know what you're going to get", but you can bet the farm that there'll be "accommodating" service and a "romantic" setting, all to ensure a most "enchanted evening"; N.B. for smaller appetites, a three-course prix fixe is also available.

Hamilton's Grill Room 25 20 21 $44
8 Coryell St. (N. Union St.), Lambertville, 609-397-4343;
www.hamiltonsgrillroom.com
"Excellent" meats and "sublime" seafood "grilled in front of your eyes" are yours courtesy of chef Mark Miller at this "wonderful" "rustic" Mediterranean BYO in Lambertville; "tucked away in an alley" near the Delaware River Canal, it's "hard to find", but folks "like it that way" since it's "crowded" enough as is on account of the "adventurous" menu and "convivial" atmosphere; update: they've recently added a glass-enclosed garden room that seats 25.

Ixora 25 21 23 $51
407 Hwy. 22 E. (Rte. 523), Whitehouse Station, 908-534-6676;
www.ixoranj.com
This Whitehouse Station "strip-mall" "sleeper" may not be one of New Jersey's "best-kept secrets" for long, not after an across-the-board jump in its ratings this year, a testimony to its "pristine sushi" and other "outstanding" items on the "innovative" Japanese-French fusion menu, as well as the "elegant, modern" decor and "helpful, unobtrusive" staff; P.S. sample some of the BYO's "wonderful teas and coffees."

Jocelyne's 27 21 24 $47
168 Maplewood Ave. (Baker St.), Maplewood, 973-763-4460;
www.jocelynesrestaurant.com
"Sweet and petite", this French BYO in Maplewood "has it all": "outstanding" fare, "wonderful" service, a "cozy", "elegant" ambiance and the "great team" of chef-owner Mitchell Altholz and his wife, Jocelyne, "whose friendly and steadying presence is an added bonus"; P.S. some reminders from regulars: "make reservations" "weeks in advance", it's dinner only, and closed Mondays and Tuesdays.

La Isla 27 10 19 $19
104 Washington St. (bet. 1st & 2nd Sts.), Hoboken, 201-659-8197;
www.laislarestaurant.com
"Ridiculously small" but packing the energy of a supernova, this "festive", "diner-esque" Hoboken BYO cooks up "the best Cuban food you've ever had" that arrives via a "quick" and "busy, busy" floor crew; the "multitudes" willing to wait for a table is evidence of its "popularity"; N.B. no reservations taken, and it's brunch-only on Sundays.

Latour   26 | 22 | 24 | $49
6 E. Ridgewood Ave. (Broad St.), Ridgewood, 201-445-5056
Chef-owner Michael Latour's "fabulous" French-American cuisine matched by "consistently top-notch" service and an "elegant", "lovely and low-key" setting have put this "quaint storefront" "by the train station" in Ridgewood on many a "must" list; it is "popular", "small" and utterly "charming" – and thus "tough to get a reservation" at.

Mazi   ▽ 23 | 17 | 21 | $35
401 Main St. (4th St.), Bradley Beach, 732-775-8828
"Where to start?" ask die-hard devotees of this "bistro-like" seasonal Bradley Beach Med BYO whose "creative" menu (with Greek and Portuguese dishes thrown in) includes "perfect piri-piri chicken" and "desserts in a league of their own"; it also helps that it's "charming" and "cute."

NICHOLAS   28 | 24 | 28 | $79
160 Rte. 35 S. (bet. Navesink River Rd. & Pine St.), Middletown, 732-345-9977; www.restaurantnicholas.com
Though the setting is "sophisticated" and "calm", the "tasting menu delivers a roller-coaster" ride "for the taste buds" at Melissa and Nicholas Harary's "spectacular" Middletown New American (No. 1 for Food in NJ); you may have to "mortgage the Shore house" to experience its "culinary masterpieces", but it's a "place to celebrate" offering a "Mercedes meal" that comes complete with an "impeccable", "unobtrusive" staff: just call it "perfect."

Origin   27 | 20 | 20 | $34
10 South St. (Morris St.), Morristown, 973-971-9933
25 Division St. (Main St.), Somerville, 908-685-1344
www.originthai.com
You may ask yourself if "the flavors are from France, Thailand or heaven"? admit those awed by these paeans to fusion fare in Morristown (the new sibling) and Somerville (the older, but recently expanded original); no matter, exult those who dub these BYOs "a delight for all five senses" and a "true adventure in eating", and even if the crowds often "overwhelm" the staff, diners are "transported by the first bite."

Perryville Inn   26 | 24 | 24 | $52
167 Perryville Rd. (I-78, exit 12), Union Township, 908-730-9500; www.theperryvilleinn.com
"A country classic" in Hunterdon County is this "perfect getaway" in a "historic" 1813 building where "consistently" "well-executed and creative" New American fare courtesy of chef-owner Paul Ingenito "hits a homer"; it makes for an "exquisitely romantic" dinner, prompting partisans to brag it's a "find off Route 78."

Pluckemin Inn, The ⊠   – | – | – | VE
359 Rte. 202/206 S. (Pluckemin Way), Bedminster, 908-658-9292; www.pluckemininn.com
High class, high concept and high prices define this New American debutante, a rebuilt Colonial-style manse that's rapidly becoming the inn place to be in Somerset Hills; chef Matthew Levin, whose pedigree includes Ryland Inn and Philly's Le Bec-Fin, unveils a cutting-edge menu, with signatures like a pastry-wrapped 'brik' of

halibut, hamachi tartare and avocado ice cream; it's supplemented by 1,200 different wines stored in a three-story tower that dominates one of the four plush, posh dining rooms.

Rat's   24 | 28 | 24 | $60
Grounds for Sculpture, 16 Fairgrounds Rd. (Sculptor's Way),
Hamilton, 609-584-7800; www.ratsrestaurant.org
A "fantasy" in every sense of the word, this piece of "magic" is decorated as a "wondrous" re-creation of Monet's fabled Giverny; "prepare for an unrushed evening of culinary and sensory delight", starting with a stroll through the "spectacular" Grounds for Sculpture (thanks, Mr. Johnson) and continuing with a "phenomenal" New French repast enhanced by "superb service"; simply put, it's "breathtaking inside and out."

RYLAND INN, THE   28 | 27 | 26 | $87
Rte. 22 W. (Rte. 523), Whitehouse, 908-534-4011;
www.rylandinn.com
"The magic of culinary excellence" inspires acolytes to worship at the "granddaddy of NJ restaurants" (No. 1 for Popularity in New Jersey), a showcase for the "gastronomic wizardry" of "brilliant" chef Craig Shelton; since 1991, devout diners have been making pilgrimages to this country inn in Whitehouse to savor "magnificent" New French fare (bolstered by the on-site organic garden), service that "misses nothing" and a "superbly" selected wine list; all of the above leaves surveyors asking "how can you improve perfection?"

Saddle River Inn ☒   27 | 25 | 25 | $59
2 Barnstable Ct. (bet. E. Allendale Ave. & W. Saddle River Rd.),
Saddle River, 201-825-4016; www.saddleriverinn.com
"Once you open the doors, the enchanted journey begins" at this Saddle River "gem" in a "quaint barn" that "oozes country elegance", a "veteran" creating "exceptional" French–New American food "without novelties", "foams or fussiness"; with a "chef-owner who really cares", and who "understands the subtleties of good service", it shouldn't shock anyone that this BYO "continues to perform at the top of its game."

Sagami   26 | 15 | 21 | $33
37 W. Crescent Blvd. (Haddon Ave.), Collingswood,
856-854-9773
"Unsurpassed sushi" and "unparalleled commitment" from the owner ensure this Collingswood Japanese remains in the "favorite" category for everyone from "Philadelphia TV news anchors" to locals who dub it their "family's special place for any occasion"; sure, the "location stinks" and its "low-profile look" doesn't titillate, but the BYO's always "worth the trip."

SCALINI FEDELI ☒   27 | 25 | 24 | $64
63 Main St. (Parrot Mill Rd.), Chatham, 973-701-9200;
www.scalinifedeli.com
"Culinary heaven on earth", this "beautiful", "world-class" Chatham Northern Italian "pampers" patrons lucky enough to get in – what can be a "three-month wait" is quickly forgotten after tasting Michael Cetrulo's "magical" prix fixe "wonders" served by a "staff that knows the right amount of schmooze"; the only issue, for many, is deciding which of the "divine" creations to order.

Serenade
27 | 26 | 26 | $66

6 Roosevelt Ave. (Main St.), Chatham, 973-701-0303;
www.restaurantserenade.com

Hitting all the high notes with surveyors, this "magnificent" New French in Chatham (from the union of "husband-chef" James Laird and "wife-in-front" Nancy Sheridan Laird) is "fabulous from start to finish", with "breathtaking" food, an "incredible wine list" shepherded by a "very user-friendly" sommelier, "understated service" and a "magical setting"; all in all, this one will "impress" "even people from the big city."

Siri's Thai French Cuisine
26 | 21 | 24 | $36

2117 Old Marlton Pike (bet. Grove St. & Sayer Ave.), Cherry Hill,
856-663-6781; www.siris-nj.com

The change of ownership that took place in 2004 had tongues wagging about this Cherry Hill Thai-French, but it's safe to say the BYO "buried in a strip mall" is still "so much better than" big-city spots in the same genre, presenting "dazzling" specialties that arrive via a "very fine" staff; "excellent on all fronts", the "tremendous value" turns this one into a "must."

Stage House Restaurant & Wine Bar
26 | 24 | 24 | $62

366 Park Ave. (Front St.), Scotch Plains, 908-322-4224;
www.stagehouserestaurant.com

Even in the post–David Drake era, "it all still works" at this "romantic" "gem on the sleepy main drag" of Scotch Plains where New French fare is served forth in a "charming" 1737 building; "walk past the herb garden" and dig into the seasonal "market menu", insiders advise, or relax "in front of a roaring fire in the winter" over dishes that are "perfectly refined and ready" for what's on the "incredible wine list."

Washington Inn
27 | 25 | 28 | $54

801 Washington St. (Jefferson St.), Cape May, 609-884-5697;
www.washingtoninn.com

"Unlike the weather, you can always count on it to be great" say diehards of this American that's "as good as it gets in Cape May", an "always on-the-money", "up-to-date" "favorite" with "fantastic" fare and an "outstanding" 900-bottle wine list; other restaurants "should send their staff here for training", since "no detail is forgotten", so even though it may be "tough on the pocketbook", the entire package is deemed "total class all the way."

Whispers
27 | 23 | 25 | $52

Hewitt Wellington Hotel, 200 Monmouth Ave. (2nd Ave.), Spring Lake,
732-974-9755; www.whispersrestaurant.com

If the "sublime" is what you seek, by all means try this chandeliered New American "wonder" in Spring Lake offering an "awesome, intimate dining experience" that's even more "memorable in the off-season"; its "heavenly" fare, BYO status and staff "on standby" to serve may soften the screams of those who say you'll need "a high credit limit" on that platinum card.

Zafra
25 | 18 | 19 | $30

301 Willow Ave. (3rd St.), Hoboken, 201-610-9801

"Close your eyes and blindly point to anything on the menu" at this "superior" Hoboken Pan-Latino with "too many delicious dishes to highlight" and too little room to make folks feel anything other

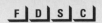
than "cramped"; still, chef-scholar Maricel Presilla makes it a "pleasure to dine" at her "colorful" BYO whose "high-quality" fare turns any meal into an "affordable" experience; in simple words, go and "wait on line" if you must.

Zoe's by the Lake　　26　23　25　$51
112 Tomahawk Trail (2 mi. east of Rte. 15), Sparta, 973-726-7226; www.zoesbythelake.com
Called "a miracle in the boondocks of northwestern New Jersey", this bi-level "find" has gushers grateful for its "seriously thoughtful" French menu that "grabs your attention" and for the "scrumptious food that keeps it"; with owners and a staff who "charm", and "classy, understated elegance" pervading the setting overlooking Seneca Lake, this one would be "outstanding anywhere."

New Orleans

At press time, New Orleans was starting its recovery from Hurricane Katrina. We are publishing this directory in the hope that the listed restaurants will soon reopen.

TOP FOOD RANKING

	Restaurant	Cuisine
27	Peristyle	Contemp. LA/French
	Bayona	New American
	Jacques-Imo's Cafe	Creole/Soul Food
	Dick & Jenny's	Creole/French
	Brigtsen's	Contemp. Louisiana
	Gabrielle	Contemp. LA/Creole
	New Orleans Grill	Continental
	Upperline	Creole
26	Sal & Judy's	Creole/Southern Italian
	Stella!*	New American
	Mosca's	Italian
	August	Continental/New French
	NOLA	Contemp. LA/Creole
	Commander's Palace	Creole
	Irene's Cuisine	Italian
	Dakota, The	Contemp. LA/New Amer.
	La Provence*	French
	K-Paul's	Cajun
	Crabby Jack's	Po' Boys/Seafood
	Clancy's	Creole

OTHER NOTEWORTHY PLACES

Restaurant	Cuisine
Antoine's	Creole/French
Arnaud's	Creole/Seafood
Brennan's	French/Creole
Eleven 79	Creole/Italian
Emeril's	Contemp. Louisiana
Galatoire's	Creole/French
Gautreau's	New French/New Amer.
Herbsaint	New French/New Amer.
Kim Son	Asian
La Petite Grocery	Contemp. LA/French
Louis XVI	French
Martinique Bistro	Caribbean/French
Mr. B's Bistro	Contemp. Louisiana
Muriel's	Creole
Nine Roses	Chinese/Vietnamese
Pelican Club	New American
René Bistrot	French Bistro
Rib Room	Continental/Steakhouse
RioMar	Seafood/Spanish
Ruth's Chris	Steakhouse

---

* Indicates a tie with restaurant above

Antoine's 🖾   22 | 24 | 23 | $52 |
713 St. Louis St. (bet. Bourbon & Royal Sts.), 504-581-4422;
www.antoines.com
The birthplace of oysters Rockefeller, this antebellum Creole-French
in the Vieux Carré is to many "New Orleans history epitomized",
a "charming, picturesque" "old-world" "bastion" "dripping with
tradition" and featuring "tuxedo-clad" servers, "elegant food"
and an "elaborate wine list"; critics counter that "time is taking
its toll", complaining of "dated" decor, "hurried" service (unless
"your waiter knows you") and "heavily sauced" cuisine; in any
event, "you'll empty your wallet filling your stomach."

Arnaud's   24 | 24 | 24 | $50 |
813 Bienville St. (bet. Bourbon & Dauphine Sts.), 504-523-5433;
www.arnauds.com
A "welcome oasis from hectic Bourbon Street", this "legendary"
"sentimental favorite" in the French Quarter has habitués hailing its
"delectable" Creole seafood and the "alert, attentive" "tuxedoed"
servers who ply their trays in "spacious dining rooms" with "tall
ceilings" and "leaded-glass windows" or in the bistro where a
Dixieland trio "swings" ("we were dancing in our chairs"); doubters
dissent, saying this "overpriced" "classic has gone so touristy."

August 🖾   26 | 27 | 25 | $54 |
301 Tchoupitoulas St. (Gravier St.), 504-299-9777;
www.restaurantaugust.com
"Ambitious" chef John Besh may be the "hottest talent in New
Orleans", cry connoisseurs who commend his "exquisite",
"imaginative but not too precious" contemporary Continental
cuisine (with a New French emphasis) "served with precision" by
"polite", "polished" staffers – which may be why this "divine"
CBDer with exposed-brick walls and crystal chandeliers is
becoming a "destination unto itself"; the petite portions can be
"hard to swallow when you're paying that much" – though the
advent of a new owner recently has led to more heaping helpings.

BAYONA 🖾   27 | 25 | 25 | $49 |
430 Dauphine St. (bet. Conti & St. Louis Sts.), 504-525-4455;
www.bayona.com
"Connoisseurs of fine food and wine" say chef Susan Spicer's
French Quarter flagship "merits all its accolades"; the "superlative"
New American cuisine is "impeccably prepared", and inside the
"old Creole cottage" with its "picturesque" patio the "gracious",
"knowledgeable" staff fosters an "intimate", "relaxing" ambiance;
it's "worth calling way ahead" for a reservation, since "it'd be a
bargain at twice the cost."

BRENNAN'S   23 | 24 | 23 | $49 |
417 Royal St. (bet. Conti & St. Louis Sts.), 504-525-9711;
www.brennansneworleans.com
"Brunch has become an art form" – and a "splurge" – at this
Creole–Classic French "institution", the "epitome of everything
New Orleans", with "sublime food" (including "knee-weakening"
bananas Foster), "amiable", "attentive" servers and a "labyrinth"
of "genteel" rooms ("explore – you'll need the exercise"); seen-
it-alls shrug, though, that it's "famous for being famous", calling
it "too high-priced, too crowded, too touristy"; N.B. a partial
renovation may outdate the above Decor score.

BRIGTSEN'S ☒ 27 | 22 | 26 | $45
723 Dante St. (Maple St.), 504-861-7610; www.brigtsens.com
"King" Frank Brigtsen still "rules" with a "deft hand" over his
"tiny kitchen" in Riverbend, creating "rooted-in-tradition yet"
"innovative" Contemporary Louisiana cuisine that's so "dazzling"
his subjects "want to lick their plates clean" ("rabbit tenderloin
makes my heart hop"); regulars report the staff's "Old South
graciousness" renders this "super-quaint" shotgun house "truly
homey"; N.B. rezzies a must.

Clancy's ☒ 26 | 20 | 24 | $41
6100 Annunciation St. (Webster St.), 504-895-1111
For "all the Creole without the tourists", "well-heeled Uptown
locals" congregate at this "lively", "*très* clubby" "hangout" "in a
residential neighborhood" (so "hidden" "you need a secret decoder
ring to find it"); the draw is "consistent", "inspired" "New Orleans
haute cuisine" (especially the "mouthwatering" oyster-and-Brie
appetizer) served by a "sarcastic" yet "friendly" staff; some,
however, complain the scene can be so "noisy" and "crowded"
"you can't hear yourself eat."

COMMANDER'S PALACE 26 | 26 | 26 | $54
1403 Washington Ave. (Coliseum St.), 504-899-8221;
www.commanderspalace.com
The city's Most Popular for the 17th year in a row, this Garden
District "celebration place" is considered by many the "unrivaled
crown jewel" in the Crescent City's culinary coronet, preserving
the "essence of New Orleans" in "stellar" "haute Creole cuisine"
(Sunday's jazz brunch is "phenomenal"); a "near-psychic" staff
and "venerable", "truly romantic" surroundings convince most
that this "classic" still "deserves its reputation" – though a few
fret that the "granddaddy" has "lost a step."

Crabby Jack's ☒ 26 | 8 | 15 | $13
428 Jefferson Hwy. (Knox Rd.), Jefferson, 504-833-2722
A lunch-only "sibling of Jacques-Imo's", this unassuming Jefferson
sandwich shop serves up "divine", "awesome po' boys" "piled
high" with slow-roasted duck, rabbit and "the plumpest, most
delicious oysters ever", plus "specials that are a bargain at twice
the price"; "limited seating" means "there's always a line", and
once you get inside the "decor is sparse", but "who cares?" – you
can always "call for takeout."

Dakota, The ☒ 26 | 21 | 24 | $40
629 N. Hwy. 190 (¼ mi. north of I-12), Covington, 985-892-3712;
www.thedakotarestaurant.com
It may be far to go north to The Dakota, but devotees really dig this
Covington "gem" for its "fresh and innovative" yet "unpretentious"
Contemporary Louisiana–New American cuisine ("can't beat the
crabmeat-and-Brie soup"), extensive wine list, "attentive" servers
and "warm and inviting ambiance."

DICK & JENNY'S ☒ 27 | 21 | 23 | $34
4501 Tchoupitoulas St. (Jena St.), 504-894-9880; www.dickandjennys.com
"Seasonal" Creole-French cuisine at "tremendous bargain" prices
entices local epicures to "revel in pure deliciousness" at this
"unpretentious" Uptown "cottage" where "gracious" service, a
"congenial" "at-home" vibe and tables that are "unbelievably

close together" combine to conjure "a dinner-party feel"; "thanks to the new expansion" the "long-but-worth-it" "waits have dwindled" but the no-reservations policy endures, so "get there early" or "phone ahead."

Eleven 79 ⑤   25 | 21 | 22 | $45
1179 Annunciation St. (Erato St.), 504-299-1179
"Fabulous veal", "rich, garlicky" pastas and other "expensive-but-worth-it" Italian-Creole specialties attract an "older crowd" to this "renovated old cottage" "under the bridge" in the Warehouse District, where "dark mahogany" decor creates an "intimate", "masculine" atmosphere and the "accommodating" servers "can be a lot of fun"; given the "small" space, though, "it's hard to get in" – if not "one of the toughest reservations in town."

EMERIL'S   25 | 23 | 24 | $55
800 Tchoupitoulas St. (Julia St.), 504-528-9393; www.emerils.com
"Don't hate it because of Emeril's overexposure", urge Lagasse loyalists who assert that his Warehouse District "flagship" still serves up "stellar" Contemporary Louisiana cuisine that's "exquisitely presented" by a "coordinated" contingent of "eager waiters"; the recently revamped, rawly modern room has a "trendy" feel, though "with no sound insulation" it can get "objectionably noisy", and given the "max-out-the-credit-card" prices, many maintain the celeb chef owes "more attention to his namesake restaurant."

Gabrielle ⑤   27 | 18 | 23 | $44
3201 Esplanade Ave. (Mystery St.), 504-948-6233;
www.gabriellerestaurant.com
"Every bite a delight", sing supporters who serenade chef-owner Greg Sonnier's "distinctive", "delectable" Creole–Contemporary Louisiana haute cuisine, which inspires them to "keep driving" till they get to the "cozy", "charming" triangular building in Faubourg St. John; a "friendly" ambiance and "unobtrusive" service help make the "tight quarters" more palatable but claustrophobes still "wish the tables were spread out more."

GALATOIRE'S   26 | 23 | 25 | $48
209 Bourbon St. (Iberville St.), 504-525-2021;
www.galatoires.com
Perhaps the only restaurant "where the waiters are more important than the chef", this beloved "epicenter" of haute French-Creole cuisine in the French Quarter is "the defining New Orleans dining experience", with "absolutely reliable renditions of old favorites" from an extensive menu that "never changes", "understated" yet "inviting decor" and "genuine" "old-style service and charm"; the renovated, reservable second floor is quieter, but locals say you "gotta sit downstairs", "especially on Fridays" for "long martini lunches and gossip."

Gautreau's ⑤   26 | 23 | 24 | $45
1728 Soniat St. (Danneel St.), 504-899-7397; www.gautreaus.net
A "culinary jewel box" with a "Paris bistro feel", this "tiny" Uptowner housed in a former antique drugstore is so "charming" it has "locals trying to keep it a secret"; surveyors savor the "superb" New French–New American cuisine (especially "wonderful appetizers") and call the "lovely interior" and "polished" service "perfect for a date" "when you really like her."

Herbsaint ⑤

25 | 20 | 22 | $40

701 St. Charles Ave. (Girod St.), 504-524-4114; www.herbsaint.com

Serial restaurateur Susan Spicer (Bayona) and chef Donald Link have concocted an "adventurous" New American–French menu of "fabulous appetizers", "small plates" and "novel twists" on "Southern-favorite" entrees for this "lovely neighborhood bistro" on the edge of the Warehouse District; it's a "mix of NY and NO" with a "chic" interior and "well-trained, personable" staff that has out-of-towners wishing they could "dine here every week."

Irene's Cuisine

26 | 20 | 22 | $37

539 St. Philip St. (Chartres St.), 504-529-8811

"Folks are waking up to this Italian sleeper" "tucked away" in the French Quarter, perhaps because of "wafting" aromas "you can smell a block away" that reveal the "succulent", "authentic" food to be had in this "dark, cozy", "romantic" refuge, administered by an "attentive but not suffocating" staff; even so, given the no-reservations policy (unless you're a large party), habitués hate to rate since the wait's already too great.

JACQUES-IMO'S CAFE ⑤

27 | 20 | 21 | $30

8324 Oak St. (S. Carrollton Ave.), 504-861-0886; www.jacquesimoscafe.com

"Definitely now *on* the beaten track", this "whimsical" Carrollton "joint" has become a "true foodie destination"; even locals still "wait here like they are being led to the Promised Land" for a chance to eat Jacques Leonardi's "sensational" Creole–soul food; "upbeat servers" help sustain the "ordered chaos" in the "rustic", colorful dining rooms while the "amiable" chef-owner "roams" "in his boxerlike shorts"; N.B. reservations for five or more accepted.

Kim Son ⑤

22 | 10 | 16 | $18

349 Whitney Ave. (Westbank Expy.), Gretna, 504-366-2489

Connoisseurs "stick to the Vietnamese" vittles when they visit this unassuming Gretna Asian for "super" spring rolls, "filling" soups and "fantastic" salt-baked crustaceans; it's "cheap and fast" but they take "no reservations" so "you may have to wait a bit."

K-Paul's Louisiana Kitchen ⑤

26 | 20 | 23 | $45

416 Chartres St. (bet. Conti & St. Louis Sts.), 504-524-7394; www.kpauls.com

Expect a line of tourists outside this "culinary shrine" to "genius of taste" Paul Prudhomme; it's a "homey" French Quarter "institution" where you can "stuff yourself" with "robust" Cajun classics like "out-of-this-world jambalaya", "fantastic duck" and "blackened fish, of course", served "with panache and personality" by "the same professional waiters year after year"; even leery locals admit that after a quarter of a century "it has found its rhythm", but prices are now "laughably high."

La Petite Grocery

– | – | – | E

4238 Magazine St. (General Pershing St.), 504-891-3377

The latest venture from chef Anton Schulte (ex Peristyle and Clancy's) is this renovated Garden District corner store (circa 1890), now a charming vintage-style cafe; wife Diane greets the foodies who flock here to dine on the maestro's Classic French fare (which focuses on regional ingredients) and imbibe from a select but eclectic wine list ($15 corkage fee if you BYO).

La Provence
26 | 24 | 22 | $45

25020 Hwy. 190 (bet. Lacombe & Mandeville), Lacombe, 985-626-7662; www.laprovencerestaurant.com

Food that's "first-class but never pretentious" is the province of this "always-a-treat" Gallic where super-chef Chris Kerageorgiou and his talented chef de cuisine Allen Heintzman proffer "pâté instead of bread and butter", "excellent" Sunday brunch and "generous" three-course prix fixe dinners; the "charming" Lacombe auberge with "stunning fireplaces ablaze" is a literally "warm" venue that feels like a "bit of French countryside right here in rural Louisiana."

Louis XVI
26 | 25 | 24 | $56

Saint Louis Hotel, 730 Bienville Ave. (bet. Bourbon & Royal Sts.), 504-581-7000; www.louisxvi.com

Don't walk into this "hidden" and "very elegant" "special-occasion venue" in the Quarter expecting a culinary commotion; instead, this "true French haute cuisine" "star" takes patrons on a "nostalgic journey into yesteryear" via "superb" "flaming entrees" prepared "tableside" and served by "tuxedoed waiters", a 300-label *carte du vin* and a "beautiful garden" view – all adding up to a pricey yet "priceless" experience.

Martinique Bistro
25 | 22 | 22 | $36

5908 Magazine St. (bet. Eleonore & State Sts.), 504-891-8495

One of the "best-kept secrets in town", this Uptown bistro remains a "longtime" favorite of locals seduced by chef Kevin Reese's "standout" "Caribbean-influenced" Gallic seafood; indoors the atmosphere is "intimate", like being in a "small French village", but dining in the "magical" courtyard "under the stars" "on a balmy evening" feels downright "enchanted"; breaking the spell, however, is "spotty", sometimes snaillike service.

Mosca's ☒⇱
26 | 10 | 18 | $36

4137 Hwy. 90 W. (bet. Butler Dr. & Live Oak Blvd.), Avondale, 504-436-9942

When hunting down this hard-to-find Italian "out on the highway" in Avondale, "go with a group" "that's not afraid of garlic", since its enormous "family-style servings" of "piquant", "luscious" seafood are "meant to be shared"; but "don't look" around, because this "rustic" "joint" has "worn" wooden floors and "decor as basic as it comes"; even so, "it's not cheap", so "bring lots of cash."

Mr. B's Bistro
24 | 22 | 23 | $40

201 Royal St. (Iberville St.), 504-523-2078; www.mrbsbistro.com

"The place to B" for "tourists and natives" alike, this "lively" and "crowded", "wood-paneled" bistro "reliably" proffers an "upscale" yet "unpretentious" Contemporary Louisiana menu, served by "friendly" teams who "handle" the "huge numbers" "admirably"; relatively "moderate prices" for the Quarter and a Sunday jazz brunch that "rocks the house" have more than a few calling it a "stellar performer."

Muriel's Jackson Square
21 | 24 | 21 | $38

Jackson Sq., 801 Chartres St. (St. Ann St.), 504-568-1885; www.muriels.com

Executive chef Erik Veney's "classic" yet "contemporary Creole" "food will revive the most jaded gourmand", gush the spellbound surveyors who haunt this historic haven on a "stunningly beautiful corner of Jackson Square"; after a meal in the "gorgeous dining rooms" "appointed with antiques" or on the wraparound balcony upstairs, settle into the "magical" séance lounge, a study in "exoticism" done up with "red tapestry and comfy sofas."

New Orleans Grill   27 | 28 | 27 | $63

Windsor Court Hotel, 300 Gravier St. (bet. S. Peters & Tchoupitoulas Sts.), 504-522-1992; www.windsorcourthotel.com

When the already-elegant Grill Room was renamed a while back, it also unveiled a $1.5 million-dollar renovation, cementing its status as a "sumptuous" CBD hotel "oasis"; meanwhile, chef Jonathan Wright, Britain's "culinary gift to the city", is still wowing high-end foodies with his "exquisite" Louisiana-influenced Contemporary American cuisine, presented by a "superb" staff; expect a "magical night", surveyors say – "for that price, it should be."

Nine Roses   24 | 16 | 17 | $18

1100 Stephens St. (Westbank Expy.), Gretna, 504-366-7665

This "friendly", "family" West Bank "can't-miss" is a "great Vietnamese choice" since it "aims to please" with a "huge menu" of "excellent" fare from "great pho" and "wonderful" hot and sour shrimp soup to "outstanding" low-fat meats, fish and vegetarian dishes; when you want to "sample a lot" of the "authentic" eats, "go with a big group or do takeout."

NOLA   26 | 23 | 24 | $48

534 St. Louis St. (bet. Chartres & Decatur Sts.), 504-522-6652; www.emerils.com

"Bam!-tastic", boom boosters blown away by the "sassy" Contemporary Louisiana–Creole "creations" and "top-notch service" at this "casual", "terrific two-story" "hot spot" in the French Quarter; sure, it's "packed with Emeril worshipers" but the "mouthwatering eats" make it "worth putting up with the hustle and bustle"; "it should be called Noise, not NOLA", blast bashers also deterred by "overzealous" servers and "tourist prices", who gripe "things ain't been the same since" the "legendary chef" "done got fame."

Pelican Club   25 | 24 | 23 | $47

312 Exchange Pl. (Bienville St.), 504-523-1504; www.pelicanclub.com

Though "still sort of undiscovered" by visitors, this "consistently winning" New American is "packed with local faces" tucking into its "enticing", "unique blend of Asian and Creole cuisines" proffered by "prompt, superb" servers in an "elegant room"; alas, the "bustling bistro atmosphere" can get "too noisy", so wise owls advise dining at dusk to enjoy what some term "the best early-bird meal in the Quarter."

PERISTYLE ⊠   27 | 24 | 26 | $52

1041 Dumaine St. (bet. N. Rampart & Burgundy Sts.), 504-593-9535

"Ambrosia" is how admirers acclaim the "amazing" French-Contemporary Louisiana cuisine from this champ, voted No. 1 for Food in New Orleans once again; set "on the fringe of the Quarter", the "bistro-esque" scene (with "sublime" bar) bustles with "cordial", "unobtrusive" servers; true, the "small" size makes it "tough to get a reservation – but it's worth fighting for"; N.B. following chef/co-owner Anne Kearney's post-*Survey* departure, new proprietor Tom Wolfe is supervising the stove.

René Bistrot
25 | 23 | 23 | $40

Renaissance Pere Marquette Hotel, 817 Common St. (Barrone St.), 504-412-2580; www.renebistrot.com

"In a word – superb", say succinct supporters of this "stylish" "surprise"; the "outstanding" French Bistro fare is "creative yet unpretentious", thanks to "magical" chef René Bajeux, and the wine list is "dazzling"; a "chic" but "comfortable" setting, "excellent service" and "great-value" prix fixe lunch and dinner are other reasons this CBD destination is such a "delightful getaway."

Rib Room
25 | – | 24 | $50

Omni Royal Orleans, 621 St. Louis St. (bet. Chartres & Royal Sts.), 504-529-7046; www.omnihotels.com

A "see-and-be-seen spot in the Quarter", this veteran Continental chophouse serves "magnificent" prime rib, "stellar" steaks and "creative seasonal offerings", along with "big, cold martinis"; an "open rotisserie so you can watch the chef", "professional" servers and "great people-watching" ("especially at lunchtime") make this "safe port" a perennial "favorite" and the epitome of "Southern elegance"; P.S. post-*Survey*, its "lovely", "old-world" setting has been given a marble-and-mahogany makeover.

RioMar ⊠
24 | 18 | 21 | $32

800 S. Peters St. (Julia St.), 504-525-3474; www.riomarseafood.com

Some of the "most creative seafood in town" is served at this "wonderful" piscatorium in the Warehouse District where the "adventurous" dishes have strong Spanish and Latin accents, including a "great assortment of seviches" and "divine serrano-wrapped tuna" washed down by "excellent", "affordable" wines; the staff's "friendly" and the setting's "casual", and even if it gets a bit "noisy" at times, that may be because "chef-owner Adolfo Garcia makes the fish positively sing."

Ruth's Chris Steak House
26 | 21 | 23 | $48

711 N. Broad St. (Orleans Ave.), 504-486-0810
3633 Veterans Memorial Blvd. (Hessmer Ave.), Metairie, 504-888-3600
www.ruthschris.com

"Nothing beats eating in the original" Broad Street flagship of the steakhouse chain, though the Metairie branch offers the same "generous" portions of "always-perfect" beef, "excellent" sides and "wonderful wines"; both spots lure "local politicians" and "power" brokers, but the "superb staff" treats "everyone like a VIP", and despite "high" prices, most agree it's "worth it."

Sal & Judy's
26 | 20 | 23 | $34

27491 Hwy. 190 (14th St.), Lacombe, 985-882-9443

Hungry North Shore pilgrims seek Sal-vation at this "superior" Italian, saying it's definitely "worth the ride" to Lacombe for "amazing", "more-than-you-can-finish" "Sicilian-type" Creole fare in an "intimate setting"; "they make you feel like one of the family" once you get in, but to reserve a place among the "inner circle of regulars", "plan on calling two to three weeks ahead."

Stella!
26 | 22 | 24 | $48

Hôtel Provincial, 1032 Chartres St. (bet. St. Philip St. & Ursuline Ave.), 504-587-0091; www.restaurantstella.com

Chef-owner Scott Boswell "puts it all together" with his slate of "superb", "imaginative" New American "fusion comfort food" at this "civilized, cute" charmer "set back from the craziness of the Quarter" that "tourists miss completely" and locals love for its "warmth, intimacy" and sophistication ("not a picture of Marlon Brando in sight"); a "professional yet friendly" staff provides "excellent service", and though high prices make a few people blanch, most simply shout "stellar!"; N.B. an expansion of the French Provincial digs may outdate the Decor score.

Upperline

27 | 24 | 25 | $42

1413 Upperline St. (bet. Prytania St. & St. Charles Ave.), 504-891-9822;
www.upperline.com

"Magnificent" meals that "consistently" "delight" surveyors ("legendary fried green tomatoes with shrimp rémoulade sauce", duck that "will forever spoil you") are the bottom line at this Uptown Creole "showplace"; the historic building (1877) is the "best salon in town" thanks to "effervescent" owner JoAnn Clevenger, her "captivating" collection of vintage NO art and a "pampering" staff; it all creates an "atmosphere conducive to unwinding" – and at "nice prices" (given the high quality); P.S. "try their theme menus."

New York City

TOP FOOD RANKING

Restaurant	Cuisine
28 Le Bernardin	French
Daniel	New French
per se	French/New Amer.
Bouley	New French
Sushi Yasuda	Japanese
Gramercy Tavern	New American
Nobu	Japanese/Peruvian
Peter Luger	Steakhouse
27 Jean Georges	New French
Gotham Bar & Grill	New American
Chanterelle	French
Babbo	Italian
Café Boulud	French
Sushi of Gari	Japanese
La Grenouille	Classic French
Masa	Japanese
Tomoe Sushi	Japanese
Roberto's	Italian
Grocery, The	New American
Il Mulino	Southern Italian
Aureole	New American
Pearl Oyster Bar	Seafood
Union Square Cafe	New American
Annisa	New American
Veritas	New American

OTHER NOTEWORTHY PLACES

Alain Ducasse	New French
Asiate	French/Japanese
Balthazar	French Brasserie
Bayard's	French/American
BLT Fish	Seafood
BLT Steak	Steakhouse
Blue Water Grill	Seafood
Café des Artistes	French
Café Gray	French Brasserie
Carnegie Deli	Deli
dévi	Indian
Matsuri	Japanese
Megu	Japanese
Milos	Greek/Seafood
Modern, The	French/American
Montrachet	French
Nobu 57	Japanese/Peruvian
Ouest	New American
Picholine	French/Med.
River Café	New American
Shun Lee Palace	Chinese
Smith & Wollensky	Steakhouse
Spice Market	Malaysian/Thai
Tavern on the Green	American
21 Club	American

Alain Ducasse ⧄   27 | 27 | 27 | $179
Essex House, 155 W. 58th St. (bet. 6th & 7th Aves.), Manhattan,
212-265-7300; www.alain-ducasse.com
Alain Ducasse's "fantastical" Central Park South "Shangri-la"
"elates" diners who "feel like overindulging" with "hours" of
culinary New French "wizardry" (courtesy of new exec chef Tony
Esnault) and "unparalleled" service in the "most glamorous" of
surroundings; "positively stunning" might equally describe the bill,
but "win the Lotto" and "go for it" – "this isn't just food, it's theater."

Annisa   27 | 23 | 26 | $65
13 Barrow St. (bet. 7th Ave. S. & W. 4th St.), 212-741-6699;
www.annisarestaurant.com
"Stealth superstar" Anita Lo "works her magic" at this "civilized"
Villager, which "enchants the senses" with "smart" New American
"artistry", "gracious service" and "spare, elegant" decor; a
"wowed" crowd urges "raise your credit card limit" 'cause it's
"worth the splurge."

Asiate   23 | 27 | 23 | $82
Mandarin Oriental Hotel, 80 Columbus Circle, 35th fl. (60th St.),
212-805-8881; www.mandarinoriental.com/newyork/
Reaching "dazzling heights", the Mandarin Oriental Hotel's "luxe"
Japanese-French "perch" with "million-dollar views" of Central
Park showcases chef Nori Sugie's "inspired", "exotic" "artistry"
in an "ethereal" window-lined space; service disputes aside
("superb" vs. "uneven"), it's "worth every dime" of the "trust-fund"
tabs; P.S. if money matters, go for the $35 prix fixe lunch.

Aureole ⧄   27 | 26 | 26 | $81
34 E. 61st St. (bet. Madison & Park Aves.), Manhattan,
212-319-1660; www.charliepalmer.com
Charlie Palmer and chef Dante Boccuzzi remain "at the top of their
game" at this "unforgettable" East Side townhouse duplex where
the "lovingly prepared" New American sets the "gold standard"
down to the "masterpiece" desserts; "highbrow" surroundings
and "classy service" bolster its "mystical status", so go for a
"spurge" or aim for "value" via the $35 lunch prix fixe.

BABBO ◗   27 | 24 | 25 | $70
110 Waverly Pl. (bet. MacDougal St. & 6th Ave.), 212-777-0303;
www.babbonyc.com
"There is no hype" at Mario Batali and Joe Bastianich's "magnifico"
Village Italian, just "unbeatable" "originality" in the "intense
flavors" that translate to "pure bliss" for "capacity" crowds;
"exemplary" service, "impressive wines" and the "rollicking"
"vibrance" of the carriage house environs help make it "the place
to be", so keep redialing because getting a table is "a blood sport."

Balthazar ◗   23 | 23 | 20 | $51
80 Spring St. (bet. B'way & Crosby St.), 212-965-1414;
www.balthazarny.com
Still "the quickest way to Paris", Keith McNally's "insanely popular"
SoHo brasserie "never loses its edge", doing a "phenomenal job"
from the "prototypical" decor to the "pitch-perfect" French fare and
"energetic" staff; it draws everyone from a "gossipy" "who's who"
to "fanny-packed tourists", so prepare for a "claustrophobic"
"hubbub" and "expect to wait unless you're Madonna."

Bayard's 🗵
24 | 25 | 24 | $64

1 Hanover Sq. (bet. Pearl & Stone Sts.), 212-514-9454; www.bayards.com
"Romance in the Financial District" is not an oxymoron thanks to this French-American "surprise" housed in the "transporting" circa-1851 India House; wonder chef Eberhard Müller (ex Le Bernardin and the late Lutèce) brilliantly employs produce "from his own North Fork farm" and owner Harry Poulakakos' "famed cellar" adds "outstanding" wines all served via a "pro" staff; "it doesn't get much better than this"; N.B. a private club at lunchtime, it also boasts "elegant" party rooms.

BLT Fish
22 | 20 | 20 | $54

21 W. 17th St. (bet. 5th & 6th Aves.), 212-691-8888; www.bltfish.com
Part of chef Laurent Tourondel's expanding BLT school, this new Flatironer's "incredible" seafood brings back "summers on Cape Cod"; really two eateries in one, it includes a glorified "clam shack" on the first floor for lobster rolls and the like, while the "formal", "*très* cool" upstairs offers "pricier", more "elegant" fare.

BLT Steak 🗵
24 | 21 | 22 | $69

106 E. 57th St. (bet. Lexington & Park Aves.), 212-752-7470; www.bltsteak.com
Giving a "twist to the steakhouse" template ("no sawdust and geriatric waiters" here), chef Laurent Tourondel's "classy" Midtown eatery attracts a "sleek moneyed crowd" for "melt-in-your-mouth" meat and "excellent sides" offered strictly à la carte; prime "people-watching" helps distract from constant crowds, "ear-splitting" noise levels and "steep" prices.

Blue Water Grill ●
24 | 22 | 21 | $50

31 Union Sq. W. (16th St.), 212-675-9500; www.brguestrestaurants.com
"Never disappoints", declare devotees of Steve Hanson's Union Square anchor where "consistently" "top-shelf" seafood, a "dramatic", "airy" former bank setting, "prompt" service and live jazz downstairs combine to "winning effect"; despite "waits even with reservations" and serious "noise levels", it's still "perfect for dates" and alfresco brunches.

BOULEY ●
28 | 26 | 27 | $87

120 W. Broadway (Duane St.), 212-964-2525; www.bouleyrestaurants.com
Star chef David Bouley is back at the top of his game at this "triumphant" TriBeCan serving "spectacular" New French cuisine in a lovely vaulted space via a "stealthily attentive" "pro" staff; connoisseurs "clear their credit cards" for this "mind-blowing", but "expensive", experience, or capitalize on the "extraordinary prix fixe lunch" deal.

Café Boulud
27 | 23 | 26 | $75

Surrey Hotel, 20 E. 76th St. (bet. 5th & Madison Aves.), 212-772-2600; www.danielnyc.com
"Aren't we lucky", sigh sated surveyors at Daniel Boulud's "more relaxed, more modern" but still "luxurious" East Side sister, after experiencing the "exquisite", "imaginative" French cuisine served against an "elegantly understated" backdrop by an "unobtrusive, courteous" staff; it all adds up to "a class act" that's "among NYC's most celebrated" – and that describes the clientele too.

Café des Artistes ◐　　　22 | 26 | 23 | $66
1 W. 67th St. (bet. Columbus Ave. & CPW), 212-877-3500;
www.cafenyc.com
"One of the city's treasures", George and Jenifer Lang's venerable
"institution" near Lincoln Center exudes "old-world elegance and
class" thanks to its "ornate" belle epoque interior resplendent
with Howard Chandler Christy's "intoxicating" "frolicking nymph"
murals; factor in "excellent" food and "caring" service, and it's
"the ultimate in romantic dining" "indulgence."

Café Gray 🅔　　　25 | 22 | 23 | $78
Time Warner Ctr., 10 Columbus Circle, 3rd fl. (60th St. at B'way),
212-823-6338; www.cafegray.com
"Thank goodness" "he's back", cry fans of chef Gray Kunz,
whose Asian-accented French brasserie in the Time Warner
Center is declared a "winner" thanks to its "brilliant" cuisine
featuring "powerful flavor combinations" backed by "unusual
wines" and "exceptional" service; however, when it comes to the
"stunning" David Rockwell–designed space overlooking Central
Park, surveyors can't help but ask "why did they put the kitchen
in front of the view?"

Carnegie Deli ◐≠　　　21 | 9 | 13 | $25
854 Seventh Ave. (55th St.), 212-757-2245; www.carnegiedeli.com
"Killer" "overstuffed" sandwiches "only a python could get its jaws
around" lure NYers and "tourists" alike to this "hectic" Midtown
"deli heaven"; noshers crammed "elbow-to-elbow" should
expect "fast, efficient and rude" service that's as "classic"
as the "can't-beat-it" cheesecake at this quintessential New
York City "landmark."

Chanterelle 🅔　　　27 | 27 | 27 | $91
2 Harrison St. (Hudson St.), 212-966-6960; www.chanterellenyc.com
"The height of understated luxe", David and Karen Waltuck's
TriBeCa French standby combines "flawless" cuisine, a "serene",
"airy" dining room dressed with "breathtaking floral displays" and
"faultless" "choreographed" service; fans call it a "first-class trip"
to "heaven-on-earth", but suggest "saving up" in advance or
checking out the "pure perfection" $43 prix fixe lunch.

DANIEL 🅔　　　28 | 28 | 28 | $108
60 E. 65th St. (bet. Madison & Park Aves.), 212-288-0033;
www.danielnyc.com
"If only life were as perfect as dinner" at "artiste" Daniel Boulud's
East Side "luxurious temple" of "fine dining", where the "flawless"
New French fare is "enthralling", the wines "wonderful", service
"seamless" and the "exquisite" room "adorned with gorgeous
flowers"; *bien sûr,* the cost is on par with "Ivy League tuition", but
gourmets recommend that you "throw caution to the winds and
order the tasting menu."

dévi　　　25 | 23 | 22 | $55
8 E. 18th St. (bet. B'way & 5th Ave.), 212-691-1300; www.devinyc.com
"Even the okra dazzles" at this Flatiron "haute Indian", where chefs
Suvir Saran and Hemant Mathur create "extraordinary" cuisine; it
may be "expensive", but no one minds much given the "gorgeous"
bi-level space and "gracious" service; P.S. insiders say the "tasting
menu's the way to go."

Gotham Bar & Grill   27 | 25 | 26 | $68
12 E. 12th St. (bet. 5th Ave. & University Pl.), 212-620-4020;
www.gothambarandgrill.com
"Year after year" this Village star "continues to shine brightly"
thanks to chef Alfred Portale's "terrific", "towering" New American
cuisine, served by a "top-notch" staff in "simple but elegant"
surroundings; in short, "everything is grand – including the check",
although the $25 prix fixe is "a wonderful thing."

GRAMERCY TAVERN   28 | 26 | 27 | $73
42 E. 20th St. (bet. B'way & Park Ave. S.), 212-477-0777;
www.gramercytavern.com
Still "magical" and still NYC's No. 1 for Popularity, this "flagship
of Danny Meyers' fleet" is the "utmost" in "sophisticated dining",
from Tom Colicchio's "dazzling", "innovative" New American
cuisine to the "refined" yet "rustic" stetting to the "flawless",
hospitable service; in sum, it's well "worth every penny" ("and
it will take a ton of them") as well as the trouble of "getting a
reservation" – though if you can't book a "month in advance", the
more "affordable" "front tavern" takes walk-ins.

Grocery, The ☒   27 | 17 | 25 | $56
288 Smith St. (bet. Sackett & Union Sts.), Brooklyn, 718-596-3335
Now that "the secret's out", you'll need to "book weeks in advance"
at this "special" Carroll Gardens spot, whose "superb" "seasonal"
New American cuisine crafted and presented by "gracious"
owners Charles Kiely and Sharon Pachter "continues to dazzle";
"caring" service, a "small", "homey" dining room and a "dream-
come-true" back garden all make the experience worth waiting for.

Il Mulino ☒   27 | 18 | 24 | $79
86 W. Third St. (bet. Sullivan & Thompson Sts.), 212-673-3783;
www.ilmulinonewyork.com
Visits to this Southern Italian Village "classic" are "a culinary
event" featuring "king-size" portions of "heavy, old-fashioned",
"always-sublime" fare served by waiters that are "the epitome of
professional"; after landing a "difficult-", if not "impossible-
to-get" reservation, hit this "dimly lit" "shoebox" with "plenty
of cash", time and appetite, because meals here last "longer than
a flight to Italy and cost about the same."

Jean Georges ☒   27 | 26 | 27 | $95
Trump Int'l Hotel, 1 Central Park W. (bet. 60th & 61st Sts.), 212-299-3900;
www.jean-georges.com
Jean-Georges Vongerichten's "prowess is entirely seductive" at
his "opulent" New French flagship on Columbus Circle, where
"highly personal cooking from a modern master" is "impeccably
presented" to "spectacular" effect; factor in "flawless" service
and Adam Tihany's "subtle" "contemporary" design, and the high
tabs are fully understandable; if price is a concern, the $20 prix
fixe lunch offered in the "less-formal Nougatine Room" and on
the terrace is probably "the best bargain in town."

La Grenouille ☒   27 | 27 | 27 | $88
3 E. 52nd St. (bet. 5th & Madison Aves.), 212-752-1495;
www.la-grenouille.com
"Regal, elegant and timeless", this East Side French classic is one
of the city's "last grande dames" supplying "superb" cuisine in

"spectacularly beautiful" quarters with "sublime fresh flower displays"; "memorable wines", "gracious" black-tie service and the chance to experience "a treasured remnant of old NY" conspire to make the $87 prix fixe dinner feel like a bargain.

LE BERNARDIN ☒   28 | 27 | 28 | $100
155 W. 51st St. (bet. 6th & 7th Aves.), 212-554-1515; www.le-bernardin.com
"Still nonpareil", Maguy LeCoze's "world-class" Midtown French is "hallowed" ground for "sophisticated" dining and an "unequaled" practitioner of the "high art of seafood subtlety"; chef Eric Ripert's "exquisite" fare (rated No. 1 in NYC) arrives in "understated" environs where the "classical" service is as "flawless" as "clockwork"; granted, prices may be steep, but it's worth a "home equity loan" for a "profound event" that "lingers in the memory", and the $48 lunch conveys the same experience for far less.

Masa ☒   27 | 23 | 25 | $356
Time Warner Ctr., 10 Columbus Circle, 4th fl. (60th St. at B'way), 212-823-9800; www.masanyc.com
Like a "trip to the moon" for "sushi worshipers", this Time Warner Center Japanese (renowned as "NY's most expensive restaurant") is overseen by star chef Masayoshi Takayama who offers exquisite, Tokyo-worthy, kaiseki-style dinners, best taken at the counter "to get the full show"; some find the "multiple credit card prices" hard to swallow ($350 prix fixe before drink, tax and tip), but most feel it's "worth every Benjamin."

Matsuri ◑   23 | 27 | 20 | $56
Maritime Hotel, 369 W. 16th St. (9th Ave.), 212-243-6400; www.themaritimehotel.com
Set in an "ultraluxurious" "aircraft hangar"–esque space, this "stunning" Japanese beneath Chelsea's Maritime Hotel lives up to its looks with chef Tadashi Ono's "always good and sometimes magical" offerings; sure, the "price tags are a little steep" but the "sexy people running around" don't seem concerned.

Megu ◑   24 | 27 | 22 | $102
62 Thomas St. (bet. Church St. & W. B'way), 212-964-7777; www.megunyc.com
"Everything's over the top" at this TriBeCa Japanese, from the "unbelievable" theatrical setting arranged around a dramatic "ice Buddha sculpture" to the "menu as long as a book"; while the food's "fantastic" and the service seamless, regulars advise you "eat slowly to savor the flavors" – and to blunt the shock of those "ouch"-inducing prices.

Milos, Estiatorio ◑   26 | 23 | 22 | $70
125 W. 55th St. (bet. 6th & 7th Aves.), 212-245-7400; www.milos.ca
"If you can't get to Mount Olympus", this "spectacular" Midtown Greek seafooder is the next best peak with "incredibly fresh fish" "simply prepared" and presented in a "stylish" space by a "top-notch" staff; to avoid the "hard-to-swallow", by-the-pound prices, some suggest staying with the sensational first courses.

Modern, The ◑   25 | 26 | 22 | $70
Museum of Modern Art, 9 W. 53rd St. (bet. 5th & 6th Aves.), 212-333-1220; www.themodernnyc.com
"A work of art within a work of art", the latest "masterpiece" from Danny Meyer is set in the reopened MoMA, where "everything has

style", from chef Gabriel Kreuther's "memorable" French-American food to the "chic", spare setting; the more formal main dining room features a prix fixe–only menu eased by "killer views" of the museum's "serene sculpture garden", but it's easier to score a seat in the still "sexy" (but cheaper) bar where the menu's à la carte.

Montrachet 🖾   26 | 20 | 24 | $68
239 W. Broadway (bet. Walker & White Sts.), 212-219-2777;
www.myriadrestaurantgroup.com
Managing to stay at the "cutting-edge" of the TriBeCa scene, Drew Nieporent's 20-year-old French "delight" shows "real staying power" with its "consistent" food and service, even if the room is a bit "lacking in style"; "no-corkage-fee Mondays draw an interesting clientele", while Friday's $20 prix fixe lunch is "not to be missed."

Nobu   28 | 23 | 24 | $78
105 Hudson St. (Franklin St.), 212-219-0500;
www.myriadrestaurantgroup.com
Still "off the charts", this TriBeCa "destination" serves "sublime" Japanese-Peruvian fusion fare in "gorgeous" digs liberally garnished with celebs; no surprise, getting a reservation is an "ordeal", but beyond that, the "expert staff" and "astronomical" prices make for an "out-of-this-world" experience; P.S. the next-door adjunct offers the "same level" of dining but is "a tad less expensive" and easier to get into since it only takes walk-ins.

Nobu 57 ●🖾   – | – | – | VE
40 W. 57th St. (bet. 5th & 6th Aves.), 212-757-3000;
www.noburestaurants.com
Nobu Matsuhisa's spin-off of his Downtown powerhouse, this must-see-to-believe David Rockwell–designed Midtown duplex is a triumph of theatrical feng shui with a downstairs bar/lounge topped by a spacious, second-floor dining room; look for the same pricey Japanese-Peruvian fusion fare that built the brand, and as for the scene, it's a safe bet to become people-watching central.

Ouest   25 | 22 | 23 | $59
2315 Broadway (bet. 83rd & 84th Sts.), 212-580-8700; www.ouestny.com
"Leading the Upper West Side fine-dining renaissance", chef Tom Valenti has "mastered the art of upscale comfort food" here with "wickedly wonderful", "just original enough" New Americana; the food's "superlatively served" in "sophisticated", "grown-up" digs dotted with "sexy red leather booths" filled with a fair share of celebs – so "good luck getting a table."

Pearl Oyster Bar 🖾   27 | 15 | 20 | $40
18 Cornelia St. (bet. Bleecker & W. 4th Sts.), 212-691-8211;
www.pearloysterbar.com
Habitués of this Village "fantasy of a Maine clam shack" can't say enough about chef Rebecca Charles' "deservedly legendary" lobster roll or her "flawless" preparation of "whatever the fish of the day is"; service is "friendly" and "efficient" but waits can be "horrendous" given the "sardine" space.

PER SE   28 | 27 | 28 | $201
Time Warner Ctr., 10 Columbus Circle, 4th fl. (60th St. at B'way), 212-823-9335; www.perseny.com
Thomas Keller's year-old "shrine to food" has acolytes "swooning" over his French–New American tasting menus, a "parade of

culinary wizardry" providing "hours of bliss"; kudos also go to the "seamless", "choreographed" service and Adam Tihany's design that's "elegance stripped to its essentials", capped by "stunning" Central Park and Columbus Circle views; sure, the price is a "shocker", but "worth every C-note" for a "temporary pass to heaven"; appropriately, getting a table takes "divine intervention."

Peter Luger Steak House ∅   28 14 19 $66
178 Broadway (Driggs Ave.), Brooklyn, 718-387-7400;
www.peterluger.com
Williamsburg's "utopia of steakdom" is NYC's No. 1 chophouse – for the 22nd year – thanks to "buttery soft" meats and "killer sides" served in a faux (verging on funky) "German biergarten" setting; they "don't take plastic", so "bring cash, and plenty of it", and if the "gruff" waiters "mock you for asking for a menu", just "order what everyone else is" – the "ultimate porterhouse."

Picholine   27 24 25 $79
35 W. 64th St. (bet. B'way & CPW), 212-724-8585
"Soigné in every way", Terry Brennan's Lincoln Center French-Med is a "West Side star" with "heavenly food", "gracious hospitality" and a "beautiful" setting, capped by a "not-to-be-missed cheese cart"; although it costs a "pretty penny", Saturday's $28 prix fixe lunch is a "steal" and, no matter what the cost, a meal in the private rooms is sure to be happily remembered.

River Café   26 27 25 VE
1 Water St. (bet. Furman & Old Fulton Sts.), Brooklyn, 718-522-5200;
www.rivercafe.com
"Dress-up destination" dining doesn't get much better than at Buzzy O'Keeffe's Brooklyn waterfront "jewel" where the New American menu is "heavenly" and the "breathtaking" views of Lower Manhattan plus spectacular flowers and piano music provoke "at least one marriage proposal per night"; though a meal here can be pricey, it's "well worth any expense", especially if you snag a coveted window table.

Roberto's   27 18 22 $45
603 Crescent Ave. (Hughes Ave.), Bronx, 718-733-9503
The "new surroundings" are "marginally better" but the food remains as "stellar" as ever at Roberto Paciullo's relocated "piece of heaven in the Bronx"; regulars "time their visit carefully" ("no reservations" taken) and "don't even think of looking at a menu", preferring to let the chef (a "real character") choose for them.

Shun Lee Palace ◑   24 20 22 $52
155 E. 55th St. (bet. Lexington & 3rd Aves.), 212-371-8844
Proving "there is such a thing as upscale Chinese food", Michael Tong's Midtown "institution" combines "striking" surroundings and "silky service" to provide plenty of "panache"; ok, it may come at "Hong Kong real estate prices", but in return you get "emperor's-quality" "gourmet" dining.

Smith & Wollensky   23 18 20 $63
797 Third Ave. (49th St.), 212-753-1530; www.smithandwollensky.com
Beef eaters agree this "clubby", "man's man" East Side steakhouse is well "worth the high price of admission" given the "gargantuan" portions and "old-fashioned NY" service – or you can always "save a few dollars" at the Grill next door (that's also "open later").

Spice Market ◐
22 | 27 | 20 | $56

403 W. 13th St. (9th Ave.), 212-675-2322; www.jean-georges.com
"Another winner in the Vongerichten empire", this "sybaritic" Meatpacking District destination purveys "haute" Thai-Malay street food in a spectacular "theatrical" duplex setting frequented by "tourists early and glamorous folk later on"; despite barbs for "birdlike portions at beastlike prices", it's still "hard as hell to get reservations", and deservedly so.

Sushi of Gari
27 | 11 | 19 | $63

402 E. 78th St. (bet. 1st & York Aves.), 212-517-5340
The food's "so creative" and the prices so high at chef Gari's "avant-garde" East Side Japanese that admirers "don't know if it belongs in a restaurant or a museum guide"; just ignore the "unpretentious surroundings" and prepare for "a wait even on a school night"; P.S. "omakase is the only way to go."

SUSHI YASUDA ⊠
28 | 22 | 24 | $76

204 E. 43rd St. (bet. 2nd & 3rd Aves.), 212-972-1001;
www.sushiyasuda.com
"Nirvana" on 43rd Street, this Grand Central–area sushi purveyor showcases the "ethereal" handiwork of "true master" chef Naomichi Yasuda; the "best does not come cheap", but "first-rate service" and "modern", Calvin Klein–esque decor are also part of the "superb" package.

Tavern on the Green
15 | 25 | 17 | $59

Central Park W. (bet. 66th & 67th Sts.), 212-873-3200;
www.tavernonthegreen.com
"Central Park meets Disneyland" at this "storybook" West Side American institution where the "picturesque surroundings" "make up for any gastronomic deficiencies"; indeed, the Crystal Room's "Fabergé egg" decor alone makes it "a must" for lunch or special occasions; while dining in the garden can be delightful, it's also great for private parties.

Tomoe Sushi ⊠
27 | 8 | 17 | $38

172 Thompson St. (bet. Bleecker & Houston Sts.), 212-777-9346
"Neither rain nor sleet nor snow" deter diehards from this Village Japanese and its "affordable", "monster-size" sushi that "melts in your mouth like buttah"; defying the "nonexistent decor" and "postage stamp" dimensions, "ouch"-inducing lines wrap "around the block" every day.

21 Club ⊠
22 | 23 | 24 | $66

21 W. 52nd St. (bet. 5th & 6th Aves.), 212-582-7200; www.21club.com
This quintessential NYC institution, a former speakeasy, still draws Midtown "power brokers" with its "classic" American menu, "impeccable" service, "old-world panache" and "money-is-no-object" pricing; though it "won't be the same without [retired maitre d'] Bruce Snyder", its traditional "jacket-and-tie" dress code, "priceless bartenders" and "great private rooms" remain; don't miss a tour of the "not-to-be-believed wine cellar."

UNION SQUARE CAFE
27 | 23 | 26 | $62

21 E. 16th St. (bet. 5th Ave. & Union Sq. W.), 212-243-4020;
www.unionsquarecafe.com
Now in its 20th year and thus one of the "elder statesmen of NYC food", Danny Meyer's "evergreen" New American off Union Square

just "gets better with age", starting with chef Michael Romano's "inspired" cooking delivered by a staff that "acts as if your showing up has made their day"; folks in need of a "morale boost" "eat at the bar" when they can't get a table, and leave "happier than when they came in."

Veritas 27 23 26 $81
43 E. 20th St. (bet. B'way & Park Ave. S.), 212-353-3700; www.veritas-nyc.com
"Getting better with each passing year", chef Scott Bryan's "impeccable" Now American cuisine has become an "equal partner" to the "best wine list out there" at this Flatiron "mecca"; given the "refined" service and "subdued" setting, it's made for "romance", so long as you "bring your wallet" – the prix fixe–only dinner is $72.

Orange County, CA

TOP FOOD RANKING

Restaurant	Cuisine
27 Ramos House	New American
Studio	Cal./New French
26 Black Sheep	French/Spanish
Basilic	French/Swiss
Zov's Bistro	Mediterranean
Pascal	French
Napa Rose	Californian
Troquet	French Bistro
Pavilion	Cal./Mediterranean
25 Hobbit, The	Continental/French

OTHER NOTEWORTHY PLACES

Abe	Japanese
Antonello	Italian
Aqua	Seafood
Cheesecake Factory	American
Golden Truffle	Caribbean/French
Houston's	American
P.F. Chang's	Chinese
Picayo	Mediterranean
Roy's	Hawaii Regional
Ruth's Chris	Steakhouse

F	D	S	C

Abe — 25 | 14 | 19 | $49

2900 Newport Blvd. (29th St.), Newport Beach, 949-675-1739; www.aberestaurant.com

Disciples descend on Balboa Peninsula to experience chef Takahashi Abe's "exceptional" sushi "masterpieces" made with "immaculate precision" from "only the freshest" fish; overlook the "sterile decor" and wash down the "perfectly balanced flavors" with "premium sakes", and if you can't swing the "incredible omakase", remember "lunch is a bargain"; P.S. a "premier Crystal Cove" branch is set to open fall 2005.

Antonello ☒ — 25 | 24 | 24 | $48

South Coast Plaza, 3800 Plaza Dr. (Sunflower Ave.), Santa Ana, 714-751-7153; www.antonello.com

"Everything is magical" at South Coast Plaza's "perennial powerhouse" for "delectable" "handmade pastas and family recipes" boosted by an "extensive wine list" and "professional old-world" service; the "labyrinthine" palazzo interior "exudes romance" that's "great for a date" but also works for "power lunches and expense-account meals"; if a handful harrumph there's "too much snoot", most retort that Antonio Cagnolo's "special place" is "a must for lovers of serious Italian."

Aqua
25 | 26 | 23 | $65

St. Regis Monarch Beach Resort & Spa, 1 Monarch Beach Resort Dr. (PCH), Monarch Beach, 949-234-3325; www.stregismb.com
"Panoramic views of the Pacific" supply a "wowie kazowie" backdrop at sunset for "amazing seafood" at this "classy" setting in Monarch Beach, where "astronomical prices" are "probably appropriate" for meals "served with just enough élan"; if wet blankets squawk "the price is so lofty the food can't live up to it", aquanuts advise "don't leave this place to the hotel guests alone."

BASILIC ⊠
26 | 19 | 26 | $51

217 Marine Ave. (Park Ave.), Newport Beach, 949-673-0570
You "can't beat the excellent staff and intimate atmosphere" at this "matchbox-sized bistro" on Balboa Island where "unassuming genius" chef-owner Bernard Althaus turns out "sophisticated" French-Swiss dinners from a "limited", but "surprising menu"; "every bite is worth every dollar", prompting acolytes to crow "tiny space, big delight"; P.S. "don't miss the monthly raclette night."

BLACK SHEEP, THE ⊠
26 | 15 | 24 | $41

303 El Camino Real (3rd St.), Tustin, 714-544-6060; www.blacksheepbistro.com
An "incredible blend" of "savory, sensual" French and Spanish "delights" from the Mediterranean and "great wines for cheap" keep followers coming baa-ack to chef/co-owner Rick Bouffard's "hidden gem" in Old Towne Tustin "year after year"; the "really unique meals", including "awesome paella" and "wonderful bouillabaisse", are served with "loving customer care", providing a "unique" "break from the chains."

CHEESECAKE FACTORY
20 | 18 | 18 | $24

Brea Mall, 120 Brea Mall (Imperial Hwy.), Brea, 714-255-0115 ☻
Irvine Spectrum Ctr., 71 Fortune Dr. (Pacifica St.), Irvine, 949-788-9998
42 The Shops at Mission Viejo (I-5), Mission Viejo, 949-364-6200
Fashion Island, 1141 Newport Center Dr. (Santa Barbara Dr.), Newport Beach, 949-720-8333
www.thecheesecakefactory.com
Even die-hard chain-haters confess to periodic "gorge-athons" at this "solid" American, voted OC's Most Popular, where the menu "goes on for miles" and the "gargantuan portions" could "feed a small army"; sure, it's a good "value", but the trade-off lies in the "hit-or-miss" service, the "noisy" scene and the "painful" wait for a table – a "purgatory" that can last "two or three eternities."

Golden Truffle, The ⊠
25 | 14 | 20 | $44

1767 Newport Blvd. (bet. 17th & 18th Sts.), Costa Mesa, 949-645-9858
"Eccentric" chef-owner Alan Greeley's following worships at this "oddball outpost" where the "eclectic" French-Caribbean menu is an "adventurous mix" of "classics" and "culinary experiments"; the "crazy" strip-mall location can't diminish the glow of meals that "wow your palate"; all said, this "great find" is "very un-Orange County – in a good way."

Hobbit, The
25 | 23 | 26 | $74

2932 E. Chapman Ave. (Malena St.), Orange, 714-997-1972; www.hobbitrestaurant.com
"Dining the way it should be" rejoice foodies who journey to Orange's "quaint" "old house" for "memorable" French-Continental

repasts with "remarkable service" that feels like "great theater"; the "divine", single seating "experience" can last for three-and-a-half hours, beginning in the "wondrous wine cellar" and proceeding though seven courses in the "main part" of the establishment; in short, this "prix fixe throwback" is "unlike any other."

HOUSTON'S   21 | 20 | 20 | $31

Park Pl., 2991 Michelson Dr. (Jamboree Rd.), Irvine, 949-833-0977; www.houstons.com

This "dark, intimate", "popular" outfit with "consistent" American eats, "enthusiastic service" and "wonderful electricity" "makes a chain feel like a real dining experience"; the "winning formula": offer "limited items" like "fall-off-the-bone ribs", "do them well" and add "new" features like the sushi bar at Santa Monica; sure, waits can be "atrocious", but reservations are taken for larger parties.

Napa Rose   26 | 25 | 26 | $56

Grand Californian Hotel, 1600 S. Disneyland Dr. (Katella Ave.), Anaheim, 714-300-7170

"The Rose has no thorns" at this "un-Disney", "beautiful Craftsman-style" Californian set "amid the hubbub" of Anaheim's "Mouse empire" in the Grand Californian Hotel; "master" chef Andrew Sutton's "kitchen shines", turning out "Napa Valley–quality" "culinary creations", while "charming" GM-sommelier Michael Jordan offers "remarkable assistance selecting wine" from the "outstanding list"; sure, you "may sit next to the ubiquitous tourist family", but few mind because "this place rocks" ("ears to you" is the decisive kudo) for "special evenings."

Pascal ☒   26 | 19 | 24 | $54

1000 N. Bristol St. (Jamboree Rd.), Newport Beach, 949-752-0107; www.pascalnewportbeach.com

"Forever wonderful", sigh smitten Francophiles of "gracious magician" chef-owner Pascal Olhats' "rock-solid performer" in Newport Beach that's "not flashy or fussy, just one of the best" for "perfectly authentic" French cooking; the "so-so strip mall" "impression fades once you step inside" the "white-washed brick room" adorned with "gorgeous roses" and taste "mouthwatering" "comfort food" served by a "knowledgeable staff."

Pavilion   26 | 26 | 27 | $60

Four Seasons Hotel, 690 Newport Center Dr. (Santa Cruz Dr.), Newport Beach, 949-760-4920; www.fourseasons.com

"Hotel dining at its best" – yes, "everything is first class" at this "celebration kind of place", from "personalized" "service that sets the standard" to the "beautiful room" with "well-spaced tables that permit conversation"; the "expert" Cal-Med dishes boast "the finest ingredients", adding to an "experience" that's "memorable in all respects" (really, "how can you go wrong at a Four Seasons?").

P.F. CHANG'S CHINA BISTRO   20 | 19 | 18 | $26

Irvine Spectrum Ctr., 61 Fortune Dr. (Irvine Center Dr.), Irvine, 949-453-1211
The Shops at Mission Viejo, 800 The Shops at Mission Viejo (Crown Valley Pkwy.), Mission Viejo, 949-364-6661
Fashion Island, 1145 Newport Center Dr. (Santa Barbara Dr.), Newport Beach, 949-759-9007
www.pfchangs.com

It may "not be authentic", but it's a "great formula" that works, attest "hordes of faithful" fans that "keep coming back" to this "lively", "cool"-looking "champ of the Chinese chains"; "after an endless wait, treat yourself" to "worth-the-trip lettuce wraps" and "delicious" dishes with "just the right spices"; "don't know what the fuss is all about", pout the put-off, who insist it "tastes corporate."

Picayo 24 | 19 | 23 | $45

610 N. PCH (Boat Canyon Dr.), Laguna Beach, 949-497-5051; www.picayorestaurant.com

"Beyond excellent" despite a "less than scenic" "strip-mall" site, Laguna's "hidden gem" "does everything right", "delighting" diners with "intimate" dinners of "inspired" Med fare, "sauces that dazzle" and "friendly" hospitality; if a few feel the "food has declined under new ownership" (Laurent Brazier is no longer a partner, but still a consulting chef) and "don't know what the hype is about", for most it's still a "memorable experience."

RAMOS HOUSE CAFE 27 | 22 | 23 | $26

31752 Los Rios St. (Ramos St.), San Juan Capistrano, 949-443-1342; www.ramoshouse.com

"Bring your GPS" to find San Juan Capistrano's "hideaway" lodged in a historic adobe hugging the train tracks where "culinary genius" chef-owner John Q. Humphreys turns out "magical" New American cuisine "with Southern flair" that ranks No.1 for Food in OC; the "tranquil patio" seating flanking the herb garden provides a "delightful respite from high-powered" options, while "enthusiastic service" and "killer Bloody Marys" only swell the popularity of this "unique" choice for breakfast and lunch, prompting fans to ask "when will they add dinner?"

ROY'S 25 | 22 | 22 | $46

Fashion Island, 453 Newport Center Dr. (San Miguel Dr.), Newport Beach, 949-640-7697; www.roysrestaurant.com

Mavens of "master-of-the-islands" Roy Yamaguchi's "heavenly" ways with "exquisite" Hawaii Regional fare flock to Fashion Island's "always-packed" branch for "spectacular" seafood and the "best" chocolate soufflé; a few feel the service is "too formal" and gasp the "prices will take your breath away", but most feel the "unforgettable" food is "worth the splurge."

RUTH'S CHRIS STEAK HOUSE 25 | 21 | 23 | $54

2961 Michaelson Dr. (Jamboree Rd.), Irvine, 949-252-8848; www.ruthschris.com

"Year after year", this "clubby", "reliable" "old-school" Irvine steakhouse chainster with a "talented staff" serves "consistently perfect" "tender, juicy" "sizzling hunks of beef" "drenched in butter"; "try to heed your greed – you'll be tempted to order all the sides, but try to refrain" because the "protein" is "filling" and it gets "pricey"; still, it's "splurge"-worthy, in fact, "hands down and forks up" it's among the "best of the chains" – you "cannot mess with a classic."

STUDIO 27 | 28 | 24 | $78

Montage Resort & Spa, 30801 S. PCH (Montage Dr.), Laguna Beach, 949-715-6420; www.montagelagunabeach.com

Though the "kitchen aspires to be the best" at Laguna's "stellar oceanside offering" "on the cliffs", it's slightly outranked by the "enchanting" vistas of "the turquoise waters of the Pacific" seen from the "elegant comfort" of the "ultradeluxe" Montage Resort wrapped in "large plate glass windows"; when not hypnotized by the "drop-dead gorgeous" scenery, acolytes coo over chef James Boyce's "superb" Cal–New French cuisine ("try the tasting menu"), the "endless wine list" and the "polished service" at this "real boon to the OC dining scene."

Troquet   26 | 23 | 23 | $53 |
South Coast Plaza, 3333 Bristol St. (Anton Blvd.), Costa Mesa, 714-708-6865; www.troquetrestaurant.com

"Not what you'd expect to find" "perched atop South Coast Plaza", Tim and Liza Goodell's "smart" "hideway" is "absolutely stellar" for "divine", "pricey" French Bistro fare backed by a "first-rate wine program"; when "you grow up", this is where "you want to go", especially for the "transcendent mall experience" of "unbelievable foie gras" on the back patio; *oui,* a few dis "hit-or-miss" service, but for most, it's "never a disappointment", "after you've survived the expense of the stores downstairs."

ZOV'S BISTRO   26 | 20 | 22 | $34 |
Enderle Ctr., 17440 E. 17th St. (Yorba St.), Tustin, 714-838-8855; www.zovs.com

"Unique in a land of sameness" swoon admirers of "acclaimed" chef-owner Zov Karamardian's "delectable", "original" take on "perfectly prepared" Med dishes "served with flair"; the "elegant yet homey" Tustin bistro is favored for "perfect dinners" with "attentive service" on the "restful patio", while the attached bakery is an "oasis" for "excellent" sandwiches or breakfast while "soaking up the sun"; "always leave room" for the "out-of-this-world" pastries that "taste even better than they look."

Orlando

TOP FOOD RANKING

	Restaurant	Cuisine
27	Le Coq au Vin	French
	Victoria & Albert's	American
	Chatham's Place	Continental
	Del Frisco's	Steakhouse
26	Manuel's on the 28th	Eclectic
	California Grill	Californian
	Flying Fish Café	Seafood/New Amer.
	Emeril's Orlando	Contemp. Louisiana
25	Maison & Jardin	Continental
	Christini's*	Northern Italian
	Roy's	Hawaii Regional
	K	Eclectic
	Morton's	Steakhouse
	Jiko	African
	Little Saigon	Vietnamese
	Palm	Steakhouse
	Thai House	Thai
24	Ruth's Chris	Steakhouse
	Antonio's La Fiamma	Italian
	Enzo's on the Lake	Italian

OTHER NOTEWORTHY PLACES

Restaurant	Cuisine
Anaelle & Hugo	Continental/American
Boma	African
Café de France	French
Charley's	Steakhouse
Cheesecake Factory	American
Chef Justin's	Floribbean
Citricos	New American
Dux	New American
Emeril's Tchoup Chop	Asian/Polynesian
Harvey's Bistro	European/New Amer.
Hue – A Restaurant	Asian/New American
Le Cellier	Steakhouse
MoonFish	Seafood/Steakhouse
Norman's	New World
Primo	Italian
Rice Paper	Vietnamese
Seasons 52	Eclectic
Vito's	Steakhouse
Wolfgang Puck Cafe	Californian
ZaBella Ristorante	Northern Italian

*   Indicates a tie with restaurant above

Anaelle & Hugo
– | – | – | M

The Fountains, 7533 W. Sand Lake Rd. (Dr. Phillips Blvd.), 407-996-9292;
www.anaelleandhugo.com

Everything from sculptural plates to Sunday jazz to the vivid colors
that accent the mahogany dining room conveys the arty attitude of
this Continental-American bistro, where chef/co-owner Francis
Metais composes dramatic dishes from ingredients new to Orlando
(salsify, red rice, porcini oil); meanwhile, commerce-conscious
customers will appreciate the reasonable prices.

Antonio's La Fiamma ⊠
24 | 21 | 24 | $37

611 S. Orlando Ave. (Maitland Ave.), Maitland, 407-645-1035;
www.antoniosonline.com

"Delicious, authentic Italian food and handsome waiters" entice
diners to this Maitland mainstay "overlooking a nearby lake"; with
"elegant" service and a "superior wine list", it all adds up to a
"delightful setting" that's "comfortable" and "romantic" – though
sometimes "noisy": you can "hear the chefs yell at the waiters
through the open kitchen door."

Boma
24 | 24 | 23 | $31

Disney's Animal Kingdom Lodge, 2901 Osceola Pkwy.
(Sherbert Rd.), Lake Buena Vista, 407-938-4722;
www.disneyworld.com

"Remember not to eat anything the entire day" before heading to
Disney's "safari" smorgasbord where everything has an "African
twist": the environment includes a thatched roof and has an "open
marketplace feel", and those with "adventurous palates" can
explore an "awesome diversity of food" that's "as wild as the
Animal Kingdom residents", including the signature Zebra Dome
dessert ("do not leave without having one"); given the "world-class
flavors", fans note, the price is "remarkably low."

Café de France ⊠
23 | 18 | 23 | $44

526 S. Park Ave. (Fairbanks Ave.), Winter Park, 407-647-1869;
www.lecafedefrance.com

Patrons of this Winter Park sidewalk bistro laud its "fabulous French
dishes", including pâtés that "should not be missed"; though the
decor is "basic", the "quaint atmosphere" is "casual" and "quiet",
and the "friendly" staff is "always willing to suggest wines"; in
short, most conclude, you get "great food in a mediocre place
at high prices."

CALIFORNIA GRILL
26 | 25 | 24 | $45

Disney's Contemporary Resort, 4600 N. World Dr., Lake Buena Vista,
407-824-1576; www.disneyworld.com

This hotel Californian, tied with Emeril's Orlando as the area's
Most Popular restaurant, is "no Mickey Mouse" joint, say smitten
surveyors; local hotshot John State serves up "delectable" fare
("great" pork tenderloin) that "sensuously melts in your mouth";
"enthusiastic" staffers "really know the menu" and 31 on-site
sommeliers oversee 100 by-the-glass offerings; views of the Magic
Kingdom's nightly fireworks are "spectacular" but can give rise to a
"boisterous" atmosphere (some respondents feel they're "sitting
in a nursery school").

Charley's Steak House
24 | 19 | 22 | $47

8255 International Dr. (Sand Lake Rd.), 407-363-0228

(continued)
Charley's Steak House
*6107 S. Orange Blossom Trail (bet. W. Lancaster & Oak Ridge Rds.),
407-851-7130*
2901 Parkway Blvd. (Space Coast Pkwy.), Kissimmee, 407-239-1270
www.charleyssteakhouse.com
Everyone knows that the "wood fire"–grilled hunks of aged prime
beef at this carnivore's-delight chainlet "melt in your mouth", but
it's "quite a surprise" to also find "fantastic" shrimp, seared tuna
and other "excellent" seafood on its "classic steakhouse" menu;
just make a selection from the 1,000-label wine list and prepare
for a "mm-mm-good", "top-notch" experience.

CHATHAM'S PLACE ⑤   27 19 25 $49
*7575 Dr. Phillips Blvd. (Sand Lake Rd.), 407-345-2992;
www.chathamsplace.com*
Seek and ye shall find this "out-of-the-way" Dr. Phillips Continental,
an "intimate and lovely" spot in an "office building location" that
loyalists like for its "perfection in flavors and offerings": signature
dishes (e.g. "excellent" pecan-topped Florida black grouper) are
"exceptional" and the staff is "anxious to please"; though the
dining room is "private and quiet", some lament "decor that's still
in the '90s"; N.B. guitar music nightly.

CHEESECAKE FACTORY ◐   21 20 19 $27
Mall at Millenia, 4200 Conroy Rd. (I-4), 407-226-0333
Winter Park Vlg., 520 N. Orlando Ave. (Lee Rd.), Winter Park, 407-644-4220
www.cheesecakefactory.com
"Excess takes on new meaning" at the South Orlando and Winter
Park links of this "festive" American chain: for the "giant" menu,
"you may require a bookmark", and each entree is a "mountain" of
"reliably good" food; also outsized, though, is the "outrageous" wait
for a table, and naysayers nix "noisy" crowds and say servers
"sometimes disappear like Houdini"; "you won't leave hungry and
you won't leave broke", but "the word 'factory' says it all."

Chef Justin's Park Plaza Gardens   23 25 23 $46
*319 Park Ave. S. (New England Ave.), Winter Park, 407-645-2475;
www.parkplazagardens.com*
"Finally, it's back!" shout fans of this "venerable" Winter Park
"bastion", insisting the fare (now Floribbean) has "gone way up
since Justin Plank took over as chef"; a "dependable" staff helps
you "dine in style", whether alfresco "out on Park Avenue" or in the
"charming" "indoor courtyard" with "huge trees in the middle of the
dining room", all making for "a little bit of heaven in the center of
town"; N.B. the Decor rating may not reflect a post-*Survey* revamp.

Christini's Ristorante Italiano   25 20 25 $55
*The Marketplace, 7600 Dr. Phillips Blvd. (Sand Lake Rd.), 407-345-8770;
www.christinis.com*
"Food doesn't get much better in Orlando", which may be why
"special-occasion" celebrants, "out-of-towners" and those "on
expense accounts" shell out at this "enjoyably over-the-top", "sorta
schmaltzy" Dr. Phillips Tuscan where staffers "take the pressure
off men by giving every woman a rose" as they seat patrons in a
"cozy and romantic", "old-world" dining room; meanwhile, "prices
require a short-term loan", complain ciao hounds, who gripe "come
on, it's Italian – do they have to charge that much?"

Citricos 24 24 24 $44
*Disney's Grand Floridian Resort & Spa, 4401 Grand Floridian Way,
Lake Buena Vista, 407-824-2712; www.disneyworld.com*
"Inspired food and incredible service", effervesce eaters about this
New American "tucked into the Grand Floridian", where chef Gray
Byrum's "culinary genius" gives rise to a "sophisticated menu" of
"creative creations" ("fish that melts in the mouth", "fantastic
desserts"); the "striking", "Manhattan-chic decor" impresses too,
as does the "accommodating" staff's "individualized attention to
detail"; "not yet fully discovered by the masses", this "foodie must"
is "so good even the locals flock to Disney."

DEL FRISCO'S 27 19 24 $54
PRIME STEAK & LOBSTER Ⓢ
*729 Lee Rd. (I-4, exit 88), Winter Park, 407-645-4443;
www.delfriscosorlando.com*
"Steaks you'll remember all your life" and "lobster tails so huge
they belong in a 1950s mutant movie" make this Winter Park beef-
barn a favorite shrine for "red-meat pilgrimages" – "especially if
someone else is paying"; 500 wines and staffers who "never say
no" add appeal to a dining room that's so "crowded, noisy and
masculine" "you expect Sinatra to walk in"; aesthetes murmur that
the decor "needs revamping" (and indeed, it has been freshened
post-*Survey*) but of course that "isn't what you go for."

Dux Ⓢ 23 22 22 $53
*Peabody Orlando Hotel, 9801 International Dr. (W. Century Blvd.),
407-345-4550*
"Who says hotel food can't be great?" ask admirers of this New
American near the convention center, where the globally accented
fare, "down to the great bread basket, is lovely" and the formal
room is "exquisite" and "quiet"; detractors dismiss the jackets-
recommended venue as "overpriced" and say it's "time to revitalize
the concept"; P.S. arrive at 5 PM to watch the Peabody ducks
"march through the lobby to their penthouse retreat."

EMERIL'S RESTAURANT ORLANDO 26 22 24 $53
*Universal Studios CityWalk, 6000 Universal Blvd. (Vineland Rd.),
407-224-2424; www.emerils.com*
Lagasse lovers laud this hot Contemporary Louisianan, tied for
Orlando's Most Popular, as "an oasis in a desert of dreck" (read:
Universal Studios CityWalk); "all superlatives apply": food that's
"beyond outstanding", a "phenomenal wine list" (650 labels),
"expertly choreographed" service and a "casual but classy" space;
but plenty deplore the need to reserve "weeks ahead" for a
"hectic" "joint" that doesn't "justify the long wait and huge tab."

Emeril's Tchoup Chop 24 28 23 $48
*Royal Pacific Hotel & Resort, 6300 Hollywood Way (Universal Blvd.),
407-503-2467; www.emerils.com*
"Oh yeah, babe", croon swooning supporters of Emeril's Asian-
Polynesian in Universal's Royal Pacific Hotel; they enthuse about
its "innovative", "enchanted", "sexy", "South Seas–style" David
Rockwell decor (complete with waterfall and pond) as well as
"delectable", "innovative" dishes and "impeccable" service; some
say the strong start suggests the "master" "has done it again",
while others caution that this three-year-old may still be "going
through some growing pains."

Enzo's On The Lake ☒   24 | 21 | 22 | $45
1130 S. Hwy. 17-92 (Wildmere Ave.), Longwood, 407-834-9872;
www.enzos.com
"Don't go if you want a quick meal – this needs to be savored",
note *amici* of this Longwood Italian with "amazing antipasto" and
other "old-world favorites" like the signature Dover sole (in season)
or sauce "to rival your nonna's", served by a "superb" staff in a
"gorgeous" waterside setting; for an even livelier outing, "come
with 15 of your closest friends" or "get Enzo to sing"; result: "it
gets pretty loud in there."

FLYING FISH CAFÉ   26 | 24 | 23 | $45
Disney's BoardWalk Inn, 2101 N. Epcot Resorts Blvd. (Buena Vista Dr.),
Lake Buena Vista, 407-939-2359; www.disneyworld.com
"Top-of-the-(fishing)-line" seafood lures loyal locals as well as
returning tourists to Disney's New American reef 'n' beefer, which
garners kudos for fin fare that "tastes like it was caught a few
moments before", "amazing" steaks and the occasional "*très
fantastique*" bananas Napoleon; the "whimsical", "oceanic"
decor draws raves, but many say it's even more fun to "watch the
chefs fling flying fish" as you dine by the open kitchen, then stroll on
a boardwalk that's "nothing like New Jersey's – thank God!"

Harvey's Bistro   22 | 21 | 22 | $30
Bank of America Bldg., 390 N. Orange Ave. (E. Livingston St.),
407-246-6560 ☒
7025 County Rd. 46a (I-4), Heathrow, 407-936-1267
www.harveysbistro.com
In the middle of Downtown, this European-leaning New American is
a "cozy bistro" with a "delightful pub atmosphere" and "reasonable
prices"; it's perfect for a "power lunch" or "pre-theater dinner",
thanks to "homestyle-mixed-with-haute-cuisine" entrees that
are "not like mom's – they're better", and the ministrations of a
"sophisticated and helpful" staff; after dark, a "great bar scene"
draws a "post-trial crowd of attorneys and businessmen"; N.B. the
new Heathrow branch is unrated.

Hue - A Restaurant ☽   23 | 24 | 20 | $42
629 E. Central Blvd. (Summerlin Ave.), 407-849-1800;
www.huerestaurant.com
"Where did all these beautiful people come from?" wonder wags
about Thornton Park's "sassy", "trendy" Asian–New American,
as much "a "hipster" "meat market" ("wear black and bring your
attitude") as it is a "solid" eatery with "creative", "avant-charred"
comestibles; noting it's "noisy as hell" – especially on Thursday
nights, when it's "the place to be" – regulars recommend "be seen
on the outdoor corner patio" and warn there's "almost always a
wait" owing to a limited reservations policy.

Jiko — The Cooking Place   25 | 26 | 25 | $45
Disney's Animal Kingdom Lodge, 2901 Osceola Pkwy., Lake Buena Vista,
407-938-3000; www.disneyworld.com
Out of Africa comes the inspiration for Disney's "rare gem of resort
dining", an "exotic", "stunning venue" where chef Anette Grecchi
Gray blends "food from many cultures" with sub-Saharan flavors
"in joyous harmony" for entrees that will make you "close your eyes
and sigh" over fare you can pair with dozens of "enjoyable" South
African wines; furthermore, gratified grazers express heart-veldt

appreciation for a "knowledgeable, enthusiastic" staff that "treats you like a friend."

K ⌀ 25 | 20 | 23 | $39
2401 Edgewater Dr. (Vassar St.), 407-872-2332;
www.krestaurantwinebar.com
K is special, say kibitzers keen on this College Park kitchen, who give chef-owner Kevin Fonzo's Eclectic "50-seat oasis" kudos for "delicious", "worldly" K rations (including "to-die-for" monthly wine dinners and killer chocolate lava cake, "the best dessert in town"), and say a "superb", "helpful" staff treats them like kin; the "arty" setting, with "cool paintings" that change monthly, is also A-ok.

Le Cellier Steakhouse 23 | 21 | 23 | $38
Epcot, Canada Pavilion, Lake Buena Vista, 407-939-3463;
www.disneyworld.com
"Who knew Canadian food was more than maple syrup and bacon?" tease visitors to this Epcot cellar; in fact, the cave draws raves for steaks "cooked to perfection" and "fish so good you can't stop eating", served by a "hardworking" staff within a "cozy", "dark" space (a "welcome respite" from "hot, flat Florida"); overall it's more do-right than dud, but a contingent of critics judges this meatery "a little small" and its menu "booooring."

LE COQ AU VIN 27 | 20 | 25 | $43
4800 S. Orange Ave. (Holden Ave.), 407-851-6980;
www.lecoqauvinrestaurant.com
Voted No. 1 for Food in the area, this South Orlando Classic French has plenty to crow about, declare diners who dote on its "rich", "sublime" dishes (including the namesake entree, which *coq* fiends call a "masterpiece", and "top-notch" soufflés); better yet, this "hidden treasure", located in a "modest" house in an offbeat neighborhood, has the "nicest servers in town" and "bargain" prices, making it "the perfect place to go if you want to avoid the tourist traps."

Little Saigon 25 | 11 | 19 | $16
1106 E. Colonial Dr. (Mills Ave.), 407-423-8539; www.littlesaigon.com
The pho-one-one on this East Orlando Vietnamese, according to the few who have found it, is that its "straightforward fare" (i.e. "filling soups full of foreign flavors", "noodle dishes with every combination of meat and seafood") is "perfect when you only have a few bucks to spend" on "dinner before hitting the clubs"; consider "carpooling to avoid the dearth of parking" or, since it's "cramped and hurried" inside, takeout is a good bet; N.B. an expansion was planned for late summer 2005.

Maison & Jardin ⌀ 25 | 24 | 26 | $53
430 S. Wymore Rd. (State Rd. 436), Altamonte Springs, 407-862-4410;
www.maisonjardin.com
"Lovingly known as the Mason Jar", this Continental stalwart in Altamonte Springs "costs a fortune, but it's so worth it", say supporters; chef Hans Spirig "thrills" a "Francophile crowd" with culinary classics like "to-die-for" beef Wellington, the wine cellar contains 1,300 labels and the "gracious", "formally attired" staff "does everything right" – though trendier types tsk that it's a "stuffy", "tired old dame" and liken a meal here to "going to the country club with your grandparents."

MANUEL'S ON THE 28TH ☒　　26 | 28 | 27 | $59

Bank of America Bldg., 390 N. Orange Ave. (Colonial Dr.), 407-246-6580;
www.manuelsonthe28th.com

The "big tab is justified" by the "million-dollar view" from the "huge windows" on the 28th floor that showcase Orlando's "burgeoning Downtown"; so "at sunset" or "when thunderstorms roll in, this is where you want to be" – especially given its "impeccable" staff, "phenomenal" Eclectic entrees and desserts that are "works of art"; in all, romantics rhapsodize, it's "the perfect place to propose"; still, despite the panorama, a few claim Manny Garcia's showpiece "doesn't live up to expectations."

MoonFish Restaurant　　　23 | 24 | 19 | $39

The Fountains, 7525 W. Sand Lake Rd. (International Dr.), 407-363-7262;
www.fishfusion.com

Proponents of this Dr. Phillips surf 'n' turfer moon about its elaborate interior, a "gorgeous" "palace" where restrooms have "spigots shaped like porpoises" and "videos of swimming fish" above the urinals; many also maintain the "food's as cool as the bathroom", including a "daring and rewarding" menu of "spicy" swimmers, "fresh, flavorful" sushi and an "extensive" array of 400 wines; but skeptics snipe this place has "nothing to really distinguish itself except the decor" and bewail "expense-account" prices.

Morton's, The Steakhouse　　25 | 20 | 23 | $57

The Marketplace, 7600 Dr. Phillips Blvd. (Sand Lake Rd.), 407-248-3485;
www.mortons.com

"Popular with the limo set", this Restaurant Row link of the national chain of upscale beefmongers is "like every other", with "fabulous steak", a "must-have" chocolate cake, a "knowledgeable staff" and a "big-city atmosphere"; foes grumble that the "testosterone level is too high" and "you have to yell at your companions" to be heard, saying that the experience is "not worth the price", but supporters suggest you "have someone bring you and make sure they're loaded."

NORMAN'S　　　　　　　　– | – | – | E

Ritz-Carlton Orlando, Grande Lakes, 4012 Central Florida Pkwy.
(John Young Pkwy.), 407-393-4333; www.normans.com

Gastronaut Norman Van Aken brings his trademark New World cookery to Central Florida audiences at this dinner-only eatery, conjuring up concoctions of Caribbean and Latin American foods (yuca, habanero chiles, plantains) accompanied by thematic cocktails like the signature Cozumelpolitan (made with cactus-pear sorbet); the dining room, a romantic, well-windowed space with an octagonal wine vault rising through the center, is Ritzy indeed.

Palm　　　　　　　　　　25 | 21 | 24 | $56

Hard Rock Hotel, 5800 Universal Blvd. (Vineland St.), 407-503-7256;
www.thepalm.com

Meat lovers give the Palm a hand, dubbing this "great installation of a NYC original" in the Hard Rock Hotel at Universal a "first-class steakhouse", with "out-of-this-world" lobster and "gargantuan sides", and therefore an "excellent" choice "for taking customers if you want to close" a deal; disregarding the "cheerful and attentive" service and the walls' celebrity caricatures, though, dissatisfied dissenters deliver a thumbs-down, deeming the place merely "functional" – not to mention "noisy, noisy, noisy and overpriced."

Primo
– | – | – | E

JW Marriott Orlando, Grande Lakes, 4040 Central Florida Pkwy.
(John Young Pkwy.), 407-393-4444; www.primorestaurant.com
Maine-based maestro Melissa Kelly now gladdens mouths down
South at the upscale JW Marriott Orlando Grande Lakes; her
organic, Italian-influenced menus may include such specials as
pork saltimbocca and farm-raised lamb chops (plus decadent
desserts designed by Kelly's husband/partner/pastry chef, Price
Kushner) along with an international array of some 200 wines; the
roomy Tuscan-farmhouse environs also feature terrace seating
for up to 30 people.

Rice Paper
– | – | – | I

7637 Turkey Lake Rd. (Sand Lake Rd.), 407-352-4700
Just steps from Restaurant Row, this newcomer takes Vietnamese
vittles to a new level for Orlando: it infuses such exotic and
authentic ingredients as saw-leaf and lemongrass into enticing
soups and stir-fries, plates them dramatically and presents them
in a chic two-room space.

Roy's Orlando
25 | 23 | 24 | $48

Plaza Venezia, 7760 W. Sand Lake Rd. (Dr. Phillips Blvd.), 407-352-4844;
www.roysrestaurant.com
"So much for a jaded palate", lei people say of their meals at Roy
Yamaguchi's "pricey" Plaza Venezia outpost of his Hawaii Regional
chain; "inspired, almost over-the-top" seafood entrees and the
signature "oozy chocolate soufflé" "with a molten lava center"
wake up "weary taste buds"; meanwhile, an "attentive but not
obtrusive" staff steers patrons through this Pacific passage amid
an atmosphere that some call "lively" and others "loud."

Ruth's Chris Steak House
24 | 22 | 23 | $53

7501 W. Sand Lake Rd. (Turkey Lake Rd.), 407-226-3900
Winter Park Vlg., 610 N. Orlando Ave. (Webster Ave.), Winter Park,
407-622-2444
www.ruthschris.com
Whether you "hang out in the bar and eat solo" or "take a big group
and get a private room", you can't help but have a "wonderful
experience" at these Bay Hill and Winter Park meateries, according
to acolytes of the "huge martinis", "big, juicy steaks" and "to-die-
for sides"; if a few wonder "what all the fuss is about" and reproach
its "everything's-à-la-carte" approach, the majority simply sings
the praises of its "serious beef" whose "quality holds true."

Seasons 52
23 | 25 | 23 | $36

Plaza Venezia, 7700 W. Sand Lake Rd. (Dr. Phillips Blvd.), 407-354-5212
The Altamonte Mall, 463 E. Altamontle Dr. (Palm Springs Dr.),
Altamonte Springs, 407-767-1252
www.seasons52.com
"It's like sin and forgiveness all in one" at these Eclectics from the
ex chef and manager of California Grill, thanks to "craveworthy"
entrees all "under 475 calories" and "almost guilt-free desserts"
served in shot glasses; "warm wood" and "inviting textures"
make the lakeside Bay Hill locale "one of Orlando's prettiest"
(Altamonte Springs diners must make do with patios) and the
"polite" staff "tries hard"; still, antagonists dislike what they call
the "bland food", and the promise of low-cal luxury attracts so
many weight-watchers you may have to "wait, wait, wait."

Thai House ⌧ 25 | 16 | 21 | $22
2117 E. Colonial Dr. (N. Hillside Ave.), 407-898-0820
The "spartan" decor at this East Colonial Thai "neighborhood favorite" is just "ok" (if not "dumpy"), but "this place is all about the food, and it is fantastic", agree adherents, urging readers to delve into "inexpensive" dishes that are "packed with flavor" with the assistance of "friendly" staffers who "encourage" visitors "to try something new."

VICTORIA & ALBERT'S 27 | 26 | 27 | $85
Disney's Grand Floridian Resort & Spa, 4401 Grand Floridian Way, Lake Buena Vista, 407-939-3463; www.disneyworld.com
Ecstatic epicures "feel like well-fed royalty" at this formal American (jacket required) in the Magic Kingdom, where a gaslight-era "night of delights" includes a "maid-and-butler" duo who "anticipate every need", an "exquisite" six-course meal you can "embellish" with picks from the 700-label wine list and sometimes even a harpist; fans rave it's "worth the six-month wait" to sit at Scott Hunnel's chef's table for a personalized "plethora of delicacies"; though to a few the whole experience seems "slightly contrived", by consensus it's "the best splurge in Orlando."

Vito's Chop House 23 | 21 | 20 | $46
8633 International Dr. (Austrian Row), 407-354-2467; www.vitoschophouse.com
"Perfectly aged" and "seasoned" chops "served just as you like them" plus a "staggering" wine list (950 entries) entice I-Drive conventioneers to this "Italian-influenced steakhouse" lauded for "lower-than-average prices"; just beware of "pushy" servers and laissez-faire management "oriented toward the tourist."

Wolfgang Puck Cafe 22 | 20 | 19 | $34
Downtown Disney West Side, 1482 E. Buena Vista Dr. (Hotel Plaza Blvd.), Lake Buena Vista, 407-938-9653; www.wolfgangpuck.com
It's "not quite Spago, but what is?" observe patrons of this Downtown Disney casual Californian; still, it offers "the best pizza this side of the Atlantic", "super-fresh sushi" and "eclectic yet safe" entrees; the decor is "cool" and "colorful", but be prepared for "slow" service – and "bring earplugs."

ZaBella Ristorante – | – | – | M
1234 N. Orange Ave. (Oak Rd.), Winter Park, 407-628-2333; www.zabella.com
Chef/co-owner Todd Holender's trattoria tantalizes taste buds with this Winter Park address, which offers a well-tuned repertoire of robust Northern Italian treats ranging from panzanella to pasta to prosciutto, all using ultrafresh ingredients; favorites both new and old are served up in a stylishly modern, yet warm, art-studded room.

Palm Beach

TOP FOOD RANKING

	Restaurant	Cuisine
27	11 Maple St.	New American
	Chez Jean-Pierre	French
	Four Seasons	Floribbean
	Little Moirs Food Shack	Seafood
26	Kathy's Gazebo	Continental
	Cafe Chardonnay	New American
	Café Boulud	French
	New York Prime	Steakhouse
	Le Mistral	French
25	Café L'Europe	Continental

OTHER NOTEWORTHY PLACES

Addison	Continental
Cheesecake Factory	American
Houston's	American
Ke-e Grill	Seafood
La Vieille Maison	French
Marcello's La Sirena	Italian
Morton's	Steakhouse
P.F. Chang's	Chinese
Ta-boo	Continental/New Amer.
32 East	New American

F	D	S	C

Addison, The

23	27	22	$54

2 E. Camino Real (S. Dixie Hwy.), Boca Raton, 561-395-9335;
www.theaddison.com
The epitome of "special-occasion" dining is this "romantic" Boca Raton Continental set in Addison Mizner's restored 1925 office building; though the "consistently good" fare pleases patrons, it's the "stunning", "fairy-tale" setting enhanced by the "gorgeous courtyard" complete with banyan tree that wins over the hearts of many; surveyors split over service (from "excellent" to "erratic"), but the majority concurs that a "memorable" evening's in store.

Café Boulud

26	27	25	$71

Brazilian Court Hotel, 301 Australian Ave. (Hibiscus Ave.), 561-655-6060;
www.danielnyc.com
Daniel Boulud's "sophisticated" Palm Beach French (a satellite of the NYC original) in the Brazilian Court Hotel "makes a lasting impression" with "magical" fare paired with "wonderful" wines and "perfect service", and offers a crowd "dripping in diamonds" the option of dining in either the "beautiful outdoor patio" or in the "elegant" dining room; the prices, not surprisingly, are strictly "haute"; N.B. open for breakfast, and jackets suggested in season for dinner.

Cafe Chardonnay   26 | 22 | 24 | $52

Garden Square Shoppes, 4533 PGA Blvd. (Military Trail),
Palm Beach Gardens, 561-627-2662; www.cafechardonnay.com
It's "hard to believe" it's in a strip mall, but this Palm Beach Gardens
"jewel" defies expectations with "divine" New American food
delivered by an "excellent staff", a "stellar wine list" and "pretty
decor" that contributes to an overall "unpretentious" ambiance; all
in all, it's a "winner", albeit one that comes with a "high price" tag.

CAFÉ L'EUROPE   25 | 27 | 25 | $70

331 S. County Rd. (Brazilian Ave.), 561-655-4020; www.cafeleurope.com
"Even after 25 years", Palm Beach's "grande dame" is still "on
top" of her game, offering its "society clientele" "outstanding",
"beautiful presentations" of Continental food complemented by a
"killer", 2,400-label wine list and a "pampering" floor crew who
"attend to every detail" in the "best looking dining room" in town;
it's "chichi to the nth degree, so expect "unparalleled people-
watching" and to catch up on area "drama and gossip"; P.S. better
"bring your banker" to pay for it.

CHEESECAKE FACTORY ◑   20 | 18 | 19 | $26

5530 Glades Rd. (Butts Rd.), Boca Raton, 561-393-0344
CityPlace, 701 S. Rosemary Ave. (Okeechobee Blvd.), West Palm Beach,
561-802-3838
www.thecheesecakefactory.com
The "best chain – ever", aver acolytes of these South Florida
Americans whose "encyclopedic" menus feature "giant-sized
portions" of everything, from "burgers to Thai", and the "ultrarich",
"unbelievable" namesake desserts, served by a "cheerful",
"efficient" staff; sure, "the line goes all the way to I-95" and it's so
loud you'd better "bring your megaphone", but the "consistent",
reasonably priced fare and "kid-friendly" credo make it a "winner."

CHEZ JEAN-PIERRE BISTRO ▨   27 | 21 | 25 | $67

132 N. County Rd. (bet. Sunrise & Sunset Aves.), 561-833-1171
"Chez incredible!" exclaim enthusiasts about the "undisputed
champion"of French dining in Palm Beach, a redoubt of "old-time",
"magnificent" Gallic dishes ("flawless Dover sole") delivered by
"classy", "friendly" servers; owners Nicole and Jean-Pierre
Leverrier "take care of their patrons" and see to it that the ambiance
is "perfect without being pretentious", so "plan ahead", and "if you
can eat only one meal out", "eat it here."

11 MAPLE STREET   27 | 24 | 25 | $53

3224 NE Maple Ave. (11th Ave.), Jensen Beach, 772-334-7714
"It all works" at this Jensen Beach New American that nabs Palm
Beach's No.1 ranking for Food for the second straight year given
chef-owner Mike Perrin's "unique", "consistently wonderful"
cuisine that employs the "freshest ingredients" possible and
includes "imaginative" options for vegetarians; the "unobtrusive"
service works its magic in a "beautifully appointed", "funky old
house" setting; N.B. closed Mondays and Tuesdays.

FOUR SEASONS – THE RESTAURANT   27 | 27 | 27 | $73

Four Seasons Resort, 2800 S. Ocean Blvd. (Lake Ave.), 561-533-3750;
www.fourseasons.com\palmbeach
A hotel restaurant to "judge others by", this "pearl" perched
oceanside in Palm Beach beckons with "genius"-chef Hubert

Des Marais' "outstanding Floribbean" food that manages to be "comforting and innovative"; the "perfection" trickles down to the "superb" staff, "elegant" setting and nightly live piano; while you may have to "break the piggy bank" to foot the bill, it's "worth it" considering this "treasure" "succeeds on all fronts."

HOUSTON'S   21 | 20 | 21 | $32 |
1900 NW Executive Center Circle (Glades Rd.), Boca Raton, 561-998-0550; www.houstons.com
Floridians fare well at this Boca chain link known for "rock-solid" American food, especially "great burgers" and the now legendary "fabulous" spinach dip; the "comfortable", "clubby" setting, "consistently good service" and "active bar scene" is a testament to their popularity and reason for many to endure such "long waits."

KATHY'S GAZEBO CAFE ☒   26 | 22 | 23 | $59 |
4199 N. Federal Hwy. (Spanish River Rd.), Boca Raton, 561-395-6033; www.kathysgazebo.com
"So civilized" and "old school", this "classy" Continental in Boca Raton is still "worth dressing up for" after nearly 25 years in light of the "wonderful" menu featuring time-tested signatures such as "outstanding" Dover sole; though the "white-glove treatment" seems "stuffy" to some, and others opine that "reservations need to be honored on time", the majority maintains "you can't find better" in its class – just "bring money, and then bring more money."

KE-E GRILL   24 | 22 | 21 | $42 |
17940 N. Military Trail (bet. Champion Ave. & Clint Moore Rd.), Boca Raton, 561-995-5044
14020 US 1 (Donald Ross Rd.), Juno Beach, 561-776-1167
"Fabulously fresh fish" paired with "excellent sides" can be had at these Palm Beach County seafooders; the "friendly", "efficient service" (the "check arrives with the coffee – get it?") and "great" "South Pacific"–style setting make waiting in season on "way-too-long lines" a "no-brainer"; N.B. reservations taken at only the Boca location.

La Vieille Maison   25 | 26 | 24 | $66 |
770 E. Palmetto Park Rd. (NE Olive Way), Boca Raton, 561-391-6701
A fixture on Palm Beach County's dining scene for nearly 30 years, this French "classic" in Boca Raton continues to satisfy supporters with "superb" meals, a "beautiful", "sophisticated" multiroomed setting that makes you "feel like you're in a private château" and a staff that "treats first-timers like guests of honor"; if critics chastise it for "losing its luster", far more maintain it's "easy to see why it's been in business so long."

Le Mistral   26 | 19 | 21 | $57 |
Sound Advice Plaza, 12189 US 1 (PGA Blvd.), North Palm Beach, 561-622-3009
This "piece of Provence" has *le tout* North Palm Beach swooning with delight thanks to "lovingly prepared" classic French dishes served in "romantic" quarters; the "caring" owners and staff "always remember you" and make dining here a "treat"; tip: don't let the "wonderful" summer prix fixe menu blow by you.

LITTLE MOIRS FOOD SHACK 🗷   27 | 14 | 20 | $27
103 US 1 (E. Indiantown Rd.), Jupiter, 561-741-3626;
www.littlemoirsfoodshack.com
Prepare yourself for "funky", "beachy", "chintzy" digs and
"some of the best food in the county" at this "secret" Jupiter
seafooder where locals in-the-know put up with "terrible waits"
and jam into the "small", "noisy" space to get their hands on
"fresh", "exciting" fish preparations with "zing"; "slow service"
is an afterthought when you consider this "shack" provides a
"cheap" ticket to a "great meal."

Marcello's La Sirena   25 | 18 | 22 | $55
6316 S. Dixie Hwy. (Forest Hill Blvd.), West Palm Beach, 561-585-3128;
www.lasirenaonline.com
"A breath of fresh air" in a sea of "strip plazas", this West Palm
Beach Italian offers food "so delicious you could never produce it at
home", a "welcoming" vibe and an "intimate" setting; cognoscenti
crow that the "good" Boot-centric vino selections come at
"uninflated prices", and even if the "attentive" service "slows
down" at times, this "jewel" is on many "repeat-visit" lists.

Morton's, The Steakhouse   24 | 21 | 23 | $59
Phillips Point Office Bldg., 777 S. Flagler Dr. (Lakeview Ave.),
West Palm Beach, 561-835-9664; www.mortons.com
"Many compete, but few deliver" as well as this "premium" West
Palm Beach outpost of the steakhouse chain, where business types
with expense accounts and other carnivores herd in to a typically
"clubby" atmosphere for "mouthwatering filets" that require
nothing more than "a butter knife", "delicious sides" and "decadent
desserts" all served by a "professional" staff; even critics cowed
by "obscene" prices are willing to fork over the cash and say
it's "worth it."

New York Prime   26 | 22 | 22 | $64
2350 Executive Center Dr. NW (Glades Rd.), Boca Raton, 561-998-3881;
www.newyorkprime.com
Carnivores "count up the ways" they "love" this "cavernous" Boca
steakhouse where a "noisy" crowd of "glitterati" and "celebs"
"dressed to the nines" wolf down "fabulous" steaks, "delicious
sides" and a chocolate cake "to die for"; critics, however, counter
that the "wallet-busting" goods are served by a staff that's well
aware of "the pecking order."

P.F. CHANG'S CHINA BISTRO   21 | 21 | 18 | $29
The Gardens, 3101 PGA Blvd. (Campus Dr.), West Palm Beach,
561-691-1610; www.pfchangs.com
The fare may be "hardly authentic", but it's still "reasonably priced"
and "consistently delicious" at this "contemporary" Chinese chain
servicing South Florida sinophiles who stick out "long waits" for
a table; the handful of salty sorts who see "spotty service" and
"commercial"-grade food are overruled.

Ta-boo   22 | 21 | 21 | $49
221 Worth Ave. (bet. Hibiscus Ave. & S. County Rd.), 561-835-3500;
www.taboorestaurant.com
A "must" for residents and visitors alike, this "classy" Worth
Avenue "old-timer" is lauded for its "wonderful" Continental–New
American fare and "excellent lunches" that are a "tough ticket in

season", and for an "attentive staff"; the "elegant", "sparkling" setting's ready-made for a "beautiful", "dressed-for-a-fashion-show" crowd that picks up on the "delicious conversations" at the other tables; P.S. you may have to "beware the man eaters" at the "active bar."

32 East   25 | 20 | 22 | $48

32 E. Atlantic Ave. (bet. SE 1st & Swinton Aves.), Delray Beach, 561-276-7868; www.32east.com

This crowd-"pleaser" on Delray Beach's "hot" Atlantic Avenue "continues to shine" with chef Nick Morfogen's "imaginative" New American food, "first-rate service", a "great wine list" and "soothing", wood-appointed quarters suitable for both "romance" and "people-watching"; even those who think the prices are "more NYC" than FLA consider it "fabulous"; P.S. the "happening bar scene" means it "can get loud."

Philadelphia

TOP FOOD RANKING

Restaurant	Cuisine
28 Fountain	Continental/New French
Le Bec-Fin	French
Le Bar Lyonnais	French Bistro
Django	Eclectic
Birchrunville Store	French/Italian
Lacroix/Rittenhouse	French
Vetri	Italian
27 Gilmore's	French
Morimoto	Japanese
Buddakan	Asian Fusion
Bluefin	Japanese
La Bonne Auberge	French
Deux Cheminées	French
26 Swann Lounge	New French/New Amer.
Citrus	Eclectic
High St. Caffé	Cajun-Creole
Savona	French/Italian
¡Pasión!	Nuevo Latino
Brasserie Perrier	New French
24 Mainland Inn	New American

OTHER NOTEWORTHY PLACES

Restaurant	Cuisine
Alison at Blue Bell	New American
Blue Sage	Vegetarian
Dmitri's	Med./Seafood
General Warren Inne	American
Jake's	New American
L'Angolo	Italian
Little Fish	Seafood
Meritage	Eclectic/European
Nan	New French/Thai
Ota-Ya	Japanese
Overtures	French/Med.
Peking	Chinese/Japanese
Pif	French Bistro
Prime Rib	Steakhouse
Shiao Lan Kung	Chinese
Southwark	New American
Sovalo	Italian
Susanna Foo	Chinese/New French
Totaro's	Eclectic
Washington Square	New American

Alison at Blue Bell ⌧⌀   25 | 15 | 21 | $42 |
721 Skippack Pike (Penllyn-Blue Bell Pike), Blue Bell, 215-641-2660;
www.alisonatbluebell.com
"Superbly done fish" by Striped Bass founder Alison Barshak
attracts the Montco "scene-and-heard" herd to this "minimalist"
New American BYO, where they're tended by "knowledgeable"
staffers "without an ounce of pretension"; though the "corporate-
center" setting can be "as noisy and crowded as the cafeteria at
Beverly Hills High", and a few cynics fret that the chef "tries to
get too cute with basic stuff", most surveyors give thanks for
this "suburban salvation."

BIRCHRUNVILLE STORE CAFE ⌧⌀   28 | 22 | 25 | $45 |
1403 Hollow Rd. (Flowing Springs Rd.), Birchrunville, 610-827-9002;
www.birchrunvillestorecafe.com
Francis Trzeciak lures city slickers out to the "bucolic" "wilds
of Chester County" with his "superb", "classical yet innovative"
"fusion of haute cuisine" from France and Italy that leaves "taste
buds happy"; as a result, his "charming", "relaxed", cash-only BYO
in a "converted country store" (circa 1792) is one of the highest-
rated rooms outside the metropolis; you'll have to reserve a table
"at least a month in advance" – so "don't go if you're in a hurry";
N.B. closed Sunday–Tuesday, and reservations only.

Bluefin ⌧   27 | 15 | 23 | $32 |
1017 Germantown Pike (Virginia Rd.), Plymouth Meeting, 610-277-3917;
www.sushibluefin.com
"No superlative is excessive" for this "tiny", "quaint" Japanese
BYO in a Plymouth Meeting mini-mall, where the "wonderful" sushi
chef "builds a meal you could only dream of" from his 89 menu
offerings; pick up a "six-pack of Japanese beer" or "your own
sake", to round off an "unquestionably" "fabulous" meal; the place
is a mere "hole-in-the-wall", however, so "do make reservations"
to avoid "terrible waits on busy nights."

Blue Sage Vegetarian Grille ⌧   26 | 13 | 22 | $24 |
772 Second Street Pike (Street Rd.), Southampton, 215-942-8888;
www.bluesagegrille.com
"Wow! who cares that it's a vegetarian place?" rhapsodize
respondents about Mike and Holly Jackson's "friendly" Bucks
County BYO; the "unassuming" "strip-mall location" may "not
look like much", but the local "king of veggie fare" exhibits such
"exceptional", "artful" takes on the green stuff ("like jazz
improvisations") that even committed carnivores "swoon" and
marvel that he "eschews tofu, seitan and mock-anything";
N.B. open Sundays in summer.

Brasserie Perrier   26 | 24 | 24 | $52 |
1619 Walnut St. (bet. 16th & 17th Sts.), 215-568-3000;
www.brasserieperrier.com
"Even New Yorkers" venture south to "linger, dine, enjoy" (and
"impress the in-laws") at Georges Perrier's "Le Bec-Fin lite" on
Restaurant Row; chef-partner Chris Scarduzio's "phenomenal"
New French cuisine pleases "discriminating palates", while
aesthetes adore the "sexy, sumptuous" art deco–inspired dining
room, where "cultured" staffers deliver "stellar" service without
"pretense"; meanwhile, the "happening" lounge bursts with
"personality, from clamor to glamour."

BUDDAKAN
| 27 | 27 | 23 | $49 |

325 Chestnut St. (bet. 3rd & 4th Sts.), 215-574-9440; www.buddakan.com
"Believe the hype", avow disciples who still swoon ("I died and went to a higher plane") over Stephen Starr's "ab fab", "über-cool" Old City Asian fusion "wonder", rated No. 1 for Popularity in Philly; connoisseurs "just don't get tired of" chef Scott Swiderski's "creative", "delicious" dishes, served in the shadow of a 10-ft. golden Buddha by "fast-paced" "young 'uns"; steeply mounting tabs can end up "a little on the completely outrageous side", so most achieve true "serenity" only when "on an expense account."

Citrus ⊠⼾
| 26 | 14 | 21 | $30 |

8136 Germantown Ave. (bet. Abington Ave. & Hartwell Ln.), 215-247-8188
Vegetarians squash in to this "tiny", "quirky", earth-friendly Eclectic BYO in Chestnut Hill to relish its "amazing" cuisine ("incredible bananas Foster") for surprisingly few greenbacks; because of a no-res policy, however, "plan to wait" or "have a drink across the street and leave your cell number"; but cynical carnivores are soured on "pretentious" "political signs" that say "you can't wear fur", "yet they serve fish" (but not meat or poultry).

Deux Cheminées ⊠
| 27 | 27 | 26 | $76 |

1221 Locust St. (bet. 12th & 13th Sts.), 215-790-0200; www.deuxchem.com
"Chef-owner Fritz Blank "continues to outdo himself" and "never ceases to amaze" with the "sublime" French fare in his "opulent" 1875 townhouse in Center City; cognoscenti count on a "perfect romantic meal" with "flawless execution" all around ("you'll hug [Blank] after dinner" – then ask to see his cookbook collection); the four-course prix fixe dinner is $85, but even if a "home-equity loan may be necessary", it's "worth every cent" to enjoy this "rare treat."

DJANGO
| 28 | 19 | 25 | $41 |

526 S. Fourth St. (South St.), 215-922-7151
"Get your speed-dial ready 30 days in advance" if you plan to djingle Bryan Sikora and Aimee Olexy's "hard-to-get-into", 38-seat, Euro-style Eclectic BYO; despite its "understated storefront" setting off South Street, meteoric Food ratings testify to Sikora's "complex", "inventive combinations"; savants suggest "save room" for the "ambrosial cheese course" with Olexy's commentary, just one aspect of the "expert service."

Dmitri's
| 24 | 13 | 19 | $28 |

2227 Pine St. (23rd St.), 215-985-3680
795 S. Third St. (Catharine St.), 215-625-0556 ⼾
Dmitri Chimes' "inexpensive" Med seafood sibs bear a family likeness – "über-fresh", "no-frills", "top-notch plates" ("divine" grilled octopus), "frazzled" yet "efficient" servers who "deserve Olympic medals for gymnastics in cramped spaces" and "loud, loud, loud" acoustics – but the Queen Village original is a cash-only BYO "shoebox" where regulars cheerfully "wait in line before opening" so they can "sit in their neighbors' laps", while the slightly larger Fitler Square branch takes cards and serves liquor.

FOUNTAIN RESTAURANT
| 28 | 28 | 29 | $76 |

Four Seasons Hotel, 1 Logan Sq. (bet. Benjamin Franklin Pkwy. & 18th St.), 215-963-1500; www.fourseasons.com
Once again voted No. 1 for Food, the Four Seasons' "always-superb" culinary "mecca" continues to be Philadelphia's favorite

venue for "impressing the date or closing the deal"; maestro Martin Hamann's "heavenly" Continental–New French cuisine seems "impervious to the trends du jour"; "experienced" staffers display "brilliant attention to minuscule details", and the "elegant" room "glistens"; in all, "what a grand experience" – of course "you do pay for such excellence"; N.B. jacket required.

General Warren Inne ⧈   25 | 25 | 24 | $47
General Warren Inne, Old Lancaster Hwy. (Warren Ave.), Malvern, 610-296-3637; www.generalwarren.com
A Main Liners' "mainstay" in Malvern, this "subdued" American in a "comfortable old" Revolutionary-era (1745) house "takes you back in time" for "classic favorites" ("crab cakes dispatched from heaven") while "knowledgeable, professional" attendants "make you feel like a million bucks"; fresh-air folks "love the patio out back in spring."

Gilmore's ⧈   27 | 23 | 26 | $51
133 E. Gay St. (bet. Matlack & Walnut Sts.), West Chester, 610-431-2800; www.gilmoresrestaurant.com
"Why did Georges Perrier ever let this man leave?" puzzle foodies who find Le Bec-Fin alum Peter Gilmore's Classic French cuisine "as imaginative" as it is "spectacular" when they celebrate "special occasions" at his "adorable" BYO in West Chester; "warm" staffers are "excellent" as well, though it's almost "impossible to get a reservation" due to the restaurant's 35-seat capacity (so "cramped" you might "eat your neighbor's salad" and "so noisy the chef probably couldn't hear our compliments").

High Street Caffé   26 | 18 | 22 | $32
322 S. High St. (Dean St.), West Chester, 610-696-7435; www.highstreetcaffe.com
It might be "decorated like a New Orleans cathouse" ("very small and very purple", with big mirrors on the walls) but this "funky" Cajun-Creole BYO in West Chester has one of the area's most "creative" kitchens, conjuring up "spicy", "mystical creations" that will leave you "begging for more" ("don't order 'voodoo' anything without medication"); waiters are "so friendly you want to take them home", and the "noisy, delightfully young", Big Easy–esque vibe is enhanced by "swank jazz" on weekends.

Jake's   26 | 21 | 24 | $51
4365 Main St. (bet. Grape & Levering Sts.), 215-483-0444; www.jakesrestaurant.com
Patrons proclaim "you can never go wrong" at Bruce Cooper's "Manayunk mainstay", which keeps getting a "thumbs-up" for "consistently" "splendid" New American cuisine that makes you want to "lick the plates clean"; "charm to the max" and "stellar service" will "take the worry out of entertaining – for business or pleasure"; however, at busy times, patrons are "packed in like sardines", and parking still seems to be "a royal pain."

La Bonne Auberge   27 | 26 | 24 | $68
Village 2 Apartment Complex, 1 Rittenhouse Circle (Mechanic St.), New Hope, 215-862-2462; www.bonneauberge.com
"Close your eyes and you are on the Continent" exclaim enthusiasts of this "intimate" haute cuisine French; actually, it's located in a New Hope condo complex, but still "worth the effort to find" for "special-occasion" dining, most maintain, due to Gerard Caronello's

"fantastic" cooking and the "warm, attentive" service; some urge "eat before you go", though, because of "small" portions that don't justify "high price tags"; N.B. open Thursday–Sunday, dinner only.

LACROIX AT THE RITTENHOUSE   28   27   26 $74
Rittenhouse Hotel, 210 W. Rittenhouse Sq. (bet. Locust & Walnut Sts.), 215-790-2533; www.rittenhousehotel.com
"Ooh-la-la!" gush gleeful gastronomes over Jean-Marie Lacroix's "sleek", formal Classic French "masterpiece" in the Rittenhouse Hotel; they love his "extraordinary concept": "scrumptious" tasting menus of three ($60), four ($69) or five ($78) small plates (lunch, "a foodie's bargain", is $24 for four courses); the "airy" "minimalist" design and view of the Square are "as conducive to a romantic dinner as to a power lunch", and a "congenial" staff "overlooks nothing"; it's "worth every dollar your platinum card is debited."

L'Angolo   25   17   21 $31
1415 Porter St. (Broad St.), 215-389-4252
"I wish it could stay a secret", sigh stalwarts who "love" Davide and Katheryn Faenza's "tiny, charming" BYO, an "offbeat oasis" "not far from the stadiums" in South Philly; they cherish "authentic" "basics" from The Boot ("killer pasta") that will satisfy even "your picky Italian father" and "amiable service"; "if you haven't been there yet, good luck getting a table", but when you do "you're going to be happy"; N.B. the Decor score may not reflect post-*Survey* renovations.

LE BAR LYONNAIS ⊠   28   23   25 $54
1523 Walnut St. (bet. 15th & 16th Sts.), 215-567-1000; www.lebecfin.com
Beloved by Botox types who "take someone they want to seduce", this "clubby" bistro/bar hidden in Le Bec-Fin's "glamorous cellar" is the "casual alternative" to the main room upstairs; bargain-hunters beam it's a way to "get a taste of Perrier" – LBF's "wonderful French fare" and "impeccable" service – at "half the price" ("one can go in jeans and leave with one's shirt"); still, some sing sadly, "smoke gets in your eyes."

LE BEC-FIN ⊠   28   28   28 $120
1523 Walnut St. (bet. 15th & 16th Sts.), 215-567-1000; www.lebecfin.com
"To hell with carbs, fats and money" – Georges Perrier's *très* "elegant" Center City "institution" (a "magnificent dinosaur, thank God") is the "perfect splurge" during a "bull market"; his legions laud "*le best*" French cuisine ("every morsel a thrill" – plus a "Volkswagen-size dessert cart"), "toned-down" decor and a staff so "attentive" "you'll feel like a movie star"; in all, it's "better" and "cheaper than flying to Paris" – though with three-figure dinner prices, it's "not for the thin of wallet."

Little Fish ⊅   25   11   21 $31
600 Catharine St. (6th St.), 215-413-3464
"As crowded as a can of sardines" ("you can seat more people in your car"), John Tiplitz's "charming" "one-man" seafood BYO in Queen Village nevertheless does a whale of a job with "inspired" surf suppers and "unobtrusive" service; staffers "pay attention to you but also stay back" when not needed, and, hey, "if you have a question for the chef, he's right there"; P.S. the "small size means reservations are absolutely required."

Mainland Inn   26 | 23 | 25 | $46
17 Main St. (Sumney Town Pike), Mainland, 215-256-8500
"Business dinners", "birthdays" and other "special occasions"
draw diners to this "consistent" "old friend", a "beautifully
decorated" "traditional" New American in central Montco
that's among the "best of the burbs"; a "stellar" menu, "elegant"
ambiance and staff that "bends over backwards and sideways" all
make it popular with big spenders whose "Porsches, Mercedeses
and BMWs [sit] lined up in the lot like steeds awaiting their riders."

Meritage Philadelphia 図   – | – | – | VE
500 S. 20th St. (Lombard St.), 215-985-1922;
www.meritagephiladelphia.com
Davio's alums James Colabelli and Taylor Barneby not only run
this *très élégant* Euro-Eclectic jewel box in Center City, but they
also wait tables to assure perfection; the menu is stocked with
modern twists on old-school faves and there's a 350-label wine
list; N.B. it's pronounced to rhyme with 'heritage.'

Morimoto   27 | 27 | 25 | $74
723 Chestnut St. (bet. 7th & 8th Sts.), 215-413-9070;
www.morimotorestaurant.com
From 'Iron Chef' Japanese' Masaharu Morimoto and Stephen Starr,
this storefront near Washington Square is a "transporting visual
and culinary experience" not unlike a tongue-"titillating" "*Star
Trek*" episode; "sensual" "techno-funk" interiors attract "Philly's
who's who" for "ambrosial" omakase ("omigodzi!"); service,
while "skilled", seems to some "too rehearsed" and the meal will
"cost you $2 per bite", but after tasting and judgment almost all
agree the Food Network star "reigns supreme."

Nan 図   25 | 16 | 20 | $36
4000 Chestnut St. (40th St.), 215-382-0818; www.nanrestaurant.com
"This is why Philly is so fat", sigh surveyors who savor Kamol
Phutlek's "splendid" specialties, deploying "French culinary
techniques" and Thai flavor combinations with "fantastic" results;
at his "casual", "relaxing" BYO in an "aesthetically challenged"
slice of University City, service is "friendly" (if "abysmally slow");
P.S. renovations to address nan-descript, "one-step-up-from-a-
luncheonette" digs may outdate the Decor score.

Ota-Ya   26 | 17 | 22 | $33
10 Cambridge Ln. (Sycamore St.), Newtown, 215-860-6814;
www.ota-ya.com
"Bring your copy of the *Tale of Genji*" and "all the sake you can
drink" to this "genuine-article" Japanese in Newtown, which
makes only a "few concessions to Western cuisine" (fortunately,
"forks are available if needed"); you're sure to "recognize the
regulars" eating "imaginative sushi" and "creative specials"
ferried about the "low-key" room by "attitude"-free staffers.

Overtures   25 | 22 | 23 | $46
609 E. Passyunk Ave. (bet. Bainbridge & South Sts.), 215-627-3455
It "deserves a standing-O", rhapsodize respondents who sing arias
about this "charming" French-Med BYO "oasis" "off South Street";
they savor the "*saveur*" of "elegant" fare "done very well every
time" ("the midweek fixed-price menu may be the best bargain in
the city"), a "courteous", "unpretentious" staff and "grand yet

intimate" atmosphere ("you want romance, this is romance"); the only sour note: a menu that changes infrequently.

¡Pasión!
26 | 24 | 24 | $55

211 S. 15th St. (bet. Locust & Walnut Sts.), 215-875-9895
People are "passionate" about the "swimmingly delish" seviche and other "inventive", "flavorful" fare at Guillermo Pernot's "sexy", "highbrow" Nuevo Latino in Center City; sit in the airy, shuttered dining room to "feel like you're in the tropics" or at the "open kitchen's counter" to "watch the action"; even novices and fish haters can trust the "informative, helpful" staff, so "come with an adventurous palate" – and, if possible, an expense account.

Peking
25 | 19 | 21 | $28

Granite Run Mall, 1067 E. Baltimore Pike (Middletown Rd.), Media, 610-566-4110; www.margaretkuos.com
"The food is always a wow" at Margaret Kuo's high-class Asian where "creative" Chinese and Japanese menus allow "wonderful combinations" ("sushi followed by Peking duck") and "servers try to be as helpful as possible"; in short, "get over" the Granite Run Mall location – hey, it "saves a trip to Center City" – because this is not one of those "greasy" "red-and-gold" Delco joints.

Pif
25 | 14 | 22 | $42

Italian Mkt., 1009 S. Eighth St. (bet. Carpenter St. & Washington Ave.), 215-625-2923
"Don't publish this!" beg fans of this "hard-to-get-into" BYO French bistro in "the heart of Italian South Philly"; "gastronomic artist" David Ansill has a "delightful European touch" and "just enough attitude" when he "wanders" the "cramped" dining room, while staffers provide "personal" attention; even with "no froufrou" environs and a "lack of scenesters", rising tabs suggest the proprietors have "priced themselves out of the neighborhood."

Prime Rib
25 | 25 | 24 | $61

Radisson Plaza Warwick Hotel, 1701 Locust St. (17th St.), 215-772-1701; www.theprimerib.com
If you're primed for a *Flintstones*-size slab" of "tender, flavorful" beef, "step back in time" to this "carnivore's dream-come-true" in Center City's Warwick Hotel, a "luxe", "swanky" chain link "reminiscent of '40s supper clubs"; live piano music and a dress code (gentlemen must wear jackets) "make it even more special" and well-trained, tuxedoed attendants "set a high bar for service", though a few recalcitrant razzers rib it's "stodgy" and "starchy."

Savona
26 | 26 | 25 | $64

100 Old Gulph Rd. (Rte. 320), Gulph Mills, 610-520-1200; www.savonarestaurant.com
You "feel like you've entered another world" at this "exotic" and "lovely" Riviera-inspired Main Line Franco-Italian, where "high rollers" "rub elbows" over "sublime" cuisine (including "standout seafood" dishes), a "fantastic wine list" and "impeccable service" from a "knowledgeable staff"; given the "private-jet prices", though, it's a "splurge" best enjoyed on "someone else's tab."

Shiao Lan Kung ●
25 | 8 | 17 | $20

930 Race St. (bet. 9th & 10th Sts.), 215-928-0282
"Never mind the decor – just try the salt-baked" shrimp ("utter perfection"), "excellent hot pots" or other "unusual items prepared

sizzling and fresh" at this "no-frills" but "insanely great and authentic" Chinatown BYO packed with "many Chinese patrons"; its "friendly staff" "isn't flustered by crowds", fortunately, and it's open "after midnight" to "satiate late-night cravings."

Southwark
– | – | – | E |

701 S. Fourth St. (Bainbridge St.), 215-238-1888

A husband-and-wife team created this casual, yet sophisticated New American bistro in Queen Village that's grabbed a fair amount of attention since it opened; chef Sheri Waide's food (including the cheese and charcuterie on the farmhouse platter) and her other half's smooth manner behind the mahogany bar are easy to dig; N.B. the concise, well-parsed wine list includes a number of offerings by the glass.

Sovalo ⊠
– | – | – | VE |

702 N. Second St. (bet. Brown St. & Fairmount Ave.),
215-413-7770

One of the city's brightest newcomers and easily the poshest restaurant in fast-growing Northern Liberties, this romantic, sumptuously outfitted Italian is a showcase for chef Joseph Scarpone (who once toiled at Napa Valley's much-lauded Tra Vigne) and his modern, ever-changing menu; oenophiles take note of a cellar centered on labels from California and Italy.

Susanna Foo
26 | 24 | 24 | $57 |

1512 Walnut St. (bet. 15th & 16th Sts.), 215-545-2666;
www.susannafoo.com

You'll be "smiling for hours after" dining at this "sophisticated", "polished" Asian-French "standout" on Restaurant Row, according to acolytes of "wonderful chef" and "innovator" Susanna Foo, who challenges patrons to "put aside all preconceptions about Chinese food" with "breathtaking" dishes that take many "to new heights of rapture"; still, Foo fighters find the "petite portions" "ridiculously small" ("you might need two entrees") and say it's best "if someone else pays."

Swann Lounge ●
26 | 27 | 27 | $50 |

Four Seasons Hotel, 1 Logan Sq. (Benjamin Franklin Pkwy. & 18th St.),
215-963-1500; www.fourseasons.com

"If you want the Fountain without the formality" (or the cost), this "other restaurant in the Four Seasons" will "wow" you with "great dining" amid more "casual" yet still "lovely" environs; count on "delicious" New American–New French food and "unpretentiously superb" service from your vantage point "overlooking the beautiful Benjamin Franklin Parkway"; P.S. "the Sunday brunch is a little slice of heaven."

Totaro's
25 | 13 | 20 | $47 |

729 E. Hector St. (bet. Righter & Walnut Sts.), Conshohocken,
610-828-9341; www.totaros.com

"From the outside, you'd never guess" this "intimate" Italian-leaning Eclectic in a Conshohocken bar is thought to be "one of the best" in the region, but respondents rave "wait till you taste the food"; the kitchen consistently turns out "obscenely decadent" cuisine (including "interesting game" such as rabbit, buffalo and ostrich) "presented with panache" by a "cordial", "well-trained" staff; meanwhile, devotees debate whether it's "overpriced or under-decorated."

Vetri ☒   28 | 23 | 27 | $73 |
1312 Spruce St. (bet. Broad & 13th Sts.), 215-732-3478

"Leave your preconceptions about Italian food out on Spruce Street" and just "put yourself in Marc Vetri's hands", because he'll put on an "astounding" "virtuoso display of creative cooking", while "personalized service" "anticipates your every need", at this "elegant" brownstone in Center City; a few grumble that "the portions are teeny, the place too small and the bill too big"; nevertheless, it's still "easier to hit Powerball than to secure a reservation" here for Saturday night – and indeed, you may need the jackpot to cover the tab.

Washington Square   – | – | – | VE |
210 W. Washington Sq. (bet. Locust & St.James Sts.), 215-592-7787;
www.washingtonsquare-restaurant.com

Owner Stephen Starr has changed gears and concepts at his bustling yearling on Philly's long-overlooked Washington Square; "global street food" from NYC's Marcus Samuelsson (Aquavit, Riingo) has given way to New American cuisine from Franklin Becker (also an NYC alum); you enter through a dramatic, all-white garden created by Todd Oldham that leads into three rooms designed by Manhattan's Rockwell Group; all told, one of the more stylish spots in the city.

Phoenix/Scottsdale

TOP FOOD RANKING

Restaurant	Cuisine
28 Pizzeria Bianco	Pizza
Sea Saw	Japanese
27 Marquesa	Mediterranean
Binkley's	New American
Barrio Café	Mexican
T. Cook's	Mediterranean
Mary Elaine's	New French
Drinkwater's City Hall	Steakhouse
26 Mastro's	Steakhouse
Cyclo	Vietnamese

OTHER NOTEWORTHY PLACES

Atlas Bistro	Eclectic
Eddie V's Edgewater	Seafood/Steakhouse
elements	Asian/New American
Los Sombreros	Mexican
Michael's at the Citadel	New American
P.F. Chang's	Chinese
Rancho Pinot	New American
Roaring Fork	American
Roy's	Hawaii Regional
Vincent Guerithault	New French/SW

F	D	S	C

Atlas Bistro   25 | 15 | 24 | $39
2515 N. Scottsdale Rd. (E. Wilshire Dr.), Scottsdale, 480-990-2433
Though it's "small" and "nondescript", this South Scottsdale site unites gourmets and over-the-moon oenophiles in "paradise", thanks to its "excellent" Eclectic eats and "extraordinary wine selections" available at "the adjacent wine store" (the restaurant itself is BYO); N.B. closed Sundays–Tuesdays.

BARRIO CAFÉ   27 | 17 | 22 | $29
2814 N. 16th St. (Thomas Rd.), Phoenix, 602-636-0240;
www.barriocafe.com
"Come early or late" or "bet on a wait" at this "small", "popular" Mexican "gem" dishing "exciting", "nuevo" renditions of Mexican standards that draw crowds unafraid to venture "beyond the burrito"; if the "amazing guacamole" (prepared tableside during dinner) and "scrumptious churros" aren't enough, take the edge off with some "sangria with a hit of Jack Daniels."

BINKLEY'S RESTAURANT 🖼   27 | 20 | 25 | $54
6920 E. Cave Creek Rd. (1/2 mile west of Tom Darlington Dr.), Cave Creek,
480-437-1072; www.binkleysrestaurant.com
"Fresh", "fabulous" and "fastidiously prepared" cuisine comes to gastronomy starved Cave Creek thanks to chef-owner Kevin

Binkley (ex Napa's French Laundry, Inn at Little Washington in VA) and his "sophisticated" "art-filled" New American; indeed, this "rising culinary star" has the "energy" to revise the menu daily and invent "splendid tasting menus" to sate "serious foodies" who make a trip to the man they're dubbing the "Gary Danko of the desert."

Cyclo ⊠ 26 15 20 $18
1919 W. Chandler Blvd. (Dobson Rd.), Chandler, 480-963-4490
Expect "plenty of sass" and "charm" from "fashionable" proprietor/menu designer/server Justina Duong, who "makes everyone feel like a lifelong friend" at her "casual" Vietnamese BYO in a Chandler strip mall; since the "amazing", reasonably priced food is as "fresh" and "lovely" as its owner, this "small" "piece of Saigon" is always "worth the wait."

Drinkwater's City Hall Steakhouse 27 24 25 $54
6991 E. Camelback Rd. (Goldwater Blvd.), Scottsdale, 480-941-4700
Scottsdale citizens soak up the "dark" and "sexy" atmosphere at this beloved beefery, whose backers crown it the "king of Arizona's steakhouses"; the "unbeatable" chops are as "juicy" as a scene that's abetted by "great martinis", live music and a "terrific bar area" where a "spunky" crowd works off the "huge portions" on the dance floor; "if you have to go somewhere, make this the place."

Eddie V's Edgewater Grille 26 25 24 $47
20715 N. Pima Rd. (E. Thompson Peak Pkwy.), Scottsdale, 480-538-8468; www.eddiev.com
Find some surf on desert turf at this "large", "clubby" seafood-steak combo in North Scottsdale serving "fresh", "fantastic" sea fare and "excellent" chops for red-meat mavens; budget-seekers baited by the "amazing 35-cent oysters" and selected half-price appetizers at happy hour forsake the "vibrant dining room" for the "happening" jazz lounge.

elements 25 27 24 $52
Sanctuary Resort Camelback Mountain, 5700 E. McDonald Dr. (bet. Scottsdale Rd. & Tatum Blvd.), Paradise Valley, 480-607-2300; www.elementsrestaurant.com
"Request a window table at sunset" and treat yourself to a "breathtaking view" and "romantic" dinner at this "stunning" Asian–New American at Sanctuary Resort tucked away on the northern slope of Camelback Mountain; the "spectacular architecture" and "contemporary", "Zen-like" decor echo the menu, which offers "divine", "healthy" fare in "artful", "minimalist" presentations; all things considered, it's certifiably "perfect" for a "special occasion."

Los Sombreros 25 19 20 $28
2534 N. Scottsdale Rd. (bet. Oaks St. & Thomas Rd.), Scottsdale, 480-994-1799
Chef-owner Jeff Smedstad turns out "authentic", yet "original" takes on regional Mexican food so "absolutely amazing" that many "hate to share" this South Scottsdale eatery with anyone else, considering it the "best of its kind" in AZ; P.S. since you may find the "cozy" digs "packed" on any given day, try to score a spot in the "fabulous" patio.

MARQUESA
27 | 27 | 27 | $59

Fairmont Scottsdale Princess, 7575 E. Princess Dr.
(bet. Hwy. 101 & N. Scottsdale Rd.), Scottsdale, 480-585-4848;
www.fairmont.com/scottsdale

"Absolutely beautiful", this "top-notch" North Scottsdale Mediterranean is a "foodie's delight", "from the imaginative appetizers" to the "exotic" entrees to the "fabulous desserts"; the "flawless" service means that guests are "treated like royalty", resulting in a "truly marvelous experience that makes any meal a special occasion"; of course, it comes with a "big price tag", but otherwise, "what's not to love?" here; P.S. its marketplace-style Sunday brunch, set outside in the courtyard, is "second to none."

MARY ELAINE'S ☒
27 | 28 | 27 | $82

The Phoenician, 6000 E. Camelback Rd. (N. 60th St.), Scottsdale,
480-423-2530; www.thephoenician.com

Setting the standard for a "special-occasion" experience, this "elegant", "ultrafancy" room at The Phoenician is where the city views are "heavenly", the wine list "extraordinary" and Bradford Thompson's "exquisite" New French fare way up there with "the best in the country"; the "unparalleled" service "anticipates every desire", so even though you'll need to bring "buckets of cash", it's "more than worth it"; N.B. jackets required, and summer hours are limited.

MASTRO'S STEAKHOUSE
26 | 24 | 24 | $59

La Mirada, 8852 E. Pinnacle Peak Rd. (N. Pima Rd.), Scottsdale,
480-585-9500

Meat mavens award this North Scottsdale "paradise" an "A+" for serving up "mouthwatering" steaks, "excellent sides" and a "seafood tower that's not to be missed", while scene-seekers say the "lively bar" (fully stocked with "eye candy") amps up both the "East Coast vibe" and "noise levels"; even the "high rollers" concede it's "expensive", but they, like most, can't help "loving it."

Michael's at the Citadel
25 | 24 | 24 | $53

The Citadel, 8700 E. Pinnacle Peak Rd. (N. Pima Rd.), Scottsdale,
480-515-2575; www.michaelsrestaurant.com

It may be "a bit of a hike", but this "sophisticated" New American in Pinnacle Peak makes it "well worth it" considering chef Michael DeMaria's "exceptional" cooking and "stunning decor" featuring an indoor waterfall, "lovely fireplace" and patio (complete with tropical plants and fountains); although curmudgeons carp the "big price tag" raises "value-for-money" issues, the majority says it all adds up to a "spectacular" experience.

P.F. CHANG'S CHINA BISTRO
21 | 20 | 20 | $29

Chandler Fashion Ctr., 3255 W. Chandler Blvd. (bet. Chandler Villlage Dr. &
Rte. 101), Chandler, 480-899-0472
Kierland Commons, 7132 E. Greenway Pkwy. (N. Scottsdale Rd.),
Scottsdale, 480-367-2999
740 S. Mill Ave. (E. University Dr.), Tempe, 480-731-4600
www.pfchangs.com

"Wear comfortable shoes" to help cushion yourself for the invariably "unbearable waits" at these "busy" Asian outposts of a national chain; while purists pan the provisions as "Americanized

Chinese", partisans praise the "dependably delicious" fare, singling out the "fabulous lettuce wraps" as edible proof.

PIZZERIA BIANCO ⊠   28 | 20 | 21 | $25

Heritage Sq., 623 E. Adams St. (N. 7th St.), Phoenix, 602-258-8300
"Believe the hype": copping the No. 1 rating for Food in AZ is Chris Bianco's "adorable" "pizza temple" that draws droves of devotees who deem the "outstanding" pies ("they make life worth living") to be "the best in the country"; with all the recent publicity, though, the "mind-numbing waits" are even longer, so insiders suggest sipping wine at the adjacent Bar Bianco.

Rancho Pinot   25 | 20 | 24 | $47

Lincoln Vlg., 6208 N. Scottsdale Rd. (E. Lincoln Dr.), Scottsdale, 480-367-8030; www.ranchopinot.com
"Creative" "comfort food" abetted by a "comfortable", "rustic" ranch setting turn this "low-key" Scottsdale New American into an "all-around winner"; owner Tom Kaufman's "fantastic wine list" paired with wife Chrysa's "excellent" cooking mean that, despite its strip-mall locale, "you owe it to yourself" to make a trip here.

Roaring Fork   25 | 24 | 24 | $43

4800 N. Scottsdale Rd. (Chaparral Rd.), Scottsdale, 480-947-0795; www.roaringfork.com
Locals "love" this American "favorite" where chef-owner Robert McGrath elevates "cowboy cooking" to a "fine-dining" level; that it's known as a "happy-hour" "hangout" (the "great" huckleberry margaritas are a must) also helps corral fans into its "Western"-decorated digs; P.S. their "big-ass burger" is "legendary."

ROY'S   24 | 22 | 22 | $44

J. W. Marriott Desert Ridge Resort & Spa, 5350 E. Marriott Dr. (bet. Deer Valley Rd. & Tatum Blvd.), Phoenix, 480-419-7697
Scottsdale Seville, 7001 N. Scottsdale Rd. (Indian Bend Rd.), Scottsdale, 480-905-1155
www.roysrestaurant.com
Fusion fare lands in the desert at Roy Yamaguchi's "gorgeous" duo serving "magical", "cutting-edge" Hawaii Regional food, including "beautifully prepared fish" and downright "sinful desserts"; though some find they "don't compare" to the original locations, most swim with the tide, declaring the pair "meets the highest standards."

SEA SAW   28 | 18 | 25 | $61

7133 E. Stetson Dr. (E. 6th Ave.), Scottsdale, 480-481-9463; www.seasaw.net
"Take out a loan" if necessary before visiting this spartan, 30-seat "foodie destination" in Oldtown Scottsdale for "astonishing" Japanese tapas and "unsurpassed sushi" prepared in "ways you never thought possible"; an "incredible" 2,500-plus-label wine list and the "best sake selection in town" help put it in the "inspirational" category.

T. COOK'S   27 | 28 | 26 | $56

Royal Palms Resort and Spa, 5200 E. Camelback Rd. (bet. N. Arcadia Dr. & N. 56th St.), Phoenix, 602-808-0766; www.royalpalmsresortandspa.com
"All around", it "doesn't get better" than this "romantic" retreat in the Royal Palms – the Most Popular place in AZ – that "blows away" admirers with its "beautiful hacienda-style" setting and "luxurious" atmosphere; it's also impossible to overlook chef

Gregory Casale's "marvelous" Mediterranean creations and the "professional staff", making a trip here "a must for out-of-town guests" and "lots of locals" alike.

Vincent Guerithault on Camelback ⊠ 26 | 22 | 24 | $58
3930 E. Camelback Rd. (N. 40th St.), Phoenix, 602-224-0225;
www.vincentsoncamelback.com
Considered a "classic" by its many fans, this "elegant" Camelback Corridor stalwart still "charms" with Vincent Guerithault's "terrific", "innovative" Gallic interpretation of Southwestern fare and "elegant", "upscale" country French decor; if it's "tired" to a few, this piece of "gastronomic heaven" in the desert remains "at the top" to most.

Portland, OR

TOP FOOD RANKING

Restaurant	Cuisine
27 Genoa	Italian
Paley's Place	French/Pacific NW
Higgins	Pacific Northwest
Saburo's	Japanese
Heathman	French/Pacific NW
26 Pho Van	Vietnamese
El Gaucho	Continental/Steakhouse
Castagna	French/Italian
Lemongrass	Thai
Caffe Mingo	Italian

OTHER NOTEWORTHY PLACES

Andina	Peruvian
Bluehour	Med./New American
Caprial's Bistro	Pacific Northwest
clarklewis	Pacific NW/New Amer.
Giorgio's	Italian
Jake's Famous Crawfish	Seafood
Joel Palmer House	Pacific Northwest
McCormick & Schmick's	Seafood
Park Kitchen	Pacific NW/New Amer.
Wildwood	Pacific Northwest

F	D	S	C
–	–	–	E

Andina
Pennington Bldg., 1314 NW Glisan St. (13th Ave.), 503-228-9535; www.andinarestaurant.com
Offering a taste of Peru in the Pearl, this expensive eatery presents Portlanders with *novoandina* cuisine, which marries the best of the country's ancient recipes with its emergent flashy cooking style; the modern-rustic, high-ceiling dining room houses a bar that serves tapas, house sangria and killer passion fruit cocktails.

Bluehour
22	25	21	$43

Wieden & Kennedy Headquarters, 250 NW 13th Ave. (Everett St.), 503-226-3394; www.bluehouronline.com
With its "gorgeously chic setting", this "hip, hip, hip" "hot spot" in the "trendy Pearl District" offers "a bit of New York in Portland", where the smitten swoon for chef-partner Kenny Giambalvo's "creative menu" of Mediterranean–New American dishes such as "excellent scallops" wrapped in bacon and "to-die-for gnocchi with truffle sauce"; still, it must be said that some skeptics are "underwhelmed" by the "sometimes inconsistent" kitchen and certain "snooty" staffers that seem like "supermodels who forgot to smile."

Caffe Mingo
26 | 20 | 22 | $29

807 NW 21st Ave. (Johnson St.), 503-226-4646
Despite "tables practically on top of each other", the "creative,
rustic" cucina and "laid-back" servers ensure this "tiny" trattoria
"beats out its fancier neighbors" on "Northwest's Italian Restaurant
Row"; while the "no-reservations [policy for parties under six] can
be a hassle", it's "worth the wait" – just "stand outside and enjoy a
good glass of wine", soaking up the "cognoscenti cool" at the bar.

Caprial's Bistro ☒
26 | 20 | 23 | $36

7015 SE Milwaukie Ave. (Bybee Blvd.), 503-236-6457;
www.caprialandjohnskitchen.com
The "PBS celebrity" chef's "zest is evident" in her often "Asian-
inspired" "Pacific NW cuisine with zing", served by "attentive
staffers" in this "light, airy" Westmoreland venue she co-owns
with husband John "in a lovely neighborhood"; but it may be the
"walls lined with wines" "at store prices" that prompt Pence-ive
proponents to proclaim "Caprial, we love you!"

Castagna/Cafe Castagna
26 | 21 | 24 | $43

1752 SE Hawthorne Blvd. (18th Ave.), 503-231-7373 ☒
1758 SE Hawthorne Blvd. (18th Ave.), 503-231-9959
www.castagnarestaurant.com
When seeking a "place to take food-loving friends", look no further
than Ladd's Addition and this "elegant" eatery, acclaimed for its
"consistently stunning" French-Italian fare created "with a loving
eye on local sources" and dished by "super-efficient servers";
the sensitive sense an "aloof" "attitude" in the "high prices" and
"stylish" if "sterile" decor, but no one minds that "you don't have
to struggle with parking Downtown"; N.B. the Cafe next door at
1758 Hawthorne offers casual bistro dishes.

clarklewis ☒
– | – | – | E

Eastbank Commerce Ctr., 1001 SE Water Ave. (bet. Taylor &
Yamhill Sts.), 503-235-2294; www.ripepdx.com
Bucking convention, this yearling on the industrial East Side
provides guests with flashlights for menu reading in its dim,
cavernous dining area; departure from the norm continues in the
kitchen, where ever-inventive chef Morgan Brownlow creates
rave-worthy Pacific NW–New American dishes (offered in three
different portion sizes), including homemade pastas, house-smoked
meats and fried vegetables fairy-dusted with batter.

El Gaucho ☻
26 | 22 | 26 | $51

The Benson Hotel, 319 SW Broadway (bet. Oak & Stark Sts.),
503-227-8794; www.elgaucho.com
Carnivores crow over the "mouthwatering steaks" at this "barely
lit", "trendy" Downtown "men's club" where business tycoons and
pro athletes enjoy the "royal treatment", with everything from "live
Latin guitars" to Continental "creations" "prepared tableside" with
"retro" flair; of course, all this costs "obscene amounts of money",
causing the cost-conscious to call it "El Gouge-o."

GENOA
27 | 21 | 27 | $71

2832 SE Belmont St. (bet. 28th & 29th Aves.), 503-238-1464;
www.genoarestaurant.com
"Be prepared to devote an entire evening to dining bliss" declare
devotees of this "intimate", "elegant-yet-unpretentious" "grande

dame" on funky Belmont Street that's "perennially Portland's best"
(No. 1 for Food); it's "expensive but worth saving for", given its
"haute Italian" prix fixes "served dotingly by people" who "describe
the courses like the parts of their lover's body"; those who decry
the digs ("need updating") should be "delighted" by a recent redo
(not reflected in the Decor score).

Giorgio's
24 | 23 | 24 | $36

1131 NW Hoyt St. (12th St.), 503-221-1888; www.giorgiospdx.com
"Beautiful presentation" and a "panoply of tastes" mark the "out-
of-this-world" Italian faro prepared with French technique by
chef Michael Clancy at this "pearl in the Pearl" with tile floors,
brocaded banquettes and a bar that's "right out of Rome"; owner
Giorgio Kawas, "a warm and personable man", along with his
"genial staff", "treats everyone like family" within the "intimate,
romantic" "welcoming space."

HEATHMAN
27 | 24 | 25 | $43

The Heathman Hotel, 1001 SW Broadway (Salmon St.), 503-790-7752;
www.heathmanhotel.com
"Every plate is a masterpiece" in the "delicious marriage of
French and healthy Pacific Northwest" fare in chef Philippe
Boulot's hotel dining room, which also offers an "extensive wine
list" and a beloved brunch presided over by a "stellar" staff;
smack-dab in the center of the Cultural District's "sidewalk
action", it's "a great place to take out-of-towners", whether for
jazz and "winter-season high tea" in the "elegant" historic lobby
or a light "before-show dinner" in the Marble Bar.

HIGGINS RESTAURANT & BAR ◑
27 | 23 | 25 | $39

1239 SW Broadway (Jefferson St.), 503-222-9070
"Prof. [Greg] Higgins, I could have dined all night" – so sing
supporters of the chef-owner's "dark, woody" Cultural District
Downtowner dedicated to "distinctively Oregonian" (and often
organic), seasonal "haute comfort food" served by an "exceedingly
knowledgeable, well-trained staff"; however, "to keep the tab
affordable", regulars recommend dining in the "cozy adjoining
bar", a "respite for foodies in need of a beer" (there's "an amazing
selection") and "a fabulous stop before or after the theater."

JAKE'S FAMOUS CRAWFISH
24 | 21 | 23 | $35

401 SW 12th Ave. (Stark St.), 503-226-1419;
www.jakesfamouscrawfish.com
"Nothing is more venerable" than this Downtown "institution",
"still bustling and noisy" after 113 years with "nonstop tourist
crowds" consuming "super-fresh fish" and "old-faithful" fare
("pan-fried oysters and local beers"), served by "waiters who are
'lifers'" amid "historic paintings" and "wood paneling" (wags
wager the "decor hasn't changed since 1899 or so"); some salty
dogs sniff it's "spendy", but they're swamped by satisfied sailors
who proclaim it Portland's Most Popular.

Joel Palmer House ☒
25 | 23 | 23 | $44

600 Ferry St. (6th St.), Dayton, 503-864-2995; www.joelpalmerhouse.com
"Everyone should make a pilgrimage" to this "beautiful" and
"historic house" "in the heart of wine country", where Jack
Czarnecki, "the nation's foremost mycologist/chef", "shares
mushroom-hunting stories" and a "heavy" Northwest menu of
"wonderful dishes" that feature fungi, including "fresh-picked

black-and-white truffles", along with "outstanding Oregon pinots";
despite occasionally "immature" service, most get happily high
on this "shrine to 'shrooms in all their glory."

Lemongrass ⊠⊅
26 | 18 | 17 | $24

1705 NE Couch St. (17th Ave.), 503-231-5780
It's "well worth the wait" that "will whet your appetite" at what
Northeast natives call the "best Thai west of the Mississippi",
where "the curries are fabulous" and the "perfectly balanced"
"flavors of each dish are explosive"; just be aware that the kitchen
crew really "means business when they say 'hot'" and members
of the "shorthanded [staff] can be slow", as they navigate the
"funky old house."

MCCORMICK & SCHMICK'S
23 | 21 | 22 | $36

235 SW First Ave. (bet. Oak & Pine Sts.), 503-224-7522;
www.mccormickandschmicks.com
"The original McCormick's" that spawned a nationwide school of
seafooders, this Downtown "Portland classic" is a "traditional
but not stuffy" destination for a "large selection" of "reliable",
"fresh" surf 'n' turf and "cheap happy-hour eats", served in the
"dark-paneled elegance" of an "old-style" "cavernous room."

PALEY'S PLACE BISTRO & BAR
27 | 22 | 25 | $43

1204 NW 21st Ave. (Northrup St.), 503-243-2403
At this "quaint Victorian house" in the Nob Hill district, the
"fabulous" Northwest-sourced and "French-influenced menu"
comes with "stellar wine selections" and a "personal welcome";
the "convivial atmosphere" may "make intimate conversation
difficult", given that "you seem to be on top of your neighbors",
but it's all part of the pleasure of this piece of "Paris in Portland."

Park Kitchen
– | – | – | M

422 NW 8th Ave. (bet. Flanders & Glisan Sts.), 503-223-7275;
www.parkkitchen.com
Situated across from bocce courts in the leafy North Park Blocks,
this lively debutante boasts easily elegant decor, crisp, competent
service and a creative Pacific NW kitchen with a sense of humor
(think chickpea fries dipped in pumpkin ketchup and fruit crisp with
licorice ice cream); chef-owner Scott Lolich and his team make
abundant use of seasonal, local ingredients, catering to a clientele
that likes to be surprised each time it returns to a restaurant.

Pho Van
26 | 24 | 23 | $23

1012 NW Glisan St. (10th Ave.), 503-248-2172 ⊠
1919 SE 82nd Ave. (bet. Division & Stark Sts.), 503-788-5244
11651 SW Beaverton Hillsdale Hwy. (Canyon Rd.), Beaverton,
503-627-0822
These "pho-nominal" hot spots "put Vietnamese food on the
haute-cuisine map"; the fare is "reasonably priced", so they're
"packed at lunchtime", and be aware that the "friendly, polished
service" "can be slow when [things] get hopping"; N.B. after a
thorough renovation, the 82nd Avenue branch unveiled a menu
emphasizing street foods.

SABURO'S SUSHI HOUSE
27 | 11 | 16 | $21

1667 SE Bybee Blvd. (bet. 16th & 17th Aves.), 503-236-4237
"What more could you want", wonder worshipers of this Bybee
Boulevard favorite, than the "freshest" "and biggest sushi portions

in the city" ("you could take some home and throw it on the grill for a second meal") offered at the "cheapest prices"; true, the no-reservations policy and some staffers' "attitude" can be "trying", but the waits are not as "interminable" since a post-*Survey* expansion of the formerly "nondescript, cramped location" nearly doubled seating capacity.

WILDWOOD
25 | 23 | 23 | $41

1221 NW 21st Ave. (Overton St.), 503-248-9663;
www.wildwoodrestaurant.com

Almost "everyone in Portland serves Northwest fare", but fans still go wild for the "fresh, inventive" dishes – including "the best skillet-roasted mussels anywhere" – turned out by celebrity chef, author and "local treasure Cory Schreiber" in his "fast-moving exhibition kitchen"; his "always-crowded", "noisy dining room", complete with works by "the region's best artists", is "a place to be seen" in the Nob Hill area, so be prepared for "fancy food and a side of 'tude" when you come.

Salt Lake City & Mountain Resorts

TOP FOOD RANKING

	Restaurant	Cuisine
27	Tree Room	Regional American
	Red Iguana	Mexican
	Mariposa	New American
26	Michelangelo	Italian
	Seafood Buffet	Seafood
	Glitretind	New American
	Fresco Italian Cafe	Northern Italian
	Metropolitan	New American
	Martine	Mediterranean
25	Chez Betty	Continental/American

OTHER NOTEWORTHY PLACES

Restaurant	Cuisine
Bambara	New American
Chimayo	Southwestern
Cucina Toscana	Northern Italian
Log Haven	New American
Lugano	Northern Italian
Market St. Grill	Seafood
New Yorker Club	American
Snake Creek Grill	American
Takashi	Japanese
Wahso	Asian Fusion

F	D	S	C

Bambara 24 | 25 | 24 | $36

Hotel Monaco, 202 S. Main St. (200 South), 801-363-5454; www.bambara-slc.com

"Bringing energy and style to Downtown", this "hip" "favorite" in the "trendy Hotel" Monaco boasts a "busy open kitchen" helmed by "talented chef" Robert Barker, whose "dynamite" New American cuisine "excites foodies' imaginations"; with "swanky decor" and a "hip atmosphere", its "great space" (the historic Continental Bank lobby) is a "nice place to impress your date", but it's "not for a quiet romantic dinner" and "not if you're in a hurry" – so just "sit back, have a drink and take it all in."

Chez Betty 25 | 18 | 24 | $45

Copper Bottom Inn, 1637 Short Line Rd. (Deer Valley Dr.), Park City, 435-649-8181; www.chezbetty.com

"You can Betty" that this "jewel" (named after its resident goldfish) "off Main Street" in Park City's Copper Bottom Inn is "a delight" thanks to its "consistent", "creative kitchen's" "innovative menu" of "delicious" Continental-American fare; partisans praise the "superb, personal service" from the "warm, friendly" staff and "romantic, cozy, intimate" environs that "feel like an auberge", even if a few feel that the decor "needs updating"; P.S. there's "always at least one delicious vegetarian plate" on offer.

CHIMAYO
24 | 25 | 22 | $43

368 Main St. (4th St.), Park City, 435-649-6222;
www.chimayorestaurant.com

"You're immediately engulfed by a ritzy vibe" and "warm ambiance" "reminiscent of Santa Fe in winter" at this Main Street "Park City favorite" where the "charming" decor (recently renovated) and "aromas set the perfect mood"; connoisseurs are "impressed with" the "wonderful flavors" featured in its "expensive" but "unusual spins on traditional Southwestern food", which are "innovative without being weird" and include "great wild-game selections" such as "the best elk in town"; all told, it's "a must-visit."

Cucina Toscana ⊠
24 | 21 | 24 | $33

307 W. Pierpont Ave. (300 West), 801-328-3463;
www.cucina-toscana.com

The "warm, welcoming staff" will "make you feel at home" when you visit this "gem" "in the Downtown arts district", where *ciao*-hounds dig into "excellent Northern Italian fare" that's "authentic" ("not that sweet, creamy American stuff") and served in a "bustling and fun" "if noisy environment" ("you almost always strike up a conversation about the food with the patrons dining next to you"); the "electric atmosphere" makes it an experience "not to miss", and it's a "great value" to Boot.

Fresco Italian Cafe
26 | 22 | 24 | $38

1513 S. 1500 East (bet. Emerson & Kensington Aves.), 801-486-1300;
www.frescoitaliancafe.com

Adoring *amici* swoon over the "fresh", "tasty Northern Italian" dishes – now overseen by chef Dave Jones (ex Log Haven) – on offer at this "romantic little spot" set in a "secluded former home" "tucked away in a quiet Eastside residential neighborhood"; those who find its "intimate" interior a bit "cramped" say it's "best in summer" when one can dine on the "darling patio" surrounded by "beautiful grounds"; P.S. "the place draws a loyal clientele, so be prepared to wait" – and "make your reservations way in advance."

Glitretind Restaurant
26 | 24 | 26 | $52

Stein Eriksen Lodge, 7700 Stein Way (Royal St.), Deer Valley,
435-645-6455; www.steinlodge.com

Even those who "can't pronounce the name" "love" ascending to the "beautiful alpine setting" of this "Deer Valley treasure" "in the Stein Eriksen Lodge", where a "professional, polished and polite" staff caters to "discerning diners" with "beautifully presented", "manicured meals" of "wonderful, inventive" New American cuisine, accompanied by a "killer wine list" and offered in a "European-feeling" room that's "formal yet comfortable for après-ski"; P.S. if it's "pricey" for your pocketbook, "wait for the summer two-for-one coupons."

Log Haven
– | 27 | 23 | $44

6451 E. 3800 South (Wasatch Blvd.), 801-272-8255; www.log-haven.com

"A magical place" "high in the mountains", this "secluded", "rustic cabin" boasts a "beautiful Millcreek Canyon setting" "complete with waterfall"; in summer of 2005, new chef Frank Mendoza introduced his New American menu that makes good use of local fish, game and produce; given his résumé, which includes stints at Metropolitan and San Francisco's La Folie, a visit here should remain an "exceptional experience" "to remember."

Lugano   25 | 19 | 24 | $31
3364 S. 2300 East (3300 South), 801-412-9994; www.luganorestaurant.com
"It's not uncommon to see" "magnificent chef" and owner Gregory Neville "among the tables" of this "cozy, upscale" Northern Italian in Holladay, "working the crowd" and "ensuring diners a quality experience"; devotees declare that his "reasonably priced", "seasonally changing menu" and "attentive", "knowledgeable staff" "deserve the accolades" regularly "piled upon" them, even if the "lively, upbeat atmosphere" can be more than a little "noisy" ("don't expect to hear everything your date says").

MARIPOSA, THE   27 | 25 | 25 | $58
Silver Lake Lodge, Deer Valley Resort, 7600 Royal St. (Rte. 224), Deer Valley, 435-645-6715; www.deervalley.com
Smitten surveyors sum up this "special-occasion" spot in the "world-class Deer Valley" Resort's Silver Lake Lodge as "one of Park City's treasures", touting its "uniformly" "exquisite" New American fare (including a "very good vegetarian tasting menu"), "wonderful wine" list and "consistently superb service"; lauders love the "informal elegance" and the "fabulous" "mountain appeal" of its alpine interior, and if you get too "hot sitting next to the fireplace", the signature Chocolate Snowball dessert will cool you off nicely; N.B. open December through mid-April.

MARKET STREET GRILL   24 | 21 | 22 | $30
2985 E. 6580 South (3000 East), 801-942-8860
48 Market St. (West Temple St., bet. 300 South & 400 South), 801-322-4668
www.gastronomyinc.com
Collectively ranked Most Popular among Utah restaurants, this "terrific" twosome "sets the standard" for "excellent seafood" with its "expansive" selection of "reasonably priced" "fresh fish" dishes ("start with" the "superior clam chowder" – a "classic favorite"); whether visiting the "fun Downtown" "institution" or its younger sibling "in the suburbs", which "wows" with "great mountain and creek views", expect "friendly service" and a "packed", "noisy", "high-energy" environment; P.S. the "early-bird special is a wondrous thing."

Martine ⊠   26 | 23 | 23 | $33
22 E. 100 South (bet. Main & State Sts.), 801-363-9328
Happy habitués hail the "innovative menu" of "top-notch" "Med food with serious influences from Morocco and Spain" (including "inventive tapas") that "leaves diners pleased" at this "Salt Lake classic" set in a "cozy Downtown brownstone"; "romantics" report it's a "great place to bring your main squeeze" thanks to "refined service" from an "attentive staff" and "fine ambiance that feels like a great small restaurant in San Francisco or Boston."

Metropolitan ⊠   26 | 25 | 24 | $52
173 W. Broadway (300 South, bet. 200 West & West Temple St.), 801-364-3472; www.themetropolitan.com
"Fine-art platings" of "exquisite food" matched with "incredible wine pairings" are the hallmark of this "excellent-albeit-expensive New American", a "chic" "favorite" whose "cool", "cosmopolitan" interior is manned by "a hip host" and "funky" staffers providing

"impeccable service"; contrarians contend it "falls short" of its "pretensions", but acolytes aver it's Downtown's "definition of high-end dining"; P.S. its "casual bistro is an escape to NYC, but at SLC prices."

MICHELANGELO RISTORANTE ⊠   26 | – | 21 | $27 |

Hyland Plaza Mall, 2156 S. Highland Dr. (2100 South), 801-466-0961; www.michelangeloristorante.com

"Excellent risottos and housemade pastas" are among the "outstanding" offerings that "consistently impress" at this "authentic" "little trattoria" "in a hard-to-find" Eastside location; fans "love" that it's manned by "actual Italian waiters" in a new, and comparatively elegant setting (i.e. the old plastic plants have been exchanged for real ones).

NEW YORKER CLUB ⊠   25 | 24 | 24 | $45 |

60 W. Market St. (West Temple St., bet. 300 South & 400 South), 801-363-0166; www.gastronomyinc.com/ny

The "grand patriarch of Downtown SLC restaurants", this "tasteful, elegant" "classic" is the "always reliable, always appropriate" choice of "well-dressed", "mature" Utahns celebrating "special occasions" and "power brokers" looking to "seal the deal" over "excellent" Traditional American fare (including "great steaks" and "to-die-for soufflés") delivered by a "top-notch" staff; some sigh over the "steep prices", but most say it's "a pleasure" ponying up the nominal membership fee to "join the club."

RED IGUANA, THE   27 | 12 | 20 | $17 |

736 W. North Temple St. (800 West), 801-322-1489; www.rediguana.com

Though the "amazing moles" are "the most flavorful north of the border", you "can't go wrong with any dish" from the "impressive menu" of "authentic Mexican" treats at "this crowded joint" in a "sketchy neighborhood" west of Downtown, where the "friendly waiters" keep the "focus on customer service"; sure, it's a bit of a "dive", and you might have to "wait outside" "on the sidewalk" ("the line often snakes down the block"), but for 20 years now, spicy-food fanatics "have fantasized about" its "fantastic food."

SEAFOOD BUFFET ⊠   26 | 18 | 22 | $56 |

Snow Park Lodge, 2250 Deer Valley Dr. (Mellow Mountain Rd.), Deer Valley, 435-645-6632, www.deervalley.com

"Serious overeaters" "skip the slopes" and simply slalom to this "seafood-aficionados paradise", a "high-end buffet" and bastion of "conspicuous consumption" where the "abundant variety" of "excellent-quality" ocean fare ("incredible fresh fish, oysters, sushi, crab, smoked salmon") and "desserts galore" are an "all-you-can-eat bargain" offered "in a casual atmosphere" that's "great for families and groups"; "pace yourself", though, as "this kind of indulgence requires stamina"; P.S. sadly, it's solely a "ski-season" "event" – "if only it were open year-round!"

Snake Creek Grill   24 | 18 | 23 | $35 |

650 W. 100 South (6th W.), Heber City, 435-654-2133; www.snakecreekgrill.com

"Worth the scenic drive to Heber City", this "hidden" "treasure" in a faux Old Town just off the main drag, is "must-visit for anyone serious about food"; the "homestyle meals" remind some of "an old-fashioned dinner at mom's house" thanks to Traditional American fare that's "consistently" "delicious but not pretentious" and served by some of "the nicest, friendliest people" around in a "homey, welcoming atmosphere"; the "reasonable prices" make it "a real bargain", to boot.

Takashi ⊠　　　　　　　　　　– | – | – | M

18 W. Market St. (West Temple St., bet. 300 South & 400 South), 801-519-9595

Chef Takashi Gibo helms this Japanese showcase where sushi subjects sample his exquisite offerings, all served with premium sakes, wines and brews; the enamored crowds haven't subsided since day one, packing into the contemporary, arty Downtown space (once the site of Au Bon Appetit) that features a giant mesh fish by local sculptor Willy Litig.

TREE ROOM　　　　　　　　27 | 27 | 26 | $45

Sundance Resort, Scenic Rte. 92 (Hwy. 189), Sundance, 801-223-4200; www.sundanceresort.com

"Even the most sophisticated guests are invariably charmed by" this "special place" "surrounded by the splendor of the Sundance Resort" whose "flawless" Regional American eats have earned it the No.1 spot for Food in Utah; "outstanding service" and the "rustic", "romantic", "relaxed ambiance" with "Native Indian art all around" "only enhance" the "absolutely memorable dining experience", which is made even more "magical" by "frequent Robert Redford sightings" – and yes, there's "a tree growing through the dining room."

WAHSO　　　　　　　　　　25 | 26 | 23 | $48

577 Main St. (Heber Ave.), Park City, 435-615-0300; www.wahso.com

Slip into "one of the secluded curtained booths for a nice romantic escape" at this "oh-my-God! good" Asian fusion palace where "the decor is stunning and inventive", the "impeccable" fare features "fabulous flavors and textures", the saketinis and other "cocktails are fantastic" and the staff is "informed, friendly and attentive"; gourmets gush that it's chef-owner "Bill White's best restaurant", and the one to "try if you have time for only one Park City restaurant."

San Diego

TOP FOOD RANKING

	Restaurant	Cuisine
27	Pamplemousse Grille	New French/New Amer.
	El Bizcocho	French
26	Tapenade	New French/Provençal
	Sushi Ota	Japanese
	WineSellar & Brasserie	New French
	Mille Fleurs	New French
	Taka	Japanese
	Sky Room	New French
	Donovan's	Steakhouse
25	Arterra	New American

OTHER NOTEWORTHY PLACES

A.R. Valentien	Californian
Dobson's	Californian
George's at the Cove	Californian
Laurel	French/Med.
Osetra	Seafood/Steakhouse
Rainwater's on Kettner	Seafood/Steakhouse
Region	New American
Roppongi	Asian Fusion
Ruth's Chris	Steakhouse
Sammy's Woodfired	Pizza

F	D	S	C

Arterra

25	21	22	$46

San Diego Marriott Del Mar, 11966 El Camino Real (Carmel Valley Rd.), Del Mar, 858-369-6032; www.arterrarestaurant.com
"Can't believe it's in a Marriott" declare disciples of this Del Mar dining room, whose "imaginative, savory" New American menu is designed by "favorite chef" Bradley Ogden and supervised by local talent Carl Schroeder; some note that "given the prices, they could have done better with the decor" ("too many hard surfaces for a quiet meal") and scold the "inconsistent service"; nevertheless, it's now "*the* lunch spot for San Diego's high-tech movers and shakers."

A.R. Valentien

25	26	24	$52

The Lodge at Torrey Pines, 11480 N. Torrey Pines Rd. (Torrey Pines Golf Course), La Jolla, 858-777-6635; www.lodgetorreypines.com
"Right on the famous Torrey Pines golf course", this "distinctive, Craftsman-style [hotel] restaurant" is an "architectural must-see", with "romantic" "views of the magnificent pines" and ocean; the "formal room" offers "exceptional" Cal cuisine ("the use of local, seasonal produce gives everything a kick"), "elegantly served"; some say it's the "best 19th hole ever", but "if you have to ask the price, wait for a raise" first – or "try lunch on the patio" instead.

Dobson's ☒   25 | 19 | 23 | $43
956 Broadway Circle (2nd Ave.), 619-231-6771;
www.dobsonsrestaurant.com
Owner Paul Dobson "works a room better than Sinatra", which
explains why this "local tradition" Downtown remains, "after all
these years", a "high-powered, hobnob spot"; the Cal kitchen
"serves up delicious, innovative food, along with old standbys"
("have the mussel bisque and think of heaven"); some cavil about
the "cramped" digs, but the savvy simply head for the mezzanine
tables above the "lively" bar, which provide "a great view, like
watching a soap opera" enacted by the suits and "city-hall crowd"
at lunch and the "pre-theater diners" at dusk.

Donovan's Steak & Chop House ☒   26 | 24 | 24 | $55
4340 La Jolla Village Dr. (Genesee Ave.), 877-611-6688;
www.donovanssteakhouse.com
In La Jolla's trendy Golden Triangle, this "dark" cow palace is "like
stepping back in time to a men's club" – one populated by those
on "expense-account budgets" since, as steakhouse tradition also
dictates, tabs are "pricey"; but the "beef's unsurpassed", and the
"warm, wood-paneled decor" and "courteous staff" combine to
create a "classy atmosphere", which explains why some simply
"don't eat steaks anywhere else."

EL BIZCOCHO   27 | 27 | 26 | $57
Rancho Bernardo Inn, 17550 Bernardo Oaks Dr. (Rancho Bernardo Rd.),
Rancho Bernardo, 858-675-8550; www.jcresorts.com
The grande dame "can still tap dance", says the "old-money
crowd as well as young in-the-know foodies" who treasure this
"luxurious", "romantic" Rancho Bernardo Inn dining room with a
mood "as formal as San Diego can muster these days"; what with
"live piano music", "rich" French fare "cooked to perfection"
(especially at "the beautiful Sunday brunch") and "impeccable"
service, it's "deliciously dazzling" on all levels and a "pinnacle
experience" perfect "for a splurge" or "to bring guests."

GEORGE'S AT THE COVE   25 | 25 | 24 | $50
1250 Prospect St. (bet. Cave St. & Ivanhoe Ave.), La Jolla, 858-454-4244;
www.georgesatthecove.com
"A special-occasion place" (with "special-occasion prices"), this
"romantic" "pearl" above La Jolla Cove is "so recommended" for
"exceptional", "imaginative" Cal cuisine by Trey Foshee (a "chef
who knows his stuff") backed by a "breathtaking view" without
and "beautiful decor" within; "whether dining on the casual rooftop
[terrace], in the bar or in the more formal downstairs", the "chic
crowd" agrees San Diego's Most Popular stop is not only a "must-
go", it's a "place you never want to leave."

Laurel   – | – | – | E
505 Laurel St. (5th Ave.), 619-239-2222;
www.laurelrestaurant.com
By Balboa Park's ceremonial entrance, the city's "signature
upscale" eatery has been revitalized by fresh management, which
has given it a chic, black-and-white decor; augmenting the new
look is a new menu by chef Fabrice Poigin, who adds the occasional
Asian touch to his French-Med bill of fare (e.g. wasabi-tobiko caviar
relish on raw oysters); the "impressive wine list" remains, and all's
served by a youngish staff that's San Diego–style friendly but

knowledgeable and efficient, too; P.S. "free shuttle" service to the Old Globe Theatre makes it ideal pre-curtain.

Mille Fleurs
26 | 25 | 25 | $66

Country Squire Courtyard, 6009 Paseo Delicias (Del Dios Hwy.), Rancho Santa Fe, 858-756-3085; www.millefleurs.com

"I only wish my pocketbook could afford this luxury more often", sigh supporters of celebrity owner "Bertrand Hug's original masterpiece" in "posh", "quaint Rancho Santa Fe"; it's "perfect for that romantic occasion", with chef Martin Woesle's New French "works of culinary art" served by an "elegant, refined" staff amid "auberge-style" decor with "miles of pretty Portuguese tiles"; malcontents mutter it can be "snooty", but maybe they just haven't stayed for after-dinner "singing around the piano bar."

Osetra the Fishhouse
– | – | – | VE

904 Fifth Ave. (bet. Broadway & E St.), 619-239-1800; www.osetrathefishhouse.com

Named for a grade of caviar (plenty of which is in supply here), this extravagant double-decker occupies the lower floors of a century-old building on a prime Gaslamp Quarter corner; the many-paged menu plays the opulence angle to the hilt with deluxe seafood presentations mixed with mammoth cuts of prime meats; while the interior's designed to engage the eye in every direction, the focal point is a central wine tower that soars above the ice-topped bar, populated by female 'wine angels' flying about on electric winches.

PAMPLEMOUSSE GRILLE
27 | 22 | 24 | $55

514 Via de la Valle (Jimmy Durante Blvd.), Solana Beach, 858-792-9090; www.pgrille.com

"Star of Del Mar Jeffrey Strauss" "stays on top of everything" at his race track–side establishment, which finishes No.1 for Food in San Diego; decorated with "wonderful murals" ("check out the biker painting by the restrooms"), it "attracts all the beautiful people" with a "nice variety" of "consistently extraordinary and creative" New French–New American dishes, served by a "friendly" staff; being "a bit noisy" is its "only fault" – but even so, it's "everyone's secret for a special evening."

Rainwater's on Kettner
25 | 22 | 23 | $48

1202 Kettner Blvd. (W. B St.), 619-233-5757; www.rainwaters.com

"They spoil you" at this ultra-"clubby", "East Coast–style" steak-and-seafoodery Downtown, "a great place to drink whiskey and eat hearty"; though it's known for beef, all of the "simple, upscale fare" "possesses a special flair" (including the "unbelievable meatloaf"), further smoothed by a "wine list that goes on and on" and "refined service"; granted, "this place ain't cheap", but it's an "elegant way to spend an evening" whether you're hosting "picky out-of-town guests" or "helping a business deal along."

Region ⊠
– | – | – | E

3671 5th Ave. (Pennsylvania Ave.), 619-299-6499; www.regionrestaurant.com

At this Hillcrest New American, chef Michael Stebner transforms local farm-fresh products into picture-perfect palate-pleasers, while co-toque Allyson Colwell wheedles the best provender out of top specialty growers and the pastry chef wows with baked-to-order desserts; its servers dress even more casually than its clientele (no mean feat in come-as-you-are San Diego), but the easygoing mood keeps it jiving until a later hour than most.

ROPPONGI | 25 | 23 | 22 | $42 |

875 Prospect St. (Fay Ave.), La Jolla, 858-551-5252;
www.roppongiusa.com

"Takes Asian fusion to [the level of] a true art form", fawn followers of this "loud and happening" "place to be seen" (especially by the "outside fire pit" patio) in beautiful Downtown La Jolla; regulars recommend you begin with the "sake sampler", then "stick to" the "selection of starter foods" – "order for the table, share and keep ordering" – being sure to "save room for" "one of the divine desserts"; though "fun" "just about anytime", it's "phenomenal at happy hour" when the "awesome tapas are half-price"; N.B. a sushi bar was recently added.

RUTH'S CHRIS STEAK HOUSE | 25 | 20 | 23 | $52 |

1355 N. Harbor Dr. (Ash St.), 619-233-1422
11582 El Camino Real (San Dieguito Rd.), Del Mar, 858-755-1454
www.ruthschris.com

These two chain steakeries are "always a pleasure" for their "meat masterpieces" – "piping hot, butter-broiled beauties" "so good you forget the cholesterol count", along with "sure-to-please side dishes"; despite its "great views of San Diego Bay", "the Downtown locale has poor acoustics", causing some to find "the Del Mar location superior", "but the well-trained staff is a delight" in either place.

SAMMY'S WOODFIRED PIZZA | 20 | 15 | 17 | $21 |

Mission Valley Ctr., 1620 Camino de La Reina (Mission Center Rd.),
619-298-8222
770 Fourth Ave. (F St.), 619-230-8888
Costa Verde, 8650 Genesee Ave. (bet. La Jolla Vlg. & Nobel Drs.),
858-404-9898
10785 Scripps Poway Pkwy. (east of I-15), 858-695-0900
5970 Avenida Encinas (bet. I-5 & Palomar Airport Rd.), Carlsbad,
760-438-1212
Del Mar Highlands, 12925 El Camino Real (Del Mar Heights Rd.),
Del Mar, 858-259-6600
565 Pearl St. (Draper Ave.), La Jolla, 858-456-5222
www.sammyspizza.com

Purveyor of the "best original wood-fired pizza in San Diego", this homegrown chain garners "long lines" for its "traditional" and "designer" pies, "unique chopped salads" and trademark "messy sundaes" ("a sinful delight"), consumed on "beautiful patios with ample plants" (at most branches); the "servers tend to be young, so service may vary", and since it's "a casual, family favorite", "the atmosphere is seriously lacking for evening dining" (despite a post-*Survey* redo); but "if you're hungry", "it's never a letdown."

Sky Room | 26 | 26 | 27 | $62 |

La Valencia Hotel, 1132 Prospect St. (Herschel Ave.), La Jolla,
858-454-0771; www.lavalencia.com

A "perfect place for a special occasion", this "intimate" room on the 10th floor of La Jolla's fabled La Valencia Hotel is "just like heaven", with "excellent" New French fare, famously "romantic" decor and "gracious, professional" service; given the "formal and elegant" ambiance, it's understandably "pricey", but "it's worth any price" if you "book for sundown" and what may be the "best ocean view in Southern California"; N.B. the Food rating may not reflect a post-*Survey* chef change.

SUSHI OTA

26 | 12 | 18 | $36

4529 Mission Bay Dr. (Bunker Hill), 858-270-5670
Count on "advance planning" ("businessmen call ahead from Japan") to snare a seat for "the best sushi in San Diego" at "artistic" "genius" Yukito Ota's "hidden gem" near Pacific Beach; "all locals agree" the difficulty of obtaining reservations for a place with often-"abrupt service" and "ho-hum decor" ("ambiance? what ambiance?") may make you feel like you're "living in a *Seinfeld* episode", but think of it as "the price you pay" for a nearly "perfect product" – "and it's not even the most expensive" in town.

Taka

26 | 19 | 22 | $40

555 Fifth Ave. (Market St.), 619-338-0555; www.takasushi.com
Taka "a seat at the counter and they'll take very good care of you" at this "urban-chic" sushi source often cited as "the best in Downtown" for fish that tastes "like it jumped out of the ocean and into the hands of the chefs" who, like the servers, are "fast, friendly and no-nonsense"; the "too-small" digs quickly grow "crowded", but if you "get there early, and with reservations", it'll be "the perfect place to start the evening before heading out into the Gaslamp Quarter chaos."

TAPENADE

26 | 20 | 23 | $52

7612 Fay Ave. (bet. Kline & Pearl Sts.), La Jolla, 858-551-7500; www.tapenaderestaurant.com
Chef-owner Jean-Michel Diot "does tradition proud", serving guests "masterly" modern French cuisine "with a Provençal accent" at his "unpretentious" place in Downtown La Jolla; it's "a perennial favorite", drawing an "elegant and intelligent crowd" not only for its "just perfect" cuisine but for its "gorgeous Gallic waiters" (who may be "surfers by day"); however, given the "casual decor", some feel "prices are a bit high" – though not if you go for the "bargain prix fixe lunch" or dinner.

WINESELLAR & BRASSERIE ⌧

26 | 18 | 25 | $52

9550 Waples St. (bet. Mira Mesa Blvd. & Steadman St.), 858-450-9557; www.winesellar.com
"Brasserie charm in an industrial-park setting?" – it's possible at this "wine-lover's paradise" whose "quirky location" in Sorrento Mesa doesn't deter disciples from the "fabulous" New French cuisine paired with "sublime" labels "offered at 20 percent above retail" from "the shop on the first floor" ("their whole store is their wine list"); though "hard to find, it's guaranteed to wow your date or spouse", especially given the "impeccable attention" provided by the staff.

San Francisco Bay Area

TOP FOOD RANKING

	Restaurant	Cuisine
29	Gary Danko	New American
28	French Laundry	French/New American
	Manresa	New French/New Amer.
	Erna's Elderberry House	Cal./New French
	Sushi Ran	Japanese
	Masa's	New French
	Farmhouse Inn	Californian
27	Fleur de Lys	New French
	La Folie	New French
	Sierra Mar	Cal./New French
	Michael Mina	New American
	Chez Panisse Café	Californian/Med.
	Cafe La Haye	Cal./New American
	Marché	New French
	Rivoli	Californian/Med.
	Chapeau!	French Bistro
	Le Papillon	French
	Chez Panisse	Californian/Med.
	Terra	New American
	Hana	Japanese

OTHER NOTEWORTHY PLACES

Restaurant	Cuisine
Aqua	Seafood
Bistro Jeanty	French Bistro
Boulevard	French/New American
Campton Place	French/Med.
Cyrus	New French
Delfina	Northern Italian
Fifth Floor	New French
Greens	Vegetarian
Jardinière	Californian/French
Lark Creek Inn	American
La Toque	French
Marinus	Cal./New French
Myth	New American
Oliveto	Italian
Press	Steakhouse/American
Quince	French/Italian
Restaurant Budo	New American
Ritz-Carlton Din. Rm.	New French
Slanted Door	Vietnamese
Zuni Café	Mediterranean

Aqua

26 | 25 | 25 | $69

252 California St. (bet. Battery & Front Sts.), 415-956-9662;
www.aqua-sf.com

"Under Laurent Manrique", this "sophisticated" Downtown Cal-French has continued to serve "splendid meals from the sea" plus "superb" "interpretations of foie gras", paired with wines from an "excellent" list; "meticulous" servers minister to a "chic clientele (celebs included)" that's "packed like sardines" in the "elegant, contemporary" dining room; a few fear this "frenetic" "fish house" is "drowning in foo-foo", but most folks come ready and willing to "turn up the hearing aid" and "break the bank."

Bistro Jeanty

26 | 21 | 23 | $46

6510 Washington St. (Mulberry St.), Yountville, 707-944-0103;
www.bistrojeanty.com

Philippe Jeanty's "rustic, homey" Yountville outpost feels like a "casual and friendly" "French country inn" right down to the "vintage posters" on the walls, "accommodating" service and "heavenly", "hearty" Gallic classics; the fare may be "as rich as a Lotto winner" but you don't have to be, and though it's still "tough as ever to get a reservation", walk-ins can sit at the large communal table or at the bar "rubbing elbows with Napa wine notables."

BOULEVARD

27 | 25 | 24 | $60

Audiffred Bldg., 1 Mission St. (Steuart St.), 415-543-6084;
www.boulevardrestaurant.com

"No restaurant symbolizes SF better" than this French–New American on the Embarcadero; "magnificent Bay Bridge views", "the hustle and bustle" and "gorgeous belle epoque" interior "make it an exciting place to dine", while staffers provide "flawless service" ("like perfectly matched skaters in an Olympic ice dance"); better yet, Nancy Oakes' "gutsy" cuisine, complemented by a "killer wine list", remains "fabulously consistent"; sure, it's "hard to get reservations" and it's "pricey, but aren't you worth it?"

Cafe La Haye ☒

27 | 20 | 24 | $45

140 E. Napa St. (bet. 1st & 2nd Sts.), Sonoma, 707-935-5994;
www.cafelahaye.com

Gourmets have a haye-day at John McReynolds' and Saul Gropman's "pocket bistro" ("not much bigger than a couple of phone booths") just "off the square" in Sonoma; the "arty" venue is typically filled with "more locals than tourists" but it's "worth its own trip from the city"; the "microkitchen" "consistently" and "miraculously" produces "superb", "sophisticated" Cal–New American dishes, the boutique bottles are "fairly priced" and the "professional" crew is "as much in love with the food as you are."

Campton Place

26 | 25 | 26 | $70

Campton Place Hotel, 340 Stockton St. (bet. Post & Sutter Sts.),
415-955-5555; www.camptonplace.com

This "luxe" Downtowner near Union Square may be "calm" and "sumptuously decorated" in the traditional "damask-tablecloth mode", but you should be prepared to be "blown away" "visually and gastronomically" by chef Daniel Humm, who keeps the place humming with "sublime" French-Mediterranean "foamy food" ("each course a concentrated marvel") presented with "formality and efficiency"; still, a few faultfinders cite "breathtaking prices" for "tiny portions."

Chapeau!
27 | 18 | 26 | $44

1408 Clement St. (15th Ave.), 415-750-9787

"Hats off" to Philippe Gardelle, the "hardest-working" restaurateur in San Francisco, "who cooks, works the dining room, acts as sommelier and choreographs the staff" at his "humble" Inner Richmond "sardine can"; servers who work "with Parisian perfection" proffer "spectacular" bistro classics (the prix fixe dinners are "a great value") plus an "affordable" wine list that "encourages adventurousness"; as you leave, ladies get a "kiss on the cheek from the charming proprietor" himself.

Chez Panisse ⵥ
27 | 23 | 26 | $75

1517 Shattuck Ave. (bet. Cedar & Vine Sts.), Berkeley, 510-548-5525;
www.chezpanisse.com

Chef-owner Alice Waters' "celebrated" "cathedral to organic", "just-off-the-tree" "pristine" Californian ingredients still draws devout "pilgrims" who peer into the open kitchen as if "watching the bishop give communion"; the "Draconian this-is-what-you'll-have" preset Med menu "leaves little to choice but much to savor" in the "gorgeous" Berkeley bungalow, so while heretics grumble "nothing much has changed" true believers counter "nothing much changes in the Sistine Chapel either."

CHEZ PANISSE CAFÉ ⵥ
27 | 23 | 25 | $45

1517 Shattuck Ave. (bet. Cedar & Vine Sts.), Berkeley, 510-548-5049;
www.chezpanisse.com

"Alice Waters for the rest of us", this "relaxed" "Arts and Crafts" "attic hidden above Chez Panisse" presents "locally grown", "simple" Cal-Med creations (with a dose of "moral superiority") "as scrumptious" as the mother ship's – "only cheaper" and offered à la carte – presented by a "knowing" yet "authentically friendly" staff; long-in-the-tooth longhairs muse it's "a lot like downstairs before the place became a mecca", and what's more, this is one "major treat" that "even a graduate student can afford every now and then."

Cyrus
▽ 27 | 27 | 28 | $84

Les Mars Hotel, 29 North St. (Healdsburg Ave.), Healdsburg,
707-433-3311; www.cyrusrestaurant.com

If you think Sonoma County dining means casual, this pricey prix fixe–only Contemporary French in Healdsburg's new Les Mars Hotel will come as a salutary surprise; owners Nick Peyton and chef Douglas Keane (veterans of Gary Danko and Jardinière, respectively) are aiming for flat-out luxury, from the Burgundian-style room's vaulted ceiling to a caviar and champagne cart; N.B. namesake Cyrus Alexander pioneered the nearby Alexander Valley wine region, though the extensive cellar covers the globe.

Delfina
26 | 19 | 23 | $43

3621 18th St. (bet. Dolores & Guerrero Sts.), 415-552-4055;
www.delfinasf.com

Not "extravagant" or "pretentious", just "damn good", this Mission trattoria "always" "hits the mark" thanks to Craig Stoll's "delfinately delicious" "five-star" "seasonal Tuscan" fare "at three-star prices", "served by rocker chicks with a deep knowledge of food and wine"; ok, it's "as cramped as a phone booth" and "booked eons in advance", but now that they've set aside a counter for walk-ins "you're a fool if you don't go."

ERNA'S ELDERBERRY HOUSE   28 | 27 | 28 | $80
48688 Victoria Ln. (Hwy. 41), Oakhurst, 559-683-6800;
www.elderberryhouse.com
Although this Oakhurst "jewel" is "nestled in the hills" "a few
miles from Yosemite", you'll be "magically transported to Europe"
when you step inside its "elegant", "palace"-like interior, where
you're "treated like royalty" right down to the "handwritten menus"
that record every "exquisite" course of your costly prix fixe
Californian–New French meal; perhaps the only way to "make your
dinner even better" is to "stay overnight at the château" "after
consuming all the well-selected wines."

Farmhouse Inn & Restaurant, The   28 | 25 | 27 | $58
Farmhouse Inn, 7871 River Rd. (Wohler Rd.), Forestville, 707-887-3300;
www.farmhouseinn.com
It's easy to keep 'em down on the farm at this Forestville "favorite"
"in the Russian River area" that's "exactly what one would hope
for in wine country" in a "tranquil", "country-chic" inn, it
showcases "sublime" Cal cuisine and "top-notch" local wines,
proffered by a "knowledgeable", "pampering" staff that practically
holds a "personal seminar over the cheese course" served
tableside from rolling carts; N.B. open Thursday–Sunday only.

Fifth Floor   26 | 25 | 25 | $81
Hotel Palomar, 12 Fourth St. (Market St.), 415-348-1555;
www.hotelpalomar.com
"After many chef changes", this "swanky" "citadel of fine cuisine"
at SoMa's hip Hotel Palomar now boasts Melissa Perello (ex the
late Charles Nob Hill) as top toque; her "fabulous", "inventive" New
French fare is "impeccably" served by a "top-notch" staff and
paired with "perhaps the best wine list" around (though with "too
many" bottles "in the three- and four-digit range") – all of which
adds up to "astounding" tabs (tip: "arrive in a Brink's truck").

Fleur de Lys ⊠   27 | 27 | 26 | $87
777 Sutter St. (bet. Jones & Taylor Sts.), 415-673-7779;
www.fleurdelyssf.com
Step right up to the greatest show on Nob Hill and be seated
under a "romantic circuslike tent" for culinary feats of derring-
do – Hubert Keller's "spectacular" prix fixe French dinner is an
"epic performance" ("foie gras, truffles and caviar coming out of
your ears", but "even vegetarians" can easily partake of the
"magic"); it's all staged by a "pampering" staff and "marvelous
sommelier", making an evening here a "civilized splurge" that
rewards "the effort of wearing a coat and tie."

FRENCH LAUNDRY, THE   28 | 26 | 27 | $154
6640 Washington St. (Creek St.), Yountville, 707-944-2380;
www.frenchlaundry.com
Thomas Keller's "countryside" Yountville cottage is home to
"outstanding" "dinner theater in the best sense of the phrase"; "the
service is a ballet, and the food a symphony" of "exquisite" tasting
meals (some vegetarian) in which "magnificent" French–New
American cuisine is paired with "stunning" wines by "sommeliers
who read minds"; yes, the reservations system is a "hassle" and
the meal will cost you "an arm and a leg", but after "the best five
hours ever spent" "you will agree that you didn't need that extra
arm or leg anyway."

GARY DANKO 29 | 27 | 28 | $91

800 N. Point St. (Hyde St.), 415-749-2060; www.garydanko.com
A "foodie who hasn't" worshipped at this "temple of gastronomy" – ranked No. 1 for Food and Popularity in SF – is "like an art lover who hasn't been to the Louvre"; "Gary Swanko" is a "master" of "perfection and finesse" whose "multihour", "design-it-yourself" New American meals end with a visit from the "extraordinary" artisanal cheese cart, all served without a "scintilla of pomposity" by "telepathic" waiters; though a few critics deconstruct the modern, almost minimalistic digs near the Wharf, most maintain "everything is superlative" – which is why reservations remain as elusive as the Mona Lisa's smile.

Greens 23 | 22 | 21 | $38

Fort Mason Ctr., Bldg. A (Buchanan St.), 415-771-6222; www.greensrestaurant.com
After 26 years there's not as much novelty at this "veggie nirvana", but thanks to "imaginative" meat-free "haute cuisine" plus a slew of organic and sustainable wines, "even carnivores" happily "veg out" at this "ample, lofty" Marina institution; for Saturday's prix fixe dinners the "remarkably healthy-looking staff" "pulls out the stops", and "views of the Golden Gate Bridge at sunset" just make "everything taste better"; trenchermen harrumph "portions are for hummingbirds" but still cost you a lot of green.

Hana Japanese Restaurant 27 | 17 | 21 | $41

Doubletree Plaza, 101 Golf Course Dr. (Roberts Lake Rd.), Rohnert Park, 707-586-0270; www.hanajapanese.com
"Omakase, oh my god", sigh salivating surveyors who sagely let chef-owner Ken Tominaga "do his thing" for them at his "tiny" Rohnert Park place next to the Doubletree Plaza, "easily" one of the "best Japanese restaurants north of SF"; proffered by "unobtrusive" staffers, the "impeccable sashimi and sushi" and "Asian-European dishes" are downright "swoon-worthy", so while more pretentious spots "may have better decor" (this one "reeks of plastic strip-mall") the Sonoma County chefs who "flock" here "on their days off" couldn't care less.

Jardinière 26 | 26 | 24 | $63

300 Grove St. (Franklin St.), 415-861-5555; www.jardiniere.com
No garden-variety eatery this: Traci Des Jardins' "Jazz Age"–like supper club in Hayes Valley remains a "rhapsodic" spot for the "culture crowd", though some suggest "skip the theater" and "sit upstairs" "by the band" to "watch the show below" at the "glamorous" bar; the "brilliant" Cal-French menu with veggies "straight from the *jardin*" "wows" diners, while a "superb" staff can help "divine what you're actually longing for" – now if only you had "the proverbial rich uncle" to fund it.

La Folie ☒ 27 | 23 | 25 | $80

2316 Polk St. (bet. Green & Union Sts.), 415-776-5577; www.lafolie.com
Folie artist Roland Passot's "incomparable" fine-dining folly in Russian Hill is a true "spoil-someone kind of place"; his "sublime" French prix fixe menus "pay homage to all things rich", "sinful" and "surreal" ("every time they put down a plate, I wanted to take out my camera") and are "served expertly" by an "exceptional" crew; add in the "elegance" of the "recently redone front room" and the result is a "world-class restaurant."

Lark Creek Inn, The
26 | 25 | 25 | $51

234 Magnolia Ave. (Madrone Ave.), Larkspur, 415-924-7766;
www.larkcreek.com

"Set in an 1889 Victorian" "nestled among beautiful gardens and
redwoods", Bradley Ogden's Larkspur legend "feels far away
from the city" – but relax, it's "only 20 minutes" to this "secluded"
spot, HQ for his signature "homey" yet "artful", "direct-from-the-
market" American fare ("sublime Sunday brunches") and list of
U.S. wines; with "pampering" staffers creating a "genteel", "clubby
and genial" vibe, Marin mavens maintain "it would be hard to do
better than this."

La Toque
27 | 24 | 26 | $103

Rancho Caymus Inn, 1140 Rutherford Rd. (east of Hwy. 29), Rutherford,
707-963-9770; www.latoque.com

"Plan on spending three-plus hours" enjoying the prix fixe French
dinners ("high art") and "remarkably humane service" at Ken
Frank's "spacious" "version of a Burgundian farmhouse" in
Rutherford – and plan to splurge and "go all the way with wine"
pairings "matched better than most couples"; the experience
may "cost as much as Napa Valley real estate", but since there's
"none of the snobbiness" or "drama of getting a reservation"
found at nearby rivals, at least you won't feel like you've been
"taken to the cleaners."

Le Papillon
27 | 23 | 26 | $67

410 Saratoga Ave. (Kiely Blvd.), San Jose, 408-296-3730;
www.lepapillon.com

It may be "adjacent to a strip mall" but "when you walk into this"
"quiet, elegant", almost-30-year-old San Jose French, "you'll
think you've entered the Ritz"; longtime lepidopterists have
"nothing but the highest praise" for the "phenomenal" "special
tasting menus" and "increasingly interesting wine pairings"; very
proper yet "accommodating" staffers "often surprise diners with
a treat, compliments of the chef", but the cash-conscious caution
"break that piggy bank before you go" 'cause this butterfly
sure ain't free.

MANRESA
28 | 24 | 25 | $87

320 Village Ln. (bet. N. Santa Cruz & University Aves.), Los Gatos,
408-354-4330; www.manresarestaurant.com

At his "foodie paradise" in Los Gatos, toque David Kinch ("half
ingredient-driven chef and half mad scientist") concocts "far and
away the most remarkable fare in Silicon Valley"; his "fearlessly
innovative" New American–New French tasting menus served
in a modern, "sexy" room keep a "sophisticated clientele"
"guessing" for "three hours of bliss"; though many maintain the
sometimes "superb" service "still has room to improve" and
oenophiles whine the *carte du vin* "falls short of the standard set
by the cuisine", overall this evening of "food entertainment" is
"worth every dime."

Marché ⊠
27 | 25 | 25 | $64

898 Santa Cruz Ave. (University Dr.), Menlo Park, 650-324-9092

As "Menlo Park's answer to fine dining in the city" ("without the
traffic or parking problems"), this "elegant yet modern" New French
is "increasingly the choice" of "billionaire VCs" for celebrating
and "deal-making"; its *marché*-driven tasting menus ("inventive

combinations") "compete with an equally fabulous à la carte" selection, while a "gracious" staff "suggests the perfect wine pairing"; wage slaves warn it helps "if you have a corporate credit card", because "in light of the dot-com bust", mere mortals find it "overpriced."

Marinus 　　　27　26　27　$83
Bernardus Lodge, 415 Carmel Valley Rd. (Laureles Grade Rd.), Carmel, 831-658-3500; www.bernardus.com
For the "best meal between Gary Danko and Los Angeles", "bring a compass" and navigate east to this "remote" retreat at Bernardus Lodge that "puts Carmel Valley on the culinary map"; "settle in" near the limestone fireplace, let the "expert" staff present "extraordinary" "French-style" creations "adapted to the New World" and "trust the sommelier" to steer you through the "outstanding wine" list (1,850 labels); though a few finicky types opine it's "overpriced", most mariners maintain the meal was "worth it."

Masa's ☒ 　　　28　25　27　$92
Hotel Vintage Ct., 648 Bush St. (bet. Powell & Stockton Sts.), 415-989-7154
When and if you dine at this "extraordinary" Contemporary French in Downtown's Hotel Vintage Court, "throw caution to the wind" – "splurge" on French Laundry alumnus Gregory Short's "breathtaking" nine-course tasting menu, which "lasts three hours and turns into about 12 courses after the amuses bouches and over-the-top dessert cart"; the casual cavil that the minimalist room seems "formal by San Francisco standards" (a jacket is required) but "they treat you like a star" "regardless of who you are" so "save your Benjamins" – "it's a must-do at least once, preferably more."

Michael Mina 　　　27　24　26　$107
Westin St. Francis, 335 Powell St. (bet. Geary & Post Sts.), 415-397-9222; www.michaelmina.net
"Gary Danko, watch your back", grin fanatical foodies who favor this new "monument to conspicuous consumption" Downtown; its "choreographed" staffers "energetically" present "extravagant" New American "multipart tastings" ("amazing trios") matched with "Rajat Parr's outstanding wine pairings"; however, aesthetes find it "hard to believe they spent millions" on this "beautifully appointed airplane hangar" plagued by "constant noise from the hotel lobby"; P.S. Mina's Aqua "classics" (e.g. lobster pot pie) "have moved here."

Myth ☒ 　　　24　25　23　$52
470 Pacific Ave. (bet. Montgomery & Sansome Sts.), 415-677-8986; www.mythsf.com
"So hard to get into you'd think" it didn't really exist, this "stunning" Jackson Square newcomer has been "hyped to mythic proportions" and largely lives up to the legend, thanks to Gary Danko alum Sean O'Brien's "inventive", "subtle" New American cuisine, a "sultry" scene "worthy of *Sex and the City*", "professional, pleasant" staffers and an "owner who makes everyone feel like a VIP"; what's more, dinner here won't "break the bank", owing in part to "superb wines" priced "almost at cost."

Oliveto Cafe & Restaurant　25　22　22　$48

5655 College Ave. (Shafter Ave.), Oakland, 510-547-5356;
www.oliveto.com

Supporters salute "brilliant", "passionate" chef/co-owner Paul
Bertolli, deeming his rustic Rockridge Italian "great in general"
and downright "trekworthy" when there's a "special" "epicurean
event" on; though the "unpretentious" dishes (rotisserie meats,
"breathtaking homemade pastas") are "outstanding" and the
service "professional", the bill may "cause you to stop breathing";
by contrast, the casual Cafe downstairs provides a less "precious",
less pricey yet still "delightful respite."

Press　－　－　－　VE

587 St. Helena Hwy. (White Ln.), St. Helena, 707-967-0550;
www.pressthelena.com

Despite its homey farmhouse-style decor and its superficially
straightforward American menu, this luxe St. Helena newcomer
is definitely the place to impress in Napa Valley; the dream
team behind the venue is vintner Leslie Rudd, who oversees the
exclusive Napa Valley wine list, and former White House chef
Keith Luce, who prepares a seasonal ingredient–driven repertoire
of pricey prime roasts and grill items from the custom-built
rotisserie, many of which are finished and carved tableside.

Quince　27　23　25　$61

1701 Octavia St. (bet. Bush & Pine Sts.), 415-775-8500;
www.quincerestaurant.com

Though admittedly "expensive", Pacific Heights' "precious little
boîte" is "wonderful in all respects"; its "muted decor" enables
diners to "focus" on the "delicately flavored", "über-fresh" French-
Italian fare and "outstanding wines"; bring a "dictionary to decipher
the menu" – or enlist the "extraordinarily well-trained" servers –
but do "leave Atkins behind" because the "ethereal" "handmade
pastas are clearly where the chef's heart is."

Restaurant Budo ⧉　▽ 26　27　22　$70

1650 Soscol Ave. (bet. 1st St. & Lincoln Ave.), Napa, 707-224-2330;
www.restaurantbudo.com

Word on the grapevine is this Napa neophyte is the valley's "new
star"; chef/co-owner James McDevitt (formerly of Scottsdale's
Restaurant Hapa) has crafted the "closest thing to a NYC restaurant
north of the Bay", pairing "innovative" Asian-accented New
American fare with wines from a "marvelous" "50-page" list;
pessimists pronounce the cluster of "sleek but warm" rooms "too
fancy" for the area, but early adopters optimistically opine they
"can't wait to go back" next summer to dine on the "great patio."

Ritz-Carlton Dining Room ⧉　27　27　28　$87

Ritz-Carlton Hotel, 600 Stockton St. (bet. California & Pine Sts.),
415-773-6198; www.ritzcarlton.com

The arrival of Ron (aka "I-Ron" Chef) Siegel, who has incorporated
his "love for Japanese seafood" into the "enchanting" New French
menu, "has added the final ingredient" to this "heaven on Nob
Hill"; an "impeccable" staff that "grants your every desire, even
reading glasses", and an "elegant" "old-world" ambiance ("so
quiet you can hear your ice melt") appeal to an older crowd, but
"the candy cart makes a kid out of anyone"; given that it's the
"Rolls-Royce of SF dining", expect similar sticker shock.

Rivoli
27 | 23 | 25 | $43

1539 Solano Ave. (bet. Neilson St. & Peralta Ave.), Berkeley, 510-526-2542; www.rivolirestaurant.com

At this Berkeley "oasis", revelers rejoice in Wendy Brucker's "wonderfully innovative" Cal-Med "comfort food", which can be paired with bottles from an "enviable wine list" with the assistance of "personable", "perfectly professional" staffers; meanwhile, there's a "raccoon floor show" taking place in the "lighted back garden", so though a minority grouses "the tables are too damn crowded", nature lovers declare the "delightful" experience "rivals those at the East Bay's big-name restaurants."

Sierra Mar
27 | 29 | 26 | $72

Post Ranch Inn, Post Ranch/Hwy. 1 (30 mi. south of Carmel), Big Sur, 831-667-2800

Perched 1,200 feet up "on the cliffs of Big Sur", the "all-glass dining room" at the Post Ranch Inn provides a "God's-eye view" of the Pacific Ocean that earns it the No. 1 ranking for Decor in the San Francisco Bay Area; aside from the "incomparable" seascape, admirers also adore this "secluded" aerie for its "irresistible", internationally inflected Californian cuisine, a 4,000-label wine list allowing for "wonderful pairings" and service that's "just right"; all of these elements add up to a "profoundly peaceful" and "unforgettable" gastronomic experience.

SLANTED DOOR, THE
25 | 22 | 20 | $43

The Embarcadero, 1 Ferry Bldg., #3 (Market St.), 415-861-8032; www.slanteddoor.com

Charles Phan's Vietnamese powerhouse still knocks the "socks, shoes, pants, shirt and even underwear off" its many phans; since its relocation to a "sleek", "glass-and-steel" Ferry Building space with "sweeping Bay Bridge views" its crowd is more "touristy", but the "sassy" "spin" on Saigon street food and "eclectic wine list" "still rock" and servers are "helpful", if harried, in the "deafening" environs; the only "slant in the door" remains "reservation frustration" but the adjacent "small take-out" shop helps somewhat.

SUSHI RAN
28 | 21 | 22 | $46

107 Caledonia St. (bet. Pine & Turney Sts.), Sausalito, 415-332-3620; www.sushiran.com

This Sausalito "treasure" has it all: "solicitous service", "calming decor", an "incredible sake selection" and, of course, "exquisite", "sublime" selections of sushi and sashimi ("like you're eating music"); rhapsodic regulars also recommend the "out-of-the-(bento)-box" cooked plates ("highly imaginative without being absurd"); "yes, you may have to wait, but with the wine bar next door that's not a hardship."

Terra
27 | 24 | 25 | $61

1345 Railroad Ave. (bet. Adams & Hunt Sts.), St. Helena, 707-963-8931; www.terrarestaurant.com

Even San Franciscans claim it's "worth the pilgrimage" to this "fabulous restored 19th-century stone building" "off the main drag in St. Helena" for Hiro Sone's "deeply satisfying", "spectacularly original" New American fare (incorporating Italian, French and Japanese flavors), wife Lissa Doumani's desserts that "dance on your palate", the "extensive wine list" and the attentions of an "exceptional" staff; of course, "if you're already in town, it's a slam dunk."

Zuni Café ☽   24 | 20 | 20 | $43

1658 Market St. (bet. Franklin & Gough Sts.), 415-552-2522

"One restaurant where you actually should get the chicken", Judy Rodgers' Hayes Valley Mediterranean is a "miracle of consistency" where "straightforward" ingredients are "prepared brilliantly without extravagance"; what's more, the "buzzing bar" in this "chic" yet "comfortable" "fishbowl" is HQ for SF "movers and shakers" ("the way everyone checks one another out, I thought it was a gay bar"), so though critics complain service is "abrupt" and "smug", devotees doggedly defend this "venerable" venue.

Seattle

TOP FOOD RANKING

Restaurant	Cuisine
29 Mistral	New French/New Amer.
28 Cafe Juanita	Northern Italian
Nishino	Japanese
Herbfarm, The	New American
Tosoni's	Continental
Rover's	New French
27 Harvest Vine	Spanish
Campagne	French
Inn at Langley	Pacific Northwest
Izumi*	Japanese
JaK's Grill	Steakhouse
Lampreia	Pacific NW/New Amer.
26 Shiro's Sushi	Japanese
Canlis	Pacific NW/American
Shoalwater	Pacific NW/Seafood
Dahlia Lounge	Pacific Northwest
Monsoon	Vietnamese
Il Terrazzo Carmine	Italian
Kingfish	Soul Food/Southern
Cafe Campagne	French Bistro

OTHER NOTEWORTHY PLACES

Brasa	Mediterranean
Cascadia	Pacific Northwest
Crush	New American
El Gaucho	Steakhouse
Flying Fish	Seafood
Georgian, The	Pacific Northwest
Lark	New American
Le Gourmand	French
Le Pichet	French Bistro
Lola	Greek/Mediterranean
Metropolitan Grill	Steakhouse
Nell's	Pacific NW/New Amer.
Oceanaire Seafood	Seafood
Palace Kitchen	New American
Ray's Boathouse	Pacific NW/Seafood
Restaurant Zoë	New American
Szmania's	German
Union	New American
Volterra	Italian
Wild Ginger	Pacific Rim

---

* Indicates a tie with restaurant above

Brasa ◗   25 | 24 | 22 | $45
2107 Third Ave. (bet. Blanchard & Lenora Sts.), 206-728-4220;
www.brasa.com
"Everything's a winner" – from the "unforgettable, creative"
Med cuisine to the "sleek", "beautiful interior" "glowing with
golden light" to the "attentive, discreet" service – at this Belltown
"class act"; chef/co-owner Tamara Murphy's "imaginative" dishes
are all the more "memorable" when paired with choices from the
"thoughtful wine list" "filled with obscurities"; P.S. bargain-hunters
ballyhoo the "amazing bar menu", which goes half-price during
the "best happy hour in town."

Cafe Campagne   26 | 23 | 22 | $33
Pike Place Mkt., 1600 Post Alley (bet. First & Pine Sts.), 206-728-2233;
www.campagnerestaurant.com
"In some ways more fun" than Campagne, its "grown-up brother"
upstairs, this casual Pike Place Market "favorite" provides the
"perfect combination" of *"romantique"*, "you're-in-Paris" vibe
and "excellent French Bistro fare" (*"vive le steak frites!"* and the
"pâté of champions"); its "great list of Gallic wines", "gracious
service", sidewalk seating and "reasonable prices" only add
to the appeal.

CAFE JUANITA   28 | 22 | 26 | $44
9702 NE 120th Pl. (97th St.), Kirkland, 425-823-1505;
www.cafejuanita.com
"It just keeps getting better", gush groupies of chef-owner Holly
Smith's "magical" Northern Italian that's Seattle's "best" of The
Boot and considered "a must" for special celebrations ("secluded",
"hidden" location notwithstanding); "transporting" "meals to
remember" here are composed of "sublime", "perfectly" prepared
cuisine making "great use of seasonal ingredients", "outstanding
wine" selections and "terrific service"; P.S. "are we sure this is
Kirkland and not Liguria?"

Campagne   27 | 24 | 25 | $51
Pike Place Mkt., 86 Pine St. (1st Ave.), 206-728-2800;
www.campagnerestaurant.com
"Still one of the best in Seattle", this Pike Place Market country
French "classic" is "strong all around", from the "take-your-breath-
away quality" of its "sophisticated" cuisine and "superior" wine
list to its "elegant" interior to its "formal but relaxed" service;
sure, it's "expensive", but devotees resoundingly vote it "worth
every penny", especially for celebrating "special occasions", so
"save up, skip lunch" and indulge; P.S. there's also a "wonderful
bar menu", served until midnight.

CANLIS ☒   26 | 27 | 27 | $60
2576 Aurora Ave. N. (Halladay St., south of Aurora Bridge), 206-283-3313;
www.canlis.com
"Family-owned" for more than 50 years, this "Seattle institution"
"perched above Lake Union" is the "ultimate" "special-occasion"
destination due to its "can't-be-beat ambiance" and "phenomenal
view", "divine" NW-accented surf 'n' turf menu, which "pleases
every palate" by managing to be "old-fashioned and modern at
the same time", 1,000-plus-label wine list brimming with "endless
charms" and "gracious", "intuitive" service; so, though it's *très*
spendy, this "classic" just "grows better with age."

Cascadia ☒
24 | 26 | 24 | $63

2328 First Ave. (bet. Battery & Bell Sts.), 206-448-8884;
www.cascadiarestaurant.com

"Absolutely wonderful", rave reviewers of this Belltown NWer where chef-owner Kerry Sear's "spectacular" cuisine composed of "seasonal" ingredients from the Cascade Mountain region is nothing less than a "lesson in culinary craft" (especially the "not-to-be-missed" tasting menu options), backed by an "excellent" wine list overseen by "helpful" staffers who brim with "great pairing" suggestions; "beautiful" decor (including a waterfall) completes the "truly amazing" experience; N.B. a three-course prix fixe dinner and bar menu offer less-spendy options.

Crush ☒
– | – | – | E

2319 E. Madison St. (23rd Ave.), 206-302-7874;
www.crushonmadison.com

It's quite a crush at this restored 1902 Capitol Hill farmhouse – its urban-chic dining room decorated with curvy Verner Panton mid-century furniture, dark floors and white tabletops – where chef-owner Jason Wilson's (ex Jeremiah Tower's Stars in Seattle) posh New American cuisine holds sway; the tiny drinking/dining bar, with a view into the kitchen, is a perch for see-and-be-seensters from all over the city.

DAHLIA LOUNGE
26 | 25 | 23 | $42

2001 Fourth Ave. (Virginia St.), 206-682-4142;
wwww.tomdouglas.com

"Still strong after all these years", Tom Douglas' "first" (and "best") establishment continues to set hearts swooning with its "bold" "showcase of Northwest flavors" reflecting a Pacific Rim "twist", "warm yet sophisticated" interior (complete with "sumptuous red walls") and a "sterling" staff; yes, everyone "loves the coconut cream pie", which is available to go from "the Dahlia Bakery next door."

El Gaucho ◑
25 | 24 | 24 | $63

2505 First Ave. (bet. Vine & Wall Sts.), 206-728-1337
2119 Pacific Ave. (S. 21st St.), Tacoma, 253-272-1510
www.elgaucho.com

Imagine a "NY supper club straight out of a Frank Sinatra flick" and you've got this "dark, sexy", "retro"-styled Belltown steakhouse (with a Tacoma sibling) "known for its prime beef" and "near-perfect" Caesar salads "expertly prepared tableside"; for such "swanky" experiences, including "superb", "prepare-to-be-pampered" service, it's no surprise tabs are "very spendy" ("go on an expense account" or brace for "el oucho in the pocketbook").

Flying Fish ◑
25 | 21 | 22 | $39

2234 First Ave. (Bell St.), 206-728-8595;
www.flyingfishseattle.com

Christine Keff and her team "make anything that swims taste divine" at this "vibrant" Belltown standout, "Seattle's best seafooder" thanks to its "interesting, eclectic" twists, often with "an Asian flair", on "exotic and local fish" ("love the whole fried snapper") – all of which "match well" with selections from the "excellent" wine list; it's also a "great late-night" choice, though the "festive" quarters can get "cramped" and "noisy as the evening" wears on; it's equally "fun" just for "apps at the bar."

Georgian, The
26 | 26 | 27 | $52

Fairmont Olympic Hotel, 411 University St. (bet. 4th & 5th Aves.), 206-621-7889

The yellow-toned interior of this "grand old" Downtown "hotel dining room" remains "one of the classiest" "fancy" places in Seattle, but "without being too stuffy"; the "top rate" NW cuisine with its "beautiful presentations", extensive, regionally focused wine list and "exquisite service" conspire to make "special occasions extra-special" at this ultimate "place to impress."

Harvest Vine, The
27 | 17 | 22 | $36

2701 E. Madison St. (27th Ave.), 206-320-9771

At Joseph Jimenez de Jimenez's "tiny Madison Park Basque", the "best seats are at the copper-topped bar" where "the chefs in front of you" craft "exquisite tapas" "like nothing else", so "taste everything they offer", choose from the "extensive wine list" and don't forget to "save room for pastry chef Carolin Jimenez's creations"; the "waits can be long" in the restaurant, but at least they take reservations now.

HERBFARM, THE
28 | 26 | 26 | $152

Willows Lodge, 14590 NE 145th St. (Woodinville-Redmond Rd.), Woodinville, 206-784-2222; www.theherbfarm.com

Prepare for the "meal of a lifetime" at this "legendary" Woodinville New American where "four-hour-plus" prix fixe evenings are centered around "master" chef Jerry Traunfeld's "rigorously seasonal" "nine-course gourmet wonders" that celebrate "the bounty of the NW" "in new and often startling ways", with "herbs in everything" down to "the sparkling wine"; truly "nothing is lacking" here, from the "superb" service to the "wonderful atmosphere" to the substantial tab; P.S. for the ultimate getaway, "plan to stay the night" at the Lodge.

Il Terrazzo Carmine ⊠
26 | 24 | 25 | $44

411 First Ave. S. (bet. Jackson & King Sts.), 206-467-7797; www.ilterrazzocarmine.com

"Astounding" "traditional Italian" cuisine featuring "simple preparations and the best ingredients" is what comes out of the kitchen at this "friendly" "jewel in the middle of Pioneer Square"; "upscale" but "not stuffy" decor, "honest-to-goodness pro waiters" and a "wonderful wine list" add up to truly "delightful evenings", whether "entertaining clients" or hosting "special occasions."

Inn at Langley
27 | 22 | 24 | $63

Inn at Langley, 400 First St. (bet. Anthes & Park Aves.), Langley, 360-221-3033; www.innatlangley.com

Simply "outstanding" "fresh and creative" seasonal NW cuisine is showcased in "six-course extravaganzas" at this Whidbey Island inn, where evenings are centered around the "spectacle" of "watching" chef-innkeeper Matt Costello prepare the meal before diners' eyes as he "comments on ingredients and techniques"; it's an all-around "wonderful dining experience."

Izumi
27 | 17 | 24 | $22

Totem Lake West Ctr., 12539 116th Ave. NE (124th St.), Kirkland, 425-821-1959

It's "hard to beat" the "excellent sushi" sliced up at this popular, "traditionally" appointed Japanese unexpectedly located in a

Kirkland strip mall, where the "witty chef" might just give you "things to try that aren't on the menu" while you're "sitting at the bar" trying to choose among the myriad "catch-of-the-day" options; in addition to the "very fresh" fish, regulars appreciate being "treated extremely well" by the "friendly", knowledgeable staff.

JaK's Grill
27 | 17 | 22 | $32

4548 California Ave. SW (bet. Alaska & Oregon Sts.), 206-937-7809
3701 NE 45th St. (37th Ave.), 206-985-8545
14 Front St. N. (Sunset Way), Issaquah, 425-837-8834
www.jaksgrill.com

The "superb" beef in "tremendous" portions served up at this "terrific neighborhood steakhouse" trio not only "competes with the big names", it leads the local herd, too; given such "marvelous" quality, no-attitude service and atmosphere, not to mention "excellent-value" prices, it's no wonder it's made "regulars" even of surveyors who "relish the food" ("even the hamburger is incredible") – though not the "no-reservations" policy that ensures a "long wait" unless you "get there early."

Kingfish
26 | 22 | 20 | $27

602 19th Ave. E. (Mercer St.), 206-320-8757

"Heaven-sent" soul food to "remind a Southern boy of home" draws diners in droves to this Capitol Hill "favorite" boasting a "simple yet sophisticated" setting and "gracious" service; the only thing to "hate" is "the long wait" ("be there when they open to get a table"), but for most it's more than "worth it"; P.S. "save room for" the red velvet cake.

Lampreia ⊠
27 | 20 | 22 | $58

2400 First Ave. (Battery St.), 206-443-3301; www.lampreiarestaurant.com

"Genius" chef-owner Scott Carsberg has "perfected his art" and "continues to innovate" at this "sophisticated", albeit pricey, Belltown Pacific Northwest–New American where the "exquisite" cuisine employing "beautiful", "interesting ingredients" is considered the ultimate for "celebrating a special occasion"; still, despite its undisputed gustatory "excellence" and generally solid Service score, some gripe this "food church" serves a "heaping helping of attitude" along with its other "sublime" offerings.

Lark
– | – | – | E

926 12th Ave. (bet. Marion & Spring Sts.), 206-323-5275

At this Capitol Hill spot owned by celebrated chef Johnathan Sundstrom, his wife J.M. Enos and partner Kelly Ronan, you can expect a regional, seasonal emphasis on its New American menu, including bread from neighbor La Panzanella and coffee roasted just blocks away at Caffe Vita; warm colors and textures set the mood for a comforting dining experience; N.B. no reservations.

Le Gourmand ⊠
26 | 20 | 26 | $54

425 NW Market St. (6th Ave.), 206-784-3463

"You'd never suspect" that "one of the finest dining experiences in Seattle" is on a busy Ballard thoroughfare "hidden behind an extremely unassuming facade"; but once inside this "secret hideaway" you'll find a pleasantly "non-pompous" setting for "wonderful seasonal" French fare "with a bit of NW" flair à la chef-owners Bruce and Sara Naftaly; the menu's "reasonably priced", the "wine list excellent" and the staff near-"perfect", meaning that while it may "not be the trendiest" place in town, it certainly is one of the most "amazing"; N.B. the next-door bar/ casual eatery, Sambar, *is* one of the trendiest spots in town.

Le Pichet ●

23 | 20 | 21 | $30

Pike Place Mkt., 1933 First Ave. (Virginia St.), 206-256-1499
"The fastest and cheapest way to visit France" without leaving Pike Place Market, this "slice-of-Paris" "charmer" is home to "French Bistro cuisine at its best", providing "pâté fixes" amid an "authentically" "noisy", "jam-packed", zinc-bar-and-banquette-appointed interior; the "terrific fun" here is enhanced by an "unpretentious" wine list that allows you to "experiment" with different sizes of *pichets* (pitchers); N.B. snackers take note: the *casse-croûte* menu's served all day long.

Lola

– | – | – | E

2000B Fourth Ave. (Virginia St.), 206-441-1430; www.tomdouglas.com
Owners Tom Douglas and Jackie Cross and chef Eric Tanaka have collaborated to create a menu of modern Greek and Med family-style plates at this snazzy Downtown venue serving breakfast, lunch and dinner; the tall-windowed, high-ceilinged room (caramel trimmed with pewter) is bright and airy during the day and sultry later on when the lights dim.

METROPOLITAN GRILL

26 | 21 | 23 | $50

820 Second Ave. (Marion St.), 206-624-3287; www.themetropolitangrill.com
"Where the power elite come to eat meat", this "pricey" Downtown "quintessential traditional steakhouse" "never disappoints" with its "whole-cow" portions of "thick, well-marbled", "cooked-to-perfection" beef and "delicious" sides supported by a "fabulous" 600-label wine list; add the pleasingly "old-school" "chophouse atmosphere" ("busy", "noisy") and "knowledgeable, courteous" service, and it's no wonder the "fat cats" who frequent this "Seattle classic" don't mind opening their wallets for the privilege.

MISTRAL ⌨

29 | 23 | 25 | $85

113 Blanchard St. (bet. 1st & 2nd Aves.), 206-770-7799; www.mistralseattle.com
"Out of this world" (and No. 1 for Food in Seattle), the cuisine at this Belltown New French–New American is simply "outstanding in every way" thanks to "exacting" chef-owner William Belickis' "uncompromising" use of "seasonal ingredients" and "creative" techniques imparting an "astonishing" "clarity of flavors" and resulting in "one-of-a-kind" "gastronomic experiences"; the multicourse format lends itself to "relaxing" dinners that amount to an "evening's entertainment" – and are priced accordingly.

Monsoon

26 | 20 | 20 | $30

615 19th Ave. E. (bet. Mercer & Roy Sts.), 206-325-2111; www.monsoonseattle.com
At this "destination" eatery in an out-of-the-way Capitol Hill "enclave", chef-owner Eric Banh produces "excellent Vietnamese food with flair", "delighting the senses" with an "ever-changing" menu of "innovative, well-prepared" dishes plus "specials that are worth exploring"; the "stark", "contemporary" room can get "noisy", but that doesn't deter the "crowds" from coming, meaning there's often an "unbearable wait" for a table; P.S. check out the "first-rate wine list."

Nell's
25 | 21 | 25 | $47

6804 E. Green Lake Way N. (bet. 2nd & 4th Aves.), 206-524-4044; www.nellsrestaurant.com
"Even if you're totally jaded", this Green Lake New American's "exceptional" cuisine will "break through" your gustatory cynicism with an "innovative" "menu that sings" with distinctive NW touches from "superb" chef-owner Philip Mihalski (his "excellent-value tasting menu" is a "gourmand's delight"); its "oasis-of-serenity" interior and "friendly" pro service are the crowning touches on an evening that's "first-class" all the way.

NISHINO
28 | 22 | 24 | $38

3130 E. Madison St. (Lake Washington Blvd.), 206-322-5800
"No need to fish for compliments" here – they abound from finatics who say this "elegant, relaxed" Madison Park Japanese offers "a virtually perfect sushi experience", not to mention "divine" cooked dishes; for many the multicourse "omakase meal remains a reason to wake up in the morning" ("remember to order it 24 hours ahead"): just "turn your taste buds over" to "creative" chef-owner Tatsu Nishino and "you won't go wrong."

Oceanaire Seafood Room
24 | 23 | 24 | $44

1700 Seventh Ave. (Olive Way), 206-267-2277; www.theoceanaire.com
An "outstanding" "contender" on the "fish house" scene, this "bustling" Downtown link of a national chain "has it all down" – "fantastic", "very fresh" seafood notable for its "inventive but not way-out" preparations and "mammoth portions" (regulars suggest "splitting"), truly "impeccable service" that's already among the best in town and "classy", "retro"-style decor replete with "red leather and wood."

Palace Kitchen ◐
25 | 22 | 22 | $36

2030 Fifth Ave. (Lenora St.), 206-448-2001; www.tomdouglas.com
"Food fit for royalty in a laid-back setting" is the allure of this Downtown New American, the "best" of the Tom Douglas–owned eateries, some say; considering the "great cocktails" and "highly creative", "sensational food", it's no wonder this "energetic, vibrant" place is "always bustling", especially "late-night" (the kitchen's open till 1 AM); all in all, it's considered the "quintessential Seattle experience."

Ray's Boathouse
24 | 24 | 22 | $38

6049 Seaview Ave. NW (Market St.), 206-789-3770; www.rays.com
"Always tops", this "old-school" Shilshole "institution" is among the "best places for visitors to get their fill of really good salmon" and other "fantastic" seafood prepared with "classic NW" touches while taking in a "million-dollar view over Puget Sound to the Olympic Mountains"; also contributing to the "pleasurable experiences" here is a "voluminous wine list" offering myriad "domestic and import choices" for oenophiles.

Restaurant Zoë
26 | 23 | 24 | $40

2137 Second Ave. (Blanchard St.), 206-256-2060; www.restaurantzoe.com
"One of Belltown's best", this "happening" Contemporary American succeeds on the strength of its "stellar", "creative" cuisine based on local, seasonal ingredients, "fantastic" pro service and "warm, glowing, inviting" ambiance, all overseen by chef-owner Scott

Staples, "a great guy" who "always seems to know what's going on in his dining room"; though all appreciate the "hip", "see-and-be-seen" setting and its choice "people-watching" opportunities, tender ears just wish they could "cut the decibels" a bit.

ROVER'S ⌧
28 | 23 | 27 | $88

2808 E. Madison St. (28th Ave.), 206-325-7442; www.rovers-seattle.com
Expect "an unforgettable dining experience" at chef-owner Thierry Rautureau's "world-class" Madison Valley New French showing "first-rate" "attention to detail", from the "perfectly executed" cuisine with "wonderful matched wines" to the "impeccable" staff to the "elegant" decor that's "unexpectedly relaxed for formal dining"; just find "somebody else to pay the bill" because it's "breathtakingly expensive", though "worth every penny."

Shiro's Sushi
26 | 15 | 20 | $35

2401 Second Ave. (Battery St.), 206-443-9844
Some of "the best sushi in Seattle" is sliced up at this Belltown Japanese where chef-owner Shiro Kashiba ("a true master") works "inventive" spins on "succulent", pristinely "fresh" fish, "setting the bar that others aspire to"; such "top-quality" tastes "almost make you forget" the "spartan" surroundings and service that, while "friendly", can lack polish.

Shoalwater
26 | 24 | 26 | $43

Shelburne Inn, 4415 Pacific Hwy. (45th St.), Seaview, 360-642-4142;
www.shoalwater.com
"Owner Tony Kischner knows how to treat you and your appetite right" at this Long Beach Peninsula destination for "fabulous NW cuisine" with an emphasis on seafood; the "beautiful historic setting" of the landmark Shelburne Inn, near-"miraculous wine list" and top-notch service are the crowning touches on the overall "outstanding" experiences here; N.B. check out the winemaker dinner series.

Szmania's
25 | 24 | 23 | $37

3321 W. McGraw St. (34th Ave.), 206-284-7305; www.szmanias.com
Jäger
Kirkland Waterfront Market Bldg., 148 Lake St. S. (Kirkland Ave.),
Kirkland, 425-803-3310; www.jagerrestaurant.com
At this "innovative" Magnolia Deutschlander (with a separately named sibling in Kirkland), "charming", "deft" chef-owner Ludger Szmania's "fabulous schnitzel" and other "top-notch" dishes "elevate German food to a high gourmet level" while "making good use" of NW ingredients, and a "well-trained staff" and "fun" vibe round out the "enjoyable dining experiences" here; P.S. aspiring toques seek out the "seasonal cooking demonstration dinners."

TOSONI'S ⌧
28 | 16 | 26 | $41

14320 NE 20th St. (bet. 140th & 148th Aves.), Bellevue,
425-644-1668
"One of Bellevue's best-kept secrets", this Continental "diamond in the strip-mall rough" is where "welcoming" chef-owner Walter Walcher creates "outstanding" retro classics like steak tartare and duck à l'orange (he really "knows his craft"), but "just don't ask for a menu" because the lineup changes daily and the ordering process is primarily "verbal"; add "very personal service" and a "great wine list", and it's all "worthy of a splurge", even if the "interior is a little tired."

Union
− | − | − | E

1400 First Ave. (Union St.), 206-838-8000; www.unionseattle.com
This inviting New American is a stylish venue for dining Downtown,
with a menu that's in constant flux, much of it varying daily to
follow the ebb and flow of seasonal ingredients; the idea is to
allow chef-owner Ethan Stowell full creative freedom to follow his
delicious whims (his multicourse prix fixe is easily one of the best
dining deals in town).

Volterra
− | − | − | M

5411 Ballard Ave., NW (22nd. Ave.), 206-789-5100;
www.volterrarestaurant.com
Reservations are already a must at this newcomer, named after
a Tuscan hillside town, where chef-owner Don Curtiss' lush,
imaginative eats bring a breath of fresh air to the local Italian
restaurant scene; occupying a century-old Ballard house, the
tiled, contemporary room (accented with light fixtures from its
namesake) rings with the voices of the happy hordes, wining,
dining or sipping cocktails, including one featuring housemade
limoncello; N.B. there's a dandy weekend brunch too.

WILD GINGER
26 | 23 | 21 | $36

1401 Third Ave. (Union St.), 206-623-4450
Once again voted the Most Popular restaurant in Seattle, this
simply "superb" Downtown "Pacific Rim delight" "continues to
charm" with "the best fragrant duck" and other "innovative,
delicious dishes" savored amid "big, noisy", "high-energy" yet
"elegant" environs; given such "stunning" "excellence", it's no
wonder that the throng of "too-chic-for-words" patrons "never
dwindles", meaning it "can be hard to get a table" (even booking
ahead, regulars report a certain "indifference to reservation
times") – though "once you get past the hostess it's smooth sailing."

St. Louis

TOP FOOD RANKING

	Restaurant	Cuisine
27	Tony's	Italian
	Sidney St. Cafe	New American
	Trattoria Marcella	Italian
26	Crossing, The	New American
	Dominic's	Italian
	Al's Restaurant	Seafood/Steakhouse
	Nippon Tei	Asian Fusion
	Kemoll's	Continental/Italian
	Zinnia	New American
	Giovanni's	Italian

OTHER NOTEWORTHY PLACES

Restaurant	Cuisine
American Place	American
Annie Gunn's	American
Arthur Clay's	New American
Atlas Restaurant	French/Italian
1111 Mississippi	Californian/N. Italian
Frazer's	New American
Harvest	New American
Monarch	Eclectic
Red Moon	Asian/French
Remy's Kitchen	Mediterranean

F	D	S	C

Al's Restaurant ⊠   26 | 19 | 24 | $51
1200 N. First St. (Biddle St.), 314-421-6399; www.alsrestaurant.net
Despite the death of longtime owner Al Baroni, visiting this "classic" steakhouse – a Downtown "benchmark" with a "men's club feel" – is still "like stepping back in time"; one of the city's oldest restaurants, it's been serving "superb meat and seafood" in the same way since 1925: instead of a menu, the "accommodating staff" presents "a fabulous platter" of raw materials that can be prepared with all the "fixings"; if a few yawn it's a "bit tired", fans find it "reassuring" that it "never changes."

American Place, An ⊠   – | – | – | E
800 Washington Ave. (8th St.), 314-418-5800; www.aapstl.com
In the classic corner lobby of a restored 1917 hotel Downtown, chef Larry Forgione makes his Midwest debut – and already St. Louis is lining up for his American classics with a twist; always a supporter of local suppliers (whose names are listed on the menu), the maestro uses regional wares in such dishes as Missouri pork tenderloin with Ozark bacon, while bowing to his mentor in the signature dessert, James Beard's strawberry shortcake; the wine list, which emphasizes Syrahs and Pinot Noirs, offers 20 labels by the glass.

ANNIE GUNN'S
25 | 21 | 22 | $36

16806 Chesterfield Airport Rd. (Baxter Rd.), Chesterfield, 636-532-7684; www.smokehousemarket.com

Chef Lou Rook "keeps the Chesterfield–West County set happy" with his "sublime" American fare, including "hearty portions" of "heavenly" steaks and the "freshest fish" "served with hospitality" offset by an "extensive wine list"; couples appreciate the "snuggle booths", "clubby atmosphere" and "attached Smokehouse Market" for "high-end grocery items"; call weeks ahead for weekend reservations or "be prepared" for an "unbearable wait."

Arthur Clay's ⌧
– | – | – | E

7266 Manchester Rd. (Southwest Ave.), Maplewood, 314-645-0300

Yet another reason Maplewood's Manchester Road is becoming a diners' destination district is this New American from Stephen and Kerri Scherrer and their veteran staff; though the slate changes daily, expect to find global flourishes (spaetzle, sticky rice, edamame), vegetarian options and an interesting 80-label wine list; the dining room has classic exposed brick and hardwood floors, with a few 21st-century accents (hanging metal art, a concrete bar), and sidewalk seating provides an alfresco alternative.

Atlas Restaurant & Cafe ⌧
– | – | – | M

5513 Pershing Ave. (Belt Ave.), 314-367-6800

It's in Central West End, but there's a continental feel to this small storefront establishment, whose French and Italian specialties find favor with fans of such classics as steak frites and fritto misto; theatergoers appreciate the appetizer and dessert menu served until midnight.

CROSSING, THE ⌧
26 | 20 | 25 | $43

7823 Forsyth Blvd. (Central Ave.), Clayton, 314-721-7375; www.thecrossingstl.com

"Breathtaking from every angle", this "chic", candlelit New American "star of Clayton" brings together regional ingredients from around the country, dishing up a "sublime experience" with "phenomenal" fare and a "tasting menu to die for"; chef-owner Jim Fiala was "trained in New York and you can tell", beam boosters who make a beeline to "savor every mouthful."

DOMINIC'S ⌧
26 | 24 | 26 | $44

5101 Wilson Ave. (Hereford St.), 314-771-1632; www.dominicsrestaurant.com

"Still a must if you enjoy classic Italian cuisine", this "fab" family-owned "favorite" "place to celebrate" "that special occasion" in the Hill district is also a "top choice for a romantic night out"; it's "elegant in every respect", from the "impeccable service" and "large portions" of "flavorful food" to the "lovely", "outstanding decor" and "wonderful atmosphere" – indeed, gastronomes gush, it's "worth the splurge."

1111 Mississippi ⌧
– | – | – | E

1111 Mississippi (Chouteau Ave.), 314-241-9999; www.1111-m.com

Once a shoe factory, this 1922 brick building in Lafayette Square has been rehabbed into an upscale eatery with an open kitchen, two fireplaces, a loft lounge and a glass-enclosed, eat-in wine cellar; chef Ivy Magruder's Tuscan-Californian cuisine (signature

dishes include potato-wrapped grouper) and an American-
and Italian-heavy wine list all come to your table courtesy of a
carefully schooled staff.

Frazer's ⊠   23 | 18 | 21 | $28
1811 Pestalozzi St. (Lemp Ave.), 314-773-8646;
www.frazergoodeats.com

Frazer Cameron's "offbeat" "little place on Pestalozzi" in Benton
Park, across the highway from Anheuser-Busch, has "vaulted"
"up a notch" spacewise, growing from "hip" to even "hipper";
nevertheless, the "really original" Med and "New Orleans–type"
New American food stays consistently "delicious" – "and the
crowds waiting for tables know it"; admirers adore the "relaxed
vibes and arty decor" as well as the "passionate staff", advising
"count on them to direct" your "dining experience."

Giovanni's ⊠   26 | 23 | 25 | $44
5201 Shaw Ave. (Marconi Ave.), 314-772-5958;
www.giovannisonthehill.com

"The crown of the Hill, worthy of a president's palate" (Reagan,
Bush, Clinton, to date), this "excellent, expensive", "elegant"
Italian "top performer" offers a "wonderful romantic experience"
replete with "tableside finishing of dishes" and "primo", "polished
but not fussy service"; longtime owner Giovanni Gabriele has
turned the kitchen reins over to son Francisco Paolo, who whips
up "sublime food" that's "perfect for a special occasion" (hint: it's
one of "the best places to impress a woman").

HARVEST   24 | 23 | 23 | $39
1059 S. Big Bend Blvd. (Clayton Rd.), Richmond Heights, 314-645-3522;
www.harveststlouis.com

"Talented chef"-owner Steve Gontram operates "a well-run
restaurant" in the Clayton–Richmond Heights corridor with an
"always changing" seasonal New American menu "that has
something to offer all eaters", "excellent wine choices" and a
"homey atmosphere", "especially in the winter when the fire is
going"; it's a "favorite" for "soulfully satisfying inventive dishes"
(including "bread pudding like manna") that "really make you feel
like you're somewhere special"; still, a smattering snipe "everything
is nice but the noise level."

Kemoll's ⊠   26 | 24 | 25 | $41
Metropolitan Square Bldg., 1 Metropolitan Sq. (Pine St.), 314-421-0555;
www.kemolls.com

An "oldie but goodie", this fourth-generation, family-owned
Italian-Continental "treasure", in the marble lobby of Downtown's
Metropolitan Square Building, "deserves its status" as a "local
legend"; the smitten swoon over the "superb service" and
"sumptuous surroundings" as well as the "delicious food" (the
"divine" "cheese garlic bread is worth the trip" alone); granted,
it "ain't cheap", but it's a "great place for a fancy night out."

Monarch ⊠   – | – | – | E
7401 Manchester Rd. (Sutton Ave.), Maplewood, 314-644-3995;
www.monarchrestaurant.com

Owners Jeff Orbin and Aaron Teitelbaum hope to make Downtown
Maplewood the next must-visit neighborhood with this imaginative
Eclectic that boasts an elegant dining room and a trendy bistro
coexisting around a comfortable bar; in the kitchen, well-regarded

chef Brian Hale brings a range of flavors, from Asian to French, to his dishes – all stylishly presented and accompanied by a fine, well-priced wine list.

Nippon Tei　　　　　　　　26　24　22　$28

14025 Manchester Rd. (Weidmann Rd.), Ballwin, 636-386-8999; www.nippontei-stl.com

A "wonderful respite from the everyday grind", everything "you hope for in Asian-fusion cuisine" is here at this Ballwin "favorite", from "creative tableside sukiyaki" and shabu-shabu to "some of the best sushi around"; "the greetings you receive are warm", "the service outstanding" and the "presentation superb", plus the "elegant setting" boasts "hip" colorful, "transporting decor" – so "don't be fooled by the strip-mall location."

Red Moon　　　　　　　　–　–　–　E

1500 St. Charles Ave. (15th St.), 314-436-9700; www.redmoon-stl.com

Spearheading the Downtown renaissance almost single-handedly, this busy year-old, red-hued establishment serves the best of both worlds with its Asian-French menu and a wine list that roams from the Pacific Rim to France; from cocktails to dessert, there's lots of lychee on the menu, along with such fusion fare as wok-fried red snapper and Cornish hen with coconut lime broth.

Remy's Kitchen & Wine Bar ⊠　　24　20　22　$30

222 S. Bemiston Ave. (bet. Bonhomme Ave. & Forest Park Pkwy.), Clayton, 314-726-5757; www.remyskitchen.net

Offering a "refreshing interpretation of Med cuisine" paired with "fun flights of wine", Tim Mallett's "casual, comfortable" Clayton boîte with a "beautiful bar" is "appropriate for business occasions, a date" or "late-night snacking"; the "clever cuisine" comes in "unique entrees", but they play "second fiddle" to the "tapaslike", "inventive" "small plates" boasting "wonderful" "flavors, textures and spices"; N.B. free vino tastings are held Tuesday nights.

SIDNEY STREET CAFE ⊠　　27　24　26　$38

2000 Sidney St. (Salena St.), 314-771-5777; www.sidneystreetcafe.com

"Tucked away in an old building" dating back to 1885, this "oh-so-romantic" storefront Benton Park beacon with "exposed-brick walls" and "flickering candles" "continues to live up to its reputation" for "innovative" New American cuisine; the "friendly staff" presents the menu on a chalkboard and bestows "baskets of steaming hot, impossibly soft beignets" (don't "overdose"); "reserve in advance, as they book up quickly", and remember: it's also "fun to sit" in the "cool" "old bar."

TONY'S ⊠　　27　25　27　$57

410 Market St. (4th St.), 314-231-7007; www.tonysstlouis.com

"Still the king of the town in Food" and Popularity, as evidenced by its No.1 ranking in both categories, this Downtown "icon" "sets the bar for all other St. Louis restaurants", with "superlative", "classic" Italian fare that's "never less than absolutely divine", bolstered by "very visible" owners and an "unobtrusive" staff that "treats you like royalty"; it's "definitely a destination for special celebrations" (*the* "place to go to drop serious money on dinner"), but thankfully, "portions are hearty for such a fancy place"; N.B. for more casual occasions, there's Anthony's, its bar-turned-bistro across the lobby.

TRATTORIA MARCELLA 🅢 | 27 | 19 | 24 | $33 |
3600 Watson Rd. (Pernod Ave.), 314-352-7706
Brothers Steve and Jamie Komorek "have a great thing going" at their recently expanded but still "cozy", "bistro-style" Italian "gem" on the South Side, where fans flock for "tremendously good", "rustic" yet "innovative meals" capped with a "fine choice of wine" and "hip service"; while grumblers gripe it can be as "loud as a hockey game", especially on the "newer side", and "dang hard to get into", mavens maintain it's "worth it."

Zinnia | 26 | 20 | 25 | $35 |
7491 Big Bend Blvd. (Shrewsbury Ave.), Webster Groves, 314-962-0572; www.zinniarestaurant.com
A perennial "purple" "favorite" "year in and year out", this "charmingly decorated" "gourmet delight" set in a "converted gas station" in Webster Groves "lives up to its reputation" with "daring" New American "preparations that make for a superb evening"; the "quaint" porch-style "patio is one of the best places to dine", plus the "very helpful staff" is "great at pacing a pre-theater meal"; P.S. "make reservations – it's not that big."

Tampa/Sarasota

TOP FOOD RANKING

	Restaurant	Cuisine
28	Beach Bistro	Floribbean
	Restaurant B.T.	French/Vietnamese
27	SideBern's	New American
26	Six Tables	New French/Continental
	Selva Grill	Peruvian
	Pane Rustica	Bakery
	Bijou Café	Continental
	Black Pearl	New American
	Euphemia Haye	Eclectic
	Armani's	Northern Italian

OTHER NOTEWORTHY PLACES

Bern's	Steakhouse
Campiello	Italian
Ceviché Tapas Bar/Rest.	Spanish
Columbia	Cuban/Spanish
Fred's	New American
Michael's on East	New American
Mise en Place	New American
Ophelia's	Continental
Pelagia Trattoria	Mediterranean
Zoria	Continental/Eclectic

F	D	S	C

ARMANI'S ⧖ — 26 | 26 | 25 | $60

Grand Hyatt Tampa Bay, 2900 Bayport Dr. (Hwy. 60), Tampa, 813-207-6800; www.armanisrestaurant.com

"Wear Armani" and arrive "one hour before sunset" for "a spectacular view of Tampa Bay" from this "swanky" Northern Italian atop the Grand Hyatt; the "veal is the specialty" but the "antipasto from heaven" is also a "must"; a staff that "treats you like a big shot" and a setting that's "elegant" "without feeling musty" make this the place to "celebrate and impress", though some gripe about sticker-shock prices and a "snooty" attitude; N.B. the arrival of chef Patrick Schaefer, a veteran of several Disney restaurants, may outdate the Food score.

BEACH BISTRO — 28 | 23 | 27 | $58

6600 Gulf Dr. (66th St.), Holmes Beach, 941-778-6444; www.beachbistro.com

At this Anna Maria Island cubbyhole, voted No. 1 for Food on the Gulf Coast, "a chef with sand between his toes" conjures up "exceptional" Floribbean fare (plus Med marvels like bouillabaisse that "even the French can't duplicate"), accompanied by 300-plus wines and served by a "personable" staff; though it can be "crowded and noisy", not to mention "expensive", bistrophiles say "it's worth it": "even death would be a treat if these folks had cooked it!"

BERN'S STEAK HOUSE 25 | 19 | 26 | $55
1208 S. Howard Ave. (bet. Marjory Ave. & Watrous St.), Tampa, 813-251-2421; www.bernssteakhouse.com
"Red meat, red wine and red walls": such are the robust joys of this "iconic" "carnivores' delight" (voted the Gulf Coast's Most Popular), with its "plate-sized" steaks, hundreds of thousands of bottles and "Barbary Coast/brothel" interiors; "well-versed" servers lead "unbelievable" kitchen and cellar tours, and for sugar junkies the dessert room upstairs is "as much fun as you can have" – even if prices leave you in the red; P.S. walk-ins can eat in the bar and "enjoy the experience on a budget."

BIJOU CAFÉ 26 | 24 | 25 | $47
1287 First St. (Pineapple Ave.), Sarasota, 941-366-8111; www.bijoucafe.net
No longer a diamond in the rough, this Downtown Continental (once a gas station) is now a "beautifully remodeled" "little jewel", gratifying regulars with "rack of lamb to die for" and shrimp piri piri courtesy of chef-owner Jean-Pierre Knaggs, who's laid in a large wine list from his native South Africa, and a "precise, friendly" staff that "treats you like family"; book way ahead in winter to beat opera-bound crowds worried about curtain time.

Black Pearl 26 | 21 | 26 | $44
315 Main St. (Broadway St.), Dunedin, 727-734-3463; www.theblackpearlofdunedin.com
Explorers who have discovered this "rare pearl" in the "delightful small town" of Dunedin say the tiny New American is an "excellent value" for its "delicious" twice-cooked Long Island duck and Maryland crab, served up by a "superbly knowledgeable" staff; dining here is "like eating at a close friend's house", but if you want to woo your honey at this "cozy, quiet and romantic" hideaway, better "make reservations well in advance of Valentine's Day."

Campiello Ristorante 23 | 25 | 21 | $44
1177 Third St. S. (Broad Ave.), Naples, 239-435-1166; www.campiello.damico.com
Old Naples' "see-and-be-seen crowd" gathers at the "open-air" bar of this "chic-looking" Italian "charmer", drawn by the Third Street South "energy" as well as the "dependable" pastas, salads and "well-prepared" daily specials (not to mention 20 types of martinis); it's "a huge hit", so expect "long waits."

Ceviché Tapas Bar & Restaurant ◗ 22 | 20 | 18 | $32
Bayshore Royal, 2109 Bayshore Blvd. (S. Howard Ave.), Tampa, 813-250-0203; www.cevichetapas.com
"A very NYC-ish vibe" pervades this "intimate" yet "bustling" little Tampa tapas joint where the "best" sangria and a huge small-plates menu "amaze" patrons; in-the-know amigos "go in a group" to share the "big flavors" in those little dishes and revel in the "noisy", "lively" "fun."

COLUMBIA 20 | 21 | 19 | $33
1241 Gulf Blvd. (½ mi. south of Sand Key Bridge), Clearwater, 727-596-8400
411 St. Armands Circle (Blvd. of the Presidents), Sarasota, 941-388-3987
(continued)

(continued)
COLUMBIA
St. Petersburg Pier, 800 Second Ave. (Beach Dr.), St. Petersburg, 727-822-8000
2117 E. Seventh Ave. (bet. 21st & 22nd Sts.), Ybor City, 813-248-4961
www.columbiarestaurant.com
"If it didn't exist, Hemingway would have invented it": this venerable indoor/outdoor Ybor City Cuban-Spanish, the first of the Gonzmart family's statewide chain, delivers a "festive", "authentic" Iberian interlude (with flamenco dancers, even!) in a historic tiled building; perennial dishes like the 1905 salad (so called to commemorate the restaurant's founding), black bean soup, paella and sangria are strongest here, but St. Petersburg's pier view and the people-watching at Sarasota's St. Armands Circle are compensations.

Euphemia Haye   26 | 22 | 24 | $53 |
5540 Gulf of Mexico Dr. (Gulf Bay Rd.), Longboat Key, 941-383-3633; www.euphemiahaye.com
"Blink and you'll miss the turn" for chef-owner Raymond Arpke's "expensive" Eclectic, "hidden in the trees" on Longboat Key; admirers adore its "prime pepper steak" and duck "still on the wing", served by a "loyal" staff in a formal dining room that's "like a private club in the tropics", but skeptics ask "what the Haye happened?" – this "old standby" "ain't what she used to be"; P.S. for lighter dishes and "fabulous" desserts, there's the casual HayeLoft upstairs.

Fred's   22 | 23 | 21 | $39 |
1917 S. Osprey Ave. (bet. Hillview & Hyde Park Sts.), Sarasota, 941-364-5811; www.epicureanlife.com
The glitzy copper ceiling, black-and-white-checked tile floor and Murano glass lamps say "sophisticated" and "young", and so do the crowds of "beautiful", "trendy" people who meet and greet at this Southside Village New American; while critics cry it's "too loud" and "overpriced", fans focus on the "homey" bacon-wrapped meatloaf and other "excellent" (if "pricey") dishes on a menu filled with "unusual", sumptuous spins on comfort foods; N.B. a new Lakewood Ranch branch is slated to open this winter.

Michael's On East ⊠   25 | 24 | 24 | $48 |
1212 East Ave. S. (Bahia Vista St.), Sarasota, 941-366-0007; www.bestfood.com
Sarasota's "sleek, stylish and consistent" New American certainly has "high snob appeal" ("take your mother-in-law, boss or betrothed" to "watch the crowd strut about"); aficionados applaud "one of the best kitchens in the region", "exceptional wines" from the sibling shop next door and "attentive" staffers; but detractors demur, calling it "trendy but not always wonderful" and charging that this "flashy" "joint" "suffers" because owners Phil Mancini and Michael Klauber are "more focused on catering."

Mise en Place ⊠   25 | 22 | 23 | $44 |
442 W. Kennedy Blvd. (Grand Central Pl.), Tampa, 813-254-5373; www.miseonline.com
"This is where Niles and Frasier would dine in Tampa", declare gourmands who glorify chef-owner Marty Blitz's New American Downtowner, a "solid price-performer" where "any foodie worth

his sea salt" can find cuisine that "rewards an adventurous palate";
meanwhile, a "doting" staff maintains the "high energy" at this
"chichi" "watering hole"; a few cavil, though, that "ingredients
can be overly complicated" (jokers jest "does everything have to be
served with a purée of glazed walnuts and blueberry chutney?").

Ophelia's on the Bay　　24 24 23 $48
9105 Midnight Pass Rd. (south of Turtle Beach), Siesta Key, 941-349-2212;
www.opheliasonthebay.net
Sit near a window or on the bayside patio for "breathtaking water
views", courtesy of this "pearl" at the south end of Siesta Key; it
may be "expensive", but for a "special occasion" diners can expect
a "charming", "quiet setting without tourist kitsch"; the Continental
menu's "sophisticated" and "creative" and the staff is "friendly",
but in the end "atmosphere is what it's all about."

Pane Rustica　　26 – 19 $13
3225 S. MacDill Ave. (Bay to Bay Blvd.), Tampa, 813-902-8828
"The angels bake bread here", say loaf-ers who love the "world-
class artisanal" goodies at this Tampa lunch favorite: "thin and
crispy" pizzas, "spectacular" sandwiches and homemade soups
"make eating carbs fashionable again", even if the "creative and
friendly staff" does sometimes "run out of the best daily choices";
"finding a table" during peak hours can be "difficult", but hey,
there's always takeout; N.B. it moved to its larger South MacDill
Avenue address post-*Survey*.

Pelagia Trattoria　　– – – E
Renaissance Tampa Hotel Intl. Plaza, 4200 Jim Walter Blvd. (Bay St.),
Tampa, 813-313-3235; www.pelagiatrattoria.com
Contained in the Renaissance Tampa Hotel International Plaza,
this sophisticated trattoria draws a stylish crowd clamoring for
chef Fabrizio Schenardi's lush Mediterranean cuisine; a bold,
colorful dining room, with hand-glazed tiles, custom ironwork and
an open-air courtyard, recalls the region as well.

RESTAURANT B.T. ☒　　28 – 24 $34
(fka Cafe BT)
1633 W. Snow Ave. (S. Rome Ave.), Tampa, 813-258-1916;
www.restaurantbt.com
They picked up and moved to Old Hyde Park Village, but this Tampa
French-Vietnamese serves the same "simply superb" concoctions
that help make it an "excellent" choice "for a light dinner" thanks
to the "artist in the kitchen"; dazzled devotees declare the "chef's
seafood specials" paired with beer, wine or cocktails create a
"refreshing experience for the taste buds", now enhanced with an
elegant interior that features mesh curtains, a gleaming stainless-
steel bar and Avedon-esque black-and-white photo portraits.

SELVA GRILL　　26 – 20 $34
1345 Main St. (N. Palm Ave.), Sarasota, 941-362-4427;
www.selvagrill.com
"Viva Peru!" cheer the happy few who have explored this Peruvian
dinner-only "gem", now ensconced in new larger, vibrantly colored
digs Downtown; chef-owner Darwin Santa Maria "cooks with great
gusto", "speaking fluent cilantro" with a Nuevo Latino accent and
creating special seviche that manages to be "very flavorful" yet
"not too spicy for aging taste buds"; a "charming staff" makes it
"a pleasure to go there."

SIDEBERN'S ●⊠   27 | 24 | 23 | $45

2208 W. Morrison Ave. (S. Howard Ave.), Tampa, 813-258-2233;
www.bernssteakhouse.com

This "offspring" of Bern's Steak House "should make the parent proud"; surveyors call it a "gastronomic tour de force" thanks to chef-partner Jeannie Pierola's "masterful" New American "creations" (e.g. "to-die-for" dim sum and desserts "that draw stares"); sure, prices are a bit steep, but this "contemporary stunner" brings in an "upbeat, fast-paced" crowd and staffers meet "your every need"; N.B. thrifty oenophiles buy a bottle of wine at the attached store, pay the corkage fee and save big.

SIX TABLES   26 | 21 | 28 | $70

1153 Main St. (Pinehurst Rd.), Dunedin, 727-736-8821
The Peninsula Inn & Spa, 2937 Beach Blvd. (54th St.), Gulfport,
(727) 346-9800 ⊠
118 W. Bay Dr. (west of RR tracks), Largo, 727-518-1123
4267 Henderson Blvd. (south of JFK Blvd.), Tampa, 813-207-0527
www.sixtables.com

At these prix fixe New French–Continentals – each serving half a dozen parties at one nightly seating (two on Saturday) – chef-founder Roland Levi, once Brooke Astor's private toque, puts forth a sextet of "impeccably prepared" courses, including baked Chilean sea bass, sole meunière and duckling à l'orange; thanks to his "detailed" presentations in the "intimate", "quiet" and "very romantic" dining rooms, "gastrically blessed" respondents feel like "invited guests" who are "eating at a good friend's house."

Zoria ●   25 | 24 | 23 | $44

1991 Main St. (bet. Links Ave. & US 301), Sarasota, 941-955-4457;
www.zoria.net

Formerly of Hillview Street, this Continental-Eclectic has redeemed a once-jinxed Downtown Sarasota location; the "chic clientele" calls the move a "huge improvement", "watching the movie crowd" while seated at the covered outdoor tables and praising the "much quieter digs inside"; meanwhile, the three chef-owners' "fusion of exotic and familiar flavors" in "exquisite" dishes served by a "cheerful", "knowledgeable" staff still impresses, and the expanded bar offers a menu that's "great for a light bite."

Tucson

TOP FOOD RANKING

	Restaurant	Cuisine
28	Dish, The	New American
26	Vivace	Northern Italian
	Grill at Hacienda del Sol	New American
	Le Rendez-Vous	French
	Cafe Poca Cosa	Mexican
25	Ventana Room	New American
	Feast	Eclectic
	Janos	French/Southwestern
24	Beyond Bread	Bakery/American
	Wildflower	New American

OTHER NOTEWORTHY PLACES

Restaurant	Cuisine
Acacia	New American
Arizona Inn	Continental
Bistro Zin	New American
Bluefin	Seafood
Cuvée World Bistro	Eclectic
J Bar	Nuevo Latino
Kingfisher	Seafood/New American
McMahon's Prime	Steakhouse
Tavolino	Northern Italian
Terra Cotta	Southwestern

F	D	S	C

Acacia — 23 | 24 | 23 | $46

St. Philip's Plaza, 4340 N. Campbell Ave. (E. River Rd.), 520-232-0101; www.acaciatucson.com

With "brilliant" cuisine via chef-owner Albert Hall (formerly of Hacienda del Sol), this New American newcomer in a "peaceful haven" in St. Philip's Plaza is shaping up as "one of the best" Tucson has to offer; though the "stunning", "superbly lit" interior (featuring "colorful paintings and sculptures") "raises the decor bar a notch", Old Pueblans are just as apt to opt for "terrific patio dining under the trees" where they may catch some mighty "fabulous" live jazz.

Arizona Inn — 23 | 27 | 24 | $46

Arizona Inn, 2200 E. Elm St. (bet. N. Campbell Ave. & N. Tucson Blvd.), 520-325-1541; www.arizonainn.com

For a taste of "Old Tucson", head to this "classy" 1930 "landmark", a "true throwback to yesteryear" boasting "beautiful grounds" – including a "delightful courtyard" – that provide an "idyllic" setting for breakfast; though the Continental cuisine may not be "gourmet" (it's "bland" and a "little dated" to some), supporters salute an "excellent Sunday brunch" served by staffers who "care about the details."

Beyond Bread　　　　24 | 15 | 19 | $11
3026 N. Campbell Ave. (Blacklidge Dr.), 520-322-9965
Monterey Vlg., 6260 E. Speedway Blvd. (Wilmot Rd.), 520-747-7477
www.beyondbread.com
"Knead we say more?" for "fabulous", "freshly baked" goods, these Tucson bakery/cafes go "above and beyond" the call of duty by purveying "amazing" breads, sandwiches and pastries to those who "plan their day around" visits there; P.S. they're "popular", so "call ahead" to avoid the "bustle" and settle in for a thoroughly "dependable" breakfast and lunch.

Bistro Zin　　　　24 | 22 | 22 | $39
1865 E. River Rd. (Campbell Ave.), 520-299-7799
So "very NYC", this "cramped", "stylish" New American bistro (aka "Bistro Din") is a second home to the "young and beautiful" who drop by for "delicious" French-inspired comestibles including "sinful desserts"; but the bigger draw may be the "wonderful" wine selection (with "extensive" by-the-glass options), where grape groupies can choose from 25+ flights.

Bluefin　　　　– | – | – | E
Casas Adobes Plaza, 7053 N. Oracle Rd. (W. Giaconda Way),
520-531-8500; www.bluefinseafoodbistro.com
With its brick walls, winding staircase and wrought-iron balcony, this modern, sultry seafooder (from the owners of Kingfisher) channels New Orleans, right down to the live jazz on the weekends; meanwhile, the menu covers all the fishy bases, including Parmesan-crusted scallops, wild salmon, trout and rotating lobster specials (Sunday–Thursday nights).

CAFE POCA COSA ☒　　　26 | 21 | 22 | $28
Santa Rita Hotel, 88 E. Broadway Blvd. (Scott Ave.),
520-622-6400
"Bring an open mind and empty stomach" to Suzana Davila's "colorful", "funky" and sometimes "frantically" paced Downtown "must-visit" Mexican (Tucson's Most Popular) where Oaxacan masks and bright walls complement the "exciting" food that blends the "homestyle" with the "innovative"; the daily-changing, chalkboard menu showcasing a slew of "interesting moles" helps make a meal here "magical."

Cuvée World Bistro ☒　　　23 | 21 | 21 | $34
Rancho Ctr., 3352 E. Speedway Blvd. (bet. Alvernon Way &
Country Club Blvd.), 520-881-7577; www.cuveebistro.com
"A real find", this "trendy" Midtown bistro from chef-owner Mitch Levy lures locals with "terrific" temptations in the way of "artistically presented" Eclectic eats and a "friendly staff" that makes everyone "feel at home" – even those who "dine alone"; the "great wine list" (and wine pairings with each course) is an additional "treat."

DISH, THE ☒　　　28 | 20 | 26 | $44
3200 E. Speedway Blvd. (Country Club Rd.), 520-326-1714;
www.dishbistro.com
"Reservations are a must" at this "tiny", "romantic" "hideaway" that's ranked No. 1 for Food in Tucson – no surprise, considering each "fabulous" course on its New American menu is a "treasure"; a "discreet" atmosphere enhanced by a "wonderful staff" helps

ensure an "exceptional evening" at the town's "best-kept secret";
P.S. being hitched to the Rum Runner wine shop has its advantages,
namely "unlimited wine potential."

Feast 25 16 20 $24
4122 E. Speedway Blvd. (bet. Alvernon Way & Columbus Blvd.),
520-326-9363; www.eatatfeast.com
Revered as a take-out destination (it's "tiny", and doesn't take
reservations), this "festive" Eclectic bistro is perpetually
"packed" with loyalists who fight for one of the "few tables" and
who can't get enough of "happy chef" Doug Levy's "inventive",
"vegetarian-friendly" food that's "heaven on a plate"; the
"fantastic wine wall" and "casual" atmosphere make it feel like
you're in "San Fran."

GRILL AT HACIENDA DEL SOL 26 27 25 $55
Hacienda del Sol, 5601 N. Hacienda del Sol (bet. E. River Rd. &
E. Sunrise Dr.), 520-529-3500; www.haciendadelsol.com
A "romantic" representative of "quintessential Old Arizona",
this perennially popular New American, situated in a "historic"
"resort of the golden-age Hollywood crowd", wins bravos for
its "beautiful" interior and "stunning" setting that features some
"magnificent city views" and an enviable perch for catching a
"great sunset"; if the "divine" food appears a little "pricey", save
this "star in the desert" for "those special nights when only the
best will do."

JANOS ⊠ 25 25 25 $63
Westin La Paloma, 3770 E. Sunrise Dr. (bet. N. Campbell Ave. &
N. Swan Rd.), 520-615-6100; www.janos.com
Dinner at this "top-notch" hotel restaurant in the foothills is
always "an event", thanks to its "guru", chef-owner Janos
Wilder, whose "superb", "cutting-edge" French-inspired
Southwestern cooking gets "extra points" for using "local
ingredients"; although a few lament prices "in orbit", most insist
that the "wild man" and his "special-occasion" place deserve
their reputation as one of the "Southwest's best"; P.S. the wine
list is "a feast in itself."

J Bar ⊠ 23 21 21 $34
Westin La Paloma, 3770 E. Sunrise Dr. (bet. N. Campbell Ave. &
N. Swan Rd.), 520-615-6100; www.janos.com
"Can't afford Janos?" try its "trendy" "little brother" next door,
a "lively" Nuevo Latino offshoot where "every bite" from the
open kitchen "amazes", making it for some "as good as its
relative" at a "fraction of the cost"; supporters who "love that
happy hour" rave about "out-of-sight" margaritas and add
that the "cool view" from the balcony makes this "hipster" a
"wonderful place to hang."

Kingfisher Bar & Grill ◗ 22 17 21 $36
2564 E. Grant Rd. (N. Tucson Blvd.), 520-323-7739;
www.kingfisherbarandgrill.com
"Even coastal seafood snobs would be impressed" with the
"imaginatively prepared" fish at this "funky" New American
"neighborhood hangout"; although surveyors split on the decor
("dark and dreary" versus "swanky and cool"), there's no argument
about the "exceptional wine list" and "wonderful late-night menu"
for post-theater eaters.

LE RENDEZ-VOUS
26 | 17 | 20 | $45

3844 E. Ft. Lowell Rd. (N. Alvernon Way), 520-323-7373;
www.lerendez-vous.com

"By all means the place to go" for the closest thing to a "trip to France", this "favorite" offers a "delicious" lineup of "rich", "old-time" Gallic classics; while a finicky faction suggests the decor "needs a face-lift", fawning Francophiles shrug *c'est la vie* and testify that "amazing sauces" and a "to-die-for Grand Marnier soufflé" help turn this place into "a must"; N.B. closed Mondays.

McMahon's Prime Steakhouse
23 | 24 | 22 | $51

2959 N. Swan Rd. (bet. E. Ft. Lowell Rd. & E. Glenn St.), 520-327-2333;
www.metrorestaurants.com

This "clubby", "traditional" steakhouse turns out "fabulous" "melt-in-your-mouth" meat in portions so "overly generous" that they give new meaning to "diet-busting" fare; if the price rubs some the wrong way (it's a "budget breaker"), others factor in the "fantastic wine selection" and "top-notch cigar bar" and agree it's perfect for "expense-account dining."

Tavolino ⊠
▽ 25 | 16 | 23 | $33

Safeway Shopping Ctr., 7090 N. Oracle Rd. (Ina Rd.),
520-531-1913

Chef-owner Massimo Tavolino and wife Deborah have "their act together" at their "small" new Northern Italian where each dish is "inventive without being contrived"; cognoscenti caution "Italophonies" to take heed, since the menu is "scampi"-free and "sophisticated" enough to remind some of "an upscale restaurant in Italy."

TERRA COTTA
22 | 23 | 21 | $37

3500 E. Sunrise Dr. (Campo Abierto), 520-577-8100;
www.dineterracotta.com

Denizens declare "the fire is back" (after a real one put it out of commission for a while) at this "reinvented" and relocated Southwestern "mainstay" that's "better than ever", serving a combo of "fantastic" standards (the garlic custard appetizer is "sensuous") and newer items; if the disaffected deride "uneven" food and service, others are "glad they're open again."

Ventana Room ⊠
25 | 26 | 25 | $65

Loews Ventana Canyon Resort, 7000 N. Resort Dr. (N. Kolb Rd.),
520-299-2020; www.ventanaroom.com

It's "no contest", crow culinary cognoscenti who put this altogether "spectacular" New American hotel restaurant in the foothills at the "top of the heap" for its "breathtaking views", "impeccable service" and "artful presentations" of "fabulous" food; sure, it may be a little "stodgy" (and "expensive"), but that's part and parcel of a "first-class" experience; N.B. jackets required.

VIVACE ⊠
26 | 23 | 24 | $41

St. Philip's Plaza, 4310 N. Campbell Ave. (River Rd.),
520-795-7221

"Memorable" in more than a few ways, this "charming" Tucson Northern Italian is considered an "all-around" winner by locals who point to chef-owner Daniel Scordato's "creative cooking" driven by the "finest", "freshest" ingredients; indeed, many marvel at "reasonable prices" given the "excellent quality" of the

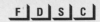
dishes (served by the "responsive staff"); P.S. alfresco dining in the "pretty courtyard" complete with fountain is "a plus."

WILDFLOWER   24 | 21 | 22 | $33

Casas Adobes Plaza, 7037 N. Oracle Rd. (W. Ina Rd.), 520-219-4230; www.foxrestaurantconcepts.com

It's not just the "yuppie flock" that flies to this perennially "popular", "ultratrendy" New American, which "overcomes its strip-mall locale" with an "unbeatable combination" of "excellent", "unique" food and a "snappy", "modern" setting that features a "relaxing patio"; insiders insist it's "especially good for lunch" when the "energetic staff" has a better chance of becoming less "flustered."

Washington, DC

Restaurant	Cuisine
28 Makoto	Japanese
Inn at Little Washington	New American
Maestro	Italian
Citronelle	New French
L'Auberge Chez François	French
27 Marcel's	Belgian/French
Gerard's Place	New French
2941	New American
L'Auberge Provençale	French
Obelisk	Italian
Ray's the Steaks	Steakhouse
26 Kinkead's	Seafood/New American
Prime Rib	Steakhouse
La Bergerie	French
Rabieng	Thai
Asia Nora	Pan-Asian
El Pollo Rico	Peruvian
Nora	New American
Galileo/Il Laboratorio	Italian
25 Heritage	Indian

OTHER NOTEWORTHY PLACES

Bis	French Bistro
Bread Line	Bakery/Cafe
Café Atlántico	Nuevo Latino
Cashion's Eat Place	New American
Ceiba	Nuevo Latino
CityZen	New American
DC Coast	New American
Equinox	New American
Eve	New American
IndeBleu	New French/Indian
Jaleo	Spanish/Tapas
Johnny's Half Shell	Seafood
Palena	New American
Pizzeria Paradiso	Pizza
1789	New American
Taberna del Alabardero	Spanish/Tapas
TenPenh	Pan-Asian
Tosca	Northern Italian
Vidalia	New American
Zaytinya	Mediterranean

Asia Nora ⌧   26 | 24 | 23 | $51
2213 M St., NW (bet. 22nd & 23rd Sts.), 202-797-4860; www.noras.com
An "air of luxury and mystery" pervades Nora Pouillon's West End "subterranean gem" where, arguably, DC's "most inventive" Pan-Asian fare comes from a kitchen that "takes sourcing seriously", with ingredients as organic and "local as possible"; "tiny portions" of "succulent appetizers" and "gorgeous entrees" are as "elegant" as the "intimate" surroundings; they're staffed by "attentive", though somewhat "pretentious", servers, causing devotees to sigh "loved everything but the price, though it was worth it."

Bis   24 | 23 | 21 | $48
Hotel George, 15 E St., NW (bet. N. Capitol St. & New Jersey Ave.),
202-661-2700; www.bistrobis.com
Stop by this "stunning", "modern" bistro near the Capitol "at lunch when the Senate checks in", along with CNN, and experience a "power dining spot if ever there was one", a "stylish" yet "relaxed" operation with "comfy nooks" and a "hoppin' bar"; the "fine" reinterpreted "French favorites" "shine", and the "knowledgeable" sommelier will guide you through "wonderful" regional wines and "tremendous" cheese selections, all "preferably expensed."

Bread Line ⌧   23 | 9 | 13 | $14
1751 Pennsylvania Ave., NW (bet. 17th & 18th Sts.), 202-822-8900
"Crusty" loaves "star" at this White House–area bakery/cafe where "everything is inventive" and "homemade", from "terrific" knishes to "fantastic fries", "savory" soups, "incredible" salads and "bread-oriented" belly busters; "organized chaos" makes for an "eat-and-run" setting and tabs are "pricey", but it's "hard to go back to a regular tuna sandwich after trying theirs."

Café Atlántico   23 | 22 | 21 | $42
405 Eighth St., NW (bet. D & E Sts.), 202-393-0812; www.cafeatlantico.com
"Walk on the wild side" in this "stylish" Penn Quarter Nuevo Latino's "airy, multilevel" digs; its offerings range from "divine guacamole made tableside" to "outstanding" 'dim sum' brunch and a "most impressive" pre-theater deal; at its copper-clad, six-seat "experimental" Minibar influenced by Spain's fabled El Bulli, "30 or more unique bites" jump-start "jaded foodies" who testify, if some dishes are "too creative", and "service is sometimes a little lax", you'll "never be bored."

Cashion's Eat Place   25 | 20 | 21 | $42
1819 Columbia Rd., NW (bet. Biltmore St. & Mintwood Pl.), 202-797-1819;
www.cashionseatplace.com
Adams Morgan's "chic" Contemporary American "treasure" is "fabulously" yin-yang: daily, "inventive use" of "the most fresh ingredients" "stretches the boundaries" "without getting scary", the "delightful" staff is "there when needed", the decor strikes a "balance with masculine dark wood and soothing soft lights and fabrics", and though the "tables can be close", the "high ceiling makes things feel spacious"; its "fantastic" brunch is "the best way to start a tired Sunday."

Ceiba ⌧   24 | 24 | 23 | $45
701 14th St., NW (G St.), 202-393-3983; www.ceibarestaurant.com
"Daringly" different, this "vibrant" Downtown "hot spot" from the TenPenh team wows with "clever" takes on Latin "flavors from

mild to wild" in "sophisticated" surroundings accented with dark woods, arty photos and "tropical" touches; servers act as your "adventure" guides, "taking the time" to explain "what's what" on a "surprising" menu; sure, it has some "kinks", but reviewers rave that "all the excitement about it is justified."

CITRONELLE
28 | 25 | 26 | $80

(aka Michel Richard's Citronelle)
Latham Hotel, 3000 M St., NW (30th St.), 202-625-2150;
www.citronelledc.com
"Playful" Michel Richard plates "dazzling" dishes that look "almost too creative to eat, but [taste] too good not to" at this top French; add a "classy", jacket-required Georgetown setting with a color-changing mood wall, "impeccable" staff and a "wonderful wine cellar", and the result is an "expensive" yet "truly fabulous dining experience" that you'll "never want to end" and "will never forget"; P.S. foodies seeking a "gastronomic epiphany" reserve the chef's table in the see-in kitchen.

CityZen
– | – | – | VE

Mandarin Oriental, 1330 Maryland Ave., SW (bet. 12th & 14th Sts.),
202-787-6006; www.cityzenrestaurant.com
In the ultrachic Mandarin Oriental hotel, this yearling showcases the pricey French-influenced, Cal-inspired cooking of chef Eric Ziebold (former chef de cuisine at Napa's famed French Laundry) in three-, five- and occasionally seven-course prix fixe dinner menus; the earth-toned dining room is dramatic but inviting, and the sleek lounge, highlighted by a 30-ft. 'wall of flames' behind the bar, is a glam destination in its own right for sophisticated cocktails and an equally intriguing roster of dishes.

DC Coast ⊠
25 | 23 | 22 | $48

Tower Bldg., 1401 K St., NW (14th St.), 202-216-5988; www.dccoast.com
A bar swimming with "young sophisticates" is awash in "the energy of the city" at this "swanky" Downtown Contemporary American that offers "the best of everything": "fantastic seafood", "style, service and presentation" coupled with a "sweeping, bustling" deco-detailed room; it's a "great scene if you're looking down from the balcony" where it's a bit "quieter"; downstairs the "buzz" makes it "hard to converse", but the "delicious food more than makes up for it."

El Pollo Rico ⊄
26 | 5 | 17 | $9

932 N. Kenmore St. (Fairfax Dr.), Arlington, VA, 703-522-3220
2541 Ennalls Ave. (Veirs Mill Rd.), Wheaton, MD, 301-942-4419
The "fragrant, perfectly seasoned", "cravable" spit-roasted chicken and "great" fries are an "unbeatable value" at these Peruvian "cult favorites" with "zilch" ambiance and "lines out the door"; amid Wheaton's "strip-mall funk" or newer, "bigger digs" in Arlington, the "lip-smacking", "super-juicy" birds are "served fast and hot" and mostly for takeout to a "diverse clientele."

Equinox
25 | 19 | 23 | VE

818 Connecticut Ave., NW (bet. H & I Sts.), 202-331-8118;
www.equinoxrestaurant.com
It's "no frills, just thrills" at this "welcoming" White House–area spot Todd Gray co-owns with wife Ellen; the New American dinner tasting menus show what a "confident chef at the top of his game can do" with "top-notch ingredients"; a "delightful staff" makes

diners "comfy" in an enclosed terrace and rooms where "you can actually talk", and "those who pooh-pooh aesthetics" that need "pizzazz" should try a "group dinner in their wine cellar – it rocks!"

Eve Ø   – | – | – | E

110 S. Pitt St. (bet. King & Prince Sts.), Alexandria, VA, 703-706-0450; www.restauranteve.com

Chef-owner Cathal Armstrong (ex Bis) and wife Meshelle have fashioned a multifaceted Old Town showplace for his seasonal New American fare using local ingredients, some of which have been specially grown for the restaurant; there's a lounge, a tasting room with daily-changing prix fixe menus and a bistro with a brick fireplace and garden (natch) where comforting cuisine is served.

Galileo/Il Laboratorio del Galileo   26 | 22 | 22 | $69

1110 21st St., NW (bet. L & M Sts.), 202-293-7191; www.galileodc.com

The namesake astronomer "would be proud": "Roberto Donna isn't a star – he's a whole galaxy" at this "superlative" Italian in the Golden Triangle; inside Il Laboratorio, the glass-walled dine-in kitchen, he performs tasting-menu "magic" matched by "stunning" wines for an "experience like no other", "and priced accordingly"; even critics who decry the main room's "dull" decor, "stuffy" service and "inconsistent" fare agree it's "unmatched when it's on"; N.B. the Osteria bar area offers bargain, rustic meals.

Gerard's Place Ø   27 | 21 | 24 | $69

915 15th St., NW (bet. I & K Sts.), 202-737-4445

At his Downtown "culinary destination", "genius" Gerard Pangaud creates New French "interpretations of the classics" in a "serene" setting that's "mindful" of the small, "charming" boîtes in Paris and Lyons; it's the "perfect place for that special dinner" when "privacy", "pristine quality", "wonderful" wines and "unobtrusive" service matter most and an "expensive" tab matters not; P.S. the $29.50 prix fixe lunch "cannot be beat for taste or price."

Heritage India   25 | 21 | 19 | $34

1337 Connecticut Ave., NW (bet. Dupont Circle & N Sts.), 202-331-1414
2400 Wisconsin Ave., NW (Calvert St.), 202-333-3120

"Excellent" subcontinental dishes make this "formal" Glover Park place one of Washington's top Indian addresses, with "rich" "classics" and "unique specialties" that are "so good, even relatives straight from Delhi demand more"; still, "service is a mixed bag", "from fawning to forgetting", and "up-sells" can be "heavy-handed"; N.B. the trendy Dupont Circle sibling serves tapas and fusion dishes at a late-night bar scene.

IndeBleu   – | – | – | M

707 G St., NW (bet. 7th & 8th Sts.), 202-333-2538; www.bleu.com

Exec chef Vikram Garg melds French food with exotic Indian flavors at this glamorous Penn Quarter restaurant/bar; in the sexy, sunken downstairs lounge, fabric-covered mattresses curve up to the ceiling, while upstairs the sumptuous, ivory-toned dining room features a chef's table and views of the National Portrait Gallery.

INN AT LITTLE WASHINGTON   28 | 28 | 28 | $129

The Inn at Little Washington, Main & Middle Sts., Washington, VA, 540-675-3800; www.theinnatlittlewashington.com

"It's all been said and it's still that good" – for over 25 years, this "luxurious" Virginia inn has hosted a "gastronomic heaven" where Patrick O'Connell transforms the "freshest" ingredients into an "exceptional" New American prix fixe; "stunning" platings, "total pampering" and "rich", "romantic", "theatrical" decor add up to a "truly fantastical experience" "worth the journey" and "every penny"; to fully realize the "dream of paradise", "stay overnight."

JALEO   23 | 20 | 19 | $31

480 Seventh St., NW (E St.), 202-628-7949 ◗
7271 Woodmont Ave. (Elm St.), Bethesda, MD, 301-913-0003
2250A Crystal Dr. (23rd St. S.), Arlington, VA, 703-413-8181;
www.jaleo.com

With a name meaning both 'merriment' and 'uproar', these "vibrant" tapas spots are "buzzing" with "big groups" ordering little plates with "many different" "zesty" Spanish flavors; "don't worry about choosing something you don't like – there'll be something else coming right behind it" during "sangria-filled dinners outside" in Bethesda, in Penn Quarter "after a show at the Shakespeare" or most recently in burgeoning Crystal City; on certain nights, entertainers "do a mean flamenco."

Johnny's Half Shell ☒   23 | 16 | 20 | $37

2002 P St., NW (bet. 20th & 21st Sts.), 202-296-2021;
www.johnnyshalfshell.com

This "unpretentious" Dupont Circle "favorite" serves "splendid" seafood, "crisp white wines" and much more, "without a huge price tag"; it's "wonderfully alive", with "first-rate" cooking, a "classic" oyster house feel and a "neighborly" bar good for "wonk sightings and soft-shell crab"; "deterrents" like "long waits" mean reserve or go for "great po' boys and hot dogs" at lunch.

KINKEAD'S   26 | 21 | 24 | $55

2000 Pennsylvania Ave., NW (I St.), 202-296-7700; www.kinkead.com

"You may run into your congressman" dining on "fabulous seafood" at DC's perennial Most Popular, Bob Kinkead's "venerable" New American for "high rollers and power brokers" in Foggy Bottom; the "best ingredients, creativity and presentation" "matched by solicitous service" and a "wine list from heaven" make for a meal made to "impress a client"; since a mid-*Survey* "face-lift", the atmosphere is more "inviting and airy", but the place still has "attitude", as the "less fabulous are often relegated to Siberia."

La Bergerie   26 | 21 | 25 | $54

218 N. Lee St. (bet. Cameron & Queen Sts.), Alexandria, VA, 703-683-1007;
www.labergerie.com

Fans of "traditional" methods say "a lesson in how French cooking should be done" can be had at this "elegant" establishment; "if you are fond of goose livers", "real quenelles" and "scrumptious soufflés", its "exquisitely prepared" dishes and "sophisticated" ambiance add up to "a truly adult experience" that "makes you want to get dressed up"; perhaps they're "a little stuck up", but what do you expect when they keep hearing they're "the tops in Old Town"?

L'AUBERGE CHEZ FRANÇOIS   28 | 27 | 28 | $68

332 Springvale Rd. (Beach Mill Rd.), Great Falls, VA, 703-759-3800;
www.laubergechezfrancois.com

The Haeringer family's "magical *esprit*" pervades its "enchanting" Alsatian farmhouse "tucked in the windy roads of Great Falls"; a "memorable" evening includes "delicious" regional dishes, "gracious" treatment and "just the right amount of homey-ness" in the "charming", rustic rooms and "gorgeous garden", leading devotees to declare it's a "special place from an earlier time that hugs you like grandma did when you were little"; N.B. Saturday reservations are accepted up to four weeks in advance.

L'AUBERGE PROVENÇALE   27 | 26 | 26 | VE |

L'Auberge Provençale, 13630 Lord Fairfax Hwy. (Rte. 50), Boyce, VA, 540-837-1375; www.laubergeprovencale.com

Your "short ride" through the Virginia countryside is "just enough time to anticipate the surroundings and fabulous fare" at this "wonderful" Provençal-style "country inn" where the French cuisine and rare wines are "heaven on the tongue"; the prix fixe meal is so "breathtaking", you "won't want the evening to end" – but let it "if you are staying the night", as you have "an over-the-top fantastic breakfast" to look forward to in the morning.

MAESTRO 🗷   28 | 27 | 28 | $98 |

Ritz-Carlton Tysons Corner, 1700 Tysons Blvd. (International Dr.), McLean, VA, 703-917-5498; www.maestrorestaurant.com

Take a "front-row seat" near "star" Fabio Trabocchi's open kitchen to watch "elegant precision" and "amazing" creativity in action; "interpretive" cuisine with a "depth of flavor" on a par with "Italy's best", plus "fantastic sommelier" Vincent Feraud's "beyond-extensive" wine list, gives frontrunners like "The Inn at Little Washington a run for their money" in the ratings, while the "impeccable" staff at this "luxurious" Ritz-Carlton "splurge" provides top service.

MAKOTO   28 | 22 | 27 | $61 |

4822 MacArthur Blvd., NW (U St.), 202-298-6866

"Nothing is lost in translation" in the Palisades, where the "exquisite" omakase tasting menu "is a work of art, with subtle flavors, lots of textures and beautiful composition", leading voters to rank this No. 1 for Food in DC; the "black town cars disgorging Japanese diplomats" attest to a "dedication to excellence", so "take off your shoes and surrender" to it as it is "authentically served" in a "tiny", rustic studio akin to "an old Kyoto *kappo*", complete with "packing-box" seats that "typify the tortured Eastern aesthetic of pleasure and pain."

Marcel's   27 | 23 | 25 | $67 |

2401 Pennsylvania Ave., NW (24th St.), 202-296-1166; www.marcelsdc.com

For "divine" dining "before the Kennedy Center", try the "best-value" prix fixe at this "luscious" Belgian-French; chef-owner Robert Wiedmaier's "blend of tastes explodes with flavor", while the digs are "lovely for a date or a duty dinner" fueled by "notable" wines; after the performance, catch its free limo and come back for piano jazz and drinks.

Nora 🗷   26 | 22 | 24 | $56 |

2132 Florida Ave., NW (bet. Connecticut & Massachusetts Aves.), 202-462-5143; www.noras.com

"Organic before it was in", Nora Pouillon's "exceptional" Dupont Circle New American uses the "freshest" seasonal ingredients in "innovative" dishes that are "indulgent" and "delicious", yet leave her fans feeling that they've "done something healthy" for themselves; there are "DC hotshots everywhere you look", soaking up the "picture-perfect" carriage-house setting complete with "handmade quilts"; nevertheless, critics carp this "special-occasion" spot is "skating by on reputation."

Obelisk ☒   27 | 20 | 26 | $65

2029 P St., NW (bet. 20th & 21st Sts.), 202-872-1180

At this "popular" Dupont Circle townhouse, Peter Pastan's "Italian sensibilities" allow "superb ingredients to shine with a minimum of fuss" in daily-changing, five-course prix fixe menus; "no-attitude" "foodie waiters" help diners "explore" "flawless, multilayered flavors" and "excellent" wines from small vintners in a "spare" but "lovely" and "intimate" room "perfect" for a "culinary romance"; the only complaint is that it's hard to "get in" the *piccolo* place.

Palena ☒   25 | 21 | 22 | $58

3529 Connecticut Ave., NW (bet. Ordway & Porter Sts.), 202-537-9250;
www.palenarestaurant.com

"Prepare to be amazed" at "perfectionist" Frank A. Ruta's "civilized" Cleveland Park New American where "value for money" means the option of "marvelous" "bar food in the front" at an under-$10 "steal"; in the "luxuriously cozy" back room, "a conversation can be had" over a "superb" prix fixe that reminds *bec fins* of "intimate European" destinations; desserts are equally "fantastic", but "slow service" irritates impatient eaters.

Pizzeria Paradiso   24 | 15 | 17 | $21

3282 M St., NW (bet. 32nd & 33rd Sts.), 202-337-1245
2029 P St., NW (bet. 20th & 21st Sts.), 202-223-1245

"Pizza delivery is a thing of the past" after the "first slice" of a wood-baked pie from these Dupont Circle and Georgetown "boutiques" boasting the "best", "freshest" ingredients atop "crispy", "smoky crusts" accompanied by "wonderful antipasto" and "rustic wines by the glass" at "cozy" tables that "invite conversation"; the "only problem is crowds", so "go at off hours."

Prime Rib ☒   26 | 24 | 25 | $62

2020 K St., NW (bet. 20th & 21st Sts.), 202-466-8811; www.theprimerib.com

"Deals get done over a nice, juicy" namesake cut of beef that's the "size of a sofa" along with a "can't-be-beat" wine list at this Golden Triangle "swanky" steakhouse; the "grand supper club" setting – "leopard-print, chrome, black leather", a baby grand piano and bass – means guys must be "dressed in jackets and ties"; hipsters might call it a "stuffy" "time warp", but traditionalists say it's "the last vestige of civilization in an age of casual-gone-amok."

Rabieng   26 | 17 | 20 | $23

Glen Forest Shopping Ctr., 5892 Leesburg Pike (Glen Forest Dr.),
Falls Church, VA, 703-671-4222; www.duangrats.com

A Falls Church "gem that sparkles", this "fantastic" Thai offers a "wide and varied" menu of "perfectly balanced flavors"; the "skillful kitchen's" "spicy" stuff is "not for the faint of tongue", but the "cheap" prices are perfect for the faint of wallet, and an "attentive" staff "seals the deal."

Ray's The Steaks   27 | 11 | 21 | $36

Colonial Village, 1725 Wilson Blvd. (Rhodes St.), Arlington, VA,
703-841-7297

The "lights are bright", the "walls are white", but the steak is "as good as you can get in DC", for "much less money" than the "expense-account" joints; "charming owner, knowledgeable sommelier" and crack chef Mike (Ray) Landrum "walks around in a working apron and adds to the fun" of a "no-frills" Arlington strip-mall beefery where "the decor gives you nothing to focus" on but the "delicious" prime cuts.

1789
25 | 25 | 25 | $58

1226 36th St., NW (Prospect St.), 202-965-1789; www.1789restaurant.com
"The ambiance is Colonial, the clientele is Kennedy" at this "old-money" ("men in bow ties" and de rigueur jackets) "crowd-pleaser" in "the Georgetown scene"; the "service and cozy, romantic ambiance [especially downstairs] are all top-notch" for "special occasions", and chef Ris Lacoste "pleases demanding palates" with "terrific, seasonal" New American menus that have "multigenerational" appeal; just "don't look for a loud, wild time or a small tab."

Taberna del Alabardero ⊠
25 | 25 | 25 | $56

1776 I St., NW (18th St.), 202-429-2200; www.alabardero.com
"Get dressed up, put on your best manners", enter this taberna through its door on 18th Street and you're "suddenly whisked to Madrid" to "savor" "extraordinary" tapas at the bar (a "nice secret for lunch") or "wonderful", "hearty" Iberian classics "prepared with modern flair" and matched by "a great selection of top Spanish wines"; the "sumptuously decorated" dining room "sparkles" at night, and so will you when you're "coddled" in a "special-occasion" atmosphere that has expats crying "bravo."

TENPENH ⊠
25 | 24 | 23 | $46

1001 Pennsylvania Ave., NW (10th St.), 202-393-1500; www.tenpenh.com
"Call it 'Penh-ominal'" – Jeff Tunks' Downtown "crowd-pleaser" is a "treat for the senses": its "striking" decor and "intriguing" menu are filled with "unique", "successful takes" on Eastern "colors, textures and flavors"; Pan-Asian dishes so "delicious" you'll "lick your plate clean", a "staff that knows its stuff" and a "lively bar" "buzzing with energy" make it the "perfect place" to "take your New York friends to prove that DC is not a dining wasteland"; watch out, though, for "prices that match the high ceilings."

Tosca
25 | 23 | 24 | $55

1112 F St., NW (bet. 11th & 12th Sts.), 202-367-1990;
www.toscadc.com
At this "Armani" of Northern Italians, the "daring" yet "luscious" cooking "rivals the city's best", while the "sharp, contemporary" Penn Quarter room "oozes" "minimalist" "subtlety"; the "warm, welcoming" staff "knows what it's recommending", making it a "top pick" to "impress a new customer"; the "fabulous" chef's table is "not a bargain", but dining here can be "surprisingly affordable", if you take advantage of the "great-value" pre-theater menu.

2941 Restaurant
27 | 27 | 24 | $58

2941 Fairview Park Dr. (Arlington Blvd.), Falls Church, VA, 703-270-1500;
www.2941.com
This "entrancing restaurant in a Falls Church office park" is "mere seconds from the Beltway", and serves Jonathan Krinn's "marvelous" New American meals distinguished by "wonderful, rich reductions" and "quality ingredients"; a "superb" "retreat" set among trees and overlooking a lake, the "dramatic" place is a "romantic" modern "winner", from the "koi ponds as you arrive"

to the "best meeting rooms" to the take-home baguette baked by the chef's papa.

Vidalia　　　　　　　　　　25　23　24　$54

1990 M St., NW (bet. 19th & 20th Sts.), 202-659-1990; www.vidaliadc.com

"The South rises victorious from every plate" at this Golden Triangle New American where "dynamite" dishes with Dixie "flair" are served up with "passion and care"; "down-home was never this good", and a meal here now is "better than ever" since the joint has been "reinvigorated" with a "stylish makeover" – "lavish" leather banquettes, rippled glass and more "open" space with a "great grazing bar" make for "fabulous new digs" in which to enjoy "stylized cooking" and a "fantastic wine list" (35 offerings by the glass).

Zaytinya ☽　　　　　　　　25　26　21　$37

701 Ninth St., NW (G St.), 202-638-0800; www.zaytinya.com

In a "spectacular", "soaring" "glass, chrome and marble" space, this "stunning" sophisticate "has lit up the Penn Quarter", drawing "beautiful people" for a "culinary tour of the Eastern Mediterranean"; "you can't stop eating" its "incredible selection" of Greek, Lebanese and Turkish meze and sipping its "excellent", "unusual" wines, and at these "surprisingly" "affordable" prices, why should you?; "noise" and "long waits" (no reservations after 6:30 PM) cause admirers to sigh "if it weren't so trendy and popular it would be even better."

Westchester/ Hudson River Valley

TOP FOOD RANKING

	Restaurant	Cuisine
29	Freelance Café	New American
	Xaviar's at Piermont	New American
27	Rest. X & Bully Boy Bar	New American
	Blue Hill at Stone Barns	New American
	Buffet de la Gare	French
	Il Cenàcolo	Northern Italian
	Mina	New American
	La Panetière	French
26	Escoffier, The	French
	Zephs'	Eclectic/New Amer.
	La Crémaillère	French
	Coromandel	Indian
	Ocean House	New England/Seafood
	Il Barilotto	Italian
	L'Europe	Continental
	Arch	Eclectic/French
	Johnny's Pizzeria	Italian/Pizza
	Wasabi*	Japanese
	Iron Horse Grill	New American
	Busy Bee Cafe	New American

OTHER NOTEWORTHY PLACES

Restaurant	Cuisine
Aberdeen	Chinese/Cantonese
American Bounty	New American
Aubergine	French/Amer.
Cafe Mezé	Mediterranean
Caterina de Medici	Italian
Crabtree's Kittle House	New American
DePuy Canal House	New American
Equus	French/New Amer.
French Corner	French
Harvest on Hudson	Mediterranean
Koo	Japanese
Le Canard Enchainé	French Bistro
Le Pavillon	French
Mulino's of Westchester	Italian
Sonora	Nuevo Latino
Stoneleigh Creek	Eclectic
Sushi Mike's	Japanese
Terrapin	New American
Trotters	Mediterranean
Would, The	New American

---

* Indicates a tie with restaurant above

Aberdeen   25 | 17 | 22 | $27

Marriott Residence Inn, 3 Barker Ave. (Cottage Pl.), White Plains, 914-288-0188

It's as "close to China as you can get" declare devotees of this "authentic, refined" White Plains Cantonese "jewel" in the Marriott Residence Inn, which features "fresh" seafood live from the tanks (including some "unusual" choices) and "amazing" lunchtime dim sum deemed "on a par with" what you'd find in NYC's Chinatown; "courteous", "knowledgeable" service and new digs considered "more comfortable than the old Harrison location" make it "not your usual Sunday night" option.

American Bounty Restaurant ⌖   25 | 24 | 23 | $50

Culinary Institute of America, 1946 Campus Dr. (Rte. 9), Hyde Park, 845-471-6608; www.ciachef.edu

"Those kids sure can cook", declare diners of the "chefs-to-be" at this Hyde Park cooking school eatery where a "tantalizing menu" of "memorable", "near-impeccable" New American fare featuring regional produce earns CIA students an "excellent" grade; high marks also go to the "stunning", "airy" room with "gorgeous views" manned by an "eager-to-please" trainee staff, adding up to a decidedly "winning combination"; P.S. "chat it up" with your server, because "you may be talking to the next Emeril."

Arch   26 | 25 | 26 | $66

1296 Rte. 22 (end of I-684), Brewster, 845-279-5011; www.archrestaurant.com

"If you want to be pampered", head "up the winding road" to this "charming" Brewster "hideaway" and dine on "superb" French-Eclectic cuisine in "tastefully decorated" rooms; surveyors swoon it's the "epitome of elegance", with service "so refined you almost don't know it's there", so although it's "very expensive", most agree it's more than "worth the price" (and "the hike").

Aubergine   25 | 24 | 23 | $54

Aubergine Fine Food & Lodging, Rtes. 22 & 23, Hillsdale, 518-325-3412; www.aubergine.com

Chef-owner David Lawson's "excellent" French-American fare featuring "seasonal and game dishes" "in colorful puddles of berry and herb and you-name-it sauces" keeps customers coming to this "absolutely lovely" 18th-century house in Hillsdale; an "impressive wine list" (or tickets at nearby Tanglewood) may have some deciding to stay on, so just "climb the stairs to the bedrooms" – it's all "a country inn should be."

BLUE HILL AT STONE BARNS   27 | 28 | 26 | $76

Stone Barns Center for Food & Agriculture, 630 Bedford Rd. (Lake Rd.), Pocantico Hills, 914-366-9600; www.bluehillstonebarns.com

"Manhattan dining meets the countryside" at this "extraordinary" New American, which is blessed with a "magical" converted Norman-style barn setting amid a working farm/educational center in Rockefeller State Park ("thank you, Mr. Rockefeller!"); the ingredients here are "so fresh and local", the "superb" cuisine "takes on a whole new dimension", while the "warmly elegant" decor and "incredibly knowledgeable staff" complete the "culinary nights to remember" (not to mention Sunday brunches); call "far in advance" to "snare a reservation" and then "arrive early to walk the grounds."

BUFFET DE LA GARE ⊠   27   22   26 $58
155 Southside Ave. (Spring St.), Hastings-on-Hudson, 914-478-1671
A "beautifully romantic" "visit to a special place in France" is the
experience "warm hosts" Annie and Gwenael Goulet have crafted
at this *magnifique* bistro that's located "near the train station" in
Hastings, but in spirit is "as close to Paris (without the attitude)" as
you can get; a "confident, sure-footed" staff "from heaven" delivers
"first-rate" cassoulet and other classics, inspiring groupies to gush
"it doesn't get much better than this"; the only quibble: given such
"pricey tabs", "why can't they find more comfortable chairs?"

Busy Bee Cafe ⊠   26   16   21 $35
138 South Ave. (Reade Pl.), Poughkeepsie, 845-452-6800
"Don't judge a book by its cover", because contrary to appearances
this New American in a "former deli" tucked among family homes
in Poughkeepsie is a "great little bistro" serving "scrumptious"
meals to "knock your socks off"; it's "tiny", so expect "sardine"
seating, but the "thoughtful service" and "good vibe" more than
make up for the squeeze.

Cafe Mezé   24   19   21 $46
20 N. Central Ave. (Hartsdale Ave.), Hartsdale, 914-428-2400;
www.cafemeze.com
"Creative" chef Mark Filippo "always has something new and
inventive on the menu" at this "top-notch" Hartsdale Med housed
in a "boxy building that hides its pretty interior"; simply "delicious"
dishes (the artichoke ravioli and grilled octopus are "particularly
recommended") and "excellent waiters" make it "another Livanos
family triumph", even if a few curmudgeons crab it's "too loud"
during "crowded times."

Caterina de Medici ⊠   26   25   23 $47
Colavita Center for Italian Food and Wine, Culinary Institute of America,
1946 Campus Dr. (Rte. 9), Hyde Park, 845-471-6608; www.ciachef.edu
"It's all terrific", declare disciples of the "superb", "mouthwatering"
preparations by CIA chefs-to-be at this Hyde Park Italian, housed in
a "magnificent" space that looks like a "bright Tuscan villa" –
albeit one with crystal chandeliers and "de Medici crests hidden
everywhere"; although the student staff sometimes "isn't polished",
it "makes up for it with enthusiasm", contributing to a dining
experience that all in all is deemed "elegant and relaxing at the
same time"; N.B. the Al Forno room offers more casual meals
overlooking the kitchen.

Coromandel   26   16   21 $31
30 Division St. (bet. Huguenot & Main Sts.), New Rochelle, 914-235-8390;
www.coromandelcuisine.com
"Long live India!" declare devotees of this "superb" subcontinental
that serves "innovative" cuisine, providing patrons with the
chance to "discover taste buds they never knew they had"; with
"service that could not be friendlier or faster" and a "bargain lunch
buffet", you "feel like you could be in New Delhi."

CRABTREE'S KITTLE HOUSE   25   25   24 $56
Crabtree's Kittle House Inn, 11 Kittle Rd. (Rte. 117), Chappaqua,
914-666-8044; www.kittlehouse.com
"You'll feel like landed gentry" at this "beautiful, old-school"
institution in Chappaqua that "captures the eloquence of rustic

dining" – and nabs the area's Most Popular ranking – with "artfully prepared" New American cuisine "fit for a president" ("it's a fave of Bill Clinton", who lives nearby), "an exhaustive" wine list boasting some 6,000 labels and a "gorgeous", truly "romantic" "country setting"; in sum, it's a "wonderful place to take out-of-town guests", "impress the in-laws" or enjoy a "celebratory meal"; P.S. longtime chef Greg Gilbert departed post-*Survey*.

DePuy Canal House
23 | 26 | 22 | $62

Rte. 213 (Lucas Tpke.), High Falls, 845-687-7700;
www.depuycanalhouse.net
"One of the original homes of New American cuisine", this "gorgeous", "very romantic" High Falls Colonial stone building serves as the perfect backdrop for "hot dates, anniversaries" and everything in between; "elder statesman" chef-owner John Novi's "menu is always full of surprises" with "exotic flavors" making for some "unforgettable dinners", so go ahead and "splurge" – it's "a wonderful adventure."

Equus
26 | 29 | 25 | $70

Castle on the Hudson, 400 Benedict Ave. (bet. Maple St. & Martling Ave.), Tarrytown, 914-631-3646; www.castleonthehudson.com
A "glorious" "hilltop location" in Tarrytown is the "stunning" "baronial setting" for this French–New American housed in a turreted palace replete with "romantic corners for quiet, intimate meals"; sure, the "incredible" cuisine and "no-detail-overlooked" "formal" service comes with a "hefty price tag", but how else are you going to know "what it's like to eat in a castle?"; P.S. in warm weather, the terrace and gardens are "magnificent."

Escoffier, The ⊠
26 | 25 | 24 | $56

Culinary Institute of America, 1946 Campus Dr. (Rte. 9), Hyde Park, 845-471-6608; www.ciachef.edu
"Lovely high French" cuisine "served with style" "the classic way" in the "most elegant room" makes this CIA standout "the star of the Hyde Park school's marvelous restaurants", rave reviewers, noting that desserts prepared tableside "are a great show" too; "cheap it's not", but it's the perfect "place for special moments" – or get a seat overlooking the kitchen to witness "the wonders of the culinary world"; P.S. remember to "plan ahead", because "reservations are hard to come by."

FREELANCE CAFÉ & WINE BAR, THE ⊅
29 | 20 | 26 | $45

506 Piermont Ave. (Ash St.), Piermont, 845-365-3250; www.xaviars.com
"Deee-lightful", coo the "cosmopolitan" cognoscenti who collect at Xaviar's "superb" sister in Piermont, which was voted No. 1 for Food thanks to its "coconut shrimp that dreams are made of" and other truly "exquisite" New American offerings; it's more "affordable" than next door (though still "not for a freelancer's budget"), and "you've gotta love" "gracious" maitre d' Ned Kelly, who sets the tone for the "excellent service" in its tiny, "minimalist" space; yes, the no-reservations policy means the lines practically "start forming at the crack of dawn", but to most it's "worth it."

French Corner
24 | 23 | 22 | $47

3407 Cooper St./Rte. 213 W. (Rte. 209), Stone Ridge, 845-687-0810;
www.frcorner.com
"Skillful and knowledgeable" chef-owner Jacques Qualin (once of NYC's Le Perigord) makes "good use of local ingredients" to create

"delicious regional French cuisine" at this "welcome newcomer" to Stone Ridge; a few antique touches add to the chic, sleek interior, and though some find the "Manhattan prices" a tad too steep for the area, the "$25 prix fixe is a bargain" in any town.

HARVEST ON HUDSON   22 26 20 $48
1 River St. (¼ mi. north of Hastings-on-Hudson RR), Hastings-on-Hudson, 914-478-2800; www.harvest2000.com

Savor the smell of the "inviting fireplace" as you "watch the Hudson float by" at this "gorgeous" Hastings Med, whose "picturesque views of the Palisades" and "Napa Valley feel" captivate visitors as much as the "delicious" dishes "made with ingredients from on-premises gardens"; some say the kitchen "doesn't match the extraordinary setting", and there are a few complaints that the service "needs polishing", but most don't notice because "on a clear night" it's hard to find a more "enchanting" locale.

Il Barllotto   26 22 23 $44
1113 Main St. (North St.), Fishkill, 845-897-4300

"Another crowd-pleaser" from Eduardo Lauria, this "posh", "first-rate" Fishkill fave draws raves with "sophisticated" Italian fare, so when ordering "be a bit adventurous – you won't be disappointed"; the dining room in a 19th-century building is deemed "handsome", the list of boutique vinos "awesome" and the staff "professional and accommodating", so the only drawback is "it can get noisy."

Il Cenàcolo   27 21 25 $56
228 S. Plank Rd./Rte. 52 (Rte. 300), Newburgh, 845-564-4494

"Phenomenal" cooking that "explodes with complex flavors", plus a "list of specials a mile long (forget about the menu)", make this Northern Italian "the epitome of fine dining" in "gritty Newburgh" – or "anywhere"; the simple decor is enhanced by a "fantastic array of antipasti" on display, and other pluses include a "thoughtful and kind staff" and an "excellent wine selection"; yes, meals here cost "a pretty penny", but "hoo, boy are they good!"

Iron Horse Grill   26 21 24 $53
20 Wheeler Ave. (Manville Rd.), Pleasantville, 914-741-0717; www.ironhorsegrill.com

"I don't have to go to NYC anymore!" say fans of this "exquisite" Pleasantville New American where "passionate" chef-owner Philip McGrath "is a genius" who "greets you as you come in" to sample his "sublime" "seasonal" cuisine; a "confident staff" and "intimate" "restored train station" setting are other reasons this "winner" is worth "splurging on" ("wish I could afford it more often").

Johnny's Pizzeria ⊟   26 9 15 $17
Lincoln Plaza, 30 W. Lincoln Ave. (bet. N. 7th Ave. & Rochelle Terrace), Mt. Vernon, 914-668-1957

There are "no slices" to be had at this Mt. Vernon Italian, "but that's ok" because the "melt-in-your-mouth", "world-class pizza" "is so light and thin" "you can almost eat a whole pie by yourself"; never mind if "parking is next to impossible" and the rest of the menu's only "ordinary" – just focus on the house specialty.

Koo   24 20 20 $51
17 Purdy Ave. (2nd St.), Rye, 914-921-9888; www.koorestaurant.com

"Young", "cool and cosmopolitan" Rye residents suffering "Nobu withdrawal" make a beeline for this "amazing" nouveau Japanese, whose "innovative", "eclectic" cuisine is tailor-made for the "sophisticated palate" and comes via an "attentive", "welcoming" staff; you may "need a second mortgage to pay the bill", but after a couple of pours from the "top-quality" sake list, you won't notice the "New York City prices."

La Crémaillère   26 | 26 | 26 | $68
46 Bedford-Banksville Rd. (Round House Rd.), Bedford, 914-234-9647;
www.cremaillere.com
"Tucked in the backwoods of Bedford" is the Meyzen family's "first-class", "wonderful retreat" where you "wait for the waiters to lift the lids" to experience "the art of French cooking" at its "finest"; "charming decor", an "astonishing" wine list (some 14,000 bottles) and servers "that treat you like an old, valued friend" make it an especially fitting "place to get engaged (or engage in an affair!)."

LA PANETIÈRE   27 | 26 | 26 | $70
530 Milton Rd. (Oakland Beach Ave.), Rye, 914-967-8140;
www.lapanetiere.com
"You don't have to wait to get into heaven" when this "first-class" French housed in an "elegant" Rye mansion awaits; here, "sublime meals" backed by an "impeccable" wine cellar are presented amid "stunning" environs by a staff that "treats you royally", adding up to a guaranteed "evening to remember" (owner Jacques Loupiac "never disappoints"); surveyors suggest "don't just save this for a special occasion" – though you may want to "win the lottery" or take out a loan first.

Le Canard Enchainé   24 | 22 | 22 | $40
276 Fair St. (bet. John & Main Sts.), Kingston, 845-339-2003
Uptown Kingston gets a jolt of "joie de vivre" at chef-owner Jean-Jacques Carquillat's "charming" "true French bistro" where "delicious", "careful cooking" covers "all the classics" (including the "tastiest cassoulet this side of the Pond"); service comes via "fun waiters" "without attitude", "music on weekends is a nice plus" and the prix fixe lunch "can't be beat" – in sum, "it's a winner."

Le Pavillon ⊠   24 | 19 | 20 | $45
230 Salt Point Tpke./Rte. 115 (N. Grand Ave.), Poughkeepsie, 845-473-2525;
www.lepavillonrestaurant.com
"Excellent traditional French fare" served in the three "intimate" dining rooms of this "charmingly restored farmhouse" in "the back roads" of Poughkeepsie has made it "a favorite for almost 25 years"; a "thoughtful wine list", "dessert soufflés that are a hit" and "attentive" "without being snooty" service contribute to the "lovely, romantic" repasts here; N.B. tasting menus of from six to 10 courses begin at $55.

L'Europe Restaurant   26 | 22 | 25 | $60
407 Smith Ridge Rd./Rte. 123 (Tommys Ln.), South Salem, 914-533-2570;
www.leuroperestaurant.com
"Refinement lives" at this South Salem "sit-up-straight" "bastion of Continental cuisine" where a "courteous" staff presents a "fabulous", "rarely changing" menu along the lines of venison, rack of lamb and "fabulous soufflés that are not to be missed"; fittingly, the "beautiful setting" and "precise", "old-world" service (not to mention the "pricey"-but-"worth-it" tab) make you "feel like you're in Europe."

Mina | 27 | 20 | 23 | $47 |
29 W. Market St. (Rte. 9), Red Hook, 845-758-5992;
www.minarestaurant.com
"Inventive" chef Natalie DiBenedetto's "exceptional" New
American cuisine dazzles diners at this "intimate" Red Hook
storefront rife with "cool jazz ambiance"; its "devotion to local
produce" and game, "wonderful presentation", "sinful desserts"
and "great wine list", plus "gracious" staffers willing to "go to
great lengths to make you happy" add up to "really fabulous", "first-
class dining" – "it doesn't get much better than this."

Mulino's of Westchester ●🗷 | 25 | 23 | 24 | $53 |
99 Court St. (bet. Martine Ave. & Quarropas St.), White Plains,
914-761-1818; www.mulinos.us
The "power elite meet and eat" at this "special" White Plains
"throwback to the golden age of classy Italian restaurants",
which wins bravos for its "elegant" cuisine from north of The
Boot (including "delightful" touches like "chunks of Parmigiano-
Reggiano brought to the table" as a starter), "beautiful" environs
("get a table looking into the garden") and "gracious" service;
simply put, this is a "destination" voted well "worth every penny."

Ocean House | 26 | 19 | 21 | $38 |
49 N. Riverside Ave. (Rte. 9), Croton-on-Hudson, 914-271-0702
This "simple, delicious" New England "gem" of a fish house hidden
in a "tiny" Croton "converted diner" is "run by a couple who really
care"; from the "oysters that sparkle" to the "excellent chowder",
everything's "unbelievably good", but the "no-reservations policy"
has some asking "have they heard of winter on the Hudson?" – it's
way too "cold" to "stand outside waiting for a table."

RESTAURANT X & BULLY BOY BAR | 27 | 26 | 25 | $54 |
117 Rte. 303 (bet. Lake Rd. & Rte. 9W), Congers, 845-268-6555;
www.xaviars.com
From the "delectable" savory dishes and "desserts almost too
beautiful to eat" to the "fabulous wine cellar" and "gracious"
staff, "everything's simply marvelous", gush gourmands of Peter
Kelly's New American in Congers that's "more relaxed" than his
flagship Xaviar's; its three rooms are "hip but homey", "especially
when the fire is lit", and even the duck pond is rated "romantic",
so "splurge", or go for the "excellent" $20.05 prix fixe lunch,
because "these people really know how to run a restaurant."

Sonora | 25 | 23 | 22 | $46 |
179 Rectory St. (bet. Locust & Willett Aves.), Port Chester, 914-933-0200
"No need to go to the city for diversity" of flavor when right in Port
Chester is "creative chef" Rafael Palomino, who "excels" at
"delicious", "definitive" cooking, including a "wide variety" of
"excellent tapas", at this Nuevo Latino; equally "vibrant" is the
"wonderful decor" and "noisy", "festive" atmosphere, overseen by
a "helpful" staff – in short, it lives up to "the rave reviews"; P.S. don't
miss the "wonderful" tropical cocktails "with sugarcane stirrers."

Stoneleigh Creek | 25 | 19 | 23 | $43 |
166 Stoneleigh Ave. (Rte. 100), Croton Falls, 845-276-0000;
www.stoneleighcreek.com
Why "did you have to include" this Croton Falls "country house"
Eclectic "in your *Survey*"? protest possessive patrons who

consider it "their little secret" "gem in the woods" boasting "marvelous", "creative" cuisine, "very friendly" service and a "cozy" vibe that makes it a place they'd "feel comfortable every night"; it's "tiny" with "limited tables" and indeed "the word is out", so "reserve way ahead"; P.S. "the prix fixe lunch is a bargain."

Sushi Mike's   25 ▌ 14 ▌ 21 ▌ $31 ▌
146 Main St. (Cedar St.), Dobbs Ferry, 914-591-0054; www.sushimikes.com
Even Manhattan sushi snobs would savor the "spectacularly fresh and imaginative" rolls and "innovative seafood specials" at this Dobbs Ferry Japanese owned by the "ultimate host" ("we love Mike!"); "more crowded than a Tokyo subway" it may be, but for what many consider "the freshest sushi in Westchester", it's "well worth tucking your shoulders in" and braving the "ridiculous lines."

Terrapin ◐   24 ▌ 24 ▌ 20 ▌ $42 ▌
6426 Montgomery St. (bet. Chestnut & Livingston Sts.), Rhinebeck, 845-876-3330; www.terrapinrestaurant.com
Really "two fabulous restaurants in one", chef-owner Josh Kroner's "striking" Rhinebeck New American offers a "dramatic" fine dining room with a mezzanine and "divine" decor as well as a "casual, less-expensive" bistro-bar; as befits the converted church setting, both offer "heavenly meals and sinful desserts", with a few signatures (like the "superb duck quesadillas") appearing on both "imaginative" menus; the staff sometimes enters "the *Twilight Zone*" on weekends when it gets "hectic", but at least "they try."

Trotters ☒   23 ▌ 21 ▌ 21 ▌ $47 ▌
175 Main St. (Court St.), White Plains, 914-421-5012; www.trottersny.com
"Manhattan-caliber food and presentations" by a chef who is a "fanatic about quality", a "global wine list" and a "posh", "hip" setting make this "classy" Med restaurant and tapas lounge well suited to the "vibrant city that White Plains is becoming"; the "romantic" ambiance is "perfect for a date", though some complain that the "singles scene" of suits and "high-maintenance women" "can interfere with the dining experience."

Wasabi   26 ▌ 25 ▌ 23 ▌ $44 ▌
110 Main St. (Park St.), Nyack, 845-358-7977
"Nobu, watch out" – chef-owner Doug Nguyen "has scored big" with this Rockland Japanese newcomer serving "interesting combinations" of "impeccable sushi and sashimi" as well as "fabulous" "culinary adventures" like "outrageous sushi pizza" and "absolutely divine grilled yellowtail cheeks", all looking like "works of art"; "hip" "modern" decor (complete with wasabi-hued walls) gives a "cosmopolitan feel" to the "glamorous Zen scene", and even though it's a bit "heavy on the purse" for "locals' budgets", it's "worth it."

Would, The   24 ▌ 18 ▌ 20 ▌ $43 ▌
Inn at Applewood, 120 North Rd. (Rte. 9W), Highland, 845-691-9883; www.thewould.com
Set in an "oddly urban-looking building in the midst of an apple orchard" with "chickens running around", this "hidden" Ulster County New American is home to a "wonderful chef" concocting "amazing" dishes using local cheeses, vegetables and game "in imaginative ways"; a "large vegetarian selection" and "the best wine list" are extra inducements, and although a few critics carp

that the place "still shows a bit of its ex-bar roots", most praise the "warm, inviting" dining room and "attentive staff."

XAVIAR'S AT PIERMONT ⊄   29 25 28 $73
506 Piermont Ave. (Ash St.), Piermont, 845-359-7007; www.xaviars.com
"Please let the food in heaven be like this", sigh the sated at "virtuoso" chef Peter Kelly's "magical, memorable" Piermont "gem" where "exquisite" New American fare, "phenomenal waiters", "beautiful china and glassware" and a "romantic", "intimate", "simple yet elegant" dining room make it "the best on the planet, down to the last detail"; even though the $60 prix fixe ($30 at lunch) may mean you'll have to "save up, you'll be glad you did" – it's "worth every red cent"; N.B. don't forget, it's cash only.

Zephs'   26 18 24 $48
638 Central Ave. (bet. Nelson Ave. & Water St.), Peekskill, 914-736-2159
"More people should know about this" "exceptional", "off-the-beaten-path-but-well-worth-finding" Peekskill New American–Eclectic where the "gracious service" from a "friendly staff" headed by "wonderful host Michael" Zeph is only topped by the "unending appeal" of his "creative" sister Victoria's "short" but "sophisticated" "seasonal" menu, which features "delightful couplings of flavors and ingredients"; even most who fault the "nondescript room" concede it's offset by the "charming" "old-mill" location, thereby ensuring a "first-rate experience."

Indexes

CUISINES BY AREA

Atlanta

American
  Bone's
American (New)
  Aria
  Bacchanalia
  BluePointe
  Canoe
  dick and harry's
  Food Studio
  Park 75
  Quinones Room
  Rathbun's
  Restaurant Eugene
  TWO. urban licks
American (Traditional)
  Thumbs Up
Asian
  BluePointe
  Sia's
Californian
  Woodfire Grill
Chinese
  Hsu's Gourmet
Coffee Shops/Diners
  Thumbs Up
Continental
  Iris
  Nikolai's Roof
  Pano's & Paul's
  Seeger's
European
  Babette's
French
  Floataway Cafe
  Joël
  Nikolai's Roof
French (New)
  Ritz Buckhead Din. Rm.
Greek
  Kyma
Indian
  Madras Saravana
Italian
(N=Northern)
  di Paolo (N)
  Floataway Cafe
  La Grotta (N)
  La Tavola
  Sotto Sotto (N)
Japanese
(* sushi specialist)
  MF Sushibar*

Pan-Latin
  Tierra
Seafood
  Atlanta Fish
  Chops/Lobster Bar
  dick and harry's
Small Plates
  Kyma
Southern
  South City Kitchen
  Wisteria
Southwestern
  Nava
  Sia's
  TWO. urban licks
Steakhouses
  Bone's
  Chops/Lobster Bar
  McKendrick's Steak
Thai
  Nan Thai
  Tamarind
Vegetarian
  Madras Saravana

Atlantic City

American (Traditional)
  Dock's Oyster
Chinese
  P.F. Chang's
  Suilan
French
  Suilan
Italian
  Capriccio
  'Cesca
  Chef Vola's
Mexican
  Los Amigos
Sandwiches
  White House
Seafood
  Dock's Oyster
Southwestern
  Los Amigos
Steakhouses
  Brighton Steak
  Old Homestead

Baltimore/Annapolis

Afghan
  Helmand
American (New)
  Charleston
  Corks

Hampton's
Linwoods
Timothy Dean's
American (Traditional)
Cheesecake Factory
Clyde's
Crab House
Cantler's
Costas Inn Crab Hse.
Eclectic
Bicycle
French
Timothy Dean's
French (Bistro)
Les Folies
Greek
Samos
Hamburgers
Clyde's
*Italian
(N=Northern)*
Boccaccio (N)
*Japanese
(* sushi specialist)*
Joss Cafe/Sushi Bar*
Mediterranean
Pazo
Pub Food
Clyde's
Seafood
Les Folies
McCormick & Schmick's
O'Learys Seafood
Small Plates
Pazo
Steakhouses
Prime Rib
Ruth's Chris

Boston
Afghan
Helmand
American (New)
Franklin
Hamersley's
Harvest
Icarus
Meritage
Sage
Salts
Sibling Rivalry
Troquet
UpStairs on the Square
Asian Fusion
Blue Ginger
Restaurant L

Barbecue
East Coast Grill
Continental
Locke-Ober
Eclectic
EVOO
French
Mistral
No. 9 Park
French (Bistro)
Coriander Bistro
Craigie St. Bistrot
Hamersley's
Le Soir
Petit Robert Bistro
Pigalle
Troquet
French (New)
Aujourd'hui
Clio
L'Espalier
Radius
Indian
Tamarind Bay
*Italian
(N=Northern; S=Southern)*
Carmen
Grotto
Il Capriccio (N)
No. 9 Park
Sage (N)
Saporito's (N)
Taranta (S)
*Japanese
(* sushi specialist)*
Oishii*
Mediterranean
Mistral
Oleana
Rialto
Peruvian
Taranta
Seafood
B&G Oysters
East Coast Grill
Legal Sea Foods
Neptune Oyster
*Small Plates
(See also Spanish tapas
specialist)*
Meritage
*Spanish
(* tapas specialist)*
Dalí*

Charlotte

American (New)
Barrington's
Bonterra Dining/Wine
Carpe Diem
Ethan's of Elizabeth
ONEO
Sonoma
Californian
Sonoma
Continental
Noble's
Eclectic
McNinch House
French (Classic)
Patou
French (New)
Zebra Rest./Wine Bar
Greek
ilios noche
*Italian
(N=Northern)*
ilios noche
Luce (N)
Noble's
Toscana (N)
Volare
*Japanese
(* sushi specialist)*
Nikko*
Seafood
McIntosh's
Upstream
Steakhouses
McIntosh's
Mickey & Mooch
Palm
Sullivan's

Chicago

American (New)
Alinea
Blackbird
Charlie Trotter's
Green Zebra
Kevin
Le Titi de Paris
mk
Naha
North Pond
Oceanique
one sixtyblue
Seasons
Spring
302 West

Eclectic
Avenues
Eclectic
French
Bistro Banlieue
Le Vichyssois
French (Classic)
Le Français
French (New)
Ambria
Carlos'
Everest
Kevin
Les Nomades
Le Titi de Paris
NoMI
Oceanique
Ritz-Carlton Din. Rm.
Tallgrass
Tru
French Steakhouses
Morton's Steak
Hot Dogs
Hot Doug's
Italian
Spiaggia
*Japanese
(* sushi specialist)*
Japonais*
Mirai Sushi*
Mediterranean
Avec
Naha
Mexican
Frontera Grill
Topolobampo
Pan-Asian
Shanghai Terrace
Pizza
Lou Malnati
Seafood
Oceanique
Spring
Small Plates
Avec
Steakhouses
Chicago Chop Hse.
Gibsons Steak
Morton's Steak
Thai
Arun's
*Vegetarian
(* vegan)*
Green Zebra*

Cincinnati

American (New)
Palace
Palomino

Asian Fusion
Beluga

Bakeries
BonBonerie

Barbecue
Montgomery Inn

Chinese
China Gourmet

Continental
Palace

Dessert
BonBonerie

Eclectic
Aioli
Daveed's at 934
Sturkey's

French
JeanRo
Pho Paris

French (New)
Jean-Robert at Pigall's

Indian
Cumin

Italian
(N=Northern)
Boca
Nicola's (N)

Mediterranean
Palomino

Pizza
Dewey's Pizza

Seafood
South Beach Grill

Steakhouses
Jeff Ruby's
Morton's
Precinct
South Beach Grill

Tearooms
BonBonerie

Vietnamese
Pho Paris

Cleveland

American
Flying Fig

American (New)
Century
fire
Lolita
Three Birds

Cambodian
Phnom Penh

Continental
Baricelli Inn
Johnny's Bar

Eclectic
Flying Fig
Fulton Bar & Grill
Grovewood Tavern

French
Chez François
Classics
Sans Souci

Italian
(N=Northern)
Battuto
Giovanni's (N)
Johnny's Bar (N)

Japanese
(sushi specialist)*
Ginza Sushi House*

Mediterranean
Lolita
Sans Souci

Seafood
Blue Point Grille
Parallax Restaurant

Steakhouses
Hyde Park Prime
Red the Steakhouse

Connecticut

American (New)
Ann Howard
Bricco
Carole Peck's
Jeffrey's
Max Downtown
Mayflower Inn
Métro Bis
Rebeccas
Relish

American (Traditional)
City Limits Diner

Coffee Shops/Diners
City Limits Diner

Continental
Jeffrey's

French
Bernard's
Da Pietro's
Jean-Louis
La Colline Verte
L'Escale
Ondine
Rest. du Village

French (Bistro)
Cafe Routier
Le Petit Cafe
Union League

French (New)
  Cavey's
  Thomas Henkelmann
Indian
  Coromandel
Italian
(N=Northern; S=Southern)
  Bravo Bravo
  Cavey's (N)
  Da Pietro's (N)
  Frank Pepe (S)
  Il Palio (N)
  Peppercorn's Grill
  Piccolo Arancio
  Valbella (N)
Japanese
(* sushi specialist)
  Mako of Japan*
Malaysian
  Bentara
Nuevo Latino
  Roomba
Pan-Asian
  Ching's Table
Pizza
  Frank Pepe
  Frank Pepe's Spot
  Sally's Apizza
Seafood
  Max's Oyster Bar
  Ocean 211
Spanish
(* tapas specialist)
  Barcelona*
  Ibiza
  Meigas*
Steakhouses
  Max Downtown

Dallas

American (New)
  Aurora
  Café on the Green
  Grape, The
  Green Room
  Hibiscus
  Iris
  Local
  Lola
  Mercury Grill
  Nana
  Tramontana
  2900
  York Street

American (Traditional)
  French Room
Brazilian
  Fogo de Chão
Chinese
  P.F. Chang's
Continental
  Hôtel St. Germain
  Old Warsaw
Eclectic
  Abacus
  2900
French
  French Room
  Hôtel St. Germain
  Old Warsaw
French (Bistro)
  Lavendou
Hawaii Regional
  Roy's
Italian
(N=Northern)
  Il Mulino
  Mi Piaci (N)
  Modo Mio Cucina
Japanese
(* sushi specialist)
  Nobu Dallas
  Steel
  Tei Tei Robata Bar*
  Teppo*
Mediterranean
  Suze
Pan-Asian
  Steel
Pan-Latin
  La Duni Latin Café
Peruvian
  Nobu Dallas
Seafood
  Café Pacific
  Oceanaire
Southeast Asian
  Steel
Southwestern
  Mansion on Turtle Creek
Steakhouses
  Al Biernat's
  Bob's
  Capital Grille
  Chamberlain's
  Del Frisco's
  Fogo de Chão
  Pappas Bros.
Thai
  Chow Thai

Denver Area & Mountain Resorts

American
Alpenglow Stube

American (New)
Emma's
Flagstaff House
Highlands Garden
John's
Kevin Taylor
Keystone Ranch
Mel's Rest./Bar
Mizuna
Montagna
Opus
Potager
Q's
Six89 Kitchen/Wine
Solera Rest./Wine
Sweet Basil
Syzygy
240 Union

American (Regional)
Grouse Mountain Grill
Piñons

Asian
Zengo

Brazilian
Cafe Brazil

Colombian
Cafe Brazil

Eclectic
Flagstaff House
Kitchen, The

French
L'Atelier
Left Bank

French (New)
La Tour

German
Alpenglow Stube

Indian
India's

Italian (N=Northern)
Barolo Grill (N)
Frasca (N)
Full Moon Grill (N)
Luca d'Italia
Panzano (N)

Japanese (* sushi specialist)
Matsuhisa*
Sushi Den*

Mediterranean
Rioja

Nuevo Latino
Zengo

Seafood
Jax Fish House
240 Union

Small Plates
Rioja

Steakhouses
Capital Grille
Del Frisco's
Morton's

Vietnamese
New Saigon

Detroit

American
Oslo Sushi
Sweet Georgia Brown

American (New)
Beverly Hills Grill
Five Lakes Grill
Grill/Ritz-Carlton
West End Grill

American (Traditional)
Opus One
Rugby Grille

Continental
Lark, The
Opus One
Rugby Grille

Delis
Steve's Deli
Zingerman's

Dessert
Cafe Bon Homme

Eclectic
Traffic Jam & Snug

French (Classic)
Tribute

French (New)
Cafe Bon Homme
Emily's

Italian
Bacco
Il Posto
Rist. Café Cortina

Japanese (* sushi specialist)
Oslo Sushi*

Mediterranean
Emily's

Seafood
Common Grill
No. VI Chop Hse.

Steakhouses
No. VI Chop Hse.

Ft. Lauderdale
American (New)
  Cafe Maxx
  Hi-Life Café
  Sunfish
  3030 Ocean
American (Traditional)
  Cheesecake Factory
  Houston's
Brazilian
  Chima
Chinese
  Silver Pond
Eclectic
  Cafe Maxx
Floribbean
  Johnny V's
  Mark's Las Olas
Italian
(N=Northern)
  Cafe Martorano
  Cafe Vico
  Casa D'Angelo (N)
  Josef's (N)
Japanese
(sushi specialist)*
  Galanga*
Mediterranean
  La Brochette
Mexican
  Eduardo/San Angel
Pizza
  Anthony's
Seafood
  Sunfish
  3030 Ocean
Southwestern
  Canyon
Steakhouses
  Chima
  Ruth's Chris
Thai
  Galanga

Ft. Worth
American (New)
  Bistro Louise
  Cafe Aspen
  62 Main Restaurant
American (Regional)
  Lonesome Dove
American (Traditional)
  Babe's Chicken
  Classic Cafe
Barbecue
  Angelo's Barbecue

Brazilian
  Boi NA Braza
  Texas de Brazil
Creole
  Bonnell's
Eclectic
  Pegasus
French
  Cacharel
  Saint-Emilion
Hamburgers
  Kincaid's
Italian
  La Piazza
  Piccolo Mondo
Mediterranean
  Bistro Louise
  Pegasus
Mexican
  Joe T. Garcia's
Southwestern
  Bonnell's
  Reata Restaurant
Steakhouses
  Del Frisco's
  Ft. Worth Chop House
  Texas de Brazil

Honolulu
American
  Orchids
Asian
  Indigo
Dessert
  3660 on the Rise
Eclectic
  Indigo
French (Classic)
  Michel's
French (New)
  Chef Mavro
  La Mer
Fusion
  Hiroshi Eurasian
Greek
  Olive Tree Café
Hawaii Regional
  Alan Wong's
  Chef Mavro
  Pineapple Room
  Roy's
  Roy's Ko Olina
Japanese
(sushi specialist)*
  Sansei*
Mediterranean
  Olive Tree Café

Pacific Rim
Bali By The Sea
Hoku's
L'Uraku
Sansei
3660 on the Rise

Seafood
Duke's Canoe Club
Nick's Fishmarket
Sansei

Steakhouses
Hy's Steak House
Ruth's Chris

Houston

American (New)
Aries
Artista
benjy's
Daily Review Café
Mark's American Cuisine
Mockingbird Bistro
Quattro
Ruggles
Shade
Zula

American (Regional)
Rainbow Lodge

Barbecue
Goode Co. Texas BBQ

Brazilian
Fogo de Chao

Cajun
Tony Mandola's

Continental
Tony's

Creole
Brennan's of Houston

Eclectic
Shade

European
Charivari

French
Brennan's of Houston
Chez Nous

Indian
Ashiana
Indika

Italian
(N=Northern)
Da Marco
Damian's Cucina Italiana
La Griglia
La Mora Cucina (N)
Quattro
Simposio (N)
Tony Mandola's

Japanese
(sushi specialist)*
Azuma*
Kubo's*

Mediterranean
t'afia

Mexican
Hugo's
Mama Ninfa's

Nuevo Latino
Julia's Bistro

Seafood
Goode Co. Texas Seafood
Pesce
Tony Mandola's

South American
Américas
Churrascos

Southwestern
Cafe Annie

Steakhouses
Capital Grille
Churrascos
Fleming's Prime
Fogo de Chão
Pappas Bros.
Ruth's Chris

Tex-Mex
Mama Ninfa's

Kansas City

American
Room 39

American (New)
American Rest.
Bluestem
Café Sebastienne
Circe
40 Sardines
1924 Main
Starker's Reserve
zin

American (Traditional)
Stroud's

Barbecue
Danny Edwards'
Fiorella's Jack Stack
Oklahoma Joe's

Delis
d'Bronx

Eclectic
Grand St. Cafe

French
Tatsu's

French (Bistro)
Le Fou Frog

Italian
(N=Northern)
    Lidia's (N)
Pizza
    d'Bronx
Seafood
    McCormick & Schmick's
Steakhouses
    Plaza III

Las Vegas
American (New)
    Aureole
    Bradley Ogden
    Medici Café
    Rosemary's
    Sterling Brunch
Asian
    Malibu Chan's
Cajun
    Commander's Palace
    Emeril's
Californian
    NOBHILL
Chinese
    Mayflower Cuis.
Continental
    Michael's
    3950
Creole
    Commander's Palace
    Emeril's
Eclectic
    Bellagio Buffet
    Mix
French
    Alex
    Andre's
    Eiffel Tower
    Mayflower Cuis.
    Mix
    Pamplemousse
French (Bistro)
    Bouchon
French (Brasserie)
    Daniel Boulud
French (New)
    Alizé
    Le Cirque
    Picasso
Hawaii Regional
    Roy's
Italian
(N=Northern)
    Gaetano's (N)
    Osteria del Circo (N)
    Piero's Italian (N)
    Valentino (N)

Japanese
(* sushi specialist)
    Hyakumi*
    Nobu*
    Shintaro*
Pacific Rim
    Malibu Chan's
Seafood
    Craftsteak
    Emeril's
    Michael Mina
    NOBHILL
    Piero's Italian
    Seablue
    3950
Small Plates
(See also Spanish tapas
specialist)
    Rosemary's
Spanish
(* tapas specialist)
    Firefly*
Steakhouses
    Craftsteak
    Del Frisco's
    Delmonico Steak
    Prime
    Steak House
    3950
Thai
    Lotus of Siam

Long Island
American (New)
    Barney's
    Chachama Grill
    Coolfish
    Della Femina
    Mill River Inn
    On 3
    Panama Hatties
    Piccolo
    Plaza Cafe
    Polo
    Starr Boggs
American (Traditional)
    American Hotel
    Cheesecake Factory
Chinese
    Orient
Dessert
    Cheesecake Factory
Eclectic
    Frisky Oyster
    La Plage
    Maroni Cuisine
    Mill River Inn
    Mirko's

French
American Hotel
Barney's
Le Soir
Mirabelle
Stone Creek
French (Bistro)
Kitchen a Bistro
French (New)
Louis XVI
Italian
(N=Northern)
Dario (N)
Da Ugo (N)
Harvest on Ft. Pond (N)
Il Mulino
La Pace (N)
La Piccola Liguria (N)
Maroni Cuisine
Mio (N)
Piccolo
Rialto (N)
Robert's
Trattoria Diane (N)
Japanese
(* sushi specialist)
Kotobuki*
Mediterranean
Harvest on Ft. Pond
Nick & Toni's
Stone Creek
Seafood
Coolfish
Frisky Oyster
Kitchen a Bistro
Plaza Cafe
Starr Boggs
Tellers Chophouse
Steakhouses
Bryant/Cooper Steak
Jimmy Hay's
Peter Luger
Tellers Chophouse
Thai
Siam Lotus

Los Angeles

American (New)
Belvedere
Grace
Josie
Mélisse
Saddle Peak
American (Traditional)
Cheesecake Factory
Grill on the Alley
Asian
Chaya Brasserie
Chinois on Main

Asian Fusion
Shiro
Californian
A.O.C.
Café Bizou
Campanile
Derek's
Hotel Bel-Air
JiRaffe
Joe's
Shiro
Spago
Continental
Brandywine
Delis
Brent's Deli
Dessert
Cheesecake Factory
Spago
Eclectic
Chaya Brasserie
Depot
French
A.O.C.
Chinois on Main
Derek's
Hotel Bel-Air
L'Orangerie
Maison Akira
Mélisse
French (Bistro)
Café Bizou
Frenchy's Bistro
Mimosa
French (New)
Joe's
La Cachette
Sona
Italian
Angelini Osteria
Capo
Giorgio Baldi
Valentino
Japanese
(* sushi specialist)
Hamasaku*
Katsu-ya*
Maison Akira
Matsuhisa*
Mori Sushi*
Nobu Malibu*
Sushi Sasabune*
Mediterranean
A.O.C.
Campanile
Christine

Pacific Rim
  Christine
Sandwiches
  Brent's Deli
Seafood
  Providence
  Water Grill
Small Plates
  A.O.C.

Miami

American (New)
  Mark's South Beach
  Nemo
  River Oyster
  Talula
  Wish
American (Traditional)
  Cheesecake Factory
  Houston's
Argentinean
  Graziano's Parrilla
Asian
  Azul
Brazilian
  Porcão
Caribbean
  Ortanique on Mile
Chinese
(* dim sum specialist)
  Tropical Chinese*
Cuban
  Versailles
Eclectic
  Chef Allen's
  Restaurant at the Setai
  Vix
French
  La Sandwicherie
French (New)
  Pascal's on Ponce
  Palme d'Or
French Seafood
  River Oyster
Haitian
  TapTap
Italian
(N=Northern)
  Osteria del Teatro (N)
  Romeo's (N)
  Timo
Japanese
(* sushi specialist)
  Bond St. Lounge*
  Matsuri*
  Nobu Miami Beach*

  Shoji*
  Toni's Sushi*
Mediterranean
  AltaMar
  Azul
  Timo
New World
  Norman's
Nuevo Latino
  Cacao
  Carmen the Restaurant
Pan-Asian
  Lan
Peruvian
  Francesco
  Nobu Miami Beach
Sandwiches
  La Sandwicherie
Seafood
  AltaMar
  Francesco
  Joe's Stone Crab
  La Dorada
  Prime One Twelve
Spanish
(* tapas specialist)
  La Dorada
  Mosaico/Salero*
Steakhouses
  Capital Grille
  Graziano's Parrilla
  Porcão
  Prime One Twelve
Thai
  Tamarind

Milwaukee

American (New)
  Bacchus
  Dream Dance
  Heaven City
  Sanford
American (Traditional)
  Eddie Martini's
  Riversite
Asian Fusion
  Roots
Californian
  Roots
Chinese
  P.F. Chang's
Eclectic
  Immigrant Room
French (Bistro)
  Coquette Cafe
  Lake Park Bistro
Indian
  Dancing Ganesha

Cuisines by Area

Italian
(N=Northern; S=Southern)
   Maggiano's (S)
   Osteria del Mondo (N)
   Ristorante Bartolotta (N)
Seafood
   Eddie Martini's
   Moceans
   River Lane Inn
Serbian
   Three Brothers
Steakhouses
   Eddie Martini's
   Mr. B's: Steak
Thai
   Singha Thai

Minneapolis/St. Paul

American (New)
   Alma
   Bayport Cookery
   Levain
   Lucia's
   20.21
   Zander Cafe
American (Regional)
   Dakota Jazz
   Heartland
American (Traditional)
   St. Paul Grill
Bakeries
   Bakery on Grand
Eclectic
   Cosmos
French (Bistro)
   Bakery on Grand
   Vincent
French (New)
   La Belle Vie
Italian
(N=Northern)
   D'Amico Cucina (N)
   Ristorante Luci
   Zelo
Japanese
(sushi specialist)*
   Origami*
Mediterranean
   La Belle Vie
Seafood
   Oceanaire
Spanish
(tapas specialist)*
   Solera*
Steakhouses
   Manny's

New Jersey

American (New)
   Amanda's
   Bernards Inn
   Daniel's on B'way
   Dining Room
   Frog & Peach
   Nicholas
   Perryville Inn
   Pluckemin Inn
   Saddle River Inn
   Whispers
American (Traditional)
   Latour
   Washington Inn
Cuban
   La Isla
Eclectic
   Anthony David's
   Cafe Matisse
   Cafe Panache
   Green Gables
French
   Chez Catherine
   Ixora
   Jocelyne's
   Latour
   Origin
   Saddle River Inn
   Siri's Thai French
   Zoe's
French (New)
   Rat's
   Ryland Inn
   Serenade
   Stage House
Greek
   Mazi
Italian
(N=Northern; S=Southern)
   Anthony David's (N)
   Augustino's (S)
   Fascino
   Giumarello's (N)
   Scalini Fedeli (N)
Japanese
(sushi specialist)*
   Ixora*
   Sagami
Mediterranean
   Hamilton's Grill
   Mazi
Pan-Latin
   Zafra
Pizza
   DeLorenzo's

Portuguese
  Bistro Olé
  Mazi
Seafood
  Blue Point
  Bobby Chez
  Daniel's on B'way
Small Plates
  Cucharamama
South American
  Cucharamama
Spanish
  Bistro Olé
Thai
  Origin
  Siri's Thai French

New Orleans
American (New)
  Bayona
  Dakota
  Gautreau's
  Herbsaint
  Pelican Club
  Stella!
Cajun
  K-Paul's
Caribbean
  Martinique Bistro
Chinese
  Kim Son
  Nine Roses
Contemporary Louisiana
  Brigtsen's
  Dakota, The
  Emeril's
  Gabrielle
  La Petite Grocery
  Mr. B's Bistro
  NOLA
  Peristyle
Continental
  August
  New Orleans Grill
  Rib Room
Creole
  Antoine's
  Arnaud's
  Brennan's
  Clancy's
  Commander's Palace
  Dick & Jenny's
  Eleven 79
  Gabrielle
  Galatoire's
  Jacques-Imo's
  Muriel's Jackson Square
  NOLA

  Sal & Judy's
  Upperline
French
  Antoine's
  Dick & Jenny's
  Galatoire's
  La Provence
  Louis XVI
  Peristyle
French (Bistro)
  Martinique Bistro
  René Bistrot
French (Classic)
  Brennan's
  La Petite Grocery
French (New)
  August
  Gautreau's
  Herbsaint
Italian
(S=Southern)
  Eleven 79
  Irene's Cuisine
  Mosca's
  Sal & Judy's (S)
Po' Boys
  Crabby Jack's
Seafood
  Arnaud's
  Crabby Jack's
  Martinique Bistro
  RioMar
Soul Food
  Jacques-Imo's Cafe
Spanish
(tapas specialist)*
  RioMar*
Steakhouses
  Rib Room
  Ruth's Chris
Vietnamese
  Kim Son
  Nine Roses

New York City
American (New)
  Annisa
  Aureole
  Gotham B&G
  Gramercy Tavern
  Grocery
  Modern, The
  Ouest
  per se
  River Café
  Union Sq. Cafe
  Veritas

American (Traditional)
    Bayard's
    Tavern on Green
    21 Club
Chinese
    Shun Lee Palace
Delis
    Carnegie Deli
French
    Asiate
    Bayard's
    Café Boulud
    Café des Artistes
    Chanterelle
    La Grenouille
    Le Bernardin
    Modern, The
    Montrachet
    per se
    Picholine
French (Brasserie)
    Balthazar
    Café Gray
French (New)
    Alain Ducasse
    Bouley
    Daniel
    Jean Georges
Greek
    Milos
Hamburgers
    Peter Luger
Indian
    dévi
Italian
(S=Southern)
    Babbo
    Il Mulino (S)
    Roberto's
Japanese
(* sushi specialist)
    Asiate
    Masa*
    Matsuri
    Megu
    Nobu*
    Nobu 57*
    Sushi of Gari*
    Sushi Yasuda*
    Tomoe Sushi*
Malaysian
    Spice Market
Mediterranean
    Picholine
Peruvian
    Nobu
    Nobu 57

Sandwiches
    Carnegie Deli
Seafood
    BLT Fish
    Blue Water
    Le Bernardin
    Milos
    Pearl Oyster
Steakhouses
    BLT Steak
    Peter Luger
    Smith & Wollensky
Thai
    Spice Market

Orange County, CA
American (New)
    Ramos House
American (Traditional)
    Cheesecake Factory
    Houston's
Californian
    Napa Rose
    Pavilion
    Studio
Caribbean
    Golden Truffle
Chinese
    P.F. Chang's
Continental
    Hobbit
Dessert
    Cheesecake Factory
    Zov's Bistro
French
    Basilic
    Black Sheep
    Golden Truffle
    Hobbit
    Pascal
French (Bistro)
    Troquet
French (New)
    Studio
Hawaii Regional
    Roy's
Italian
    Antonello
Japanese
(* sushi specialist)
    Abe*
Mediterranean
    Pavilion
    Picayo
    Zov's Bistro
Seafood
    Aqua

Spanish
  Black Sheep
Steakhouses
  Ruth's Chris
Swiss
  Basilic

Orlando

African
  Boma
  Jiko/The Cooking Place
American (New)
  Citricos
  Dux
  Flying Fish Café
  Harvey's Bistro
  Hue/A Restaurant
American (Traditional)
  Anaelle & Hugo
  Cheesecake Factory
  Victoria & Albert's
Asian
  Emeril's Tchoup Chop
  Hue/A Restaurant
Californian
  California Grill
  Wolfgang Puck Cafe
Canadian
  Le Cellier
Contemporary Louisiana
  Emeril's Orlando
Continental
  Anaelle & Hugo
  Chatham's Place
  Maison & Jardin
Dessert
  Cheesecake Factory
Eclectic
  K
  Manuel's on the 28th
  Seasons 52
European
  Harvey's Bistro
Floribbean
  Chef Justin's
French
  Le Coq au Vin
French (Bistro)
  Café de France
Hawaii Regional
  Roy's Orlando
Italian
(N=Northern)
  Antonio's La Fiamma
  Christini's Rist. Italiano (N)

Enzo's On The Lake
Primo
ZaBella Ristorante (N)
New World
  Norman's
Polynesian
  Emeril's Tchoup Chop
Seafood
  Flying Fish Café
  MoonFish
Steakhouses
  Charley's
  Del Frisco's
  Le Cellier
  MoonFish
  Morton's
  Palm
  Ruth's Chris
  Vito's Chop Hse.
Thai
  Thai House
Vietnamese
  Little Saigon
  Rice Paper

Palm Beach

American (New)
  Cafe Chardonnay
  11 Maple St.
  Four Seasons
  Ta-boo
  32 East
American (Traditional)
  Cheesecake Factory
  Houston's
Chinese
  P.F. Chang's
Continental
  Addison
  Café L'Europe
  Kathy's Gazebo
  Ta-boo
Floribbean
  Four Seasons
French
  Café Boulud
  Chez Jean-Pierre
  La Vieille Maison
French (Classic)
  Le Mistral
Italian
  Marcello's La Sirena
Seafood
  Ke-e Grill
  Little Moirs
Steakhouses
  Ke-e Grill
  La Vieille Maison

Morton's Steak
New York Prime

Philadelphia

American (New)
Alison/Blue Bell
Jake's
Mainland Inn
Southwark
Swann Lounge
Washington Square

American (Traditional)
General Warren

Asian Fusion
Buddakan

Cajun
High St. Caffé

Californian
Sovalo

Chinese
Peking
Shiao Lan Kung
Susanna Foo

Continental
Fountain

Creole
High St. Caffé

Eclectic
Citrus
Django
Meritage
Totaro's

European
Meritage

French
Birchrunville Store
Deux Cheminées
Gilmore's
La Bonne Auberge
Lacroix/Rittenhouse
Le Bec-Fin
Overtures
Savona

French (Bistro)
Le Bar Lyonnais
Pif

French (New)
Brasserie Perrier
Fountain
Nan
Susanna Foo
Swann Lounge

Italian
(N=Northern)
Birchrunville Store
L'Angolo
Savona (N)
Sovalo
Vetri

Japanese
(sushi specialist)*
Bluefin*
Morimoto
Ota-Ya*
Peking*

Mediterranean
Dmitri's
Overtures

Nuevo Latino
¡Pasión!

Seafood
Citrus
Dmitri's
Little Fish
Savona

Small Plates
Lacroix/Rittenhouse
Washington Square

Steakhouses
Prime Rib

Thai
Nan

Vegetarian
Blue Sage

Phoenix/Scottsdale

American (New)
Binkley's Restaurant
elements
Michael's at Citadel
Rancho Pinot

American (Regional)
Roaring Fork

Asian
elements

Chinese
P.F. Chang's

Eclectic
Atlas Bistro

French (New)
Mary Elaine's
Vincent Guerithault

Hawaii Regional
Roy's

Italian
(N=Northern)
Pizzeria Bianco (N)

Japanese
Sea Saw

Mediterranean
Marquesa
T. Cook's

Mexican
Barrio Café
Los Sombreros

Pizza
Pizzeria Bianco

Seafood
  Eddie V's Edgewater
Southwestern
  Vincent Guerithault
Steakhouses
  Drinkwater's City Hall
  Eddie V's Edgewater
  Mastro's
Vietnamese
  Cyclo

Portland, OR

American (New)
  Bluehour
  clarklewis
  Park Kitchen
Continental
  El Gaucho
French
  Castagna/Cafe Castagna
  Heathman
  Paley's Place
Italian
  Caffe Mingo
  Castagna/Cafe Castagna
  Genoa
  Giorgio's
Japanese
(* sushi specialist)
  Saburo's Sushi*
Mediterranean
  Bluehour
Pacific Northwest
  Caprial's Bistro
  clarklewis
  Heathman
  Higgins Rest./Bar
  Joel Palmer
  Paley's Place
  Park Kitchen
  Wildwood
Peruvian
  Andina
Seafood
  Jake's Famous Crawfish
  McCormick & Schmick's
Steakhouses
  El Gaucho
Thai
  Lemongrass
Vietnamese
  Pho Van

Salt Lake City & Mountain Resorts

American (New)
  Bambara
  Glitretind

  Log Haven
  Mariposa, The
  Metropolitan
American (Regional)
  Tree Room
American (Traditional)
  Chez Betty
  New Yorker Club
  Snake Creek Grill
Asian Fusion
  Wahso
Continental
  Chez Betty
Italian
(N=Northern)
  Cucina Toscana (N)
  Fresco Italian Cafe (N)
  Lugano (N)
  Michelangelo
Japanese
(* sushi specialist)
  Takashi*
Mediterranean
  Martine
Mexican
  Red Iguana
Seafood
  Market St. Grill
  Seafood Buffet
Small Plates
  Takashi
Southwestern
  Chimayo

San Diego

American (New)
  Arterra
  Pamplemousse Grille
  Region
Asian Fusion
  Roppongi
Californian
  A.R. Valentien
  Dobson's
  George's at Cove
French
  El Bizcocho
  Laurel
French (New)
  Mille Fleurs
  Pamplemousse Grille
  Sky Room
  Tapenade
  WineSellar & Brasserie

Japanese
(* sushi specialist)
   Sushi Ota*
   Taka*
Mediterranean
   Laurel
Pizza
   Sammy's Woodfired
Seafood
   Osetra the Fishhouse
   Rainwater's on Kettner
Steakhouses
   Donovan's
   Osetra the Fishhouse
   Rainwater's on Kettner
   Ruth's Chris

San Francisco Bay Area

American (New)
   Boulevard
   Cafe La Haye
   French Laundry
   Gary Danko
   Manresa
   Michael Mina
   Myth
   Rest. Budo
   Terra
American (Traditional)
   Lark Creek Inn
   Press
Californian
   Aqua
   Cafe La Haye
   Chez Panisse
   Chez Panisse Café
   Erna's Elderberry Hse.
   Farmhouse Inn
   Jardinière
   Rivoli
   Sierra Mar
French
   Aqua
   Boulevard
   Campton Place
   French Laundry
   Jardinière
   La Folie
   La Toque
   Le Papillon
French (Bistro)
   Bistro Jeanty
   Chapeau!
French (New)
   Cyrus
   Erna's Elderberry Hse.
   Fifth Floor

Fleur de Lys
Manresa
Marché
Marinus
Masa's
Quince
Ritz-Carlton Din. Rm.
Italian
(N=Northern)
   Delfina (N)
   Oliveto
   Quince
Japanese
(* sushi specialist)
   Hana Japanese*
   Sushi Ran*
Mediterranean
   Campton Place
   Chez Panisse
   Chez Panisse Café
   Rivoli
   Zuni Café
Seafood
   Aqua
Steakhouses
   Press
Vegetarian
   Fleur de Lys
   French Laundry
   Greens
Vietnamese
   Slanted Door

Seattle

American (New)
   Crush
   Herbfarm
   Lampreia
   Lark
   Mistral
   Nell's
   Palace Kitchen
   Restaurant Zoë
   Union
American (Traditional)
   Canlis
Continental
   Tosoni's
French
   Campagne
   Le Gourmand
French (Bistro)
   Cafe Campagne
   Le Pichet
French (New)
   Mistral
   Rover's

German
  Szmania's/Jäger
Greek
  Lola
Italian
(N=Northern)
  Cafe Juanita (N)
  Il Terrazzo Carmine
  Volterra
Japanese
(* sushi specialist)
  Izumi
  Nishino
  Shiro's Sushi*
Mediterranean
  Brasa
  Lola
Pacific Northwest
  Canlis
  Cascadia
  Dahlia Lounge
  Georgian
  Inn at Langley
  Lampreia
  Nell's
  Ray's Boathouse
  Shoalwater
Pacific Rim
  Wild Ginger
Seafood
  Flying Fish
  Oceanaire
  Ray's Boathouse
  Shoalwater
Soul Food
  Kingfish
Southern
  Kingfish
Spanish
(* tapas specialist)
  Harvest Vine*
Steakhouses
  El Gaucho
  JaK's Grill
  Metropolitan Grill
Vietnamese
  Monsoon

St. Louis

American
  American Place
American (New)
  Arthur Clay's
  Crossing
  Frazer's
  Harvest

  Sidney St. Cafe
  Zinnia
American (Traditional)
  Annie Gunn's
Asian
  Red Moon
Asian Fusion
  Nippon Tei
Californian
  1111 Mississippi
Continental
  Kemoll's
Eclectic
  Monarch
French
  Atlas
  Red Moon
Italian
(N=Northern)
  Atlas
  Dominic's
  1111 Mississippi (N)
  Giovanni's
  Kemoll's
  Tony's
  Tratt. Marcella
Japanese
(* sushi specialist)
  Nippon Tei*
Mediterranean
  Remy's Kitchen/Wine
Seafood
  Al's Rest.
Steakhouses
  Al's Rest.

Tampa/Sarasota

American (New)
  Black Pearl
  Fred's
  Michael's On East
  Mise en Place
  SideBern's
Bakeries
  Pane Rustica
Continental
  Bijou Café
  Ophelia's on the Bay
  Six Tables
  Zoria
Cuban
  Columbia
Eclectic
  Euphemia Haye
  Zoria
Floribbean
  Beach Bistro

French
Restaurant B.T.
French (New)
Six Tables
Italian
(N=Northern)
Armani's (N)
Campiello Ristorante
Mediterranean
Pelagia Trattoria
Peruvian
Selva Grill
Sandwiches
Pane Rustica
Small Plates
(See also Spanish tapas specialist)
Ceviché Tapas Bar/Rest.
Spanish
(* tapas specialist)
Ceviché Tapas Bar/Rest.*
Columbia
Steakhouses
Bern's
Vietnamese
Restaurant B.T.

Tucson

American (New)
Acacia
Bistro Zin
Dish
Grill/Hacienda del Sol
Kingfisher Bar/Grill
Ventana Room
Wildflower
American (Regional)
Kingfisher Bar/Grill
Bakeries
Beyond Bread
Continental
Arizona Inn
Eclectic
Cuvée World Bistro
Feast
French
Janos
Le Rendez-Vous
Italian
(N=Northern)
Tavolino (N)
Vivace (N)
Mexican
Cafe Poca Cosa
Nuevo Latino
J Bar

Sandwiches
Beyond Bread
Seafood
Bluefin
Kingfisher Bar/Grill
Southwestern
Janos
Terra Cotta
Steakhouses
McMahon's Prime

Washington, DC

American (New)
Cashion's Eat Place
CityZen
DC Coast
Equinox
Eve
Inn/Little Washington
Kinkead's
Nora
Palena
1789
2941 Restaurant
Vidalia
Bakeries
Bread Line
Belgian
Marcel's
French
La Bergerie
L'Auberge Chez François
L'Auberge Provençale
Marcel's
French (Bistro)
Bis
French (New)
Citronelle
Gerard's Pl.
IndeBleu
Hamburgers
Palena
Indian
Heritage India
IndeBleu
Italian
(N=Northern)
Galileo/Il Laboratorio
Maestro
Obelisk
Tosca (N)
Japanese
Makoto
Lebanese
Zaytinya
Mediterranean
Zaytinya

Nuevo Latino
Café Atlántico
Ceiba
Pan-Asian
Asia Nora
TenPenh
Peruvian
El Pollo Rico
Pizza
Pizzeria Paradiso
Seafood
DC Coast
Johnny's Half Shell
Kinkead's
Small Plates
(See also Spanish tapas specialist)
Heritage India
IndeBleu
Zaytinya
Southern
Vidalia
Spanish
(* tapas specialist)
Jaleo*
Taberna/Alabardero*
Steakhouses
Prime Rib
Ray's The Steaks
Thai
Rabieng
Turkish
Zaytinya

**Westchester/
Hudson River Valley**
American
Aubergine
American (New)
American Bounty
Blue Hill/Stone Barns
Busy Bee
Crabtree's Kittle Hse.
DePuy Canal House
Equus
Freelance Café
Iron Horse Grill
Mina
Rest. X/Bully Boy Bar
Terrapin

Would
Xaviar's/Piermont
Zephs'
Chinese
(* dim sum specialist)
Aberdeen*
Continental
L'Europe
Eclectic
Arch
Stoneleigh Creek
Zephs'
French
Arch
Aubergine
Buffet de la Gare
Equus
Escoffier
French Corner
La Crémaillère
La Panetière
Le Pavillon
French (Bistro)
Le Canard Enchainé
Indian
Coromandel
Italian
(N=Northern)
Caterina de Medici
Il Barilotto
Il Cenàcolo (N)
Johnny's Pizzeria
Mulino's
Japanese
(* sushi specialist)
Koo*
Sushi Mike's*
Wasabi*
Mediterranean
Cafe Mezé
Harvest on Hudson
Trotters
New England
Ocean House
Nuevo Latino
Sonora
Pizza
Johnny's Pizzeria
Seafood
Ocean House

AREA ABBREVIATIONS

AC	Atlantic City	MI	Miami
AT	Atlanta	MN	Minneapolis/St. Paul
BA	Baltimore/Annapolis	MW	Milwaukee
BO	Boston	NJ	New Jersey
CH	Chicago	NO	New Orleans
CI	Cincinnati	NY	New York City
CL	Cleveland	OC	Orange County, CA
CR	Charlotte	OR	Orlando
CT	Connecticut	PB	Palm Beach
DA	Dallas	PH	Philadelphia
DC	Washington, DC	PO	Portland, OR
DE	Denver Area	PS	Phoenix/Scottsdale
DT	Detroit	SC	Salt Lake City Area
FL	Ft. Lauderdale	SD	San Diego
FW	Ft. Worth	SE	Seattle
HO	Honolulu	SF	San Francisco Area
HS	Houston	SL	St. Louis
KC	Kansas City	TB	Tampa/Sarasota
LA	Los Angeles	TC	Tucson
LI	Long Island	WH	Westchester/Hudson
LV	Las Vegas		

ALPHABETICAL PAGE INDEX

Abacus, DA	73	A.O.C., LA	143
Abe, OC	198	Aqua, OC	199
Aberdeen, WH	290	Aqua, SF	247
Acacia, TC	275	Arch, WH	290
Addison, The, PB	212	Aria, AT	15
Aioli, CI	54	Aries, HS	111
Alain Ducasse, NY	189	Arizona Inn, TC	275
Alan Wong's, HO	105	Armani's, TB	270
Al Biernat's, DA	73	Arnaud's, NO	180
Alex, LV	125	Arterra, SD	241
Alinea, CH	46	Arthur Clay's, SL	266
Alison at Blue Bell, PH	218	Artista, HS	111
Alizé, LV	125	Arun's, CH	46
Alma, MN	165	A.R. Valentien, SD	241
Alpenglow Stube, DE	82	Ashiana, HS	111
Al's Restaurant, SL	265	Asia Nora, DC	281
AltaMar, MI	153	Asiate, NY	189
Amanda's, NJ	171	Atlanta Fish, AT	15
Ambria, CH	46	Atlas Bistro, PS	226
American Bounty, WH	290	Atlas Restaurant, SL	266
American Hotel, LI	134	Aubergine, WH	290
American Place, SL	265	August, NO	180
American Rest., KC	119	Augustino's, NJ	171
Américas, HS	111	Aujourd'hui, BO	31
Anaelle & Hugo, OR	204	Aureole, LV	125
Andina, PO	231	Aureole, NY	189
Andre's, LV	125	Aurora, DA	73
Angelini Osteria, LA	143	Avec, CH	46
Angelo's Barbecue, FW	100	Avenues, CH	46
Ann Howard's, CT	65	Azul, MI	153
Annie Gunn's, SL	266	Azuma, HS	111
Annisa, NY	189	Azuma Rice, HS	111
Anthony David's, NJ	171	Azuma Sushi, HS	111
Anthony's Pizza, FL	96	Babbo, NY	189
Antoine's, NO	180	Babe's Chicken, FW	100
Antonello, OC	198	Babette's Cafe, AT	15
Antonio's La Fiamma, OR	204	Bacchanalia, AT	15

Alphabetical Page Index

Bacchus, MW	160	Boccaccio, BA	25
Bacco, DT	91	Boi NA Braza, FW	101
Bakery on Grand, MN	165	Boma, OR	204
Bali By The Sea, HO	105	BonBonerie, CI	55
Balthazar, NY	189	Bond St. Lounge, MI	153
Bambara, SC	236	Bone's, AT	16
B&G Oysters, BO	31	Bonnell's, FW	101
Barcelona Rest., CT	65	Bonterra Dining, CR	40
Baricelli Inn, CL	59	Bouchon, LV	126
Barney's, LI	134	Boulevard, SF	247
Barolo Grill, DE	82	Bouley, NY	190
Barrington's, CR	40	Bradley Ogden, LV	126
Barrio Café, PS	226	Brandywine, LA	143
Basilic, OC	199	Brasa, SE	257
Battuto, CL	59	Brasserie Perrier, PH	218
Bayard's, NY	190	Bravo Bravo, CT	65
Bayona, NO	180	Bread Line, DC	281
Bayport Cookery, MN	166	Brennan's, NO	180
Beach Bistro, TB	270	Brennan's of Houston, HS	112
Bellagio Buffet, LV	125	Brent's Deli, LA	143
Beluga, CI	54	Bricco, CT	65
Belvedere, LA	143	Brighton Steakhouse, AC	23
benjy's, HS	112	Brigtsen's, NO	181
Bentara, CT	65	Bryant & Cooper, LI	134
Bernard's, CT	65	Buddakan, PH	219
Bernards Inn, NJ	171	Buffet de la Gare, WH	291
Bern's Steak House, TB	271	Busy Bee Cafe, WH	291
Beverly Hills Grill, DT	91	Cacao, MI	153
Beyond Bread, TC	276	Cacharel, FW	101
Bicycle, BA	25	Cafe Annie, HS	112
Bijou Café, TB	271	Cafe Aspen, FW	101
Binkley's Restaurant, PS	226	Café Atlántico, DC	281
Birchrunville Store, PH	218	Café Bizou, LA	144
Bis, DC	281	Cafe Bon Homme, DT	92
Bistro Banlieue, CH	47	Café Boulud, NY	190
Bistro Jeanty, SF	247	Café Boulud, PB	212
Bistro Louise, FW	101	Cafe Brazil, DE	82
Bistro Olé, NJ	171	Cafe Campagne, SE	257
Bistro Zin, TC	276	Cafe Chardonnay, PB	213
Black Pearl, TB	271	Café de France, OR	204
Black Sheep, OC	199	Café des Artistes, NY	191
Blackbird, CH	47	Café Gray, NY	191
BLT Fish, NY	190	Cafe Juanita, SE	257
BLT Steak, NY	190	Cafe La Haye, SF	247
Bluefin, PH	218	Café L'Europe, PB	213
Bluefin, TC	276	Cafe Martorano, FL	96
Blue Ginger, BO	31	Cafe Matisse, NJ	172
Blue Hill/Stone Barns, WH	290	Cafe Maxx, FL	96
Blue Point Grill, NJ	171	Cafe Mezé, WH	291
Blue Point Grille, CL	60	Café on the Green, DA	73
Blue Sage, PH	218	Café Pacific, DA	74
Blue Water Grill, NY	190	Cafe Panache, NJ	172
Bluehour, PO	231	Cafe Poca Cosa, TC	276
BluePointe, AT	15	Cafe Routier, CT	66
Bluestem, KC	119	Café Sebastienne, KC	120
Bobby Chez, NJ	172	Cafe Vico, FL	97
Bob's Steak, DA	73	Caffe Mingo, PO	232
Boca, CI	55	California Grill, OR	204

subscribe to zagat.com

Alphabetical Page Index

Campagne, SE	257	Chez Panisse, SF	248
Campanile, LA	144	Chez Panisse Café, SF	248
Campiello Ristorante, TB	271	Chicago Chop House, CH	47
Campton Place, SF	247	Chima Brazilian, FL	97
Canlis, SE	257	Chimayo, SC	237
Canoe, AT	16	China Gourmet, CI	55
Cantler's Riverside, BA	25	Ching's Table, CT	66
Canyon, FL	97	Chinois on Main, LA	145
Capital Grille, DA	74	Chops/Lobster Bar, AT	16
Capital Grille, DE	82	Chow Thai, DA	74
Capital Grille, HS	112	Christine, LA	145
Capital Grille, MI	153	Christini's, OR	205
Capo, LA	144	Churrascos, HS	113
Caprial's Bistro, PO	232	Circe, KC	120
Capriccio, AC	23	Citricos, OR	206
Carlos', CH	47	Citronelle, DC	282
Carmen, BO	31	Citrus, PH	219
Carmen the Restaurant, MI	153	City Limits Diner, CT	66
Carnegie Deli, NY	191	CityZen, DC	282
Carole Peck's Cafe, CT	66	Clancy's, NO	181
Carpe Diem, CR	41	clarklewis, PO	232
Casa D'Angelo, FL	97	Classic Cafe, FW	102
Cascadia, SE	258	Classics, CL	60
Cashion's Eat Place, DC	281	Clio, BO	31
Castagna, PO	232	Clyde's, BA	26
Caterina de Medici, WH	291	Columbia, TB	271
Cavey's, CT	66	Commander's Palace, LV	126
Ceiba, DC	281	Commander's Palace, NO	181
Century, CL	60	Common Grill, DT	92
`Cesca, AC	23	Coolfish, LI	135
Ceviché Tapas Bar, TB	271	Coquette Cafe, MW	160
Chachama Grill, LI	134	Coriander Bistro, BO	32
Chamberlain's Steak, DA	74	Corks, BA	26
Chanterelle, NY	191	Coromandel, CT	66
Chapeau!, SF	248	Coromandel, WH	291
Charivari, HS	112	Cosmos, MN	166
Charleston, BA	26	Costas Inn Crab Hse., BA	26
Charley's Steak, OR	204	Crabby Jack's, NO	181
Charlie Trotter's, CH	47	Crabtree's Kittle Hse., WH	291
Chatham's Place, OR	205	Craftsteak, LV	126
Chaya Brasserie, LA	144	Craigie Street Bistrot, BO	32
Cheesecake Factory, BA	26	Crossing, SL	266
Cheesecake Factory, FL	97	Crush, SE	258
Cheesecake Factory, LA	144	Cucharamama, NJ	172
Cheesecake Factory, LI	134	Cucina Toscana, SC	237
Cheesecake Factory, MI	154	Cumin, CI	55
Cheesecake Factory, OC	199	Cuvée World Bistro, TC	276
Cheesecake Factory, OR	205	Cyclo, PS	227
Cheesecake Factory, PB	213	Cyrus, SF	248
Chef Allen's, MI	154	Dahlia Lounge, SE	258
Chef Justin's, OR	205	Daily Review Café, HS	113
Chef Mavro, HO	106	Dakota, NO	181
Chef Vola's, AC	23	Dakota Jazz, MN	166
Chez Betty, SC	236	Dalí, BO	32
Chez Catherine, NJ	172	Da Marco, HS	113
Chez François, CL	60	Damian's Cucina, HS	113
Chez Jean-Pierre, PB	213	D'Amico Cucina, MN	166
Chez Nous, HS	112	Dancing Ganesha, MW	161

Daniel, NY	191	Emily's, DT	92
Daniel Boulud, LV	126	Emma's, DE	83
Daniel's on Broadway, NJ	173	Enzo's On The Lake, OR	207
Danny Edwards', KC	120	Equinox, DC	282
Da Pietro's, CT	67	Equus, WH	292
Dario, LI	135	Erna's Elderberry Hse., SF	249
Da Ugo, LI	135	Escoffier, WH	292
Daveed's at 934, CI	55	Ethan's of Elizabeth, CR	41
d'Bronx, KC	120	Euphemia Haye, TB	272
DC Coast, DC	282	Eve, DC	283
Delfina, SF	248	Everest, CH	48
Del Frisco's, DA	74	EVOO, BO	32
Del Frisco's, DE	82	Farmhouse Inn, SF	249
Del Frisco's, FW	102	Fascino, NJ	173
Del Frisco's, LV	127	Feast, TC	277
Del Frisco's, OR	206	Fifth Floor, SF	249
Della Femina, LI	135	Fiorella's Jack Stack, KC	120
Delmonico Steak, LV	127	fire, CL	60
DeLorenzo's, NJ	173	Firefly, LV	127
Depot, The, LA	145	Five Lakes Grill, DT	92
DePuy Canal House, WH	292	Flagstaff House, DE	83
Derek's, LA	145	Fleming's Prime, HS	113
Deux Cheminées, PH	219	Fleur de Lys, SF	249
dévi, NY	191	Floataway Cafe, AT	17
Dewey's Pizza, CI	56	Flying Fig, CL	61
dick and harry's, AT	16	Flying Fish Café, OR	207
Dick & Jenny's, NO	181	Flying Fish, SE	258
Dining Room, NJ	173	Fogo de Chão, DA	75
di Paolo, AT	16	Fogo de Chão, HS	114
Dish, TC	276	Food Studio, AT	17
Django, PH	219	40 Sardines, KC	120
Dmitri's, PH	219	Fountain, PH	219
Dobson's, SD	242	Four Seasons, PB	213
Dock's Oyster House, AC	24	Francesco, MI	154
Dominic's, SL	266	Frank Pepe Pizzeria, CT	67
Donovan's, SD	242	Frank Pepe's Spot, CT	67
Dream Dance, MW	161	Franklin Café, BO	33
Drinkwater's, PS	227	Frasca Food and Wine, DE	83
Duke's Canoe Club, HO	106	Frazer's, SL	267
Dux, OR	206	Fred's, TB	272
East Coast Grill, BO	32	Freelance Café, WH	292
Eclectic, CH	47	French Corner, WH	292
Eddie Martini's, MW	161	French Laundry, SF	249
Eddie V's, PS	227	French Room, DA	75
Eduardo de San Angel, FL	98	Frenchy's Bistro, LA	146
Eiffel Tower, LV	127	Fresco Italian Cafe, SC	237
El Bizcocho, SD	242	Frisky Oyster, LI	135
elements, PS	227	Frog and the Peach, NJ	173
1111 Mississippi, SL	266	Frontera Grill, CH	48
11 Maple Street, PB	213	Ft. Worth Chop House, FW	102
Eleven 79, NO	182	Full Moon Grill, DE	83
El Gaucho, PO	232	Fulton Bar & Grill, CL	61
El Gaucho, SE	258	Gabrielle, NO	182
El Pollo Rico, DC	282	Gaetano's, LV	128
Emeril's, NO	182	Galanga, FL	98
Emeril's New Orleans, LV	127	Galatoire's, NO	182
Emeril's Orlando, OR	206	Galileo/Il Laboratorio, DC	283
Emeril's Tchoup, OR	206	Gary Danko, SF	250

Alphabetical Page Index

Gautreau's, NO 182
General Warren, PH 220
Genoa, PO 232
George's at the Cove, SD . . 242
Georgian, SE 259
Gerard's Place, DC 283
Gibsons Steakhouse, CH 48
Gilmore's, PH 220
Ginza Sushi House, CL 61
Giorgio Baldi, LA 146
Giorgio's, PO 233
Giovanni's, SL 267
Giovanni's Ristorante, CL . . . 61
Giumarello's, NJ 173
Glitretind, SC 237
Golden Truffle, OC 199
Goode Co. BBQ, HS 114
Goode Co. Seafood, HS 114
Gotham Bar & Grill, NY 192
Grace, LA 146
Gramercy Tavern, NY 192
Grand St. Cafe, KC 121
Grape, DA 75
Graziano's, MI 154
Green Gables, NJ 174
Green Room, DA 75
Green Zebra, CH 48
Greens, SF 250
Grill/Ritz-Carlton, DT 92
Grill/Hacienda del Sol, TC . . 277
Grill on the Alley, LA 146
Grocery, NY 192
Grotto, BO 33
Grouse Mountain Grill, DE . . . 83
Grovewood Tavern, CL 61
Hamasaku, LA 146
Hamersley's Bistro, BO 33
Hamilton's Grill Room, NJ . . 174
Hampton's, BA 27
Hana, SF 250
Harvest, BO 33
Harvest, SL 267
Harvest on Fort Pond, LI . . . 135
Harvest on Hudson, WH 293
Harvest Vine, SE 259
Harvey's Bistro, OR 207
Heartland, MN 166
Heathman, PO 233
Heaven City, MW 161
Helmand, BO 33
Helmand, BA 27
Herbfarm, SE 259
Herbsaint, NO 183
Heritage India, DC 283
Hi-Life Café, FL 98
Hibiscus, DA 75
Higgins Restaurant, PO 233
High Street Caffé, PH 220

Highlands Garden, DE 84
Hiroshi Eurasian, HO 106
Hobbit, The, OC 199
Hoku's, HO 106
Hot Doug's, CH 48
Hotel Bel-Air, LA 147
Hôtel St. Germain, DA 76
Houston's, FL 98
Houston's, MI 154
Houston's, OC 200
Houston's, PB 214
Hsu's Gourmet, AT 17
Hue - A Restaurant, OR 207
Hugo's, HS 114
Hy's Steak House, HO 106
Hyakumi, LV 128
Hyde Park Prime, CL 62
Ibiza, CT 67
Icarus, BO 34
Il Barilotto, WH 293
Il Capriccio, BO 34
Il Cenàcolo, WH 293
ilios noche, CR 41
Il Mulino, DA 76
Il Mulino, LI 136
Il Mulino, NY 192
Il Palio, CT 67
Il Posto Ristorante, DT 93
Il Terrazzo Carmine, SE 259
Immigrant Room, MW 161
IndeBleu, DC 283
India's, DE 84
Indigo, HO 106
Indika, HS 114
Inn at Langley, SE 259
Inn/Little Washington, DC . . 283
Irene's Cuisine, NO 183
Iris, AT 17
Iris, DA 76
Iron Horse Grill, WH 293
Ixora, NJ 174
Izumi, SE 259
Jacques-Imo's, NO 183
Jäger, SE 263
Jake's, PH 220
Jake's Famous, PO 233
JaK's Grill, SE 260
Jaleo, DC 284
Janos, TC 277
Japonais, CH 49
Jardinière, SF 250
Jax Fish House, DE 84
J Bar, TC 277
Jean Georges, NY 192
Jean-Louis, CT 67
Jean-Robert/Pigall's, CI 56
JeanRo, CI 56
Jeffrey's, CT 68

Jeff Ruby's, CI 56
Jiko, OR 207
Jimmy Hay's, LI 136
JiRaffe, LA 147
Jocelyne's, NJ 174
Joël, AT 17
Joel Palmer House, PO 233
Joe's, LA 147
Joe's Stone Crab, MI 155
Joe T. Garcia's, FW 102
Johnny's Bar, CL 62
Johnny's Half Shell, DC 284
Johnny's Pizzeria, WH 293
Johnny V's, FL 98
John's, DE 84
Josef's, FL 98
Josie Restaurant, LA 147
Joss Cafe, BA 27
Julia's Bistro, HS 115
K, OR 208
Kathy's Gazebo Cafe, PB . . .214
Katsu-ya, LA 147
Ke-e Grill, PB 214
Kemoll's, SL 267
Kevin, CH 49
Kevin Taylor, DE 84
Keystone Ranch, DE 85
Kim Son, NO 183
Kincaid's, FW 102
Kingfish, SE 260
Kingfisher, TC 277
Kinkead's, DC 284
Kitchen, The, DE 85
Kitchen a Bistro, LI 136
Koo, WH 293
Kotobuki, LI 136
K-Paul's, NO 183
Kubo's, HS 115
Kyma, AT 18
La Belle Vie, MN 167
La Bergerie, DC 284
La Bonne Auberge, PH 220
La Brochette Bistro, FL 99
La Cachette, LA 148
La Colline Verte, CT 68
La Crémaillère, WH 294
Lacroix, PH 221
La Dorada, MI 155
La Duni Latin Café, DA 76
La Folie, SF 250
La Grenouille, NY 192
La Griglia, HS 115
La Grotta, AT 18
La Isla, NJ 174
Lake Park Bistro, MW 161
La Mer, HO 107
La Mora, HS 115
Lampreia, SE 260

Lan, MI 155
L'Angolo, PH 221
La Pace Tuscan Grill, LI 136
La Panetière, WH 294
La Petite Grocery, NO 183
La Piazza, FW 102
La Piccola Liguria, LI 137
La Plage, LI 137
La Provence, NO 184
Lark, SE 260
Lark, DT 93
Lark Creek Inn, SF 251
La Sandwicherie, MI 155
La Tavola, AT 18
L'Atelier, DE 85
La Toque, SF 251
La Tour, DE 85
Latour, NJ 175
L'Auberge Chez François, DC . .284
L'Auberge Provençale, DC . . .285
Laurel, SD 242
Lavendou, DA 76
La Vieille Maison, PB 214
Le Bar Lyonnais, PH 221
Le Bec-Fin, PH 221
Le Bernardin, NY 193
Le Canard, WH 294
Le Cellier, OR 208
Le Cirque, LV 128
Le Coq au Vin, OR 208
Le Fou Frog, KC 121
Le Français, CH 49
Left Bank, DE 85
Legal Sea Foods, BO 34
Le Gourmand, SE 260
Le Mistral, PB 214
Lemongrass, PO 234
Le Papillon, SF 251
Le Pavillon, WH 294
Le Petit Cafe, CT 68
Le Pichet, SE 261
Le Rendez-Vous, TC 278
L'Escale, CT 68
Les Folies Brasserie, BA 27
Les Nomades, CH 49
Le Soir, BO 34
Le Soir, LI 137
L'Espalier, BO 35
Le Titi de Paris, CH 49
L'Europe, WH 294
Levain, MN 167
Le Vichyssois, CH 50
Lidia's, KC 121
Linwoods, BA 27
Little Fish, PH 221
Little Moirs, PB 215
Little Saigon, OR 208
Local, DA 77

Alphabetical Page Index

Locke-Ober, BO	35	McCormick & Schmick's, BA	27
Log Haven, SC	237	McCormick & Schmick's, KC	121
Lola, DA	77	McCormick & Schmick's, PO	234
Lola, SE	261	McIntosh's Steaks, CR	41
Lolita, CL	62	McKendrick's Steak, AT	18
Lonesome Dove, FW	103	McMahon's Prime, TC	278
L'Orangerie, LA	148	McNinch House, CR	41
Los Amigos, AC	24	Medici Café, LV	129
Los Sombreros, PS	227	Megu, NY	193
Lotus of Siam, LV	128	Meigas, CT	69
Louis XVI, LI	137	Mel's Restaurant, DE	86
Louis XVI, NO	184	Mélisse, LA	148
Lou Malnati's, CH	50	Mercury Grill, DA	77
Luca d'Italia, DE	86	Meritage, BO	35
Luce, CR	41	Meritage, PH	222
Lucia's, MN	167	Métro Bis, CT	69
Lugano, SC	238	Metropolitan, SC	238
L'Uraku, HO	107	Metropolitan Grill, SE	261
Madras Saravana, AT	18	MF Sushibar, AT	19
Maestro, DC	285	Michael Mina, LV	129
Maggiano's, MW	162	Michael Mina, SF	252
Mainland Inn, PH	222	Michael's, LV	129
Maison Akira, LA	148	Michael's/Citadel, PS	228
Maison & Jardin, OR	208	Michael's On East, TB	272
Mako of Japan, CT	68	Michelangelo, SC	239
Makoto, DC	285	Michel's, HO	107
Malibu Chan's, LV	128	Mickey & Mooch, CR	42
Mama Ninfa's, HS	115	Mille Fleurs, SD	243
Manny's Steak, MN	167	Mill River Inn, LI	137
Manresa, SF	251	Milos Estiatorio, NY	193
Mansion/Turtle Creek, DA	77	Mimosa, LA	149
Manuel's on the 28th, OR	209	Mina, WH	295
Marcel's, DC	285	Mio, LI	138
Marcello's La Sirena, PB	215	Mi Piaci Ristorante, DA	77
Marché, SF	251	Mirabelle, LI	138
Marinus, SF	252	Mirai Sushi, CH	50
Mariposa, The, SC	238	Mirko's, LI	138
Mark's American, HS	116	Mise en Place, TB	272
Mark's Las Olas, FL	99	Mistral, BO	35
Mark's South Beach, MI	155	Mistral, SE	261
Market Street Grill, SC	238	Mix, LV	129
Maroni Cuisine, LI	137	Mizuna, DE	86
Marquesa, PS	228	mk, CH	50
Martine, SC	238	Moceans, MW	162
Martinique Bistro, NO	184	Mockingbird Bistro, HS	116
Mary Elaine's, PS	228	Modern, The, NY	193
Masa, NY	193	Modo Mio Cucina, DA	78
Masa's, SF	252	Monarch, SL	267
Mastro's, PS	228	Monsoon, SE	261
Matsuhisa, DE	86	Montagna, DE	86
Matsuhisa, LA	148	Montgomery Inn, CI	57
Matsuri, MI	155	Montrachet, NY	194
Matsuri, NY	193	MoonFish, OR	209
Max Downtown, CT	68	Morimoto, PH	222
Max's Oyster Bar, CT	69	Mori Sushi, LA	149
Mayflower Cuisinier, LV	129	Morton's, CH	50
Mayflower Inn, CT	69	Morton's, CI	57
Mazi, NJ	175	Morton's, DE	87

Morton's, OR 209
Morton's, PB. 215
Mosaico/Salero, MI 156
Mosca's, NO 184
Mr. B's Bistro, NO 184
Mr. B's Steakhouse, MW . . .162
Mulino's, WH 295
Muriel's Jackson Sq., NO. . .184
Myth, SF 252
Naha, CH. 51
Nan, PH. 222
Nana, DA. 78
Nan Thai, AT. 19
Napa Rose, OC. 200
Nava, AT 19
Nell's, SE 262
Nemo, MI 156
Neptune Oyster, BO. 35
New Orleans Grill, NO. 185
New Saigon, DE. 87
New Yorker Club, SC. 239
New York Prime, PB 215
Nicholas, NJ. 175
Nick & Toni's, LI 138
Nick's Fishmarket, HO. 107
Nicola's, CI 57
Nikko, CR. 42
Nikolai's Roof, AT. 19
Nine Roses, NO 185
1924 Main, KC. 121
Nippon Tei, SL 268
Nishino, SE 262
NOBHILL, LV. 130
Noble's, CR 42
Nobu, LV 130
Nobu, NY 194
Nobu 57, NY 194
Nobu Dallas, DA 78
Nobu Malibu, LA 149
Nobu Miami Beach, MI 156
Nola, NO 185
NoMI, CH 51
No. 9 Park, BO 36
Nora, DC 285
Norman's, MI 156
Norman's, OR 209
North Pond, CH 51
No. VI Chop House, DT 93
Obelisk, DC. 286
Oceanaire Seafood, DA 78
Oceanaire Seafood, MN. . . .167
Oceanaire Seafood, SE. 262
Ocean House, WH. 295
Oceanique, CH. 51
Ocean 211, CT 69
Oishii, BO 36
Oklahoma Joe's, KC. 122
Old Homestead, AC 24
Old Warsaw, DA 78
Oleana, BO 36
O'Learys Seafood, BA. 28
Oliveto Cafe, SF. 253
Olive Tree Café, HO 107
Ondine, CT 69
ONEO, CR 42
one sixtyblue, CH. 52
On 3, LI 138
Ophelia's, TB 273
Opus, DE. 87
Opus One, DT 93
Orchids, HO 108
Orient, LI 139
Origami, MN. 168
Origin, NJ. 175
Ortanique, MI. 156
Osetra, SD 243
Oslo Sushi Bar, DT. 93
Osteria del Circo, LV 130
Osteria del Mondo, MW. . . .162
Osteria del Teatro, MI. 156
Ota-Ya, PH 222
Ouest, NY 194
Overtures, PH. 222
Palace, CI. 57
Palace Kitchen, SE 262
Palena, DC 286
Paley's Place, PO. 234
Palm, CR 42
Palm, OR 209
Palme d'Or, MI 157
Palomino, CI. 57
Pamplemousse, LV 130
Pamplemousse Grille, SD. . .243
Panama Hatties, LI 139
Pane Rustica, TB. 273
Pano's & Paul's, AT 19
Panzano, DE. 87
Pappas Bros., DA 79
Pappas Bros., HS 116
Parallax Restaurant, CL 62
Park Kitchen, PO 234
Park 75, AT 20
Pascal, OC 200
Pascal's on Ponce, MI 157
¡Pasión!, PH. 223
Patou, CR 43
Pavilion, OC 200
Pazo, BA. 28
Pearl Oyster Bar, NY 194
Pegasus, FW 103
Peking, PH 223
Pelagia Trattoria, TB 273
Pelican Club, NO 185
Peppercorn's Grill, CT. 70
Peristyle, NO 185
Perryville Inn, NJ. 175

per se, NY 194
Pesce, HS 116
Peter Luger, LI. 139
Peter Luger, NY. 195
Petit Robert Bistro, BO 36
P.F. Chang's, AC 24
P.F. Chang's, DA. 79
P.F. Chang's, MW. 162
P.F. Chang's, OC 200
P.F. Chang's, PB 215
P.F. Chang's, PS 228
Phnom Penh, CL 62
Pho Paris, CI 58
Pho Van, PO. 234
Picasso, LV 130
Picayo, OC. 201
Piccolo, LI 139
Piccolo Arancio, CT 70
Piccolo Mondo, FW 103
Picholine, NY. 195
Piero's Italian, LV 131
Pif, PH. 223
Pigalle, BO. 37
Pineapple Room, HO 108
Piñons, DE 87
Pizzeria Bianco, PS 229
Pizzeria Paradiso, DC. 286
Plaza Cafe, LI. 139
Plaza III, KC 122
Pluckemin Inn, NJ 175
Polo, LI 140
Porcão, MI. 157
Potager, DE 88
Precinct, CI 58
Press, SF 253
Prime One Twelve, MI 157
Prime Rib, BA 28
Prime Rib, DC 286
Prime Rib, PH 223
Prime Steakhouse, LV 131
Primo, OR. 210
Providence, LA 149
Q's, DE 88
Quattro, HS 116
Quince, SF 253
Quinones Room, AT 20
Rabieng, DC. 286
Radius, BO. 37
Rainbow Lodge, HS 116
Rainwater's, SD 243
Ramos House, OC 201
Rancho Pinot, PS 229
Rat's, NJ. 176
Rathbun's, AT 20
Ray's Boathouse, SE 262
Ray's The Steaks, DC 286
Reata Restaurant, FW 103
Rebeccas, CT 70

Red Iguana, SC. 239
Red Moon, SL 268
Red the Steakhouse, CL 63
Region, SD. 243
Relish, CT. 70
Remy's Kitchen, SL. 268
René Bistrot, NO. 186
Restaurant at the Setai, MI. . . 157
Restaurant B.T., TB 273
Restaurant Budo, SF 253
Restaurant du Village, CT . . . 70
Restaurant Eugene, AT 20
Restaurant L, BO 37
Restaurant X, WH. 295
Restaurant Zoë, SE 262
Rialto, BO. 37
Rialto, LI. 140
Rib Room, NO 186
Rice Paper, OR 210
Rioja, DE 88
RioMar, NO 186
Ristorante Bartolotta, MW . . . 163
Ristorante Café Cortina, DT . . 94
Ristorante Luci, MN. 168
Ritz-Carlton Buckhead, AT . . 20
Ritz-Carlton Din. Rm., CH. . . . 52
Ritz-Carlton Din. Rm., SF . . . 253
River Café, NY. 195
River Lane Inn, MW. 163
River Oyster Bar, MI. 157
Riversite, The, MW 163
Rivoli, SF 254
Roaring Fork, PS. 229
Roberto's, NY 195
Robert's, LI. 140
Romeo's Cafe, MI. 158
Room 39, KC 122
Roomba, CT 70
Roots, MW 163
Roppongi, SD 244
Rosemary's, LV 131
Rover's, SE. 263
Roy's, DA 79
Roy's, HO 108
Roy's, LV 131
Roy's, OC 201
Roy's, PS 229
Roy's Ko Olina, HO 108
Roy's Orlando, OR. 210
Rugby Grille, DT 94
Ruggles, HS. 117
Ruth's Chris, BA 28
Ruth's Chris, FL 99
Ruth's Chris, HO 108
Ruth's Chris, HS 117
Ruth's Chris, NO 186
Ruth's Chris, OC 201
Ruth's Chris, OR 210

Ruth's Chris, SD	244	Sonora, WH	295
Ryland Inn, NJ	176	Sotto Sotto, AT	21
Saburo's Sushi, PO	234	South Beach Grill, CI	58
Saddle Peak Lodge, LA	149	South City Kitchen, AT	21
Saddle River Inn, NJ	176	Southwark, PH	224
Sagami, NJ	176	Sovalo, PH	224
Sage, BO	37	Spago, LA	150
Saint-Emilion, FW	103	Spiaggia, CH	52
Sal & Judy's, NO	186	Spice Market, NY	196
Sally's Apizza, CT	71	Spring, CH	53
Salts, BO	38	Stage House, NJ	177
Sammy's Woodfired, SD	244	Starker's Reserve, KC	122
Samos, BA	28	Starr Boggs, LI	140
Sanford, MW	163	Steak House, LV	132
Sansei Seafood, HO	108	Steel, DA	79
Sans Souci, CL	63	Stella!, NO	186
Saporito's, BO	38	Sterling Brunch, LV	132
Savona, PH	223	Steve's Deli, DT	94
Scalini Fedeli, NJ	176	Stone Creek Inn, LI	140
Seablue, LV	131	Stoneleigh Creek, WH	295
Seafood Buffet, SC	239	St. Paul Grill, MN	168
Sea Saw, PS	229	Stroud's, KC	122
Seasons, CH	52	Studio, OC	201
Seasons 52, OR	210	Sturkey's, CI	58
Seeger's, AT	21	Suilan, AC	24
Selva Grill, TB	273	Sullivan's, CR	43
Serenade, NJ	177	Sunfish Grill, FL	99
1789, DC	287	Susanna Foo, PH	224
Shade, HS	117	Sushi Den, DE	89
Shanghai Terrace, CH	52	Sushi Mike's, WH	296
Shiao Lan Kung, PH	223	Sushi of Gari, NY	196
Shintaro, LV	132	Sushi Ota, SD	245
Shiro, LA	150	Sushi Ran, SF	254
Shiro's Sushi, SE	263	Sushi Sasabune, LA	150
Shoalwater, SE	263	Sushi Yasuda, NY	196
Shoji, MI	158	Suze, DA	79
Shun Lee Palace, NY	195	Swann Lounge, PH	224
Siam Lotus Thai, LI	140	Sweet Basil, DE	89
Sia's, AT	21	Sweet Georgia Brown, DT	94
Sibling Rivalry, BO	38	Syzygy, DE	89
SideBern's, TB	274	Szmania's, SE	263
Sidney Street Cafe, SL	268	Taberna/Alabardero, DC	287
Sierra Mar, SF	254	Ta-boo, PB	215
Silver Pond, FL	99	Taka, SD	245
Simposio, HS	117	Takashi, SC	240
Singha Thai, MW	163	Tallgrass, CH	53
Siri's Thai French, NJ	177	Talula, MI	158
Six89 Kitchen, DE	88	Tamarind, AT	21
Six Tables, TB	274	Tamarind, MI	158
62 Main Restaurant, FW	104	Tamarind Bay, BO	38
Sky Room, SD	244	Tapenade, SD	245
Slanted Door, SF	254	TapTap Haitian, MI	158
Smith & Wollensky, NY	195	Taranta, BO	38
Snake Creek Grill, SC	239	Tatsu's, KC	123
Solera, MN	168	Tavern on the Green, NY	196
Solera Restaurant, DE	89	Tavolino, TC	278
Sona, LA	150	T. Cook's, PS	229
Sonoma Modern, CR	43		

Alphabetical Page Index

Tei Tei Robata Bar, DA	79	Upstream, CR	43
Tellers American, LI	141	Valbella, CT	71
TenPenh, DC	287	Valentino, LA	150
Teppo Yakitori, DA	80	Valentino Las Vegas, LV	132
Terra, SF	254	Ventana Room, TC	278
Terra Cotta, TC	278	Veritas, NY	197
Terrapin, WH	296	Versailles, MI	159
Texas de Brazil, FW	104	Vetri, PH	225
Thai House, OR	211	Victoria & Albert's, OR	211
3950, LV	132	Vidalia, DC	288
3660 on the Rise, HO	109	Vincent, MN	169
3030 Ocean, FL	99	Vincent Guerithault, PS	230
32 East, PB	216	Vito's Chop House, OR	211
Thomas Henkelmann, CT	71	Vivace, TC	278
Three Birds, CL	63	Vix, MI	159
Three Brothers, MW	164	Volare, CR	43
302 West, CH	53	Volterra, SE	264
Thumbs Up, AT	22	Wahso, SC	240
Tierra, AT	22	Wasabi, WH	296
Timo, MI	158	Washington Inn, NJ	177
Timothy Dean's Bistro, BA	29	Washington Square, PH	225
Tomoe Sushi, NY	196	Water Grill, LA	151
Toni's Sushi Bar, MI	159	West End Grill, DT	95
Tony Mandola's, HS	118	Whispers, NJ	177
Tony's, HS	118	White House, AC	24
Tony's, SL	268	Wildflower, TC	279
Topolobampo, CH	53	Wild Ginger, SE	264
Tosca, DC	287	Wildwood, PO	235
Toscana, CR	43	WineSellar, SD	245
Tosoni's, SE	263	Wish, MI	159
Totaro's, PH	224	Wisteria, AT	22
Traffic Jam & Snug, DT	94	Wolfgang Puck Cafe, OR	211
Tramontana, DA	80	Woodfire Grill, AT	22
Trattoria Diane, LI	141	Would, The, WH	296
Trattoria Marcella, SL	269	Xaviar's at Piermont, WH	297
Tree Room, SC	240	York Street, DA	80
Tribute, DT	95	ZaBella Ristorante, OR	211
Tropical Chinese, MI	159	Zafra, NJ	177
Troquet, BO	38	Zander Cafe, MN	169
Troquet, OC	202	Zaytinya, DC	288
Trotters, WH	296	Zebra Rest./Wine, CR	44
Tru, CH	53	Zelo, MN	169
2941 Restaurant, DC	287	Zengo, DE	90
2900, DA	80	Zephs', WH	297
21 Club, NY	196	zin, KC	123
20.21, MN	168	Zingerman's Deli, DT	95
240 Union, DE	89	Zinnia, SL	269
TWO. urban licks, AT	22	Zoe's by the Lake, NJ	178
Union, SE	264	Zoria, TB	274
Union League Cafe, CT	71	Zov's Bistro, OC	202
Union Square Cafe, NY	196	Zula, HS	118
Upperline, NO	187	Zuni Café, SF	255
UpStairs on the Square, BO	39		

Wine Vintage Chart

This chart is designed to help you select wine to go with your meal. It is based on the same 0 to 30 scale used throughout this *Survey*. The ratings (prepared by our friend **Howard Stravitz**, a law professor at the University of South Carolina) reflect both the quality of the vintage and the wine's readiness for present consumption. Thus, if a wine is not fully mature or is over the hill, its rating has been reduced. We do not include 1987, 1991–1993 vintages because they are not especially recommended for most areas. A dash indicates that a wine is either past its peak or too young to rate.

	'85	'86	'88	'89	'90	'94	'95	'96	'97	'98	'99	'00	'01	'02	'03	'04
WHITES																
French:																
Alsace	24	–	22	27	27	26	25	25	24	26	23	26	27	25	22	–
Burgundy	26	25	–	24	22	–	28	29	24	23	26	25	24	27	23	24
Loire Valley	–	–	–	–	–	–	20	23	22	–	24	25	26	27	25	23
Champagne	28	25	24	26	29	–	26	27	24	23	24	24	22	26	–	–
Sauternes	21	28	29	25	27	–	21	23	25	23	24	24	28	25	26	–
German	–	–	25	26	27	25	24	27	26	25	25	23	29	27	25	25
California (Napa, Sonoma, Mendocino):																
Chardonnay	–	–	–	–	–	–	–	–	–	24	25	28	27	26	–	
Sauvignon Blanc/Sémillon	–	–	–	–	–	–	–	–	–	–	–	–	27	28	26	–
REDS																
French:																
Bordeaux	24	25	24	26	29	22	26	25	23	25	24	28	26	23	25	23
Burgundy	23	–	21	24	26	–	26	28	25	22	27	22	25	27	24	–
Rhône	–	–	26	29	29	24	25	22	24	28	27	27	26	–	25	–
Beaujolais	–	–	–	–	–	–	–	–	–	–	–	24	–	25	28	25
California (Napa, Sonoma, Mendocino):																
Cab./Merlot	27	26	–	–	28	29	27	25	28	23	26	22	27	25	24	–
Pinot Noir	–	–	–	–	–	–	–	24	24	25	24	27	28	26	–	
Zinfandel	–	–	–	–	–	–	–	–	–	–	–	26	26	28	–	
Italian:																
Tuscany	–	–	–	–	25	22	25	20	29	24	28	24	26	24	–	–
Piedmont	–	–	24	26	28	–	23	26	27	25	25	28	26	18	–	–
Spanish:																
Rioja	–	–	–	–	–	26	26	24	25	22	25	25	27	20	–	–
Ribera del Duero/Priorat	–	–	–	–	–	26	26	27	25	24	26	26	27	20	–	–